Praise for *50 Great Myths of Popular Psychology*

"True knowledge is hard won, and this timely and remarkable book shows us that stamping out falsehoods is no easy task either. The book does it all: it debunks all-too-common beliefs from the pseudoscientific fringe; it presents evidence against a variety of myths that seem like they ought to be true; it explains why people fall prey to such falsehoods; and it ends with some tantalizing facts about mind and behavior that make it clear that the truth can be every bit as amazing as fiction. These 50 myths won't disappear with the publication of this book, but those who read it will enjoy being able to set others—many others—straight."

Thomas Gilovich, Cornell University

"We have needed this compendium for some time. These factoids and popular (but fallacious) memes about psychology have been exposed in single publications, but critiques of all of them have never been brought together in one place before. The myths chosen by these authors are indeed popular ones—the very ones that psychology instructors encounter every day. The book is an incredible resource for both student and instructor. The critiques are accurate and well written. I'm sure my copy will be dog-eared within six months."

Keith E. Stanovich, author of How To Think Straight About Psychology
and What Intelligence Tests Miss

"A much-needed mythbuster for consumers and students of psychology. This engaging book reminds us that applying science to everyday psychology is not only enormously worthwhile, but fun."

Carol Tavris, coauthor of Mistakes Were Made (But Not by Me)

"Because I only use 10% of my brain, I had to play Mozart music while reading this book, and then be hypnotized to recover the memory of it because of early childhood traumas that were repressed but occasionally leaked through out-of-body experiences and ESP. And if you believe any of the above you need to read this book . . . twice if its mythbusting revelations cause you to repress the memory of it."

Michael Shermer, Publisher of Skeptic *magazine,*
monthly columnist for Scientific American,
and author of Why People Believe Weird Things

"Is it true that psychology is mostly common sense? For anyone who wonders, this amazing book—which effectively discounts 50 pop psychology myths and briefly dismisses 250 more—provides convincing answers. And it does more: it offers fascinating examples of how science works and supports critical thinking. For teachers, students, writers, and anyone who wants to think smarter, this classic-to-be will be a valuable resource and a great read."

David G. Myers, Hope College, author of Intuition:
Its Powers and Perils

"I find each and every chapter excellent and from a teaching point of view, brilliant. The way in which the history of the myths is presented up to the critical but balanced discussion of each myth, is a great achievement. Scott Lilienfeld is well-known for his user-friendly writing style, but in this text he and his co-authors reach a new level. This leads to a book which will not only be easily understandable by undergraduate, and especially first year students, but also by the general population."

Dap Louw, University of the Free State

About the Authors

Scott O. Lilienfeld is a Professor of Psychology at Emory University in Atlanta. Author of over 200 journal articles, chapters, and books, he is a recipient of the 1998 David Shakow Early Career Award for Distinguished Contributions to Clinical Psychology from Division 12 (Society for Clinical Psychology) of the American Psychological Association (APA). He is a past president of the Society for a Science of Clinical Psychology and a Fellow of the Association for Psychological Science. He is editor of the *Scientific Review of Mental Health Practice*. Dr. Lilienfeld's principal areas of research are personality disorders, psychiatric classification and diagnosis, pseudoscience in mental health, and the teaching of psychology.

Steven Jay Lynn is a Professor of Psychology and Director of the Psychological Clinic at the State University of New York at Binghamton. Dr. Lynn serves on 11 editorial boards, and he has 270 scholarly publications, including 16 books. He is past President of APA's Division of Psychological Hypnosis, and he has been the recipient of the Chancellor's Award of the State University of New York for Scholarship and Creative Activities. He is a fellow of the APA and the Association for Psychological Science, and his research has been funded by the National Institute of Mental Health. His major areas of research include hypnosis, memory, fantasy, and dissociation.

John Ruscio is an Associate Professor of Psychology at The College of New Jersey. His scholarly interests include quantitative methods for psychological research and the characteristics of pseudoscience that distinguish subjects within and beyond the fringes of psychological science. He has published more than 50 articles, chapters, and books, including *Critical Thinking in Psychology: Separating Sense from Nonsense*; serves on the editorial boards of the *Journal of Abnormal Psychology* and *Psychological Assessment*; and is an associate editor at the *Scientific Review of Mental Health Practice*.

The late **Barry L. Beyerstein** was Professor of Psychology at Simon Fraser University and chair of the British Columbia Skeptics Society. He was co-editor of *The Write Stuff* (1992), Associate Editor of the *Scientific Review of Alternative Medicine*, and co-authored many articles in the *Skeptical Inquirer* and professional journals. Dr. Beyerstein was a member of the Advisory Board of the Drug Policy Foundation (Washington, DC) and a founding board member of the Canadian Foundation for Drug Policy (Ottawa, Ontario).

50 GREAT MYTHS OF POPULAR PSYCHOLOGY

Shattering Widespread Misconceptions about Human Behavior

Scott O. Lilienfeld
Steven Jay Lynn
John Ruscio
Barry L. Beyerstein

WILEY-BLACKWELL

A John Wiley & Sons, Ltd., Publication

This edition first published 2010
© 2010 Scott O. Lilienfeld, Steven Jay Lynn, John Ruscio, and Barry L. Beyerstein

Blackwell Publishing was acquired by John Wiley & Sons in February 2007.
Blackwell's publishing program has been merged with Wiley's global Scientific,
Technical, and Medical business to form Wiley-Blackwell.

Registered Office
John Wiley & Sons Ltd, The Atrium, Southern Gate, Chichester,
West Sussex, PO19 8SQ, United Kingdom

Editorial Offices
350 Main Street, Malden, MA 02148-5020, USA
9600 Garsington Road, Oxford, OX4 2DQ, UK
The Atrium, Southern Gate, Chichester, West Sussex, PO19 8SQ, UK

For details of our global editorial offices, for customer services, and for information
about how to apply for permission to reuse the copyright material in this book
please see our website at www.wiley.com/wiley-blackwell.

The right of Scott O. Lilienfeld, Steven Jay Lynn, John Ruscio, and Barry L. Beyerstein
to be identified as the author of this work has been asserted in accordance with the
Copyright, Designs and Patents Act 1988.

Library of Congress Cataloging-in-Publication Data
50 great myths of popular psychology : shattering widespread misconceptions about
human behavior / Scott O. Lilienfeld . . . [et al.].
   p. cm.
Includes bibliographical references and index.
ISBN 978-1-4051-3111-7 (hardcover : alk. paper) — ISBN 978-1-4051-3112-4
(pbk. : alk. paper)   1. Psychology—Popular works.   2. Human behavior.
I. Lilienfeld, Scott O., 1960–   II. Title: Fifty great myths of popular psychology.
   BF145.A15 2010
   150—dc22

                                                                    2009020179

A catalogue record for this book is available from the British Library.

Set in 10/12.5pt Sabon by Graphicraft Limited, Hong Kong
Printed in Sheridan, KY, A CJK Group Company

1   2010

SKY65C52A8B-70D6-4BBA-AB33-D98612C2309E_072120

"Science must begin with myths and with the criticism of myths."

Sir Karl Popper (1957)

CONTENTS

PREFACE

Psychology is all around us. Youth and old age, forgetting and remembering, sleeping and dreaming, love and hate, happiness and sadness, mental illness and psychotherapy—for good, bad, and often both, this is the stuff of our daily lives. Virtually every day, the news media, television shows and films, and the Internet bombard us with claims regarding a host of psychological topics—brain functioning, psychics, out-of-body experiences, recovered memories, polygraph testing, romantic relationships, parenting, child sexual abuse, mental disorders, real crime, and psychotherapy, to name merely a few. Even a casual stroll through our neighborhood bookstore reveals at least dozens, and often hundreds, of self-help, relationship, recovery, and addiction books that serve up generous portions of advice for steering our path along life's rocky road. Of course, for those who prefer their psychological advice for free, there's no end of it on the Web. In countless ways, the popular psychology industry shapes the landscape of the early 21st century world.

Yet to a surprising extent, much of what we believe to be true about psychology isn't. Although scores of popular psychology sources are readily available in bookstores and at our fingertips online, they're rife with myths and misconceptions. Indeed, in today's fast-paced world of information overload, *misinformation* about psychology is at least as widespread as accurate information. Unfortunately, precious few books are available to assist us with the challenging task of distinguishing fact from fiction in popular psychology. As a consequence, we often find ourselves at the mercy of self-help gurus, television talk show hosts, and radio self-proclaimed mental health experts, many of whom dispense psychological advice that's a confusing mix of truths, half-truths, and outright falsehoods. Without a dependable tour guide for sorting out psychological myth from reality, we're at risk for becoming lost in a jungle of misconceptions.

Many of the great myths of popular psychology not only mislead us about human nature, but can also lead us to make unwise decisions in our everyday lives. Those of us who believe erroneously that people typically repress the memories of painful experiences (see Myth #13) may spend much of our lives in a fruitless attempt to dredge up memories of childhood traumatic events that never happened; those of us who believe that happiness is determined mostly by our external circumstances (see Myth #24) may focus exclusively outside rather than inside of ourselves to find the perfect "formula" for long-term satisfaction; and those of us who believe erroneously that opposites attract in romantic relationships (see Myth #27) may spend years searching for a soulmate whose personalities and values differ sharply from ours—only to discover too late that such "matches" seldom work well. Myths matter.

As science educator David Hammer (1996) noted, scientific misconceptions possess four major properties. They (1) are stable and often strongly held beliefs about the world, (2) are contradicted by well-established evidence, (3) influence how people understand the world, and (4) must be corrected to achieve accurate knowledge (Stover & Saunders, 2000). For our purposes, the last point is especially crucial. In our view, mythbusting should be an essential component of psychology education, because deeply entrenched beliefs in psychological misconceptions can impede students' understanding of human nature.

There are numerous dictionary definitions of the word "myth," but the ones that best suit our purposes derive from the *American Heritage Dictionary* (2000): "a popular [but false] belief or story that has become associated with a person, institution, or occurrence" or "a fiction or half-truth, especially one that forms part of an ideology." Most of the myths we present in this book are widely held beliefs that blatantly contradict psychological research. Others are exaggerations or distortions of claims that contain a kernel of truth. Either way, most of the myths we address in this book can seem so compelling because they fit into a broader view of human nature that many people find plausible. For example, the false belief that we use only 10% of our brain power (see Myth #1) dovetails with the belief that many of us haven't fully realized our intellectual potential; and the false belief that low self-esteem is a major cause of maladjustment (see Myth #33) fits with the belief that we can achieve just about anything if we believe in ourselves.

Many psychological myths are also understandable efforts to make sense out of our worlds. As German sociologist and philosopher of science

Klaus Manhart (2005) observed, throughout history myths have served a central function: attempting to explain the otherwise inexplicable. Indeed, many of the myths we discuss in this book, like the belief that dreams have been shown to possess symbolic meaning (see Myth #20), are efforts to grapple with some of life's perennial mysteries, in this case the underlying significance of our nighttime mental worlds.

Our book is the first to survey the full landscape of modern popular psychology, and to place common psychological misconceptions under the microscope of scientific evidence. By doing so, we hope to both dispel prevalent but false beliefs and arm readers with accurate knowledge that they can use to make better real-world decisions. Our tone is informal, engaging, and at times irreverent. We've made particular efforts to make our book accessible to beginning students and laypersons, and we presume no formal knowledge of psychology. To do so, we've kept nontechnical language to a minimum. As a consequence, this book can be enjoyed equally by specialists and nonspecialists alike.

We begin the book by surveying the vast world of popular psychology, the dangers posed by psychological myths, and 10 major sources of these myths. Then, in the body of the book, we examine 50 widespread myths of popular psychology. For each myth, we discuss its prevalence in the general population, illustrative examples from the wide world of popular psychology, its potential origins, and the research evidence bearing on it. Although one of our main goals is mythbusting, we go well beyond merely debunking myths. For each myth, we also discuss what we know to be *true* regarding each topic, thereby imparting genuine psychological knowledge that readers can take with them and apply to their everyday lives. Several of the 50 myths are accompanied by brief "Mythbusting: A Closer Look" boxes that examine a closely allied myth. Each chapter concludes with a set of other myths to explore—250 in all—along with helpful suggested references for tracking down these myths. Instructors in psychology classes may find many of these additional myths handy as presentation or term paper topics to assign to their students. To drive home the point that psychological truth is often just as fascinating, if not more, than psychological myth, the book's postscript features a David Letterman-style "Top Ten List" of remarkable psychological findings that may seem like myths, but that are in fact true. Finally, the book concludes with an Appendix containing recommended Internet resources for exploring various psychological myths.

This book, we believe, will appeal to several audiences. Students in introductory psychology and research methods courses, as well as teachers of these courses, will find the book to be of particular interest. Many students enter these courses with misconceptions concerning a host of psychological topics, so confronting these misconceptions is often an essential step toward imparting accurate knowledge. Because we have organized the book around 11 domains traditionally covered in introductory psychology courses, such as brain functioning and perception, memory, learning and intelligence, emotion and motivation, social psychology, personality, psychopathology, and psychotherapy, this book can serve as either a freestanding textbook or a textbook supplement for these courses. Instructors who use this book along with a standard introductory psychology textbook can easily assign some or all of the myths in each chapter in conjunction with the accompanying chapter in their textbook.

Laypersons interested in learning more about psychology will find the book to be an invaluable and user-friendly resource, as well an entertaining compendium of psychological knowledge. Practicing psychologists and other mental health professionals (such as psychiatrists, psychiatric nurses, counselors, and social workers), psychology educators, psychological researchers, psychology majors, and psychology graduate students should also find the book to be an enjoyable read, not to mention a valuable reference source. Finally, we modestly believe that this book should be recommended (dare we say required?) reading for all journalists, writers, educators, and attorneys whose work touches on psychological topics. This book should prevent them from falling prey to precisely the kinds of psychological misunderstandings against which we so vigorously caution our readers.

This project could never have come to fruition without the assistance of several talented and dedicated individuals. First and foremost, we sincerely thank our editor at Wiley-Blackwell, Christine Cardone, about whom we cannot say enough good things. Chris has provided invaluable guidance throughout this project, and we are deeply indebted to her for her support and encouragement. We consider ourselves remarkably fortunate to have worked with someone as competent, kind, and patient as Chris. Second, we thank Sean O'Hagen for his gracious assistance with the *Reference* section and help with the aging myth, Alison Cole for help with the midlife crisis myth, Otto Wahl for help with the schizophrenia myth, and Fern Pritikin Lynn, Ayelet Meron Ruscio, and Susan Himes for their useful suggestions on miscellaneous myths. Third, we thank Constance Adler, Hannah Rolls and Annette Abel at Wiley-Blackwell for their editorial assistance and copy-editing.

Fourth, we thank the following reviewers of drafts of the book prospectus and various chapters, whose comments, suggestions, and constructive criticisms were extraordinarily helpful to us in improving our early drafts. We are especially indebted to the following reviewers for their wise counsel: David R. Barkmeier, Northeastern University; Barney Beins, Ithaca College; John Bickford, University of Massachusetts-Amherst; Stephen F. Davis, Morningside College; Sergio Della Sala, University of Edinburgh; Dana Dunn, Moravian College; Brandon Gaudiano, Brown University; Eric Landrum, Boise State University; Dap Louw, University of the Free State; Loreto Prieto, Iowa State University; Jeff Ricker, Scottsdale Community College; and the numerous instructors who took our initial survey.

We are honored to dedicate this book to the memory of our dear friend, colleague, and co-author Barry Beyerstein. Although his contribution to this volume was cut short by his untimely death in 2007 at the age of 60, the manuscript bears the imprint of his keen mind and ability to communicate complex ideas to a wide audience. We know Barry would be extremely proud of this volume, which embodies his mission of educating the public about the promise of scientific psychology to increase our knowledge about what it means to be human, and about the pitfalls of pseudoscience. We fondly remember Barry Beyerstein's passion for life and compassion for others, and dedicate this book to him to commemorate his enduring legacy to the popularization of scientific psychology.

As authors, we very much hope you enjoy reading the book as much as we enjoyed writing it. We welcome your feedback on the book, not to mention suggestions for additional myths to discuss in future editions.

May the mythbusting begin!

ACKNOWLEDGMENTS

The authors and publisher wish to thank the following for permission to use copyright material:

Figure I.1   Copyright 1983 from McCloskey, M. (1983). Naïve theories of motion. In Gentner, D. & Stevens, A. L. (Eds.), *Mental Models*. Hillsdale, NJ: Lawrence Erlbaum Associates, pp. 299–324. Reproduced by permission of Taylor and Francis Group, LLC, a division of Informa plc.

Figure I.2   "Turning the Tables" from Shepard, R. N. (1990). *Mind sights*. New York: W. H. Freeman, 48. Reproduced by permission of the author.

Figure I.4   Photos 12/Alamy.

Figure 1.1   *Superman #37* Copyright 1945 DC Comics. All rights reserved. Used with permission.

Figure 1.2   Reuters/Corbis.

Figure 5.1   George Silk/Time Life Pictures/Getty Images.

Figure 6.1   Photos 12/Alamy.

Figure 7.1   Reuters/Vincent West.

Genesis song lyrics "Misunderstanding" by Phillip David Charles Collins, copyright TK, by permission of Hal Leonard Corporation as agent for EMI April Music Inc.

Figure 8.1   Anastasi, Anne & Urbina, Susana (1997). *Psychological testing* (7th edition), Figure 15-1, p. 413. Prentice Hall: Upper Saddle River, New Jersey. Electronically reproduced by permission of Pearson Education, Inc., Upper Saddle River, New Jersey.

Figure 9.1   Courtesy of Zazzle.com.

Figure 10.1   Photofest.

Figure 11.1   Photofest.

Every effort has been made to trace copyright holders and to obtain their permission for the use of copyright materials. The authors and publisher will gladly receive any information enabling them to rectify any error or omission in subsequent editions.

INTRODUCTION

The Wide World of Psychomythology

"Opposites attract."
"Spare the rod, spoil the child."
"Familiarity breeds contempt."
"There's safety in numbers."

You've probably heard these four proverbs many times before. Moreover, like our rights to life, liberty, and the pursuit of happiness, you probably hold them to be self-evident. Our teachers and parents have assured us that these sayings are correct, and our intuitions and life experiences confirm their wisdom.

Yet psychological research demonstrates that all four proverbs, as people commonly understand them, are mostly or entirely wrong. Opposites don't attract in romantic relationships; to the contrary, we tend to be most attracted to people who are similar to us in our personalities, attitudes, and values (see Myth #27). Sparing the rod doesn't necessarily spoil children; moreover, physical punishment often fails to produce positive effects on their behavior (see p. 97). Familiarity usually breeds comfort, not contempt; we usually prefer things we've seen many times to things that are novel (see p. 133). Finally, there's typically danger rather than safety in numbers (see Myth #28); we're more likely to be rescued in an emergency if only one bystander, rather than a large group of bystanders, is watching.

The Popular Psychology Industry

You've almost certainly "learned" a host of other "facts" from the popular psychology industry. This industry encompasses a sprawling network of sources of everyday information about human behavior, including television shows, radio call-in programs, Hollywood movies, self-help books, newsstand magazines, newspaper tabloids, and Internet sites. For example, the popular psychology industry tells us that:

- we use only 10% of our brain power;
- our memories work like videotapes or tape recorders;
- if we're angry, it's better to express the anger directly than hold it in;
- most sexually abused children grow up to become abusers themselves;
- people with schizophrenia have "split" personalities;
- people tend to act strangely during full moons.

Yet we'll learn in this book that all six "facts" are actually fictions. Although the popular psychology industry can be an invaluable resource for information about human behavior, it contains at least as much *misinformation* as information (Stanovich, 2007; Uttal, 2003). We term this vast body of misinformation *psychomythology* because it consists of misconceptions, urban legends, and old wives' tales regarding psychology. Surprisingly, few popular books devote more than a handful of pages to debunking psychomythology. Nor do more than a handful of popular sources provide readers with scientific thinking tools for distinguishing factual from fictional claims in popular psychology. As a consequence, many people—even students who graduate from college with majors in psychology—know a fair amount about what's true regarding human behavior, but not much about what's false (Chew, 2004; Della Sala, 1999, 2007; Herculano-Houzel, 2002; Lilienfeld, 2005b).

Before going much further, we should offer a few words of reassurance. If you believed that all of the myths we presented were true, there's no reason to feel ashamed, because you're in awfully good company. Surveys reveal that many or most people in the general population (Furnham, Callahan, & Rawles, 2003; Wilson, Greene, & Loftus, 1986), as well as beginning psychology students (Brown, 1983; Chew, 2004; Gardner & Dalsing, 1986, Lamal, 1979; McCutcheon, 1991; Taylor & Kowalski, 2004; Vaughan, 1977), believe these and other psychological myths. Even some psychology professors believe them (Gardner & Hund, 1983).

If you're still feeling a tad bit insecure about your "Psychology IQ," you should know that the Greek philosopher Aristotle (384–322 B.C.), who's widely regarded as one of the smartest human beings ever to walk the face of the earth, believed that emotions originate from the heart, not the brain, and that women are less intelligent than men. He even believed that women have fewer teeth than men! Aristotle's bloopers remind us that high intelligence offers no immunity against belief in psychomythology. Indeed, a central theme of this book is that we can *all* fall prey to erroneous psychological claims unless we're armed with accurate knowledge. That's as true today as it was in past centuries.

Indeed, for much of the 1800s, the psychological discipline of "phrenology" was all the rage throughout much of Europe and America (Greenblatt, 1995; Leahy & Leahy, 1983). Phrenologists believed that extremely specific psychological capacities, like poetic ability, love of children, appreciation of colors, and religiosity, were localized to distinct brain regions, and that they could detect people's personality traits by measuring the patterns of bumps on people's skulls (they thought incorrectly that enlarged brain areas create indentations on the skull). The range of psychological capacities supposedly pinpointed by phrenologists ranged from 27 to 43. Phrenology "parlors" allowing curious patrons to have their skulls and personalities measured sprouted up in many locations, giving rise to the still popular phrase "having one's head examined." Yet phrenology turned out to be a striking example of psychomythology on a grand societal scale, as studies eventually showed that damage to the brain areas identified by phrenologists hardly ever caused the psychological deficits they'd so confidently predicted. Although phrenology—depicted on this book's cover—is now dead, scores of other examples of psychomythology are alive and well.

In this book, we'll help you to distinguish fact from fiction in popular psychology, and provide you with a set of mythbusting skills for evaluating psychological claims scientifically. We'll not only shatter widespread myths about popular psychology, but explain what's been found to be true in each domain of knowledge. We hope to persuade you that scientifically supported claims regarding human behavior are every bit as interesting as—and often even more surprising than—the mistaken claims.

That's not to say that we should dismiss everything the popular psychology industry tells us. Many self-help books encourage us to take responsibility for our mistakes rather than to blame others for them, offer a warm and nurturing environment for our children, eat in moderation and exercise regularly, and rely on friends and other sources of social support when we're feeling down. By and large, these are wise tidbits of advice, even if our grandmothers knew about them.

The problem is that the popular psychology industry often intersperses such advice with suggestions that fly in the face of scientific evidence

(Stanovich, 2007; Wade, 2008; Williams & Ceci, 1998). For example, some popular talk-show psychologists urge us to always "follow our heart" in romantic relationships, even though this advice can lead us to make poor interpersonal decisions (Wilson, 2003). The popular television psychologist, Dr. Phil McGraw ("Dr. Phil"), has promoted the polygraph or so-called "lie detector" test on his television program as means of finding out which partner in a relationship is lying (Levenson, 2005). Yet as we'll learn later (see Myth #23), scientific research demonstrates that the polygraph test is anything but an infallible detector of the truth (Lykken, 1998; Ruscio, 2005).

Armchair Psychology

As personality theorist George Kelly (1955) pointed out, we're all arm-chair psychologists. We continually seek to understand what makes our friends, family members, lovers, and strangers tick, and we strive to understand why they do what they do. Moreover, psychology is an inescapable part of our everyday lives. Whether it's our romantic relationships, friendships, memory lapses, emotional outbursts, sleep problems, performance on tests, or adjustment difficulties, psychology is all around us. The popular press bombards us on an almost daily basis with claims regarding brain development, parenting, education, sexuality, intelligence testing, memory, crime, drug use, mental disorders, psychotherapy, and a bewildering array of other topics. In most cases we're forced to accept these claims on faith alone, because we haven't acquired the scientific thinking skills to evaluate them. As neuroscience mythbuster Sergio Della Sala (1999) reminded us, "believers' books abound and they sell like hot cakes" (p. xiv).

That's a shame, because although some popular psychology claims are well supported, scores of others aren't (Furnham, 1996). Indeed, much of everyday psychology consists of what psychologist Paul Meehl (1993) called "fireside inductions": assumptions about behavior based solely on our intuitions. The history of psychology teaches us one undeniable fact: Although our intuitions can be immensely useful for generating hypotheses to be tested using rigorous research methods, they're often woefully flawed as a means of determining whether these hypotheses are correct (Myers, 2002; Stanovich, 2007). To a large extent, that's probably because the human brain evolved to understand the world around it, not to understand itself, a dilemma that science writer Jacob Bronowski (1966) called "reflexivity." Making matters worse, we often cook up reasonable-sounding, but false, explanations for our behaviors after the fact (Nisbett & Wilson, 1977). As a consequence, we can persuade ourselves that we understand the causes of our behaviors even when we don't.

Psychological Science and Common Sense

One reason we're easily seduced by psychomythology is that it jibes with our common sense: our gut hunches, intuitions, and first impressions. Indeed, you may have heard that most psychology is "just common sense" (Furnham, 1983; Houston, 1985; Murphy, 1990). Many prominent authorities agree, urging us to trust our common sense when it comes to evaluating claims. Popular radio talk show host Dennis Prager is fond of informing his listeners that "There are two kinds of studies in the world: those that confirm our common sense and those that are wrong." Prager's views regarding common sense are probably shared by many members of the general public:

> Use your common sense. Whenever you hear the words "studies show"—outside of the natural sciences—and you find that these studies show the opposite of what common sense suggests, be very skeptical. I do not recall ever coming across a valid study that contravened common sense. (Prager, 2002, p. 1)

For centuries, many prominent philosophers, scientists, and science writers have urged us to trust our common sense (Furnham, 1996; Gendreau, Goggin, Cullen, & Paparozzi, 2002). The 18th century Scottish philosopher Thomas Reid argued that we're all born with common sense intuitions, and that these intuitions are the best means of arriving at fundamental truths about the world. More recently, in a *New York Times* editorial, well-known science writer John Horgan (2005) called for a return to common sense in the evaluation of scientific theories, including those in psychology. For Horgan, far too many theories in physics and other areas of modern science contradict common sense, a trend he finds deeply worrisome. In addition, the last several years have witnessed a proliferation of popular and even bestselling books that champion the power of intuition and snap judgments (Gigerenzer, 2007; Gladwell, 2005). Most of these books acknowledge the limitations of common sense in evaluating the truth of scientific claims, but contend that psychologists have traditionally underestimated the accuracy of our hunches.

Yet as the French writer Voltaire (1764) pointed out, "Common sense is not so common." Contrary to Dennis Prager, psychological studies that overturn our common sense are sometimes right. Indeed, one of our primary goals in this book is to encourage you to *mistrust* your common sense when evaluating psychological claims. As a general rule, you should consult research evidence, not your intuitions, when deciding whether a scientific claim is correct. Research suggests that snap judgments are often helpful in sizing up people and in forecasting our likes and dislikes (Ambady & Rosenthal, 1992; Lehrer, 2009; Wilson, 2004), but they can be wildly inaccurate when it comes to gauging the accuracy of psychological theories or assertions. We'll soon see why.

As several science writers, including Lewis Wolpert (1992) and Alan Cromer (1993), have observed, science is *uncommon* sense. In other words, science requires us to put aside our common sense when evaluating evidence (Flagel & Gendreau, 2008; Gendreau et al., 2002). To understand science, including psychological science, we must heed the advice of the great American humorist Mark Twain, namely, that we need to *unlearn* old habits of thinking at least as much as learn new ones. In particular, we need to unlearn a tendency that comes naturally to all of us—the tendency to assume that our gut hunches are correct (Beins, 2008).

Of course, not all popular psychology wisdom, sometimes called "folk psychology," is wrong. Most people believe that happy employees get more work done on the job than unhappy employees, and psychological research demonstrates that they're right (Kluger & Tikochinsky, 2001). Yet time and time again, scientists—including psychological scientists—have discovered that we can't always trust our common sense (Cacioppo, 2004; Della Sala, 1999, 2007; Gendreau et al., 2002; Osberg, 1991; Uttal, 2003). In part, that's because our raw perceptions can deceive us.

For example, for many centuries, humans assumed not only that the earth is flat—after all, it sure seems flat when we're walking on it—but that the sun revolves around the earth. This latter "fact" in particular seemed obvious to virtually everyone. After all, each day the sun paints a huge arc across the sky while we remain planted firmly on the ground. But in this case, observers' eyes fooled them. As science historian Daniel Boorstin (1983) noted:

Nothing could be more obvious than that the earth is stable and unmoving, and that we are the center of the universe. Modern Western science takes its beginning from the denial of this commonsense axiom . . . Common sense, the foundation of everyday life, could no longer serve for the governance of the world. (p. 294)

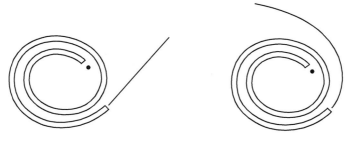

Figure I.1   A diagram from the study by Michael McCloskey (1983). What path will the ball take after exiting the spiral?
Source: McCloskey (1983).

Let's consider another example. In Figure I.1, you'll see a drawing from a study from the work of Michael McCloskey (1983), who asked college students to predict the path of a ball that has just exited from an enclosed spiral. About half of the undergraduates predicted incorrectly that the ball would continue to travel in a spiral path after exiting, as shown on the right side of the figure (in fact, the ball will travel in a straight path after exiting, as shown on the left side of the figure). These students typically invoked commonsense notions like "momentum" when justifying their answers (for example, "The ball started traveling in a certain way, so it will just keep going that way"). By doing so, they seemed almost to treat the ball as a person, much like a figure skater who starts spinning on the ice and keeps on spinning. In this case, their intuitions betrayed them.

We can see another delightful example in Figure I.2, which displays "Shepard's tables," courtesy of cognitive psychologist Roger Shepard (1990). Take a careful look at the two tables in this figure and ask yourself which table top contains a larger surface area. The answer seems obvious at first glance.

Yet believe it or not, the surfaces of both tables are identical (if you don't believe us, photocopy this page, cut out the figures, and superimpose them on each other). Just as we shouldn't always trust our eyes, we shouldn't always trust our intuitions. The bottom line: Seeing is believing, but seeing isn't always believing correctly.

Shephard's tables provide us with a powerful optical illusion—an image that tricks our visual system. In the remainder of this book, though, we'll be crossing paths with a variety of *cognitive illusions*—beliefs that trick our reasoning processes (Pohl, 2004). We can think of many or most

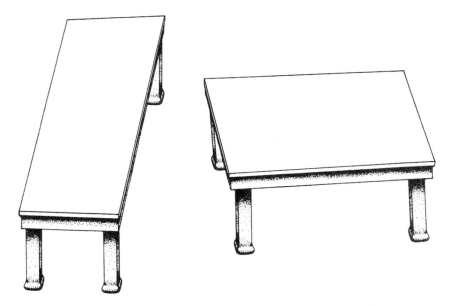

Figure 1.2 Shepard's tables. Are the two table tops the same or different?
Source: Shepard (1990).

psychological myths as cognitive illusions, because like visual illusions they can fool us.

Why Should We Care?

Why is it important to know about psychological myths? There are at least three reasons:

(1) *Psychological myths can be harmful.* For example, jurors who believe incorrectly that memory operates like a videotape may vote to convict a defendant on the basis of confidently held, but inaccurate, eyewitness testimony (see Myth #11). In addition, parents who believe incorrectly that punishment is usually an effective means of changing long-term behavior may spank their children whenever they misbehave, only to find that their children's undesirable actions become more frequent over time (see p. 97).

(2) *Psychological myths can cause indirect damage.* Even false beliefs that are themselves harmless can inflict significant indirect harm. Economists use the term *opportunity cost* to refer to the fact that

people who seek out ineffective treatments may forfeit the chance to obtain much-needed help. For example, people who believe mistakenly that subliminal self-help tapes are an effective means of losing weight may invest a great deal of time, money, and effort on a useless intervention (Moore, 1992; see Myth #5). They may also miss out on scientifically based weight loss programs that could prove beneficial.

(3) *The acceptance of psychological myths can impede our critical thinking in other areas.* As astronomer Carl Sagan (1995) noted, our failure to distinguish myth from reality in one domain of scientific knowledge, such as psychology, can easily spill over to a failure to distinguish fact from fiction in other vitally important areas of modern society. These domains include genetic engineering, stem cell research, global warming, pollution, crime prevention, schooling, day care, and overpopulation, to name merely a few. As a consequence, we may find ourselves at the mercy of policy-makers who make unwise and even dangerous decisions about science and technology. As Sir Francis Bacon reminded us, knowledge is power. Ignorance is powerlessness.

The 10 Sources of Psychological Myths: Your Mythbusting Kit

How do psychological myths and misconceptions arise?

We'll try to persuade you that there are 10 major ways in which we can all be fooled by plausible-sounding, but false, psychological claims. It's essential to understand that we're all vulnerable to these 10 sources of error, and that we're all fooled by them from time to time.

Learning to think scientifically requires us to become aware of these sources of error and learn to compensate for them. Good scientists are just as prone to these sources of error as the average person (Mahoney & DeMonbreun, 1977). But good scientists have adopted a set of safeguards—called the scientific method—for protecting themselves against them. *The scientific method is a toolbox of skills designed to prevent scientists from fooling themselves.* If you become aware of the 10 major sources of psychomythology, you'll be far less likely to fall into the trap of accepting erroneous claims regarding human nature.

Pay careful attention to these 10 sources of error, because we'll come back to them periodically throughout the book. In addition, you'll be able to use these sources of error to evaluate a host of folk psychology claims in your everyday life. Think of them as your lifelong "Mythbusting Kit."

(1) Word-of-Mouth

Many incorrect folk psychology beliefs are spread across multiple generations by verbal communication. For example, because the phrase "opposites attract" is catchy and easily remembered, people tend to pass it on to others. Many urban legends work the same way. For example, you may have heard the story about alligators living in the New York City sewer system or about the well-intentioned but foolish woman who placed her wet poodle in a microwave to dry it off, only to have it explode. For many years, the first author of this book relayed a story he'd heard many times, namely the tale of a woman who purchased what she believed was a pet Chihuahua, only to be informed weeks later by a veterinarian that it was actually a gigantic rat. Although these stories may make for juicy dinner table conversation, they're no truer than any of the psychological myths we'll present in this book (Brunvand, 1999).

The fact that we've heard a claim repeated over and over again doesn't make it correct. But it can lead us to accept this claim as correct even when it's not, because we can confuse a statement's familiarity with its accuracy (Gigerenzer, 2007). Advertisers who tell us repeatedly that "Seven of eight dentists surveyed recommended Brightshine Toothpaste above all over brands!" capitalize on this principle mercilessly. Furthermore, research shows that hearing one person express an opinion ("Joe Smith is the best qualified person to be President!") 10 times can lead us to assume that this opinion is as widely held as hearing 10 people express this opinion once (Weaver, Garcia, Schwarz, & Miller, 2007). Hearing is often believing, especially when we hear a statement over and over again.

(2) Desire for Easy Answers and Quick Fixes

Let's face it: Everyday life isn't easy, even for the best adjusted of us. Many of us struggle to find ways to lose weight, get enough sleep, perform well on exams, enjoy our jobs, and find a lifelong romantic partner. It's hardly a surprise that we glom on to techniques that offer foolproof promises of rapid and painless behavior changes. For example, fad diets are immensely popular, even though research demonstrates that the substantial majority of people who go on them regain all of their weight within just a few years (Brownell & Rodin, 1994). Equally popular are speed reading courses, many of which promise to increase people's reading speeds from a mere 100 or 200 words per minute to 10,000 or even 25,000 words per minute (Carroll, 2003). Yet researchers have found that none of these courses boost people's reading speeds without decreasing their reading comprehension (Carver, 1987). What's more, most of the reading speeds advertised by these courses exceed the maximum reading speed of the human eyeball, which is about 300 words per minute (Carroll, 2003). A word to the wise: If something sounds too good to be true, it probably is (Sagan, 1995).

(3)   Selective Perception and Memory

As we've already discovered, we rarely if ever perceive reality exactly as it is. We see it through our own set of distorting lenses. These lenses are warped by our biases and expectations, which lead us to interpret the world in accord with our preexisting beliefs. Yet most of us are blissfully unaware of how these beliefs influence our perceptions. Psychologist Lee Ross and others have termed the mistaken assumption that we see the world precisely as it is *naïve realism* (Ross & Ward, 1996). Naïve realism not only leaves us vulnerable to psychological myths, but renders us less capable of recognizing them as myths in the first place.

A striking example of selective perception and memory is our tendency to focus on "hits"—memorable co-occurrences—rather than on "misses" —the absence of memorable co-occurrences. To understand this point, take a look at Figure 1.3, where you'll see what we call "The Great Fourfold Table of Life." Many scenarios in everyday life can be arranged in a fourfold table like the one here. For example, let's investigate the question of whether full moons are associated with more admissions to psychiatric hospitals, as emergency room physicians and nurses commonly claim (see Myth #42). To answer this question, we need to

	Psychiatric hospital admission	No psychiatric hospital admission
Full moon	Ⓐ	B
No full moon	C	D

Figure 1.3   The Great Fourfold Table of Life. In most cases, we attend too much to the A cell, which can result in illusory correlation.

examine all four cells of the Great Fourfold Table of Life: *Cell A*, which consists of instances when there's a full moon and a psychiatric hospital admission, *Cell B*, which consists of instances when there's a full moon but no psychiatric hospital admission, *Cell C*, which consists of instances when there's no full moon and a psychiatric hospital admission, and *Cell D*, which consists of instances when there's no full moon and no psychiatric hospital admission. Using all four cells allows you to compute the *correlation* between full moons and the number of psychiatric hospital admissions; a correlation is a statistical measure of how closely these two variables are associated (by the way, a *variable* is a fancy term for anything that varies, like height, hair color, IQ, or extraversion).

Here's the problem. In real life, we're often remarkably poor at estimating correlations from the Great Fourfold Table of Life, because we generally pay too much attention to certain cells and not enough to others. In particular, research demonstrates that we typically pay too much attention to the *A* cell, and not nearly enough to the *B* cell (Gilovich, 1991). That's understandable, because the *A* cell is usually more interesting and memorable than the *B* cell. After all, when there's a full moon and a lot of people end up in a psychiatric hospital, it confirms our initial expectations, so we tend to notice it, remember it, and tell others about it. The *A* cell is a "hit"—a striking co-occurrence. But when there's a full moon and nobody ends up in a psychiatric hospital, we barely notice or remember this "nonevent." Nor are we likely to run excitedly to our friends and tell them, "Wow, there was a full moon tonight and guess what happened? Nothing!" The *B* cell is a "miss"— the absence of a striking co-occurrence.

Our tendency to remember our hits and forget our misses often leads to a remarkable phenomenon called *illusory correlation*, the mistaken perception that two statistically unrelated events are actually related (Chapman & Chapman, 1967). The supposed relation between full moons and psychiatric hospital admissions is a stunning example of an illusory correlation. Although many people are convinced that this correlation exists, research demonstrates that it doesn't (Rotton & Kelly, 1985; see Myth #42). The belief in the full moon effect is a cognitive illusion.

Illusory correlations can lead us to "see" a variety of associations that aren't there. For example, many people with arthritis insist that their joints hurt more in rainy than in non-rainy weather. Yet studies demonstrate that this association is a figment of their imaginations (Quick, 1999). Presumably, people with arthritis attend too much to the *A* cell of the Great Fourfold Table of Life—instances when it rains and when their joints hurt—leading them to perceive a correlation that doesn't exist. Similarly, the early phrenologists "saw" close linkages between damage to specific brain areas and deficits in certain psychological abilities, but they were wildly wrong.

Another probable example of illusory correlation is the perception that cases of infantile autism, a severe psychiatric disorder marked by severe language and social deficits, are associated with prior exposure to mercury-based vaccines (see Myth #41). Numerous carefully conducted studies have found no association whatsoever between the incidence of infantile autism and mercury vaccine exposure (Grinker, 2007; Institute of Medicine, 2004; Lilienfeld & Arkowitz, 2007), although tens of thousands of parents of autistic children are convinced otherwise. In all probability, these parents are paying too much attention to the A cell of the fourfold table. They can hardly be blamed for doing so given that they're understandably trying to detect an event, such as a vaccination, that could explain their children's autism. Moreover, these parents may have been fooled by the fact that the initial appearance of autistic symptoms—often shortly after age 2—often coincides with at the age when most children receive vaccinations.

(4)   Inferring Causation from Correlation

It's tempting, but incorrect, to conclude that if two things co-occur statistically (that is, if two things are "correlated") then they must be causally related to each other. As psychologists like to say, *correlation doesn't mean causation*. So, if variables A and B are correlated, there can be three major explanations for this correlation: (a) A may cause B, (b) B may cause A, or (c) a third variable, C, may cause both A and B. This last scenario is known as the *third variable problem*, because C is a third variable that may contribute to the association between variables A and C. The problem is that the researchers who conducted the study may never have measured C; in fact, they may have never known about C's existence.

Let's take a concrete example. Numerous studies demonstrate that a history of physical abuse in childhood increases one's odds of becoming an aggressive person in adulthood (Widom, 1989). Many investigators have interpreted this statistical association as implying that childhood physical abuse causes physical aggression in later life; indeed, this interpretation is called the "cycle of violence" hypothesis. In this case, the investigators are assuming that childhood physical abuse (A) causes adult violence (B). Is this explanation necessarily right?

Of course, in this case B can't cause A, because B occurred after A. A basic principle of logic is that causes must precede their effects. Yet we haven't ruled out the possibility that a third variable, C, explains both A and B. One potential third variable in this case is a genetic tendency toward aggressiveness. Perhaps most parents who physically abuse their children harbor a genetic tendency toward aggressiveness, which they pass on to their children. Indeed, there's good research evidence that aggressiveness is partly influenced by genes (Krueger, Hicks, & McGue, 2001). This genetic tendency (C) could result in a correlation between a childhood physical abuse history (A) and later aggression in individuals with this history (B), even though A and B may be causally unrelated to each other (DiLalla & Gottesman, 1991). Incidentally, there are other potential candidates for C in this case (can you think of any?).

The key point is that when two variables are correlated, we shouldn't necessarily assume a direct causal relationship between them. Competing explanations are possible.

(5)   Post Hoc, Ergo Propter Hoc Reasoning

"Post hoc, ergo propter hoc" means "after this, therefore because of this" in Latin. Many of us leap to the conclusion that because A precedes B, then A must cause B. But many events that occur before other events don't cause them. For example, the fact that virtually all serial killers ate cereal as children doesn't mean that eating cereal produces serial killers (or even "cereal killers"—we couldn't resist the pun) in adulthood. Or the fact that some people become less depressed soon after taking an herbal remedy doesn't mean that the herbal remedy caused or even contributed to their improvement. These people might have become less depressed even without the herbal remedy, or they might have sought out other effective interventions (like talking to a therapist or even to a supportive friend) at about the same time. Or perhaps taking the herbal remedy inspired a sense of hope in them, resulting in what psychologists call a *placebo effect*: improvement resulting from the mere expectation of improvement.

Even trained scientists can fall prey to post hoc, ergo propter hoc reasoning. In the journal *Medical Hypotheses*, Flensmark (2004) observed that the appearance of shoes in the Western world about 1,000 years ago was soon followed by the first appearance of cases of schizophrenia. From these findings, he proposed that shoes play a role in triggering schizophrenia. But the appearance of shoes could have merely coincided with other changes, such as the growth of modernization or an increase in stressful living conditions, which may have contributed more directly to the emergence of schizophrenia.

(6) Exposure to a Biased Sample

In the media and many aspects of daily life, we're often exposed to a nonrandom—or what psychologists called a "biased"—sample of people from the general population. For example, television programs portray approximately 75% of severely mentally ill individuals as violent (Wahl, 1997), although the actual rate of violence among the severely mentally ill is considerably lower than that (Teplin, 1985; see Myth #43). Such skewed media coverage may fuel the erroneous impression that most individuals with schizophrenia, bipolar disorder (once called manic depression), and other serious mental illnesses are physically dangerous.

Psychotherapists may be especially prone to this error, because they spend most of their working lives with an unrepresentative group of individuals, namely, people in psychological treatment. Here's an example: Many psychotherapists believe it's exceedingly difficult for people to quit smoking on their own. Yet research demonstrates that many, if not most, smokers manage to stop without formal psychological treatment (Schachter, 1982). These psychotherapists are probably falling prey to what statisticians Patricia and Jacob Cohen (1984) termed the *clinician's illusion*—the tendency for practitioners to overestimate how chronic (long-standing) a psychological problem is because of their selective exposure to a chronic sample. That is, because clinicians who treat cigarette smokers tend to see only those individuals who can't stop smoking on their own—otherwise, these smokers presumably wouldn't have sought out a clinician in the first place—these clinicians tend to overestimate how difficult smokers find it to quit without treatment.

(7) Reasoning by Representativeness

We often evaluate the similarity between two things on the basis of their superficial resemblance to each other. Psychologists call this phenomenon the *representativeness heuristic* (Tversky & Kahneman, 1974), because we use the extent to which two things are "representative" of each other to estimate how similar they are. A "heuristic," by the way, is a mental shortcut or rule of thumb.

Most of the time, the representativeness heuristic, like other heuristics, serves us well (Gigerenzer, 2007). If we're walking down the street and see a masked man running out of a bank with a gun, we'll probably try to get out of the way as quickly as we can. That's because this man is representative of—similar to—bank robbers we've seen on television and in motion pictures. Of course, it's possible that he's just pulling a prank or that he's an actor in a Hollywood action movie being filmed there, but better safe than sorry. In this case, we relied on a mental shortcut, and we were probably smart to do so.

Yet we sometimes apply the representativeness heuristic when we shouldn't. Not all things that resemble each other superficially are related to each other, so the representativeness heuristic sometimes leads us astray (Gilovich & Savitsky, 1996). In this case, common sense *is* correct: We can't always judge a book by its cover. Indeed, many psychological myths probably arise from a misapplication of representativeness. For example, some graphologists (handwriting analysts) claim that people whose handwriting contains many widely spaced letters possess strong needs for interpersonal distance, or that people who cross their "t"s and "f"s with whip-like lines tend to be sadistic. In this case, graphologists are assuming that two things that superficially resemble each other, like widely spaced letters and a need for interpersonal space, are statistically associated. Yet there's not a shred of research support for these claims (Beyerstein & Beyerstein, 1992; see Myth #36).

Another example comes from human figure drawings, which many clinical psychologists use to detect respondents' personality traits and psychological disorders (Watkins, Campbell, Nieberding, & Hallmark, 1995). Human figure drawing tasks, like the ever popular Draw-A-Person Test, ask people to draw a person (or in some cases, two persons of opposite sexes) in any way they wish. Some clinicians who use these tests claim that respondents who draw people with large eyes are paranoid, that respondents who draw people with large heads are narcissistic (self-centered), and even that respondents who draw people with long ties are excessively preoccupied with sex (a long tie is a favorite Freudian symbol for the male sexual organ). All these claims are based on a surface resemblance between specific human figure drawing "signs" and specific psychological characteristics. Yet research offers no support for these supposed associations (Lilienfeld, Wood, & Garb, 2000; Motta, Little, & Tobin, 1993).

(8) Misleading Film and Media Portrayals

Many psychological phenomena, especially mental illnesses and treatments for them, are frequently portrayed inaccurately in the entertainment and news media (Beins, 2008). More often than not, the media depicts these phenomena as more sensational than they are. For example, some modern films picture electroconvulsive therapy (ECT), known informally as "shock therapy," as a physically brutal and even dangerous treatment (Walter & McDonald, 2004). In some cases, as in the 1999 horror film, *House on Haunted Hill,* individuals who're strapped to ECT machines in movies experience violent convulsions. Although it's true that that ECT was once somewhat dangerous, technological advances over the past few decades, such as the administration of a muscle relaxant, have rendered it no more physically hazardous than anesthesia (Glass, 2001; see Myth #50). Moreover, patients who receive modern forms of ECT don't experience observable motor convulsions.

To take another example, most Hollywood films depict adults with autism as possessing highly specialized intellectual skills. In the 1988 Academy Award-winning film, *Rain Main,* Dustin Hoffman portrayed an autistic adult with "savant syndrome." This syndrome is characterized by remarkable mental abilities, such as "calendar calculation" (the ability to name the day of a week given any year and date), multiplication and division of extremely large numbers, and knowledge of trivia, such as the batting averages of all active major league baseball players. Yet at most 10% of autistic adults are savants (Miller, 1999; see Myth #41) (Figure I.4).

(9)   Exaggeration of a Kernel of Truth

Some psychological myths aren't entirely false. Instead, they're exaggerations of claims that contain a kernel of truth. For example, it's almost certainly true that many of us don't realize our full intellectual potential. Yet this fact doesn't mean that most of us use only 10% of our brain power, as many people incorrectly believe (Beyerstein, 1999; Della Sala, 1999; see Myth #1). In addition, it's probably true that at least a few differences in interests and personality traits between romantic partners can "spice up" a relationship. That's because sharing your life with someone who agrees with you on everything can make your love life harmonious, but hopelessly boring. Yet this fact doesn't imply that opposites attract (see Myth #27). Still other myths involve an overstatement of small differences. For example, although men and women tend to differ slightly in their communication styles, some popular psychologists, especially John Gray, have taken this kernel of truth to an extreme, claiming that "men are from Mars" and "women are from Venus" (see Myth #29).

Figure I.4 Film portrayals of individuals with autistic disorder, like this Academy Award-winning portrayal by actor Dustin Hoffman (left) in the 1988 film *Rain Man*, often imply that they possess remarkable intellectual capacities. Yet only about 10% of autistic individuals are savants.
Source: Photos 12/Alamy

(10) Terminological Confusion

Some psychological terms lend themselves to mistaken inferences. For example, the word "schizophrenia," which Swiss psychiatrist Eugen Bleuler (1911) coined in the early 20th century, literally means "split mind." As a consequence, many people believe incorrectly that people with schizophrenia possess more than one personality (see Myth #39). Indeed, we'll frequently hear the term "schizophrenic" in everyday language to refer to instances in which a person is of two different minds about an issue ("I'm feeling very schizophrenic about my girlfriend; I'm attracted to her physically but bothered by her personality quirks"). It's therefore hardly surprising that many people confuse schizophrenia with an entirely different condition called "multiple personality disorder" (known today as "dissociative identity disorder"), which is supposedly characterized by the presence of more than one personality within the same individual (American Psychiatric Association, 2000). In fact, schizophrenics possess only one personality that's been shattered. Indeed, Bleuler (1911) intended the term "schizophrenia" to refer to the fact that individuals with this condition suffer from a splitting of mental functions, such as thinking and emotion, whereby their thoughts don't correspond to their feelings. Nevertheless, in the world of popular psychology, Bleuler's original and more accurate meaning has largely been lost. The misleading stereotype of schizophrenics as persons who act like two completely different people on different occasions has become ingrained in modern culture.

To take another example, the term "hypnosis" derives from the Greek prefix "hypno," which means sleep (indeed, some early hypnotists believed that hypnosis was a form of sleep). This term may have led many people, including some psychologists, to assume that hypnosis is a sleep-like state. In films, hypnotists often attempt to induce a hypnotic state by telling their clients that "You're getting sleepy." Yet in fact, hypnosis bears no physiological relationship to sleep, because people who are hypnotized remain entirely awake and fully aware of their surroundings (Nash, 2001; see Myth #19).

The World of Psychomythology: What Lies Ahead

In this book, you'll encounter 50 myths that are commonplace in the world of popular psychology. These myths span much of the broad landscape of modern psychology: brain functioning, perception, development, memory, intelligence, learning, altered states of consciousness, emotion, interpersonal behavior, personality, mental illness, the courtroom, and psychotherapy. You'll learn about the psychological and societal origins of each myth, discover how each myth has shaped society's popular thinking about human behavior, and find out what scientific research has to say about each myth. At the end of each chapter, we'll provide you with a list of additional psychological myths to explore in each domain. In the book's postscript, we'll offer a list of fascinating findings that may appear to be fictional, but that are actually factual, to remind you that genuine psychology is often even more remarkable—and difficult to believe—than psychomythology.

Debunking myths comes with its share of risks (Chew, 2004; Landau & Bavaria, 2003). Psychologist Norbert Schwarz and his colleagues (Schwarz, Sanna, Skurnik, & Yoon, 2007; Skurnik, Yoon, Park, & Schwarz, 2005) showed that correcting a misconception, such as "The side effects of a flu vaccine are often worse than the flu itself," can sometimes backfire by leading people to be *more likely* to believe this misconception later. That's because people often remember the statement itself but not its "negation tag"—that is, the little yellow sticky note in our heads that says "that claim is wrong." Schwarz's work reminds us that merely memorizing a list of misconceptions isn't enough: It's crucial to understand the *reasons* underlying each misconception. His work also suggests that it's essential for us to understand not merely what's false, but also what's true. Linking up a misconception with the truth is the best means of debunking that misconception (Schwarz et al., 2007). That's why we'll spend a few pages explaining not only *why* each of these 50 myths is wrong, but also how each of these 50 myths imparts an underlying truth about psychology.

Fortunately, there's at least some reason to be optimistic. Research shows that psychology students' acceptance of psychological misconceptions, like "people use only 10% of their brain's capacity," declines with the total number of psychology classes they've taken (Standing & Huber, 2003). This same study also showed that acceptance of these misconceptions is lower among psychology majors than non-majors. Although such research is only correlational—we've already learned that correlation doesn't always mean causation—it gives us at least a glimmer of hope that education can reduce people's beliefs in psychomythology. What's more, recent controlled research suggests that explicitly refuting psychological misconceptions in introductory psychology lectures or readings can lead to large—up to 53.7%—decreases in the levels of these misconceptions (Kowalski & Taylor, in press).

If we've succeeded in our mission, you should emerge from this book not only with a higher "Psychology IQ," but also a better understanding of how to distinguish fact from fiction in popular psychology. Perhaps most important, you should emerge with the critical thinking tools needed to better evaluate psychological claims in everyday life.

As the paleontologist and science writer Stephen Jay Gould (1996) pointed out, "the most erroneous stories are those we think we know best—and therefore never scrutinize or question" (p. 57). In this book, we'll encourage you to never accept psychological stories on faith alone, and to always scrutinize and question the psychological stories you think you know best.

So without further ado, let's enter the surprising and often fascinating world of psychomythology.

1 BRAIN POWER

Myths about the Brain and Perception

Most People Use Only 10% of Their Brain Power

Whenever those of us who study the brain venture out of the Ivory Tower to give public lectures or media interviews, one of the questions we're most likely to encounter is, "Is it true that we only use 10% of our brains?" The look of disappointment that usually follows when we respond, "Sorry, I'm afraid not," strongly suggests that the 10% myth is one of those hopeful truisms that refuses to die simply because it would be so darn nice if it were true (Della Sala, 1999; Della Sala & Beyerstein, 2007). Indeed, this myth is widespread, even among psychology students and other well-educated people. In one study, when asked "About what percentage of their potential brain power do you think most people use?," a third of psychology majors answered 10% (Higbee & Clay, 1998, p. 471). Fifty-nine percent of a sample of college-educated people in Brazil similarly believe that people use only 10% of their brains (Herculano-Houzel, 2002). Remarkably, that same survey revealed that even 6% of neuroscientists agreed with this claim!

Surely, none of us would turn down a hefty hike in brain power if we could achieve it. Not surprisingly, marketers who thrive on the public's fond hopes for a self-improvement breakthrough continue to peddle a never-ending stream of dubious schemes and devices premised on the 10% myth. Always on the lookout for a "feel-good" story, the media has played a big role in keeping this optimistic myth alive. A great deal of advertising copy for legitimate products continues to refer to the 10% myth as fact, usually in the hopes of flattering potential customers who see themselves as having risen above their brain's limitations. For example, in his popular book, *How to Be Twice as Smart*, Scott Witt

(1983) wrote that "If you're like most people, you're using only ten percent of your brainpower" (p. 4). In 1999, an airline tried to entice potential flyers by informing them that "It's been said that we use only 10% of our brain capacity. If, however, you're flying _____ (name of company deleted) Airlines, you're using considerably more" (Chudler, 2006).

Yet an expert panel convened by the U.S. National Research Council concluded that (alas!), in this, as with other miraculous self-improvement claims, there's no good substitute for hard work when it comes to getting ahead in life (Beyerstein, 1999c; Druckman & Swets, 1988). This unwelcome news has done little to discourage millions who comfort themselves with the belief that the shortcut to their unfulfilled dreams lies in the fact that they just haven't quite caught up with the secret for tapping their vast, allegedly unused cerebral reservoir (Beyerstein, 1999c). That desired promotion, stellar grade point average, or authorship of the next bestselling novel is within your grasp, say the sellers of cerebral miracle remedies.

Even more questionable are the offerings of New Age entrepreneurs who propose to hone the psychic skills we allegedly all possess with obscure gizmos for the brain. Self-proclaimed psychic Uri Geller (1996) claimed that "In fact, most of us use only about 10 percent of our brains, if that." Promoters like Geller imply that psychic powers reside in the 90% of the brain that simple folk forced to subsist on the drudge-like 10% haven't yet learned to use.

Why would a brain researcher doubt that 90% of the average brain lies silent? There are several reasons. First of all, our brain has been shaped by natural selection. Brain tissue is expensive to grow and operate; at a mere 2–3% of our body weight, it consumes over 20% of the oxygen we breathe. It's implausible that evolution would have permitted the squandering of resources on a scale necessary to build and maintain such a massively underutilized organ. Moreover, if having a bigger brain contributes to the flexibility that promotes survival and reproduction—which are natural selection's "bottom lines"—it's hard to believe that any slight increase in processing power wouldn't be snapped up immediately by existing systems in the brain to enhance the bearer's chances in the continuous struggle to prosper and procreate.

Doubts about the 10% figure are also fueled by evidence from clinical neurology and neuropsychology, two disciplines that aim to understand and alleviate the effects of brain damage. Losing far less than 90% of the brain to accident or disease almost always has catastrophic consequences. Look, for instance, at the much-publicized controversy surrounding the nonconscious status and ultimate death of Terri Schiavo, the young Florida woman who lay in a persistent vegetative state for 15 years (Quill, 2005). Oxygen deprivation following a cardiac arrest in 1990 had destroyed about 50% of her cerebrum, the upper part of the brain responsible for conscious awareness. Modern brain science argues that "mind" equals brain function. Therefore, patients like Ms. Schiavo had permanently lost the capacity for thoughts, perceptions, memories, and emotions that are the very essence of being human (Beyerstein, 1987). Although some claimed to see signs of consciousness in Schiavo, most impartial experts found no evidence that any of her higher mental processes had been spared. If 90% of the brain is indeed unnecessary, this shouldn't have been the case.

Research also reveals that no area of the brain can be destroyed by strokes or head trauma without leaving patients with serious deficits in functioning (Kolb & Whishaw, 2003; Sacks, 1985). Likewise, electrical stimulation of sites in the brain during neurosurgery has failed to uncover any "silent areas," those in which the person experiences no perception, emotion, or movement after neurosurgeons apply these tiny currents (neurosurgeons can accomplish this feat with conscious patients under local anesthesia because the brain contains no pain receptors).

The last century has witnessed the advent of increasingly sophisticated technologies for snooping on the brain's traffic (Rosenzweig, Breedlove, & Watson, 2005). With the aid of brain imaging techniques, such as electroencepholograms (EEGs), positron emission tomography (PET) scanners, and functional magnetic resonance imaging (MRI) machines, researchers have succeeded in localizing a vast number of psychological functions to specific brain areas. With nonhuman animals, and occasionally with humans undergoing neurological treatment, researchers can insert recording probes into the brain. Despite this detailed mapping, no quiet areas awaiting new assignments have emerged. In fact, even simple tasks generally require contributions of processing areas spread throughout virtually the whole brain.

Two other firmly established principles of neuroscience create further problems for the 10% myth. Areas of the brain that are unused because of injuries or disease tend to do one of two things. They either wither away, or "degenerate," as neuroscientists put it, or they're taken over by nearby areas that are on the lookout for unused territory to colonize for their own purposes. Either way, perfectly good, unused brain tissue is unlikely to remain on the sidelines for long.

All told, evidence suggests that there's no cerebral spare tire waiting to be mounted with a little help from the self-improvement industry. So, if the 10% myth is so poorly supported, how did it get started? Attempts to track down this myth's origins haven't uncovered any smoking guns, but a few tantalizing clues have materialized (Beyerstein, 1999c; Chudler, 2006; Geake, 2008). One stream leads back to pioneering American psychologist William James in the late 19th and early 20th centuries. In one of his writings for the general public, James said he doubted that average persons achieve more than about 10% of their *intellectual potential*. James always talked in terms of underdeveloped potential, never relating it to a specific amount of the brain engaged. A slew of "positive thinking" gurus who followed weren't as careful, though, and "10% of our capacity" gradually morphed into "10% of our brain" (Beyerstein, 1999c). Undoubtedly, the biggest boost for the self-help entrepreneurs came when journalist Lowell Thomas attributed the 10% brain claim to William James. Thomas did so in the 1936 preface to one of the bestselling self-help books of all time, Dale Carnegie's *How to Win Friends and Influence People*. The myth has never lost its steam since.

The popularity of the 10% myth probably also stems partly from authors' misunderstandings of scientific papers by early brain researchers. In calling a huge percentage of the human cerebral hemispheres "silent cortex," early investigators may have fostered the mistaken impression that what scientists now call "association cortex" had no function. As we now know, association cortex is vitally important for our language, abstract thinking, and performance of intricate sensory-motor tasks. In a similar vein, early researchers' admirably modest admissions that they didn't know what 90% of the brain did probably contributed to the myth that it does nothing. Another possible source of confusion may have been laypersons' misunderstanding of the role of glial cells, brain cells that outnumber the brain's neurons (nerve cells) by a factor of about 10. Although neurons are the scene of the action with respect to thinking and other mental activities, glial cells perform essential support functions for the neurons that do the heavy lifting, psychologically speaking. Finally, those who've searched for the origins of the 10% myth frequently came across the claim that Albert Einstein once explained his own brilliance by reference to the myth. Nevertheless, a careful search by the helpful staff at the Albert Einstein archive on our behalf yielded no record of any such statement on his part. More likely than not, the promoters of the 10% myth simply seized on Einstein's prestige to further their own endeavors (Beyerstein, 1999c).

The 10% myth has surely motivated many people to strive for greater creativity and productivity in their lives, which certainly isn't a bad thing.

The comfort, encouragement, and hope that it's generated almost surely help to explain its longevity. But, as Carl Sagan (1995) reminded us (see *Introduction*, p. 11), if something sounds too good to be true, it probably is.

Myth #2 Some People Are Left-Brained, Others Are Right-Brained

The next time somebody tries to sell you a book or device for retraining your allegedly flabby right hemisphere, reach for your wallet. Then clasp it firmly to your chest and run as fast as you can. Like some other myths in this book, the one you're about to encounter has a grain of truth to it. Nevertheless, this grain can be a bit hard to find amidst the mounds of misinformation that bury it.

Are some people left-brained and others right-brained? There's good evidence that the two sides of the brain, called *hemispheres*, differ in their functions (Springer & Deutsch, 1997). For example, different abilities are more affected by injuries to one side of the brain than the other, and brain imaging techniques demonstrate that the hemispheres differ in their activity when people engage in various mental tasks. By far the most dramatic evidence for *laterality of function*—the superiority of one or the other hemisphere for performing certain tasks—comes from patients who've undergone a "split brain" operation. In this rarely performed procedure, surgeons sever the nerve tracts connecting opposite points in the brain's left and right hemispheres in a last-ditch attempt to control severe epilepsy. The large pathway connecting these hemispheres, the main target of the split-brain operation, is the corpus callosum ("colossal body").

Roger Sperry shared the Nobel Prize in 1981 for his landmark studies of split-brain patients, and a fascinating lot they are (Gazzaniga, 1998). Once they'd recovered from surgery, they appeared deceptively normal in their everyday activities. But once Sperry tested them in the laboratory, it became apparent that the two halves of their brains were working independently. Each side operated without awareness or knowledge of the other.

In Sperry's laboratory tests, patients fixate their eyes at the center of a screen, on which the researcher briefly flashes words or pictures. With the eyes immobilized, information flashed to the left of the fixation point goes to the right hemisphere and the opposite is true of information presented to the right of the fixation point (that's because the optic pathways on each side of the visual field cross over to the other side). In more ordinary situations, this separation of information doesn't occur because patients constantly move their eyes about their surroundings. As a result, the input normally reaches both hemispheres eventually. When it doesn't, though, some decidedly peculiar things can happen.

The right hemisphere receives input from and controls the movements of the left side of the body, and the left hemisphere does the same for the right. In almost all right-handers, and most lefties as well, the primary areas for language reception and production are in the left hemisphere. Thus, if we restrict new information to the right hemisphere, the left hemisphere—which is more verbal than the right—will be unable to tell us what the input was, and it may be perplexed to see the left hand acting on the segregated knowledge, for reasons it can't fathom.

For example, if the researcher shows the right hemisphere of a split-brain subject a photograph of a naked man, she may giggle. Yet when asked what she's giggling about, the subject (her left hemisphere, that is) won't be able to say. Instead, she may cook up a plausible-sounding reason ("That photo reminds me of my uncle George, who's a really funny guy"). Split-brain subjects may even do something with their right hand, like assemble a group of blocks to fit a pattern, utterly oblivious of the fact that their left hand is following a few seconds behind, undoing all the good work. This much is well established. The dispute concerns the uniqueness of the kinds of tasks handled by the two hemispheres and how they go about it. In this regard, brain researchers have become more cautious in recent years while many pop psychologists have run wild.

Using Sperry's techniques, researchers have confirmed that the left and right hemispheres are relatively better at different mental activities. Note, however, that we wrote *relatively* better. The two halves of the brain differ in how they process tasks rather than what they process (McCrone, 1999). Let's take language, for example. The left hemisphere is better at the specifics of speech, such as grammar and word generation, whereas the right hemisphere is better at the intonation and emphases of speech (what's known as "prosody"). Although the right hemisphere is better at nonlinguistic functions that involve complex visual and spatial processes, the left hemisphere plays some role in these capacities if we give it the chance. The right brain is better at dealing with a general sense of space, whereas corresponding areas in the left brain become active when the person locates objects in specific places. In many cases, it's not that one hemisphere or the other can't perform a given task; it's just that one of them can perform it faster and better than the other. So it tends to grab the assignment first.

Of course, ordinary people aren't, as left-brain/right-brain aficionados suggest, just split-brain patients who haven't gotten around to having their corpus callosums snipped. In the normal brain, the side that's first off the mark will call for help from across the way. As long as the left–right pathways are intact, the two hemispheres share information extensively. Indeed, brain imaging research shows that the two hemispheres routinely communicate during most tasks (Mercer, 2010). After a split-brain operation, this cooperation isn't possible, so the separated systems limp along as best they can.

Therefore, the ways in which the two sides of brain differ are far more limited than pop psychology's "hemisphericity" entrepreneurs suggest (Aamodt & Wang, 2008; Corballis, 1999, 2007; Della Sala, 1999). On balance, the two hemispheres are much more similar than different in their functions (Geake, 2008). Modern neuroscientists have never agreed with many New Age "hemisphere trainers," who claim that the brain's two halves house totally dissimilar minds that approach the world in radically different ways, with one (the left) side an accountant and the other (the right) side a veritable Zen master. Robert Ornstein was among those to promote the idea of using different ways to tap into our "creative" right brains versus our intellectual left brains in his 1997 book, *The Right Mind: Making Sense of the Hemispheres*. Moreover, scores of educational and business programs de-emphasize getting the "right" answers on tests in favor of harnessing creative ability. Such programs as the *Applied Creative Thinking Workshop* have trained business managers to develop the untapped capacities of their right brains (Hermann, 1996). Furthermore, the enormously successful book, *Drawing on the Right Side of the Brain* (Edwards, 1980), which has sold over 2.5 million copies, encourages readers to unleash their artistic abilities by suppressing their "analytical" left hemispheres. Even cartoonists have jumped on the bandwagon; one shows a student holding an exam emblazoned with a big "F" who tells his professor, "It's not fair to flunk me for being a right-brain thinker."

The urge on the part of pop psychologists to assign all mental abilities to unique left and right compartments probably owes more to politics, social values, and commercial interests than to science. Its detractors have dubbed this extreme view "dichotomania" because of pop psychologists' tendency to dichotomize the two hemispheres' functions (Corballis, 1999). The notion was embraced enthusiastically by New Age proponents of the 1970s and 1980s, largely because it offered a rationale for world-views that were mystical and intuitive.

Pop psychologists further embellished genuine differences in how the hemispheres process information, proclaiming the allegedly cold and rational left hemisphere "logical," "linear," "analytical," and "masculine." In contrast, they proclaimed the allegedly warm and fuzzy right hemisphere "holistic," "intuitive," "artistic," "spontaneous," "creative," and "feminine" (Basil, 1988; Zimmer, 2009). Arguing that modern society undervalues the right hemisphere's touchy-feely mode of approaching the world, dichotomizers touted fanciful schemes for boosting this hemisphere's activity. Their books and seminars promised to free us of the barriers to personal growth imposed by an inflexible school system that favors "left hemisphere thinking."

Yet an expert panel, assembled by the U.S. National Academy of Sciences, concluded that ". . . we have no direct evidence that differential hemispheric utilization can be trained" (Druckman & Swets, 1988, p. 110). The panel concluded that behavioral training could probably enhance different styles of learning or problem solving, but that such improvements were not due to differences in the two hemispheres' functioning.

If the behavioral exercises promoted for right hemisphere calisthenics might yield a few benefits, we can't say the same for the far-fetched "brain tuners" sold for the same purposes (Beyerstein, 1985, 1999a). Numerous devices of this sort allegedly harmonize or synchronize the activity of the two hemispheres. One of the most successful of these schemes was invented by a former public relations executive with no formal training in neuroscience. Like others of its ilk, the device supposedly synchronizes brain waves across the hemispheres by means of feedback signals. Probably because of the placebo effect (see *Introduction*, p. 14), the product found scores of satisfied customers. Yet even if the devices synchronized left–right brain waves, there's no reason to believe that making the two hemispheres resonate in this fashion would be good for us. In fact, if the brain is working optimally, this is probably exactly what you *wouldn't* want it to do. Optimal psychological performance usually requires differential activation rather than synchronization of the hemispheres (Beyerstein, 1999a).

The bottom line: Don't be taken in by the claims of dichotomizers with a seminar to sell or marketers of hemispheric synchronization gizmos that sound too good to be true. Current research on hemispheric differences, even by those responsible for discovering left–right specializations, focuses on showing how the normal brain works in an integrated fashion (Corballis, 2007; Gazzaniga, 1998; McCrone, 1999).

Myth #3

Extrasensory Perception (ESP) Is a Well-Established Scientific Phenomenon

Having trouble with your love life? How about money problems? Call Miss Cleo's Psychic Hotline for Free! The operators of Miss Cleo's Psychic Hot Line charged callers an astonishing $1 billion before a 2002 settlement with the Federal Trade Commission (FTC) required that they cancel $500 million in customer bills and pay a $5 million fine (Miss Cleo's psychic powers apparently failed to warn her of the FTC's impending legal action). Nearly 6 million viewers of late-night television commercials featuring the purported Jamaican soothsayer were moved to speak with her or one of her "trained psychics" by the promise of receiving 3 free minutes of revelations about their future. Callers had no reason to suspect that Miss Cleo had American parents, that she was born in Los Angeles, and that her real name was Youree Dell Harris. Nor did they realize that their calls were being charged at the rate of $4.99 a minute from the outset, and that the goal of the "psychic" on the other end of the line was to keep them talking as long as possible, thereby running up their phone bills.

Some readers skeptical of psychic abilities might assume that callers, who ended up paying an average of $60 for each call, were simply suckers. Yet this judgment doesn't consider the fact that belief in psychic abilities and extrasensory perception (ESP) is firmly entrenched in modern society. The millions of callers to "Miss Cleo" were but a tiny fraction of the Americans who believe that ESP is a firmly established scientific fact. Coined in 1870 by Sir Richard Burton, the term ESP has come to mean knowledge or perception without the use of any of the senses. According to the most recent Gallup poll on this topic (Moore, 2005), 41% of the 1,002 U.S. adults surveyed believe in ESP, 31% in the existence of "telepathy/communication between minds without using traditional senses," and 26% in "clairvoyance/the power of the mind to know the past and predict the future." Among 92 introductory psychology students, 73% said they believed that the existence of ESP was well documented (Taylor & Kowalski, 2003).

The types of experiences assessed by these surveys are also known as paranormal, or psi-related experiences. Many parapsychologists (psychologists who study the paranormal) also describe *psychokinesis* —the ability to influence physical objects or processes by the power of thought—as a paranormal ability. Nevertheless, psychokinesis is typically excluded from ESP, which includes the three capacities of (1) *telepathy* (mind reading), (2) *clairvoyance* (knowing the existence of hidden or far-away objects or people), and (3) *precognition* (predicting the future using paranormal means).

Believers in ESP aren't limited to the general public. More than half of natural scientists polled (Wagner & Monnet, 1979) reported that they believed that ESP is an established fact or a likely possibility. Starting in 1972, the U.S. government shelled out $20 million of taxpayer money to fund a program known as "Stargate" to study the ability of "remote viewers" to acquire militarily useful information from distant, inaccessible places (using clairvoyance), such as a nuclear facility in the then Soviet Union. Government agents gave remote viewers the geographical coordinates (longitude, latitude) of a specific person, place, or document, and these viewers then wrote down, drew, or described whatever they could glean mentally about the target. The government discontinued the Stargate program in 1995, apparently because it yielded no useful military information. Amidst the debate over whether the government was wasting taxpayer money on this project, a blue-ribbon subcommittee of the U.S. National Research Council reviewed the world literature on ESP and concluded that the case for psychic powers was feeble (Alcock, 1990; Druckman & Swets, 1988; Hyman, 1989). Still, the mere fact that such a program was established in the first place highlights the widespread acceptance of ESP among educated people.

If the scientific support for ESP is so weak—and we'll soon provide evidence for this verdict—why do so many people believe in it? From childhood, most of us are bombarded by favorable and unskeptical media accounts of paranormal experiences. Such television shows as the *X-Files*, *Medium*, *Fringe*, and *America's Psychic Challenge* and, before that, *Twilight Zone* and the *Outer Limits*, have portrayed ESP as part of the fabric of everyday life. Movie plots encourage belief in a wide range of paranormal powers, including clairvoyance (such as *Minority Report*, *The Dead Zone*, *Stir of Echoes*, *The Butcher's Wife*, *The Sixth Sense*), telepathy (such as *Scanners*, *Dreamscape*, *The Sender*, and *Ghostbusters*), and psychokinesis (such as *Carrie* and *X-Men*). Many popular self-help books (Hewitt, 1996; Manning, 1999) declare that we all harbor latent psychic talents and tout simple techniques to liberate these powers and achieve ESP success. The Internet features innumerable pitches for courses that promise to develop and enhance our psychic abilities. For example, an advertisement for the *Silva Ultra Mind Seminar* (2005) tells participants that they'll be paired up with other people, taught to harness their ESP following meditation, and given the skills to guess astonishing facts about each other by means of paranormal powers.

Belief in the paranormal is bolstered by strong needs to believe in something greater than ourselves, a reality that lies beyond what the "senses can sense" (Gilovich, 1991). But perhaps even more influential in spreading belief in ESP is the fact that our personal experiences occasionally seem so extraordinary that they defy ordinary explanation. In one study (Greeley, 1987), 67% of 1,500 American adults claimed to have had personal experience with clairvoyance, precognition, or psychokinesis.

The emotional impact of dramatic and unexpected coincidences is certainly one reason why so many people believe in ESP. Say you have a dream about your friend, Jessica, from whom you haven't heard in years, and Jessica calls the next morning. You might assume the coincidence is so incredible that it must be ESP. Yet people tend to underestimate how often such events could occur by chance alone. If you find yourself in a group of 25 people, what are the odds that at least 2 of them share the same birthday? Most people are shocked to learn that the answer is over 50%. If we increased the size of the group to 35, the odds of at least 2 people sharing the same birthday rises to about 85% (Gilovich, 1991). We tend to underestimate how probable most coincidences are, and we may then attribute false "psychic" significance to these events (Marks & Kammann, 1980).

As we noted in the *Introduction* (p. 11), selective perception and memory lead us to remember events that confirm our beliefs and ignore or forget events that don't (Presley, 1997). Accordingly, people who believe in ESP may be more likely to remember and attach special significance to occurrences that fall into the category of the paranormal, even though they're due merely to chance. Because the timing of Jessica's call grabbed your attention, it stood out in your memory. So if we asked you a few weeks later if you believed in ESP, her call could spring to mind as evidence for ESP.

In light of the seeming reality of ESP experiences, scientists have given them serious consideration since the late 19th century. Joseph Banks Rhine (1933) and his wife Louisa jump-started the scientific study of ESP in the United States. They established a major program of research on ESP at Duke University in the 1930s based on subjects' trying to guess one of five standard symbols (star, triangle, squiggly line, plus sign, square) on cards—named "Zener cards" after one of Rhine's colleagues. Yet other scientists couldn't replicate positive findings from Rhine and his colleagues' Zener card studies. Nor could they replicate later research involving the ability of people to transmit visual images to a dreaming person (Ullman, Krippner, & Vaughan, 1973). Skeptics dismissed rates of ESP responding that exceeded chance as due to the unintentional "leakage" of subtle sensory cues, such as seeing the vague imprint of a Zener card symbol through a sealed envelope.

Studies using the *Ganzfeld* technique have received by far the most attention from the scientific community. The mental information detected by ESP, if it indeed exists, is presumably an exceedingly weak signal. So this information is typically obscured by many irrelevant stimuli. According to the logic of the Ganzfeld method, we need to create a uniform sensory field, the Ganzfeld (from the German word meaning "whole field"), to decrease the proportion of noise relative to signal and allow the faint ESP signal to emerge (Lilienfeld, 1999).

To establish this uniform sensory field, ESP experimenters cover the eyes of relaxed subjects with ping-pong ball halves, and direct a floodlight containing a red beam toward their eyes. Meanwhile, these researchers pump white noise into subjects' ears through headphones to minimize extraneous sounds in the room. A person in another room then attempts to mentally transmit pictures to subjects, who later rate the extent to which each of four pictures matches the mental imagery they experienced during the session.

In 1994, Daryl Bem and Charles Honorton published a remarkable article on the Ganzfeld method in one of psychology's most prestigious journals, *Psychological Bulletin*. To analyze data collected previously by other investigators on this method, they used a statistical technique called *meta-analysis*, which allows researchers to combine the results of many studies and treat them as though they were one large study. Bem and Honorton's meta-analysis of 11 Ganzfeld studies revealed that participants obtained overall target "hit" rates of approximately 35%, thereby exceeding chance (25%: that's 1 in 4 targets) performance. Nevertheless, it wasn't long before Julie Milton and Richard Wiseman (1999) analyzed 30 recent Ganzfeld studies not reviewed by Bem and Honorton, and reported that the size of Ganzfeld effects corresponded to essentially chance performance.

Lance Storm and Suitbert Ertel (2001) responded to Milton and Wiseman (1999) with another meta-analysis of 79 Ganzfeld studies, dating from 1974 to 1996, and contended that their analysis supported the claim that the Ganzfeld procedure detected ESP. In the parting shot in this scientific ping-pong game (appropriate for Ganzfeld research, we might add) of arguments and counterarguments, Milton and Wiseman (2001) countered that the studies that Storm and Ertel included in their analysis suffered from serious methodological shortcomings, and had shown nothing of the kind. It's clear that the question of whether the

Ganzfeld technique will prove to be the replicable method long sought by parapsychologists is far from conclusively resolved (Lilienfeld, 1999). Still, the fact that psychologists have tried unsuccessfully for over 150 years to demonstrate the existence of ESP is hardly encouraging (Gilovich, 1991).

Many scientists argue that the scientific "bar" necessary to accept the existence of ESP should be set very high. After all, the very existence of ESP would run counter to most established physical laws related to space, time, and matter. A program of well-controlled research that yields consistent support for ESP across independent laboratories will be needed to persuade the scientific community that paranormal abilities are real. Although we shouldn't dismiss these abilities as impossible or unworthy of further scientific consideration, we recommend holding off on making any major life decisions based on that call to the psychic hot line.

Myth #4 Visual Perceptions Are Accompanied by Tiny Emissions from the Eyes

Before reading on, take a look at the world around you. If you're inside, fixate on an object, like a chair, pen, or coffee mug; if you're outside, fixate on a tree, blade of grass, or cloud. Keep staring at it.

Now answer this question: Is anything coming out of your eyes?

This question may strike you as decidedly odd. Yet surveys demonstrate that large proportions of adults believe that our visual perceptions are accompanied by tiny emissions from our eyes (Winer, Cottrell, Gregg, Fournier, & Bica, 2002).

Indeed, when researchers show college students diagrams that depict rays, waves, or particles coming either into the eye or coming out of the eye and ask them to pick the diagram that best describes visual perception, 41–67% select diagrams that show emissions emanating from the eye (Winer, Cottrell, Karefilaki, & Gregg, 1996). Even when researchers have shown college students cartoons of people's faces staring at an object and asked them to draw arrows to portray their vision, 69% drew arrows that showed visual energies emerging from the eyes (Winer & Cottrell, 1996b). These findings aren't an artifact of college students not understanding the drawings, because even when researchers ask them—without any drawings—whether or not the eye emits rays or particles that enable it to see objects, many, often 30% or more, say that it does (Winer et al., 1996).

As the great Swiss psychologist Jean Piaget (1929) noted, this belief begins early in life. Piaget even discussed the case of one child who believed that two people's looks can connect and "mix" when they meet each other. Consistent with Piaget's observations, 57% of elementary school children say that something comes out of the eye when people see (Cottrell & Winer, 1994; Winer & Cottrell, 1996a). This belief declines from the third to the eighth grade, but it remains widespread (Winer & Cottrell, 1996a).

This "extramission theory" of vision dates back at least as far as Greek philosopher Plato (427–347 B.C.), who spoke of a "fire" that emanated from the eye during vision, which "coalesces with the daylight . . . and causes the sensation we call seeing" (Gross, 1999). Later, Greek mathematician Euclid (circa 300 B.C.) described "rays proceeding from the eye" during vision. Although the Greek philosopher Aristotle (384–322 B.C.) rejected the extramission theory of vision, it remained popular for many centuries.

Indeed, beliefs about the "evil eye" (*mal ojo*) inflicting psychological harm on others have long been widespread in many countries, especially Mexico and those in the Mediterranean, Central America, and the Arab world (Bohigian, 1998; Gross, 1999; Machovec, 1976; Winer, Rader, & Cottrell, 2003). Both the Old and New testaments of the Bible refer to the evil eye, and ancient Egyptians applied eye shadow to ward off its sinister influence. Throughout the ages, poets wrote of the power of the eye to induce profound psychological effects, perhaps indirectly reflecting people's extramission beliefs (Gross, 1999). For example, Shakespeare penned that "A lover's eye will gaze an eagle blind." Even today, we speak of people giving us a "penetrating glance," a "piercing stare," or a "cutting look" (Winer & Cottrell, 1996a). Because of the representativeness heuristic (see *Introduction*, p. 15), we may over-generalize from these metaphors to the literal belief that the eye outputs energy. Interestingly, surveys suggest that 93% of college students have experienced the sense that they can "feel the stare of other people" (Cottrell, Winer, & Smith, 1996).

Biologist Rupert Sheldrake (2003) even created a stir in the scientific community by conducting research purporting to show that many people can tell they're being stared at by people they can't see, but a number of researchers have identified serious flaws in his studies, including the fact that Sheldrake's subjects may have subtly influenced people to stare back at them (Marks & Colwell, 2000; Shermer, 2005). More recently, psychiatrist Colin Ross claimed that he can harness beams from his eyes to turn on a tone from a computer. Nevertheless, preliminary testing by a neurologist revealed that Ross' eyeblinks created a brain wave artifact that was inadvertently triggering the tone (False Memory Syndrome Foundation, 2008).

Psychologists still don't understand why so many of us hold extramission beliefs, but they have a few tantalizing leads. First, popular culture, as exemplified by Superman's X-ray vision with its power to attack villains and slice through steel (Yang, 2007), may have contributed to some modern extramission beliefs, although this influence of course can't explain the origins of these beliefs in ancient culture (see Figure 1.1). Second, most of us have experienced "phosphenes," perceptions of light —often consisting of dots or patterns—created by excitation of the retina, the light-sensitive layer at the back of the eye (Neher, 1990). Pressure phosphenes, which we most often see after rubbing our eyes after awakening, are almost certainly the most common. Some writers have conjectured that phosphenes may contribute to the belief that the eye emits tiny particles to detect objects (Gross, 1999). Third, the eyes of many animals that possess good night vision contain a "tapetum lucidum," a reflective layer behind or within the retina. Many of us have seen the gleaming light generated by this layer, sometimes called "eyeshine," in cats or raccoons at night (Ollivier et al., 2004). Some have suggested that this experience may foster the misimpression that the eyes generate emissions (Yang, 2007). Nevertheless, all three speculations, although intriguing, are just that—speculations—and none has been tested systematically. The reasons for extramission beliefs remain poorly understood (Winer et al., 2003).

Can we modify extramission beliefs by education? At first blush, the answer appears to be "no." Remarkably, exposure to lectures on sensation and perception in introductory psychology courses seems to make no difference in the percentage of college students who endorse beliefs in extramission (Gregg, Winer, Cottrell, Hedman, & Fournier, 2001; Winer et al., 2002). Nevertheless, there may be a "ray" of hope, if we can be forgiven for the pun. Research suggests that presenting college students with "refutational" messages, those designed not merely to explain how the eye works but how it *doesn't* work, in this case that the eye doesn't emit rays or particles, leads to short-term reductions in extramission beliefs (Winer et al., 2002). Even here, though, these reductions aren't especially long-lasting—they've largely dissipated by 3 to 5 months—suggesting that a one-shot exposure to a refutational message may not do the trick. Repeated exposure may be needed.

In many respects, research on refutational messages mirrors the approach we're adopted throughout this book: first debunking the fictions

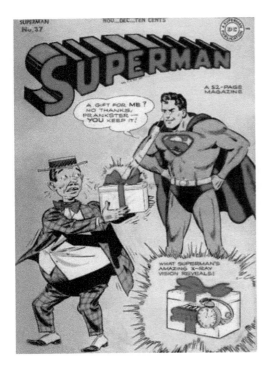

Figure 1.1 Superman's "X-ray vision" captures many people's intuitive beliefs regarding visual emissions. *Source: Superman #37.*

about the mind and brain before unveiling the facts. As Mark Twain reminded us, learning often first requires unlearning.

Myth #5   Subliminal Messages Can Persuade People to Purchase Products

Many of us know that psychologists and advertisers can present sights and sounds so briefly or so faintly that we fail to perceive them. But can those feeble stimuli influence our behavior in powerful ways? There's a profitable industry that hopes you believe the answer is "yes."

Some promoters push this kind of ultra-weak or "subliminal" messaging in the realm of advertising, whereas others have become leaders in the burgeoning self-help movement. The Internet, New Age fairs and magazines, supermarket tabloids, late-night TV "infomercials," and bookstores market subliminal audiotapes and CDs that promise to make the purchaser healthy, wealthy, and wise. Among our personal favorites we include audiotapes that promise to enlarge women's breasts, relieve constipation, improve one's sex life, or cure deafness (although the mechanism by which a deaf person could detect subliminal sounds remains truly mysterious). Given the widespread promotion of subliminal persuasion in the popular psychology world, it's hardly surprising that 59% of the psychology undergraduates sampled by Larry Brown (1983), and 83% of those sampled by Annette Taylor and Patricia Kowalski (2003), said they believed it works.

Interestingly, there's evidence that under tightly controlled laboratory conditions, psychologists can demonstrate short-lived and modest subliminal effects. In these experiments, researchers flash *priming* words or pictures on a screen so briefly that observers are unaware of what the flashes contain. In psychological lingo, priming stimuli increase the speed or accuracy with which we'll identify a later stimulus. Experimenters then determine whether the meanings or emotional content of the priming stimuli influences people's responses to the task, like completing a word with missing letters or judging the emotion of a person in a photograph. For instance, Nicholas Epley and his colleagues (Epley, Savitsky, & Kachelski, 1999) described an experiment in which researchers asked psychology graduate students to generate ideas for research projects. The investigators then exposed the students to extremely brief flashes featuring either the smiling face of a familiar colleague or the scowling face of their faculty supervisor. The students perceived the stimuli as nothing but flashes of light. Next, they rated the quality of the research ideas they'd produced. Without knowing why, subjects exposed to the flash featuring the scowling face of their supervisor rated their own ideas less favorably than those exposed to the smiling colleague's face.

Investigators can similarly influence verbal behaviors, as when a shared theme in a series of subliminally flashed priming words increases the odds that a person will choose a related word from a list of alternatives (Merikle, 1992). For example, if we present a subject with the word stem "gui _ _" and ask her to form a complete word, "guide" and "guile" are both options. Research shows that we can boost the probability of subjects choosing "guide" by priming them subliminally with words like "direct," "lead," and "escort," whereas we can boost the probability of their choosing "guile" by priming them subliminally with words like "deceit," "treachery," and "duplicity."

"Subliminal" means "under the limen." The *limen*, better known as the "sensory threshold," is the narrow range in which a diminishing stimulus goes from being just barely detectable to being just barely undetectable. If the stimulus happens to be a word or phrase, the first hurdle it must pass is the *simple detection threshold*. That's the point at which people first become dimly aware that the researcher has presented anything, even though they can't identify *what* they saw or heard. The researcher must present the stimulus for a longer interval and at a higher intensity to reach the next stage of awareness, the *recognition threshold*. At that point, people can say precisely what they heard or saw. If a stimulus has so little energy, or is so thoroughly obscured by noise that it can't trigger a physiological response in the eye's or ear's receptors, it can't affect anything the person thinks, feels, or does. Period. Messages that inhabit the gray zone between the detection and recognition thresholds, or that we simply aren't attending to, sometimes influence our emotions or behavior.

The subliminal self-help industry hopes you'll swallow the claim that your brain understands and acts on the complex meanings of phrases that are presented at vanishingly weak levels or overshadowed by stronger stimuli. Moreover, they claim that these sneaky subliminal stimuli are especially effective because they worm their way into your unconscious, where they can pull your strings like a hidden puppeteer. Should you be worried? Read on.

Modern psychology accepts that much of our mental processing goes on outside of our immediate awareness—that our brains work on many tasks at once without monitoring them consciously (Kihlstrom, 1987; Lynn & Rhue, 1994). Nevertheless, this is a far cry from the kind of non-conscious processing envisioned by pop psychology proponents of subliminal effects. Subliminal entrepreneurs are holdovers from the heyday of strict Freudian views of the unconscious, which most scientific psychologists have long abandoned (Bowers, 1987). Like Freud, subliminal enthusiasts see the unconscious as the seat of primitive and largely sexual urges that operate outside of our awareness to compel our choices.

Writer Vance Packard popularized this view of the unconscious in his 1957 smash bestseller, *The Hidden Persuaders*. Packard accepted uncritically the story of marketing consultant James Vicary, who supposedly conducted a successful demonstration of subliminal advertising at a Fort Lee, New Jersey movie theatre. Vicary claimed that during a movie, he repeated exposed cinema patrons to messages flashed on the screen for a mere 1/3,000 of a second, urging them to buy popcorn and Coca-Cola. He proclaimed that although movie-goers were unaware of these commands, sales of popcorn and Coca-Cola skyrocketed during the six-week duration of his "experiment." Vicary's findings achieved widespread popular acceptance, although he never submitted them to the scrutiny of a scientific journal, nor has anyone been able to replicate them. After much criticism, Vicary finally admitted in 1962 that he'd made up the whole story in an effort to revive his failing consulting business (Moore, 1992; Pratkanis, 1992).

Vicary's confession failed to discourage even more far-fetched accusations that the advertisers were subliminally manipulating the unsuspecting public. In a series of books with such titillating titles as *Subliminal Seduction* (1973), former psychology professor Wilson Brian Key claimed that advertisers were conspiring to influence consumer choices by embedding blurred sexual images into magazine and TV renderings of ice cubes, plates of food, models' hair-dos, and even Ritz crackers. Key gravely warned that even a single exposure to these camouflaged images could affect consumer choices weeks later. Although Key presented no real evidence to back up his claims, public alarm led the U.S. Federal Communications Commission (FCC) to look into his allegations. Although the FCC couldn't find any evidence that subliminal advertising worked, they declared it "contrary to the public interest" and warned licensed broadcasters to steer clear of it. Moreover, in an attempt to soothe public jitters, several advertising trade associations imposed voluntary restrictions, asking their members to refrain from attempts to punch below the liminal belt.

Although Vicary was an admitted fraud and Key never put his strange ideas to a proper test, some still believed that subliminal persuasion claims were worth examining. So in 1958, the Canadian Broadcasting Corporation (CBC) performed an unprecedented nationwide test. During a popular Sunday night TV program, it informed viewers that the network was about to conduct a test of subliminal persuasion. The CBC then flashed subliminally the message "phone now" on the screen 352 times throughout the show. Telephone company records indicated that phone usage didn't increase, nor did local television stations report a big upsurge in calls. Nevertheless, a few viewers, who may have known about Vicary's alleged results, called in to say they felt hungrier and thirstier following the program. The results of more carefully controlled tests of the ability of subliminal messages to influence consumer choices or voter attitudes were also overwhelmingly negative (Eich & Hyman, 1991; Logie & Della Sala, 1999; Moore, 1992; Pratkanis, 1992). To this day, there's no good evidence that subliminal messages can affect purchasers' decisions or voters' choices, let alone yield perfect memories or larger breasts.

Perhaps most bizarre of all were claims that heavy metal rock bands, such as Judas Priest, were inserting *backward* recordings of Satanic messages in their music. Alarmists claimed these messages encouraged suicidal behavior, although what conceivable purpose entertainers might have in killing off potential album buyers remains unclear. Some even asserted that it was all a plot to subvert the morality of youthful music fans. Many would maintain that youth generally manage this feat quite well without any special subliminal help, but no matter.

John Vokey and J. Don Read (1985) put the idea of subliminal backward messages to a controlled test. In one particularly amusing demonstration, they found that participants with prudish leanings, given subtle suggestions as to what they were about to hear, were likely to perceive nonexistent pornographic material in reverse-played Biblical passages. These results suggest that people who claim to hear Satanic messages embedded in commercial sound tracks are allowing their overheated imaginations to read the lewd material into meaningless sound patterns. It's all in the ear of the beholder.

Tests of self-help subliminal products have been equally discouraging. Anthony Greenwald and his colleagues (Greenwald, Spangenberg, Pratkanis, & Eskenazi, 1991) conducted a double-blind test of commercially marketed subliminal audiotapes that purport to enhance memory or self-esteem. They told half of the participants they were getting the memory boosting tapes, the other half they were getting the self-esteem boosting tapes. Within each of these groups, half got the tapes they were expecting and half got the tapes with the other message. Participants reported that they improved in ways consistent with whichever kind of tape they *believed* they received. Those who received the self-esteem tapes, believing they were the memory boosters, were just as happy with their apparent memory improvement as those who got the real McCoy, and vice versa. This curious finding led Greenwald and his colleagues to refer to this phenomenon as an *illusory placebo effect*: People didn't improve, but they thought they had.

Despite convincing debunking of the concept by the scientific community, subliminal advertisements still pop up occasionally. During the 2000 U.S. presidential election, sharp-eyed Democrats spotted, in a Republican TV attack ad aimed at candidate Al Gore, an extremely brief flash of the word "RATS" superimposed on Gore's face (Berke, 2000). The ad's creator claimed that the fact that the last four letters of the intended word "BUREACRATS" just happened to become detached from this longer word was entirely accidental (see Figure 1.2). Nevertheless, advertising production experts said that given the advanced technology used to prepare the ad, an unintentional insertion of this kind was unlikely.

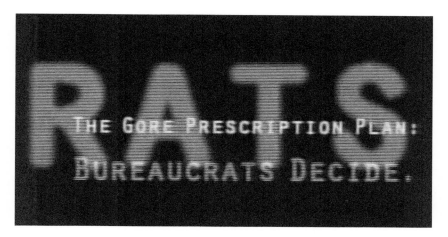

Figure 1.2 Was the inclusion of the word ("RATS"), which appeared subliminally in this 2000 Republican campaign advertisement against Democratic candidate Al Gore, intentional?
Source: Reuters/Corbis.

Perhaps the final word should go to a spokesperson for the industry that lives or dies by its ability to persuade people to buy things they may—or may not—need. Bob Garfield (1994), a columnist for *Advertising Age* magazine, summed up many people's views on the matter: "Subliminal advertising does not exist except in the public consciousness, at least not in consumer advertising. Nobody bothers with it because it's hard enough to impress people by hitting them upside the head with [blatant] images."

Chapter 1: Other Myths to Explore

Fiction	Fact
We need a full brain to function effectively.	Some people who've had one brain hemisphere surgically removed in childhood due to illness can function reasonably well in adulthood.
Modern humans have larger brains than Neanderthals.	Neanderthals' brains were probably slightly larger than ours.
Areas of activation on brain scans mean that brain regions are becoming more active.	Areas of activation on brain scans sometimes mean that some brain regions are inhibiting other regions.

Fiction	Fact
"Alpha consciousness" is associated with states of relaxation.	There's no evidence that boosting the brain's alpha waves increases relaxation; moreover, some people who aren't relaxed, such as children with attention-deficit/hyperactivity disorder, have high levels of alpha waves.
Adult humans don't grow new neurons.	Relatively recent research points to the growth of new neurons in parts of the adult brain, especially the hippocampus.
As adults, we lose about 100,000 neurons each day.	We do lose neurons each day, but the actual number is probably only about one tenth of that.
Blind people have especially well-developed senses of hearing and touch.	There's little evidence that the blind have superior abilities in other senses, including hearing, touch, or smell.
Blind people can detect obstacles at a distance by sensing heat and pressure on their foreheads.	There's no evidence for this claim.
A coma is a state of deep sleep.	People in comas are not asleep.
We can "awaken" people from comas by playing their favorite songs.	There's no scientific evidence that people can be brought out of comas by presenting them with their favorite songs or other familiar stimuli.
Biofeedback is a uniquely effective means of reducing tension.	Most studies indicate that biofeedback is no more effective than relaxation for reducing anxiety.
Humans have an invisible "body energy" that can cause psychological problems when blocked.	There's no scientific evidence for invisible energy fields in or around the human body.
Alcohol kills brain cells.	Alcohol appears not to kill brain cells themselves, although it can damage neuronal "dendrites," which are portals that bring messages into neurons.
Alcohol's primary effect is stimulating the brain.	Alcohol is primarily a depressant, and is typically a stimulant only at low doses.
Alcohol enhances sexual arousal.	Alcohol tends to inhibit sexual arousal and performance, especially at high doses.
One can always detect alcohol on the breath.	One can't always detect alcohol on the breath.

Fiction	Fact
Alcohol promotes sleep.	Although alcohol typically results in falling asleep more quickly, it usually suppresses deep sleep, often producing awakenings later in the night.
Alcohol warms the body.	Although drinking alcohol in cold temperatures can make us feel warmer, it actually results in a loss of body heat and therefore cools the body.
It's easier to get drunk at high altitudes, such as while flying in an airplane.	Studies show that higher altitudes don't result in greater intoxication.
Impaired judgment after drinking occurs only after obvious signs of intoxication.	Impaired judgment can occur well before drunkenness is apparent.
Drinking coffee is a good way to sober up after heavy drinking.	Drinking coffee won't help with a hangover; it just turns us into a "wide awake drunk."
A cold shower or exercise is a good way to sober up after heavy drinking.	Same as above.
Switching among different types of alcohol is more likely to lead to drunkenness than sticking to one type of alcohol.	The total amount, not the type, of alcohol predicts the risk of intoxication.
One can't become an alcoholic by drinking beer only.	Not true.
There's good evidence that people who smoke marijuana for many years end up apathetic.	The evidence for "amotivational syndrome" is mixed, largely in part because heavy marijuana smokers frequently use other drugs.
Most people with brain injury look and act disabled.	Most people with brain injury appear normal and act normally aside from subtle deficits on neuropsychological tests.
Following a head injury, the best prescription is rest.	Following a head injury, the best prescription is a gradual return to activity.
A head injury can't produce brain damage unless the person is knocked unconscious.	Brain damage that's detectable on neurological and neuropsychological tests can occur even with no loss of consciousness.
Prefrontal lobotomies (more popularly called "lobotomies") turn people into human "vegetables."	Most people who've received lobotomies are far from "vegetables," although they are typically apathetic.

Fiction	Fact
Humans have five senses.	Humans have several senses in addition to sight, hearing, smell, taste, and touch, including body position, temperature, and pain.
Most color-blind people see the world in black and white.	Almost all color-blind people can see at least some colors; "monochromats," who see the world in black and white, comprise only about 0.005% of the population.
Dogs see the world in black and white.	Dogs have red–green color blindness, but can perceive a number of colors, including blue and yellow.
Reading in dim light can ruin our eyesight.	Research offers no support for this claim.
The human tongue's tastes can be described as a "map" of four tastes.	Although some textbooks present a human "taste map," this map is grossly oversimplified, because receptors for the four tastes are spread throughout most of the tongue.
Consuming ice cream of other cold substances too quickly causes pain in our brains.	"Brain freeze" is caused by a constriction of blood vessels in the roof of the mouth, followed by an expansion of these vessels, triggering pain.
Magnets, like those embedded in shoe insoles, can reduce pain.	Controlled studies reveal that such magnets are useless for pain reduction.
Eating lots of turkey can make us tired.	There's no evidence that turkey is any more sleep-inducing than other foods; but because we often eat turkey on major holidays when we eat a lot and drink alcohol—both of which contribute to fatigue—we may mistakenly perceive a causal association.

Sources and Suggested Readings

To explore these and other myths about the brain and perception, see Aamodt and Wang (2008); Bausell (2007); Beyerstein (1990); Della Sala (1999, 2007); El-Hai (2005); Herculano-Houzel (2002); Hines (2003); Juan (2006); Lilienfeld and Arkowitz (2008); Vreeman and Carroll (2007).

2 FROM WOMB TO TOMB

Myths about Development and Aging

Myth # 6

Playing Mozart's Music to Infants Boosts Their Intelligence

Few qualities—or quantities—are more prized in American society than intelligence and intellectual accomplishment. When it comes to academic achievement, parents love to win bragging rights on their children's behalf. Just look at car bumper stickers: "My Child is an Honor's Student at East Cantaloupe High School," "Proud Parent of an Honor's Student at North Igloo Elementary," or for laughs, "My French Poodle is Smarter than Your Honor's Student." In today's cutthroat world, many parents are understandably eager to lend their children a competitive advantage over their classmates. This undeniable fact raises an intriguing question: Could parents give their children a jump-start by stimulating them intellectually in infancy, perhaps only a few months, weeks, or even days after birth?

This may sound like the stuff of a futuristic science fiction novel. Yet it seemingly turned into reality in 1993 with the publication of an article in one of the world's premier science journals, *Nature*. In that paper, three University of California at Irvine researchers reported that college students who listened to a mere 10 minutes of a Mozart piano sonata displayed a significant improvement on a spatial reasoning task—a test involving paper folding and cutting—compared with a group of students who listened to either a relaxation tape or to silence (Rauscher, Shaw, & Ky, 1993). The overall improvement translated into a boost of about 8 or 9 IQ points. The *Mozart Effect*—a term coined by physician Alfred Tomatis (1991) and later popularized by educator and musician Don

Campbell (1997) to refer to the supposed enhancement in intelligence after listening to classical music—was born.

The 1993 finding didn't imply anything about the long-term enhancement of spatial ability, let alone intelligence in general. It applied only to one task administered almost immediately after listening to Mozart's music. Nor did the finding imply anything about the effects of Mozart's music on infants, as the original study examined only college students.

But this didn't stop the popular press or toy companies from picking up the Mozart Effect ball and running with it. Based entirely on speculation that the original findings might apply to infants, companies soon began to market scores of Mozart Effect CDs, cassettes, and toys targeted toward babies. By 2003, Don Campbell's popular Mozart Effect CDs had sold over 2 million copies (Nelson, 2003). As of 2008, Amazon.com featured over 40 products, mostly CDs and cassettes, on the Mozart Effect, many of which proudly feature young children or newborn infants on their covers.

In addition to the mass marketing of scores of Mozart Effect products to receptive parents, another reason for this effect's popularity may stem from a confusion between correlation and causation (see *Introduction*, p. 13). Studies show that musical talent tends to be positively associated with IQ (Lynn, Wilson, & Gault, 1989). Some people may erroneously leap from this correlational finding to the conclusion that exposure to music *increases* IQ.

As psychologists Adrian Bangerter and Chip Heath (2004) observed, the Mozart Effect claim spread through society much like a message passes through a game of telephone, becoming increasingly distorted and often exaggerated over time. One 2000 article in a Chinese newspaper claimed that "According to studies conducted in the West," babies who listen to Mozart masterpieces "during gestation are likely to come out of the womb smarter than their peers" (South China Morning Post, 2000, as cited in Bangerter & Heath, 2004). Yet no published studies conducted in the West or elsewhere had ever examined the effects of Mozart's music on humans in utero. A 2001 article in the *Milwaukee Journal Sentinel* referred to "numerous studies on the Mozart effect and how it helps elementary school students, high school students, and even infants increase their mental performance," despite the fact that no researchers had investigated the effects of Mozart's music on any of these groups (Krakovsky, 2005).

These widespread media reports appear to have had an effect on public perception; two surveys revealed that over 80% of Americans were familiar with the Mozart Effect (Bangerter & Heath, 2004). A survey of introductory psychology students revealed that 73% believed that "listening to Mozart will enhance your intelligence" (Taylor & Kowalski, 2003, p. 5). Several years ago, the coach of the New York Jets football team arranged for Mozart's music to be played through loudspeakers during practice sessions in an effort to enhance their performance. A New York community college even set aside a Mozart Effect study room for its students.

The Mozart Effect eventually reached the hallowed halls of state legislatures. In 1998, then Georgia Governor Zell Miller added $105,000 to the state budget to allow each newborn child in Georgia to receive a Mozart CD or cassette free of charge, announcing his bold initiative over the inspiring strands of Beethoven's Ninth Symphony (Mercer, 2010; Sack, 1998). According to Miller, "No one questions that listening to music at a very early age affects the spatial-temporal reasoning that underlies math and engineering and even chess." Tennessee governor Don Sundquist soon followed suit, and the Florida State Senate likewise passed a bill requiring day care centers that received state funding to play classical music to infants on a daily basis (State of Florida Senate Bill 660, May 21, 1998).

But all of this implies that the Mozart Effect is real. Is it?

Several investigators who tried to replicate the original *Nature* findings reported either no effect or a miniscule one (Gray & Della Sala, 2007; McKelvie & Low, 2002). Analyses that combined the results across multiple studies revealed that the Mozart Effect was trivial in magnitude —2 IQ points or less—and of trivial duration, typically an hour or less (Chabris, 1999; Steele, Bass, & Crook, 1999). Some researchers began to claim that the Mozart Effect materialized only with certain pieces of Mozart's music, but not others, but other researchers never confirmed these assertions. Moreover, none of the published studies examined children, let alone infants, who were the supposed beneficiaries of the Mozart Effect. Georgia governor Zell Miller (1999) urged advocates of the Mozart Effect to ignore these negative findings, reassuring them not "to be misled or discouraged by some academics debunking other academics." But this is precisely how science works at its best: by refuting, correcting, or revising claims that haven't stood up to careful scrutiny.

Later researchers helped to pin down the source of the Mozart Effect. In one study, they asked students to listen to an uplifting piece by Mozart, a depressing piece by another classical composer (Albinoni), and silence (Thompson, Schellenberg, & Husain, 2001). Immediately afterwards, the investigators gave participants a paper folding and cutting task.

The Mozart piece improved performance on this task relative to the two control conditions, but it also enhanced emotional arousal relative to these conditions. When the researchers used statistical techniques to equalize for the effects of emotional arousal across the three experimental conditions, the Mozart Effect vanished. The results of another study demonstrated that listening to Mozart was no better for improving spatial ability than listening to a passage from a scary story by horror writer Stephen King (Nantais & Schellenberg, 1999).

These findings suggest an alternative explanation for the Mozart Effect: short-term arousal. Anything that heightens alertness is likely to increase performance on mentally demanding tasks (Jones, West, & Estell, 2006; Steele, 2000), but it's unlikely to produce long-term effects on spatial ability or, for that matter, overall intelligence. So listening to Mozart's music may not be needed to boost our performance; drinking a glass of lemonade or cup of coffee may do the trick.

The bottom line: The Mozart Effect may be "real" in the sense that it enhances immediate performance on certain mental tasks. But there's no evidence that this has anything to do with Mozart's music, or even music at all (Gray & Della Sala, 2007). Nor is there evidence that it increases intelligence in adults, let alone infants. Of course, introducing children to the music of Mozart and other great composers is a wonderful idea, not only because such music can be uplifting, but because it's had an immense influence on Western culture. But parents hoping to transform their babies into geniuses by exposing them to the soundtrack of *Amadeus* are best advised to save their money.

The popular craze following in the wake of the Mozart effect wasn't the first time that entrepreneurs capitalized on eager parents' desires to boost their infants' intellects. Many of these marketers seized on widespread, but poorly supported, claims that the first three years of life are especially crucial in infants' intellectual development (Bruer, 1997; Paris, 2000). In the 1980s, thousands of parents introduced their newborn infants to hours of foreign languages and advanced mathematics in a concerted effort to create "superbabies" (Clarke-Stewart, 1998). But no superbabies emerged. Today, such alleged intelligence-improving products as "Baby Einstein" toys and videos are a $100 million a year industry (Minow, 2005; Quart, 2006). Yet there's no good evidence that these products work either. To the contrary, research suggests that babies learn less from videos than from playing actively for the same time period (Anderson & Pempek, 2005).

The work of the great Russian developmental psychologist Lev Vygotsky may help to explain why these products are doomed to fail. As Vygotsky

(1978) observed, learning occurs best within a "zone of proximal development," in which children can't yet master a skill on their own but can do so with help from others. If 3-year-old children don't possess the cognitive skills to learn calculus, no amount of exposure to calculus will increase their math abilities, let alone transform them into superbabies, because calculus lies outside their zone of proximal development. Much as impatient parents might want to hear otherwise, children can't learn until their minds are ready.

Myth #7 Adolescence Is Inevitably a Time of Psychological Turmoil

In a recent weekly newspaper advice piece, an exasperated mother wrote to ask the columnist, Hap LeCrone (2007), to explain what had happened to her now 11-year-old daughter, who was until recently an easy-going and happy child. "If we like something, she hates it," the mother wrote. Her daughter "doesn't want to accompany us anywhere," and "her responses to us are not often very civil." What's more, "getting her to keep her room straight or dress nicely is likely pulling teeth," and "back talk is the norm." What on the earth, the mother wondered, is going on? LeCrone responded succinctly: "Some parents call what you are going through the disease of adolescence."

The view that adolescence is always or almost always a time of emotional turmoil is hardly new. Psychologist G. Stanley Hall (1904), the first president of the American Psychological Association, was also the first to refer to adolescence as a time of "storm and stress." Hall borrowed this term from the 18th century German "Sturm and Drang" movement in music, art, and literature, which emphasized the expression of passionate and often painful emotions. Later, Anna Freud (1958), daughter of Sigmund Freud and a prominent psychoanalyst in her own right, popularized the view that adolescent emotional upheaval is pervasive (Doctors, 2000). She wrote (A. Freud, 1958, p. 275) that "to be normal during the adolescent period is by itself abnormal" (p. 267) and "adolescence is by its nature an interruption of peaceful growth" (p. 275). For Anna Freud, the teenager who experiences minimal distress is actually pathological, and is at greatly heightened risk for psychological problems in adulthood.

Today's pop psychologists have fueled the perception that the teenage years are usually times of high family drama. For example, the promotional copy for parenting expert Dr. James Dobson's (2005) book,

Preparing for Adolescence, informs readers that it will "help teens through the rough years of adolescence" and help "parents who want to know what to say to a child who's getting ready to enter those turbulent teenage years." A television show on adolescence featuring "Dr. Phil" (Phil McGraw) warned viewers that "the teenage years can be a parent's worse nightmare" and promised to discuss "ways for parents and teens to survive adolescence."

The stereotype of the "terrible teen" years is echoed in much of the entertainment media. Dozens of films, including *Rebel Without a Cause* (1955), *Ordinary People* (1980), *Kids* (1995), *Girl, Interrupted* (1999), and *Thirteen* (2003), focus on the plight of troubled adolescents, and the title of a 2002 British television series, *Adolescence: The Stormy Decade,* speaks for itself. In addition, such bestselling novels as J. D. Salinger's *A Catcher in the Rye* (1951) capture the pain and confusion of the teenage years.

Because books and movies focus far more often on tales of troubled than healthy adolescents—a Hollywood film about an entirely normal teenager is unlikely to make for an interesting storyline, let alone hefty box office receipts—the public is routinely exposed to a biased sampling of teenagers (Holmbeck & Hill, 1988; Offer, Ostrov, & Howard, 1981). Perhaps not surprisingly, many laypersons believe that adolescence is usually a time of storm and stress. As psychologist Albert Bandura (1964) noted, "If you were to walk up to the average man on the street, grab him by the arm and utter the word 'adolescence,' it is highly probable . . . that his associations of this term will include references to storm and stress, tension, rebellion, dependency conflicts, peer-group conformity, black leather jackets, and the like" (p. 224).

Bandura's informal observations are borne out by surveys of college students. Grayson Holmbeck and John Hill (1988) found that students enrolled in an undergraduate course on adolescence scored an average of 5.2 (out of 7) on the item "Adolescence is a stormy and stressful time." Parents and teachers hold similar views (Hines & Paulson, 2006). This position is widespread even among health professionals. One survey of staff in a pediatric hospital revealed that 62% of medical residents (doctors in training) and 58% of nurses agreed that "the majority of adolescents show neurotic or antisocial behavior sometime during adolescence." In addition, 54% of medical residents and 75% nurses agreed that "Doctors and nurses should be concerned about the adjustment of the adolescent who causes no trouble and feels no disturbances," mirroring Anna Freud's position that the "normal" adolescent is actually abnormal (Lavigne, 1977).

To evaluate claims regarding adolescent storm and stress, we need to examine three domains of teen behavior: (1) conflicts with parents, (2) mood instability, and (3) risky behavior (Arnett, 1999). Research shows that like several other myths in this book, the adolescent storm and stress claim possesses a kernel of truth, which probably accounts in part for its popularity. At least in American society, adolescents are indeed at somewhat elevated risk for difficulties across all three domains (Arnett, 1999; Epstein, 2007). Conflicts with parents escalate during the teen years (Laursen, Coy, & Collins, 1998), teens report more mood changes and more extreme moods than do non-teens (Buchanan, Eccles, & Becker, 1992; Larson & Richards, 1994), and teens take more physical risks than do non-teens (Reyna & Farley, 2006; Steinberg, 2007). So it's true that adolescence can be a time of heightened psychological struggles for *some* teens.

But note that we italicized "some." The same data show overwhelmingly that each of these difficulties is confined to only a small minority of teens. Most studies indicate that only about 20% of adolescents undergo pronounced turmoil, with the substantial majority experiencing generally positive moods and harmonious relations with their parents and peers (Offer & Schonert-Reichl, 1992). Furthermore, marked emotional upset and parental conflict are limited largely to adolescents with clear-cut psychological problems, like depression and conduct disorder (Rutter, Graham, Chadwick, & Yule, 1976), as well as to adolescents who come from disrupted family backgrounds (Offer, Kaiz, Ostrov, & Albert, 2003). So the claim that adolescent angst is either typical or inevitable doesn't hold up (Epstein, 2007). To the contrary, it's the exception rather than the rule. In addition, one study that followed 73 adolescent males over a 34-year period found not a shred of evidence that well-adjusted teens are at heightened risk for psychological problems later in life (Offer et al., 2002). These findings put the lie to Anna Freud's claims that seemingly normal teens are actually abnormal and destined for psychological trouble in adulthood.

Further contradicting the view that teen storm and stress are inevitable are cross-cultural data showing that adolescence is a time of relative peace and calm in many traditional and non-Western societies (Arnett, 1999; Dasen, 2000). For example, in Japan and China, the teenage years usually pass without incident. In Japan, 80–90% of teens describe their home lives as "fun" or "pleasant" and report positive relations with their parents. We can find a similar absence of significant teenage turmoil in India, sub-Saharan Africa, Southeast Asia, and much of the Arab world (Epstein, 2007). Moreover, there's evidence that increasing

Westernization in these areas is associated with increasing adolescent distress (Dasen, 2000). We don't know why adolescent turmoil is more common in Western than in non-Western cultures. Some authors have suggested that because parents in Western cultures, in contrast to most non-Western cultures, tend to treat their teenagers more like children rather than as maturing adults with grown-up rights and responsibilities, they may rebel against their parents' restrictions and behave antisocially (Epstein, 2007).

Can erroneous beliefs about the inevitability of adolescent turmoil do any harm? Perhaps. Dismissing some adolescents' genuine problems as merely a "passing phase" or as a manifestation of a normal period of turmoil may result in deeply troubled teens not receiving the psychological assistance they sorely need (Offer & Schonert-Reichl, 1992). Admittedly, some teenagers' cries for help are manipulative ploys to garner attention, but many others are signs of desperate youths whose suffering has been ignored.

Myth #8   Most People Experience a Midlife Crisis in Their 40s or Early 50s

A 45-year-old man buys the Porsche he'd dreamt about owning for years, sports a new beard, gets hair plugs, leaves his wife for a 23-year-old woman, and takes out a chunk of his retirement savings to travel to the Himalayas to study with the guru *du jour*. Many people in our society would chalk up his uncharacteristic behaviors to a "midlife crisis," a period of dramatic self-questioning and turbulence in middle age (40 to 60 years old), as one confronts mortality, physical decline, and unfulfilled hopes and dreams.

The idea that many people experience a difficult life transition when poised roughly midway between birth and death isn't of recent vintage. In the 14th century, the first lines of Alighieri Dante's (1265–1321) epic poem the *Divine Comedy* evoked the idea of a midlife crisis:

> Midway upon the journey of our life I found
> myself within a forest dark,
> For the straightforward pathway had been lost.

But it wasn't until 1965 that Elliott Jacques coined the term "midlife crisis" to describe the compulsive attempts to remain young and defy the reality of death that he observed in middle-aged artists and composers.

Jacque served up this catchy phrase for the public and scientific community to describe virtually any unsettling life transition people experience in middle age. A decade later, Gail Sheehy's (1976) bestselling book, *Passages: Predictable Crises of Adult Life*, cemented the idea of a midlife crisis in the public imagination. By 1994, 86% of young adults surveyed believed in the reality of a "midlife crisis" (Lachman, Lewkowicz, Marcus, & Peng, 1994).

The film industry has pounced all over the idea of a turbulent period in midlife by depicting goofy and screwed up, yet likeable, middle aged guys—the protagonists are mostly male—who question the meaning and value of their lives. In *City Slickers* (1991), three men (played by Billy Crystal, Daniel Stern, and Bruno Kirby), all experiencing a midlife crisis, take a 2-week break from their humdrum lives to go on a cattle drive from New Mexico to Colorado. A more recent riff on the same theme, the movie *Wild Hogs* (2007), portrays the adventures of four middle-aged men who hit the road on motorcycles to rekindle the excitement of their youth. No movie captures the supposed rut of middle age better than *Groundhog Day* (1993), in which comedian Bill Murray portrays Phil Connors, a heavy drinking, self-absorbed weatherman, who's fated to repeat the same day, every day, until he finally "gets" that his life can have meaning when he becomes a better person. In *Bull Durham* (1988), Kevin Costner portrays baseball player "Crash" Davis, exiled to the minor leagues to coach a talented young player. Crash is keenly aware of his youth sliding away, much like his waning ability to slide safely into home plate, but he eventually finds love and fulfillment with baseball groupie Annie Savoy (played by Susan Sarandon). In the Academy Award-winning movie, *American Beauty* (1999), Lester Burnham (played by Kevin Spacey) displays all of the stereotypic hallmarks of a male midlife crisis. He quits his high pressure job to work as a burger turner, starts to use drugs and works out, buys a sports car, and becomes infatuated with his teenage daughter's girlfriend.

The Internet and books provide advice to help people negotiate not only their midlife crisis but their spouse's crisis as well. That's right: Women aren't immune to midlife angst either. The Internet site for the *Midlife Club* (http://midlifeclub.com/) warns its visitors that: "Whether it's your midlife crisis, or the midlife crisis of someone you love, whether you're a man or a woman—you're in for a bumpy ride!" The club peddles books in which men and women who "made it through the crisis" share their wisdom, strategies, and stories with one another. For $2,500, you can purchase "LifeLaunch" through the Hudson Institute of Santa Barbara (http://www.hudsoninstitute.com). For that steep price, you can obtain intensive coaching to guide you through your midlife crisis with "vision, direction, and thoughtful planning" as you "reflect on all that you bring to the next chapter of your life." At the other extreme of the price spectrum, you can buy *Overcome Midlife Crisis* for only $12.95 from HypnosisDownloads with a 100% 90-day money-back guarantee (no questions asked) and a promise that you'll "Get rid of those midlife crisis feelings and grasp life by the horns again" (http://www.hypnosisdownloads.com/downloads/hypnotherapy/midlife-crisis.html).

Psychologist Ian Gotlib (Gotlib & Wheaton, 2006) reviewed headlines and feature articles in *The New York Times Living Arts* section for 15 months. He discovered that editors used the term "midlife crisis" an average of twice a month to headline reviews of books, films, and television programs.

In addition to Internet and media coverage, another reason why the notion of a midlife crisis may persist is that it's based on a shard of truth. Psychologist Erik Erikson (1968) observed that in middle adulthood, most people grapple with finding direction, meaning, and purpose in their lives, and they strive to find out whether there's a need for a mid-course correction. We'll see that Erikson exaggerated the prevalence of a crisis in middle age, but he was right that some people experience marked self-doubt in the intermediate years of life. Yet people reevaluate their goals and priorities and experience crises in every decade of life, as evidenced by the emotional tumult some (but by no means all; see Myth #7) teens experience. Moreover, the experiences that fall under the umbrella of the "midlife crisis" are very broad—such as change of job, divorce, buying a sports car—and nebulous. As a consequence, one could consider most any upheaval or life change proof positive of a midlife meltdown.

Some "symptoms" of a midlife crisis, such as divorce, are actually more likely to occur prior to middle age. In the United States, people first divorce, on average, within 5 years of marriage, at age 33 for men and 31 for women (Clarke, 1995). Moreover, when people purchase their fantasy sports car in their 40s, it may have nothing to do with making the best of a crisis. Rather, they may finally be able to make the payments on the car for which they longed as teenagers.

Studies across cultures provide no fodder for the idea that middle age is a particularly stressful and difficult period. In a study of 1,501 Chinese married adults between 30 and 60 years old, Daniel Shek (1996) failed to find high levels of dissatisfaction approaching a "crisis" in the majority of middle-aged men and women. Researchers funded by The MacArthur Foundation studied a total of nearly 7,195 men and

Mythbusting: A Closer Look

The Empty Nest Syndrome

A mother goes into her son's bedroom to sniff his T-shirt shortly after he leaves for college for the first time. On a website (http://www.netdoctor.co.uk/womenshealth/features/ens.htm) that recounts her unusual behavior, we learn that it's a perfectly normal expression of the "empty nest syndrome," a term referring to the popular belief that most women feel disturbing pangs of depression when their children leave home or get married. The popular "Chicken Soup for the Soul" self-help series even features a book devoted entirely to helping "empty nesters" adapt to the stress of their transition (Canfield, Hansen, McAdoo, & Evans, 2008).

Actually, there's scant scientific support for the popular belief that women experience the female equivalent of the male midlife crisis when their children fly the coop, leaving the proverbial nest empty. Christine Proulx and Heather Helms (2008) interviewed 142 sets of parents after their firstborn children left home. Most parents (both men and women) made an excellent adjustment, felt the move was positive, and related more to their children as peers when they achieved greater independence. Moreover, most empty nesters actually experience an increase in life satisfaction following their newfound flexibility and freedom (Black & Hill, 1984). Recent evidence tracking marital relationships over an 18-year period points to an increase in marital satisfaction too (Gorchoff, John, & Helson, 2008).

A shift in household roles, and a sudden increase in free time, can require some adjustment for all family members. People who define themselves largely in terms of their role as parents, hold traditional attitudes toward women's roles in society and the family, and aren't employed outside the home may be particularly vulnerable to empty nest syndrome (Harkins, 1978). But a child "moving on" isn't typically a devastating experience for parents, as it's often portrayed in the media (Walsh, 1999). In fact, as children make a successful transition to young adulthood, and parents reap the rewards of many years of dedicated work raising their children, it can be an occasion for celebration.

women aged 25 to 74, of whom 3,032 were interviewed in the largest study of people at midlife (Brim, Ryff, & Kessler, 2004). Contrary to the popular stereotype, people in the 40 to 60 age range generally felt more in control of their lives and expressed greater feelings of well-being compared with the previous decade of their lives. In addition, more than three quarters of respondents rated their relationships as good to excellent. Men and women were equally likely to experience what they considered to be a midlife crisis. The researchers found that concerns about having a midlife crisis were more common than actually experiencing a crisis.

Several other findings debunk the myth of the midlife crisis. Across studies, only 10–26% (depending on how scientists define the midlife crisis) of people report they've experienced a midlife crisis (Brim, 1992; Wethington, 2000). In addition, middle age can be a period of peak psychological functioning (Lachman, 2003). Clearly, a midlife crisis isn't a prospect for everyone, or even a likely occurrence. So if you want to make radical changes in your life, and buy a red sports car or a "wild hog" motorcycle, it's never too early—and never too late—to do so.

Myth # 9 Old Age Is Typically Associated with Increased Dissatisfaction and Senility

Think of a person who matches this description: cranky, eccentric, cantankerous, afraid of change, depressed, unable to keep up with technology, lonely, dependent, physically infirm, and forgetful. We certainly wouldn't be shocked if an elderly person came to mind—perhaps hunched, shrunken, and doddering—because the descriptors we've provided fit to a T popular yet inaccurate stereotypes of the elderly (Falchikov, 1990; Middlecamp & Gross, 2002).

Many people assume that a large proportion of the elderly is depressed, lonely, and irritable, lacking in sexual desire, and either senile or displaying early signs of it. Sixty-five percent of a sample of 82 introductory psychology students agreed that "most older people are lonely and isolated" and 38% that "When people grow old, they generally become 'cranky' " (Panek, 1982, p. 105). In addition, 64% of a sample of 288 medical students said that "major depression is more prevalent among the elderly than among younger persons" (van Zuilen, Rubert, Silverman, & Lewis, 2001).

Media exposure to stereotypes—we might even say indoctrination —about the aged begins early in life (Towbin et al., 2003). In their study of Disney children's films, Tom Robinson and his colleagues (Robinson, Callister, Magoffin, & Moore, 2007) found that 42% of elderly characters like Belle's father from *Beauty and the Beast* and Madam Mim from the *Sword and the Stone* (and let's not forget "Grumpy," one of the seven dwarves in *Snow White*) are portrayed in a less than positive light, and as forgetful, angry, or crotchety. Children bombarded with these and other negative stereotypes may understandably develop unfavorable impressions of seniors that begin to crystallize at an early age.

The relentless barrage of misinformation about aging persists through adulthood. In a study of popular teen movies, most elderly characters exhibited some negative characteristics, and a fifth fulfilled only negative stereotypes (Magoffin, 2007). The depressing and occasionally frightening image of aging extends to adult-oriented cartoons, television programs, and movies. Consider Grandpa Simpson from the popular television program, who was born in the "old country" but can't seem to remember which country. Or mobster Tony Soprano's offbeat family: his mother Livia (played by Nancy Marchand in the popular television program *The Sopranos*), who tried to have Tony (played by James Gandolfini) "hit" because he put her in a nursing home (". . . it's a retirement community, Ma!"), and his demented Uncle Junior (played by Dominic Chianese), who shot Tony thinking he was an enemy who'd died 20 years earlier. In the movie *The Savages* (2007), a son and daughter, played by Philip Seymour Hoffman and Laura Linney, respectively, struggle with their ambivalence about taking care of their elderly father (played by Philip Bosco) as he deteriorates in physical and mental health, playing with his feces and becoming increasingly forgetful.

With media fear-mongering about the seemingly inevitable ravages of aging, it's scarcely any wonder that myths about senior citizens abound and prejudice against the elderly runs deep. John Hess (1991) chronicled how the media blame the elderly unfairly for many social and political ills, including high taxes, bankrupting the national budget due to the high costs of medical care and social security, and cutbacks on programs for children and the disabled. Surveys suggest that the emotion most college students feel toward the elderly is pity (Fiske, Cuddy, Glick, & Xu, 2002). Moreover, people rate memory problems in the elderly as signs of mental incompetence, but consider memory problems in younger individuals as due to inattention or a lack of effort (Cuddy & Fiske, 2002).

Sharply contradicting these perceptions, research demolishes the myth that old age (beginning at age 60–65) is typically associated with dissatisfaction and senility. One team of investigators surveyed adults between the ages of 21 and 40 or over age 60 about their happiness and the happiness of the average person at their current age, age 30, and at age 70. The young adults predicted that people in general would be less happy as they aged. Yet the older adults were actually happier at their current age than were younger respondents (Lacey, Smith, & Ubel, 2006).

Population-based surveys reveal that rates of depression are actually highest in individuals aged 25–45 (Ingram, Scott, & Siegle, 1999), and that the happiest group of people is men aged 65 and older (Martin, 2006). Happiness increases with age through the late 60s and perhaps 70s (Mroczek & Kolarz, 1998; Nass, Brave, & Takayama, 2006). In one study of 28,000 Americans, a third of 88-year-olds reported they were "very happy," and the happiest people surveyed were the oldest. The odds of being happy increased 5% with every decade of life (Yang, 2008). Older people may be relatively happy because they lower their expectations ("I'll never win a Nobel Prize, but I can be a wonderful grandparent"), accept their limitations, and recall more positive than negative information (Cartensen & Lockenhoff, 2003).

Although depression isn't an inevitable consequence of aging, it still afflicts about 15% of the elderly. But many cases of depression in this age group are probably due not to biological aging itself, but to medical and pain conditions, the side effects of medications, social isolation, and such life events as the death of a close friend (Arean & Reynolds, 2005; Kivela, Pahkala, & Lappala, 1991; Mroczek & Spiro, 2005).

Contrary to the myth of older people as lacking in sexual desire, a national survey (Laumann, Das, & Waite, in press) of about 3,000 people indicated that more than three quarters of men aged 75 to 85 and half of their women counterparts reported still being interested in sex. Moreover, 73% of people aged 57 to 64 years were sexually active, as were most people (53%) aged 64 to 74 years. Even in the oldest group, people aged 75 to 85 years, 26% reported still being sexually active. Interestingly, health problems, such as obesity and diabetes, were better predictors than aging itself of which people stayed sexually active. As overall health declined, so did sexual activity.

Although depression and ebbing sexual desire don't coincide with the arrival of an AARP card in the mail, people are naturally wary of the aging process in general, and memory loss in particular. Many websites poke fun at the elderly by quoting the *Senility Prayer*: "God, Grant me the senility to forget the people I never liked anyway, the good fortune to run into the ones I do, and the eyesight to tell the difference." Not surprisingly, popular books address, if not prey on, fears of aging. For example, Zaldy Tan's (2008) book title promises to *Age-Proof Your Mind: Detect, Delay, and Prevent Memory Loss—Before It's Too Late.* A Nintendo game called *Brain Age* supposedly permits players to lower their "brain age" through mental exercises that activate their brain's prefrontal cortex (Bennallack, 2006).

It's natural to experience some slight memory loss as we age, including minor forgetfulness and difficulty retrieving words in conversational speech. But severe memory loss associated with Alzheimer's disease and other forms of dementia that impair our ability to function isn't a typical consequence of aging. People with Alzheimer's disease experience getting lost in familiar places, personality changes, loss of language skills, difficulty in learning, and problems in completing simple daily tasks. Alzheimer's disease afflicts as many as 4 million Americans, and the disease can last from 3 to 20 years, with the average duration being 8 years (Neath & Surprenant, 2003). As people get older, their risk of Alzheimer's increases. Yet some people in their 30s and 40s develop Alzheimer's, and even after age 85, about three quarters of the elderly don't experience significant memory problems (U.S. Department of Health and Human Services, 2007).

Even at age 80, general intelligence and verbal abilities don't decline much from younger ages, although memory for words and the ability to manipulate numbers, objects, and images are somewhat more prone to age-related declines (Riekse & Holstege, 1996). Furthermore, research on creative accomplishments indicates that in some disciplines, like history or fiction writing, many people produce their highest quality work in their 50s or several decades beyond (Rabbitt, 1999). Exercising, eating a healthy diet, solving puzzles, and staying intellectually active may slow or compensate for minor losses of cognitive prowess as people age (Whitbourne, 1996), although researchers haven't established the effectiveness of "Brain Age" and similar products.

A final misconception about the elderly is that they're unable to acquire new skills or are befuddled by modern gadgets. As the saying goes, "You can't teach an old dog new tricks." In the introductory psychology student sample we mentioned earlier, 21% agreed that "older people have great difficulty learning new skills" (Panek, 1982, p. 105). The media occasionally spoofs this image of aging people. A good example is eccentric Arthur Spooner (played by Jerry Stiller) in the television program *King of Queens*, who doesn't know to use a DVD. But many older people aren't intimidated by computers, iPhones, and other "newfangled devices," and have the inclination and time to master and appreciate them. So to tweak an old (pun intended) saying, "You *can* teach an old dog new tricks . . . and a whole lot more."

Myth # 10   When Dying, People Pass through a Universal Series of Psychological Stages

DABDA.

Across the United States, scores of psychologists, psychiatrists, nurses, and social workers who work with the elderly commit this acronym to memory. DABDA stands for the five stages of dying popularized by Swiss-born psychiatrist Elisabeth Kübler-Ross (1969) in the late 1960s: *Denial, Anger, Bargaining, Depression,* and *Acceptance.* These stages, often called the "Five Stages of Grief," supposedly describe an invariant sequence of stages that all people pass through when dying (Kübler-Ross, 1969, 1974). According to Kübler-Ross, when we learn we're about to die, we first tell ourselves it's not happening (denial), then become angry at the realization that it really is happening (anger), then search in vain for some way to postpone the death, perhaps at least until we can accomplish a long-valued goal (bargaining), then become sad as the realization that we're dying sets in (depression), and finally fully come to grips with our inevitable death and approach it with a sense of serenity (acceptance).

Kübler-Ross's stages of grief are widely accepted in the medical, psychological, and nursing communities. Surveys indicate that these stages are taught to large proportions of medical, nursing, and social work students in the United States, Canada, and the UK (Downe-Wamboldt & Tamlyn, 1997; Holleman, Holleman, & Gershenhorn, 1994).

Her stages are also a common fixture in popular culture. The award-winning 1979 film *All That Jazz,* based loosely on the life of choreographer Bob Fosse, featured the five Kübler-Ross stages in a dramatization of Fosse's imagined death. In season 6 of the television program *Frasier,* Frasier passes through all five stages of grief after losing his job as a radio talk-show psychologist. In a hilarious depiction of Kübler-Ross's framework in the cartoon program *The Simpsons,* Homer Simpson passes through all five of stages in a matter of seconds after a doctor informs him (erroneously) that he's dying. These stages are even popular in the political arena. One Internet blogger likened the waning days of George W. Bush's presidency to each of the five Kübler-Ross stages (Grieser, 2008; http://www.democracycellproject.net/blog/archives/2008/02/kubler_ross_stages_as_applied_to_our_national_grief.html), and *New York Times* columnist Maureen Dowd (2008) sought to explain Hillary Clinton's reluctance to accept her Democratic nomination loss to Barack Obama in the summer of 2008 in terms of Kübler-Ross's first several stages.

Kübler-Ross's stages may be popular not merely because of the extensive media coverage they've attracted, but because they offer people a sense of predictability over the previously unpredictable—the process of dying (Copp, 1998; Kastenbaum, 1998). The thought that the often terrifying experience of death follows a standard series of stages, ending in a sense of tranquil acceptance over one's fate, strikes many of us as reassuring. Moreover, the idea that death unfolds in the same neat and tidy way for everyone is somehow appealing, perhaps because it simplifies a mysterious process. But is it true?

Given the ubiquity of the Kübler-Ross stages in popular psychology, we might think they'd been extensively validated by psychological research. If so, we should think again. In fact, as is the case for many "stage theories" in psychology, the scientific support for these stages has been at best mixed (Kastenbaum, 2004). In retrospect, this largely negative scientific evidence shouldn't have been all that surprising, because Kübler-Ross's (1969) claims regarding her five stages weren't based on carefully controlled research. In particular, her research was based almost entirely on potentially biased samples (she didn't study a broad cross-section of the population), subjective observations, and unstandardized measurements of people's emotions across time (Bello-Hass, Bene, & Mitsumoto, 2002; Friedman & James, 2008). Admittedly, some people do pass through some or even all of the Kübler-Ross stages of dying, so there's probably a grain of truth to her model that lends it a sense of credibility.

Yet research evidence suggests that many dying people don't pass through her stages in the same order (Copp, 1998). Instead, people appear to cope with their "death sentences" in many ways. Studies of dying patients reveal that many skip Kübler-Ross stages, or even pass through them in reverse order (Buckman, 1993; Kastenbaum, 1998). Some people, for example, initially accept their own death, but then later enter denial (Bello-Hass et al., 2002). Moreover, the boundaries among Kübler-Ross's stages are often blurry, and there's minimal evidence for sudden "jumps" from one stage to another.

Some writers have also attempted to apply Kübler-Ross's stages to the grief we experience following the death of a loved one, like a spouse or child (Friedman & James, 2008). Yet research doesn't bear out the validity for her stages for this kind of grief either, as grieving people don't all undergo the same fixed series of stages (Neimeyer, 2001). For one thing, not all people experience depression or marked distress following the loss of a loved one, including those about whom they care deeply (Bonanno et al., 2002; Wortman & Boerner, 2006; Wortman & Silver, 1989). Nor is there evidence that a failure to experience depression following a serious personal loss is indicative of poor mental adjustment (Wortman & Silver, 1989). Moreover, in one study of 233 people in Connecticut who'd recently lost a spouse, acceptance, not denial, was the predominant initial reaction following loss (Maciejewksi, Zhang, Block, & Prigerson, 2007). Acceptance continued to increase for the average widow or widower for 2 years following the loss.

Still other people may never fully accept the loss of their loved ones. In a study of people who'd lost a spouse or child in a motor vehicle accident, Darrin Lehman and his colleagues found that a large proportion (anywhere from 30% to 85% depending on the questions asked) of grieving people were still struggling with getting over the loss 4 to 7 years later (Lehman, Wortman, & Williams, 1987). Many said that they'd still been unable to find meaning in the tragedy.

Are there any dangers of believing in the Kübler-Ross stages? We don't know, but some grieving or dying people may feel pressured into coping with death in the sequence that Kübler-Ross described (Friedman & James, 2008). As Lehman and his colleagues noted, "When bereaved individuals fail to conform to these unrealistic expectations, others may convey that they are coping poorly or that this is indicative of serious psychological disturbance" (Lehman et al., 1987, p. 229). For example, one of the authors of your book (SJL) worked with a dying woman who felt guilt and resentment at being told by her friends that she needed to "accept" death, even though she was trying hard to continue to enjoy her life. Whether other patients experience the same apparent negative effects of belief in the Kübler-Ross stages is a worthy topic for future research.

Dying, it seems, just doesn't follow the same path for all of us. There's no uniform recipe for dying or grieving for others' death, any more than there is for living, a point that even Kübler-Ross acknowledged in her final book: "Our grief is as individual as our lives" (Kübler-Ross & Kessler, 2005; p. 1). Yet it's safe to say that for virtually all of us, death is something we'd prefer not to think about until we need to. As Woody Allen (1976) said, "I'm not afraid of dying. I just don't want to be there when it happens."

Chapter 2: Other Myths to Explore

Fiction	Fact
A mother's bad mood can lead to a miscarriage.	There's no evidence that sadness or stress in mothers increases the odds of miscarriages.
The first few minutes following birth are crucial for effective parent–infant bonding.	There is no evidence that the first few minutes after birth are essential for effective bonds to develop.
The first three years are especially critical to infant development.	There's considerable reason to doubt that the first three years are much more crucial for most psychological functions than are later years.
Children given a great deal of physical encouragement and support in walking walk earlier than other children.	The emergence of walking is influenced by children's physical development, and is largely unaffected by parental encouragement.
Newborn babies are virtually blind and deaf.	Newborns can see and hear many things.
Infants establish attachment bonds only to their mothers.	Infants establish strong attachment bonds with their fathers and other significant household figures.
Mothers who talk to their children in baby talk ("motherese") slow down their language development.	Most evidence suggests that baby talk actually facilitates children's language development.
Children exposed prenatally to crack cocaine ("crack babies") develop severe personality and neurological problems in later life.	Most children exposed to crack prenatally are largely normal in personality and neurological functioning.
Young children almost never lie.	Many young children lie about important issues, including whether they've engaged in immoral behavior or have been sexually abused.
Virtually all child prodigies "burn out" by adulthood.	Although some prodigies burn out, research shows that children with extremely high IQs have much higher levels of creative accomplishment in adulthood than other children.
Overweight children are just carrying "baby fat" that will melt away as they grow older.	Obesity in children often persists for years.
Adoption takes a negative psychological toll on most children.	Most adopted children are psychologically healthy.

Fiction	Fact
Children raised by gay parents have higher rates of homosexuality than other children.	Children raised by gay parents haven't been found to exhibit higher levels of homosexuality than other children.
Marital satisfaction increases after couples have children.	Marital satisfaction consistently plummets after couples first have children, although it typically rebounds.
People need less sleep as they get older.	The elderly need just as much sleep as the young, although because less of their sleep is consumed by "deep sleep," they tend to awaken often.
A large percentage of the elderly lives in nursing homes.	Only 7–8% adults aged 75 or older live in nursing homes.
Older people are more afraid of death than younger people.	The elderly report less fear of death, and more acceptance of death, than the young and middle aged.
Almost all senile people suffer from Alzheimer's disease.	Forty to fifty percent of people with dementia suffer from conditions other than Alzheimer's disease, such as strokes and Pick's disease.
Excessive aluminum causes Alzheimer's disease.	Controlled studies have found no support for this claim.
Many people die of "old age."	People die from accidents, violence, or disease, not from old age itself.
Terminally ill people who've given up all hope tend to die shortly thereafter.	There's no evidence for this belief.
Terminally ill people can often "postpone" their deaths until after holidays, birthdays, or other personally significant days.	There's no evidence for this belief, and perhaps even slight evidence that women with cancer are more likely to die right before their birthdays.

Sources and Suggested Readings

To explore these and other myths about human development, see Bruer (1999); Caldwell and Woolley (2008); Fiorello (2001); Furnham (1996); Kagan (1998); Kohn (1990); Mercer (2010); O'Connor (2007); Panek (1982); Paris (2000).

3 A REMEMBRANCE OF THINGS PAST

Myths about Memory

Human Memory Works like a Tape Recorder or Video Camera, and Accurately Records the Events We've Experienced

When people attend reunions or get together with childhood friends to swap "old war stories," they're often impressed with a simple fact: Their recollections of many events differ, in many cases dramatically. One person recalls a lively discussion about politics as a friendly debate; another recalls the identical discussion as a heated argument. This kind of observation should be sufficient to challenge the widespread belief that our memories work like video cameras or DVDs. If our memories were perfect, we'd never forget a friend's birthday, where we misplaced our iPod, or the exact date, time, and place of our first kiss.

Yet despite the sometimes all-too-obvious failings of everyday memory, surveys indicate that many people believe that our memories operate very much like tape recorders, video cameras, or DVDs, storing and replaying events exactly as we experienced them. Indeed, about 36% of us believe that our brains preserve perfect records of everything we've ever experienced (Alvarez & Brown, 2002). In one survey of over 600 undergraduates at a midwestern university, 27% agreed that memory operates like a tape recorder (Lenz, Ek, & Mills, 2009). Surveys show that even most psychotherapists agree that memories are fixed more or less permanently in the mind (Loftus & Loftus, 1980; Yapko, 1994).

These popular beliefs are in part residues of Sigmund Freud and others' convictions that forgotten, often traumatic, memories reside unperturbed in the murky unconscious, neither distorted by the passage of time nor by competition with other memories (Wachtel, 1977). But contrary to these claims, our memories are far from exact replicas of past events

(Clifasefi, Garry, & Loftus, 2007). The insight that our memory is imperfect and at times untrustworthy isn't recent. Before the turn of the 20th century, the great American psychologist and contemporary of Freud, William James (1890), observed that "False memories are by no means rare occurrences in most of us . . . Most people, probably, are in doubt about certain matters ascribed to their past. They may have seen them, may have said them, done them, or they may only have dreamed or imagined they did so" (p. 373).

It's true that we can often recall extremely emotional or salient events, sometimes called *flashbulb memories* because they seem to have a photographic quality (Brown & Kulik, 1977). Nevertheless, research shows that memories of such events, including the assassination of President John Fitzgerald Kennedy in 1963, the catastrophic break-up of the space shuttle *Challenger* in 1986, the death of Princess Diana in 1997, and the terrorist attacks of September 11, 2001, wither over time and are prone to distortions, just like less dramatic events (Krackow, Lynn, & Payne, 2005–2006; Neisser & Hyman, 1999).

Consider an example of a flashbulb memory from Ulric Neisser and Nicole Harsch's (1992) study of memories regarding the disintegration of the space shuttle *Challenger* about one minute after lift-off. The person, a student at Emory University in Atlanta, Georgia, provided the first description 24 hours after the disaster, and the second account 2¹/₂ years later.

> *Description 1.* I was in my religion class and some people walked in and started talking about (it). I didn't know any details except that it had exploded and the schoolteacher's students had all been watching which I thought was so sad. Then after class I went to my room and watched the TV program talking about it and I got all the details from that.

> *Description 2.* When I first heard about the explosion I was sitting in my freshman dorm room with my roommate and we were watching TV. It came on a news flash and we were both totally shocked. I was really upset and I went upstairs to talk to a friend of mine and then I called my parents.

When we compare the original memory with the memory recalled later, it's obvious that there are striking discrepancies. Neisser and Harsch found that about one third of students' reports contained similarly large differences across the two time points.

Heike Schmolck and his colleagues (Schmolck, Buffalo, & Squire, 2000) compared participants' ability to recall the 1995 acquittal of former football star O. J. Simpson—on charges of murdering his wife and her male friend—3 days after the verdict, and after a lapse of 15 or 32 months. After 32 months, 40% of the memory reports contained "major distortions." In this and other flashbulb memory studies, people were typically very confident in the accuracy of their memories, even though these memories weren't consistent with what they reported shortly after the event.

Moreover, eyewitnesses sometimes misidentify innocent individuals as criminals, even though these eyewitnesses often express their inaccurate opinions in the courtroom with utmost confidence (Memon & Thomson, 2007; Wells & Bradford, 1998). Popular beliefs notwithstanding, even eyewitnesses who get a long hard look at the perpetrator during the crime frequently finger the wrong suspect in a line-up or courtroom. What's more, the relation between eyewitnesses' confidence in their testimony and the accuracy of their memories is typically weak or even nonexistent (Kassin, Ellsworth, & Smith, 1989). This finding is deeply troubling given that jury members tend to place heavy weight on eyewitnesses' confidence when gauging the believability of their memories (Smith, Lindsay, Pryke, & Dysart, 2001; Wells & Bradford, 1998). In one recent survey, 34% of 160 American judges believed that there was a strong association between eyewitness confidence and accuracy (Wise & Safer, 2004). Disturbingly, of the 239 criminal defendants freed on the basis of DNA testing, as of June 2009 about 75% were convicted largely on the basis of inaccurate eyewitness testimony.

Even determining a memory's origins can prove elusive. About a quarter of college students find it difficult to determine whether something they distinctly remembered actually happened or whether it was part of a dream (Rassin, Merckelbach, & Spaan, 2001). Such "source monitoring confusion" may account for many of our most common memory errors, as when we accuse a friend of saying something offensive that we heard from someone else.

Today, there's broad consensus among psychologists that memory isn't *reproductive*—it doesn't duplicate precisely what we've experienced—but *reconstructive*. What we recall is often a blurry mixture of accurate recollections, along with what jells with our beliefs, needs, emotions, and hunches. These hunches are in turn based on our knowledge of ourselves, the events we try to recall, and what we've experienced in similar situations (Clifasefi et al., 2007).

Evidence for the reconstructive nature of memory derives from several lines of research. Psychologists now know that memory is *schematic*; a schema is an organized knowledge structure or mental model stored in memory. We acquire schemas from past learning and experiences, and they shape our perceptions of new and past experiences. We all possess schemas about everyday events, like ordering food at a restaurant. If a waiter asked us if we wanted our dessert before the appetizer, we'd surely find this request bizarre, as it's inconsistent with our restaurant schema or "script" for ordering food.

Stereotypes afford an excellent example of how schemas can influence our memory. Mark Snyder and Seymour Uranowitz (1978) presented subjects with a detailed case study of a woman named Betty K. After reading this information, they told some subjects that Betty K was currently living either a heterosexual or a lesbian lifestyle. Snyder and Uranowitz then gave subjects a recognition test for the material in the passage. They found that participants distorted their memory of the original information, such as her dating habits and relationship with her father, to be more in line with their schema, that is, their knowledge of her current lifestyle. We reconstruct the past to fit our schematic expectations.

Henry Roediger and Kathleen McDermott (1995) provided an elegant demonstration of our tendency to construct memories based on our schemas. They presented participants with lists of words that were all associated with a "lure word"—a single, non-presented item. For example, some participants studied a list containing the words thread, pin, eye, sewing, sharp, point, pricked, thimble, haystack, pain, hurt, and injection, all of which are associated in memory with the lure item *needle*. Roediger and McDermott found that more than half the time (55%), people recalled the lure item—needle—as having been on the list, even though it wasn't there. In many cases, participants were sure the critical non-presented items were on the list, suggesting that the false memories produced by the procedure can be as "real" to participants as their memories of the actual items. For this reason, Roediger and McDermott called these false memories "memory illusions."

Researchers have gone further to create memories of real-life events that never happened. In the "shopping mall study," Elizabeth Loftus (1993; Loftus & Ketcham, 1994) created a false memory in Chris, a 14-year-old boy. Loftus instructed Chris's older brother, Jim, to present Chris with a false event of being lost in a shopping mall at age 5 under the guise of a game of "Remember the time that . . ." To enhance its credibility, Loftus presented the false event as a vignette along with three other events that had actually occurred. Next, she instructed Chris to write down everything he remembered. Initially, Chris reported very little about the false event. Yet over a 2-week period, he constructed the following detailed memory: "I was with the guys for a second, and I think I went over to look at the toy store, the Kay-Bee toys . . . we got lost, and I was looking around and I thought, 'Uh-oh. I'm in trouble now.' . . . I thought I was never going to see my family again. I was really scared, you know. And then this old man . . . came up to me . . . he was kind of bald on top . . . he had a like a ring of gray hair . . . and he had glasses . . . and then crying, and Mom coming up and saying, 'Where were you? Don't you ever do that again!'" (Loftus & Ketcham, 1994, p. 532). When Loftus asked Chris's mother about the incident, she confirmed that it never happened.

A flood of similar studies followed, showing that in 18–37% of participants, researchers can implant entirely false memories of complex events ranging from: (a) a serious animal attack, indoor accident, outdoor accident, and medical procedure (Porter, Yuille, & Lehman, 1999), (b) knocking over a punchbowl at a wedding (Hyman, Husband, & Billings, 1995), (c) getting one's fingers caught in a mousetrap as a child (Ceci, Crotteau-Huffman, Smith, & Loftus, 1994), (d) being bullied as a child (Mazzoni, Loftus, Seitz, & Lynn, 1999), (e) witnessing a case of demonic possession (Mazzoni, Loftus, & Kirsch, 2001), to (f) riding in a hot air balloon with one's family (Wade, Garry, Read, & Lindsay, 2002).

These studies demolish the popular belief that our memories are etched indelibly into a permanent mental record. Rather than viewing our memory as a tape recorder or DVD, we can more aptly describe our memory as an ever-changing medium that highlights our remarkable ability to create fluid narratives of our past and present experiences. As the great American humorist Mark Twain is alleged to have said: "It isn't so astonishing, the number of things that I can remember, as the number of things I can remember that aren't so" (http://www.twainquotes.com/Memory.html).

<h1>Myth #12   Hypnosis Is Useful for Retrieving Memories of Forgotten Events</h1>

In 1990, George Franklin was convicted of the 1969 murder of Susan Nason. The basis of the conviction was his daughter Eileen's memories of him brutally murdering Susan, her childhood friend, some 20 years earlier. In 1996, prosecutors dropped all charges, and Franklin was released from prison. This was the first highly publicized case of "recovered traumatic memory."

In 1994, Steven Cook dropped a $10 million dollar lawsuit against the respected Cardinal Joseph Bernardin of Chicago. The suit alleged that Bernardin had molested Cook 17 years earlier.

In 2001, Larry Mayes was the 100th person to be released from prison because of DNA (genetic) testing. Unfortunately, he spent 21 years in jail for rape and robbery before a sample of his DNA was found. He was declared innocent.

Now let's consider the following facts.

- George Franklin's daughter, Janice, testified that her sister, Eileen, told her that memories of the alleged murder surfaced in therapy with the aid of hypnosis.
- The case against Cardinal Bernardin unraveled when an investigation determined that Cook's memories emerged only after a therapist who'd completed 3 hours of a 20-hour hypnosis course placed him under hypnosis. The therapist earned a master's degree from an unaccredited school run by a New Age Guru, John-Rodger, who claims to be the embodiment of a divine spirit (*Time*, March 14, 1994).
- Mayes participated in two live eyewitness line-ups and wasn't identified by the victim. But after the victim was hypnotized, she identified Mayes in another line-up, and during the trial voiced great confidence that Mayes had assaulted her.

These cases challenge the widespread idea that hypnosis unlocks the vast storehouse of memory the lies within our minds and permits accurate access to past events. In each case, there's good reason to believe that hypnosis created false memories held with virtually unshakeable conviction.

Yet the belief that hypnosis holds a special power to retrieve lost memories persists to this day. In a survey of 92 introductory psychology students, 70% agreed that "hypnosis is extremely useful in helping witnesses recall details of crimes" (Taylor & Kowalski, 2003, p. 5). In other surveys, 90% (Green & Lynn, in press) or more (McConkey & Jupp, 1986; Whitehouse, Orne, Orne, & Dinges, 1991) of college students have reported that hypnosis enhances memory retrieval, and 64% have maintained that hypnosis is a "good technique for police to use to refresh witnesses' memories" (Green & Lynn, in press).

Such beliefs are also prevalent among academics and mental health professionals. Elizabeth Loftus and Geoffrey Loftus (1980) found that 84% of psychologists and 69% of non-psychologists endorsed the statement that "memory is permanently stored in the mind" and that "... with hypnosis, or other specialized techniques, these inaccessible details could eventually be recovered." In a sample of over 850 psycho-therapists, Michael Yapko (1994) found that large proportions endorsed the following items with high-to-moderate frequency: (1) 75%: "Hypnosis enables people to accurately remember things they otherwise could not." (2) 47%: "Therapists can have greater faith in details of a traumatic event when obtained hypnotically than otherwise." (3) 31%: "When someone has a memory of a trauma while in hypnosis, it object-ively must actually have occurred." (4) 54%: "Hypnosis can be used to recover memories of actual events as far back as birth." In other surveys (Poole, Lindsay, Memon, & Bull, 1995), between about a third (29% and 34%) and a fifth (20%; Polusny & Follette, 1996) of psycho-therapists reported that they used hypnosis to help clients recall mem-ories of suspected sexual abuse.

Beliefs in the memory-enhancing powers of hypnosis have a long and at times checkered history. Hypnosis was promoted by some of the early guiding lights of psychology and psychiatry, including Pierre Janet, Joseph Breuer, and Sigmund Freud. Janet was one of the first therapists to use hypnosis to help patients recover memories of traumatic events that he assumed caused their psychological difficulties. In a famous case, Janet (1889) used hypnosis to "age regress" (mentally relive an earlier time period) his patient Marie to her childhood, when she was traumat-ized by seeing a child with a facial deformity. By consciously reliving the memory of the child's face, Marie was supposedly freed from symptoms of blindness.

The belief that hypnosis can help patients excavate buried memories of traumatic events was also the rationale for "hypnoanalysis," which many practitioners used in the aftermath of World War I to help soldiers and veterans remember events that presumably triggered their psychological disorders. Some therapists believed the chances for a com-plete recovery were optimized when the emotions associated with the recalled events were released full-blown in a so-called *abreaction* (a power-ful discharge of painful feelings), and the guilt and anger that emerged were processed in later hypnotic sessions.

Confidence in the powers of hypnosis extends to the general public, who are flooded with images of hypnosis as a memory supercharger that rivals a magical truth serum. In such movies as *In Like Flint*, *Kiss the Girls*, *Dead on Sight*, and *The Resurrection Syndrome*, witnesses recall the exact details of crimes or long-forgotten childhood events with the aid of hypnosis.

Some modern-day researchers and clinicians argue that hypnosis can mine precious nuggets of long-buried information (Scheflin, Brown, & Hammond, 1997). Nevertheless, in general, the tide of expert opinion (Kassin, Tubb, Hosch, & Memon, 2001) has turned to the point that forensic psychologists widely acknowledge that hypnosis either has no effect on memory (Erdelyi, 1994) or that it can impair and distort recall (Lynn, Neuschatz, Fite, & Rhue, 2001). In instances in which hypnosis does increase accurate memories—often because people guess and report memories when they're unsure—this increase is offset or even surpassed by an increase in inaccurate memories (Erdelyi, 1994; Steblay & Bothwell, 1994).

To make matters worse, hypnosis may produce more recall errors or false memories than ordinary recall, and increase eyewitnesses' confidence in inaccurate, as well as accurate, memories (this increase is confidence is called "memory hardening"). After all, if you expect that what you recall during a hypnosis session will be accurate in every detail, you're unlikely to hedge your bets on what you report as true. In fact, most researchers find that hypnosis inflates unwarranted confidence in memories to some degree (Green & Lynn, in press). Although highly suggestible people are most affected by hypnosis, even low suggestible individuals' recall can be impaired. Concerns that eyewitnesses who are hypnotized may resist cross-examination, and have problems distinguishing real-world fact from mental fiction, have prompted most states to ban the testimony of hypnotized witnesses from the courtroom.

Does hypnosis fare any better when it comes to remembering extremely early life experiences? A televised documentary (Frontline, 1995) showed a group therapy session in which a woman was age-regressed through childhood, to the womb, and eventually to being trapped in her mother's Fallopian tube. The woman provided a convincing demonstration of the emotional and physical discomfort one would experience if one were indeed stuck in this uncomfortable position. Although this woman may have believed in the reality of her experience, we can be quite sure that it wasn't memory-based. Instead, age-regressed subjects behave according to their knowledge, beliefs, and assumptions about age-relevant behaviors. As Michael Nash (1987) showed, adults age-regressed to childhood don't show the expected patterns on many indices of early development, including vocabulary, cognitive tasks, brain waves (EEGs), and visual illusions. No matter how compelling they may seem, "age-regressed experiences" aren't literal reinstatements of childhood experiences, behaviors, or feelings.

Some therapists go even further, claiming that current problems are attributable to previous lives, and that the treatment called for is "past life regression therapy" featuring hypnosis. For example, psychiatrist Brian Weiss (1988), who was featured on the *Oprah Winfrey Show* in 2008, published a widely publicized series of cases focusing on patients whom he hypnotized and age-regressed to "go back to" the source of a present-day problem. When Weiss regressed his patients, they reported events that he interpreted as originating in earlier lives, often many centuries ago.

Although experiences during age regression can seem convincing to both patient and therapist, reports of a past life are the products of imagination, fantasy, and what patients know about a given historical period. In fact, subjects' descriptions of the historical circumstances of their supposed past lives, when checked against known facts (such whether the country was at war or peace, the face on the coin of the realm), are rarely accurate. A participant in one study (Spanos, Menary, Gabora, DuBreuil, & Dewhirst, 1991) who was regressed to ancient times claimed to be Julius Caesar, emperor of Rome, in 50 B.C., even though the designations of B.C. and A.D. weren't adopted until centuries later, and even though Julius Caesar died several decades prior to the first Roman emperor, Augustus. When information reported about a "past life" happens to be accurate, we can easily explain it as a "good guess" that's often based on knowledge of history.

Nevertheless, not all uses of hypnosis are scientifically problematic. Controlled research evidence suggests that hypnosis may be useful in treating pain, medical conditions, and habit disorders (such as smoking addiction), and as an adjunct to cognitive-behavioral therapy for anxiety, obesity, and other conditions. Still, the extent to which hypnosis provides benefits above and beyond relaxation in these cases is unclear (Lynn, Kirsch, Barabasz, Cardena, & Patterson, 2000).

In sum, the conclusion that hypnosis can foster false memories in some people is indisputable. As tempting as it might be to contact a hypnotist to locate that favorite ring you misplaced years ago, we recommend that you just keep on looking.

Myth # 13 Individuals Commonly Repress the Memories of Traumatic Experiences

Some time ago, one of the authors of this book (SJL) was consulted by a 28-year-old female businesswoman who was considering a civil suit against three colleagues regarding a sexual assault. She related the event as follows:

Two years ago, I conducted business in China for two weeks. One night, after dancing at a club in Shanghai, I fell sound asleep. I awoke 3 hours later and thought I was having a very erotic, sexual dream. More and more, I felt like a real presence was there, over me in my bed.

I wondered what happened that night, because I couldn't recall anything in the morning. I thought I'd repressed a memory of something terrible. So I contacted someone at a medical school who was doing research with hypnosis. After the second hypnosis session, in which I tried to recall what happened, I remembered that one of the men in my company had sexually assaulted me. I was in direct competition with him for a promotion. I think this happened because he thought, "Who does this woman think she is? This will teach her a lesson."

How likely is it that she'd repressed her memories of a traumatic sexual assault? We'll soon find out, but for now we'll point out that her deep concerns touch on the controversial question of whether people can exile horrific memories to the hinterlands of consciousness where they're preserved intact, perhaps to be later recovered in therapy. Psychologists and psychiatrists refer to an inability to recall important information of traumatic or stressful events that can't be explained by normal forgetfulness as *dissociative amnesia* (American Psychiatric Association, 2000).

Debates over whether people can banish traumatic memories from awareness have sparked vigorous discussion from the glory days of Freudian psychoanalysis in the late 19th century to the present. There's little disagreement that memories that people have remembered continuously are likely to be accurate, nor that people can remember events they haven't thought about for some time, even years after they've happened. What's at issue is whether a special mechanism of repression accounts for the forgetting of traumatic material. Are memories repressed as a buffer against the aftermath of traumatic events (Scheflin et al., 1997; Erdelyi, 2006), or are repressed memories instead, "a piece of psychiatric folklore devoid of convincing empirical support," as psychologist Richard McNally argued (McNally, 2003, p. 275)?

From the way the popular media portrays repression, we'd never guess this topic was bitterly controversial in the scientific community. In films like the *Butterfly Effect* (2004), *Mysterious Skin* (2004), *Batman Returns* (1995), and *Repressions* (2007), and television programs like *Dying to Remember* (1993), repressed memories of painful events—ranging from child abuse to witnessing the murder of parents and committing a murder in a past life—would seem to be commonplace occurrences. Many popular self-help books also portray repression as a natural, if not typical, response to traumatic events. For example, Judith Blume (1990) wrote that "half of all incest survivors do not remember that the abuse occurred" (p. 81) and Renee Frederickson (1992) claimed that "millions of people have blocked out frightening episodes of abuse, years of their life, or their entire childhood" (p. 15).

Perhaps not surprisingly, many laypersons find these claims plausible. According to Jonathan Golding and his colleagues' (Golding, Sanchez, & Sego, 1996) survey of 613 undergraduates, most respondents expressed belief in repressed memories; on a 1–10 scale, men rated their likelihood at 5.8, women at 6.5. Eighty-nine percent said they'd had some experience with repressed memories either personally or through media coverage. Most felt that repressed memories should be admitted as evidence in court.

We can trace popular views of repressed memories to Sigmund Freud's belief that obsessional neuroses and hysteria are produced by the repression of sexual molestation in childhood. Freud (1894) viewed repression as the unconscious *motivated forgetting* of unpleasant memories or impulses (Holmes, 1990; McNally, 2003). Today, the idea that repressed memories must be uncovered is central to some forms of psychoanalysis (Galatzer-Levy, 1997) and memory recovery therapies (Crews, 1995). These therapies are based on the idea that clients can't resolve the root causes of their psychological problems unless they excavate repressed memories of childhood trauma, often sexual abuse. Much of this thinking appears to reflect a representativeness heuristic (see *Introduction*, p. 15): just as we must treat or remove an abscessed tooth to prevent it from festering, this reasoning goes, we must expunge repressed memories of trauma to solve our present problems.

Indeed, as of the mid 1990s, surveys suggested that many therapists were in the business of ferreting out repressed memories from the mind's hidden recesses. After surveying more than 860 psychotherapists, Michael Yapko (1994) found that almost 60% believed that repression is a major cause of forgetting, and about 40% believed that people couldn't remember much about their childhoods because they'd repressed traumatic events. Debra Poole and her collaborators (Poole, Lindsay, Memon, & Bull, 1995) surveyed 145 licensed U.S. doctoral-level psychotherapists in two studies, and 57 British psychologists in another. The researchers found that over three quarters of therapists reported using at least one memory recovery technique, like hypnosis, guided imagery, or repeated questioning and prompting (such as "Are you sure you weren't abused? Please keep thinking about it"), to "help clients remember childhood sexual abuse." Additionally, 25% of the respondents who conducted therapy with adult female clients believed that memory recovery is a key component of treatment, believed they could identify patients with repressed or otherwise unavailable memories as early as the first session, and used two or more memory recovery techniques to enhance recall of disclosure of past events. A year later, Melissa Polusny and Victoria Follette (1996) reported similar findings in another survey of therapists.

The popularity of memory recovery procedures rests more on informal clinical reports than on controlled research (Lindsay & Read, 1994; Loftus, 1993; Spanos, 1996). Indeed, there are many anecdotal reports of people seeming to recover decades-old memories of abuse in psychotherapy (Erdelyi, 1985). Nevertheless, after reviewing 60 years of research and finding no convincing laboratory evidence for repression, David Holmes (1990) wryly suggested that any use of the concept be preceded by the following statement: "Warning. The concept of repression has not been validated with experimental research and its use may be hazardous to the accurate interpretation of clinical behavior" (p. 97). More recently, after canvassing the literature in detail, Richard McNally (2003) concluded that the scientific support for repressed memories is feeble. He argued that many case histories put forward as supporting dissociative amnesia (Scheflin et al., 1997) failed to verify that the traumatic event occurred, and that we can usually explain memory loss in these cases in terms of ordinary forgetting rather than repression.

Contrary to the repression hypothesis, research shows that most people remember such traumatic events as the Holocaust and natural disasters well—sometimes all too well—in the form of disturbing flashbacks (Loftus, 1993; Shobe & Kihlstrom, 1997). Moreover, the fact that some people recover allegedly repressed memories of highly implausible undocumented events in psychotherapy, such as widespread satanic cult activity and alien abductions, casts doubt on the accuracy of many other more plausible memories that clients allegedly recover in treatment. The problem is that therapists often can't distinguish the "signal" of accurate memories from the "noise" of false memories (Loftus, 1993).

Richard McNally (2003) offered the following explanation—as an alternative to repression—for how delayed recall of child abuse can occur. As he pointed out, children may be more confused than upset by sexual advances from a relative, yet years later recall the event with revulsion as they realize that it was, in fact, an instance of abuse. The delay of recall of events isn't all that unusual in that people sometimes forget significant life events, such as accidents and hospitalizations, even a year after they occur (Lilienfeld & Loftus, 1998).

Yet another problem with studies of dissociative amnesia is the fact that people's failure to report an event doesn't mean they repressed or even forgot it (Piper, 1997). Gail Goodman and her colleagues' (Goodman et al., 2003) work is a case in point. They repeatedly interviewed 175 people with documented child sexual abuse, about 13 years after the incident. Of those interviewed across three phases of the study, 19% at first didn't report the documented incident. Nevertheless, when later interviewed by phone, 16% didn't report the incident, and by the third (in person) interview phase, only 8% failed to report it. Clearly, the events recalled were available in memory, even though participants didn't report them initially. Perhaps people were too embarrassed at first to report the abuse, or required several prompts to recall it.

The tendency to label ordinary or unexplained forgetting as repression appears to be deeply embedded in our cultural heritage. Psychiatrist Harrison Pope and his colleagues (Pope et al., 2006) offered the scientific community a fascinating challenge. They placed a notice on professional Internet sites offering a $1,000 award to the first person who could produce an example of dissociative amnesia for a traumatic event, in any work of fiction or nonfiction, in any language, prior to 1800. Although more than 100 scholars responded, none could find a single clear description of dissociative amnesia. The authors reasoned that if dissociative amnesia were a naturally occurring psychological phenomenon, like hallucinations or delusions, there should be evidence for it in nonfiction as or fictional characters. Pope and his colleagues concluded that repressed memory seems to be a relatively recent product of our culture dating from the 19th century.

In the past decade, the repressed memory controversy has de-escalated to some extent in the scientific community. A consensus has emerged that suggestive procedures, such as hypnosis, guided imagery, and leading questions, can generate false memories of traumatic events, and that delayed recall of accurate events often results from ordinary forgetting and remembering, rather than repression.

As in the case of the 28-year-old businesswoman described at the outset, it's crucial to consider alternative explanations for delayed recollections, such as being abused by a satanic cult, that strain credibility (Lanning & Burgess, 1989). For instance, the woman described in this case might have sensed someone was in her bed because of a strange yet surprisingly common phenomenon called *sleep paralysis*, caused by a disruption in the sleep cycle. As many as one third to one half of college students have experienced at least one episode of sleep paralysis (Fukuda, Ogilvie, Chilcott, Venditelli, & Takeuchi, 1998). Sleep paralysis is often associated with terror, along with the sense of a menacing figure close to or even on top of the person, who's incapable of moving. The frightening episode of sleep paralysis, combined with her attempts to reconstruct what happened during hypnosis, might have convinced her that she was sexually assaulted. When offered this explanation, she decided not to pursue a lawsuit against her colleague.

We end with a note of caution. Not all memories recovered after years or even decades of forgetting are necessarily false (Schooler, Ambadar, & Bendiksen, 1997), so psychotherapists must be careful not to dismiss all newly remembered memories of childhood abuse. Still, they shouldn't assume that recovered memories are genuine unless they're accompanied by corroborating evidence.

Myth #14 Most People with Amnesia Forget All Details of Their Earlier Lives

"Where am I?" "Who am I?"

These are probably the two questions most frequently asked in Hollywood films by characters who've awakened from a coma, that is, a prolonged period of unconsciousness. In most movies, the portrayal of amnesia—memory loss—has two major things in common. First, amnesics' most glaring problem is almost always a loss of memories of their past. They usually have little or no difficulty learning new things. Second, if amnesics have been unconscious for a long time, say a few weeks or months, they typically lose all recollection of their earlier lives. Their minds are essentially a blank slate, with much or all of their past wiped clean. More often than not, they've forgotten what year it is, where they live, to whom they're married, what they do for a living, perhaps even who they are.

Let's examine a few choice examples from the cinematic and television world. In one of the earliest depictions of amnesia on the big screen, *Garden of Lies* (1915), a newly married bride forgets everything about herself, including who she is, following a car accident (Baxendale, 2004). On a lighter note, in *Santa Who?* (2000), Santa Claus falls off his sleigh and loses his identity and, along with it, all of his previous memories. In the three films in the Jason Bourne series (*The Bourne Identity*, *The Bourne Supremacy*, and *The Bourne Ultimatum*, spanning

2002 to 2007), the hero, portrayed by Matt Damon, loses all memories of his life and assumes a new identity as a governmental assassin. Variations on this theme are especially common in Hollywood films featuring hired murderers, including the *Long Kiss Goodnight* (1996), in which a secret agent forgets everything about herself after experiencing a bump on the head. As one writer observed, profound amnesia in Hollywood films "is something of an occupational hazard for professional assassins" (Baxendale, 2004, p. 1481). And in the recent television sitcom *Samantha Who?*, starring Christina Applegate, a psychiatrist awakens from an 8-day coma following a car accident, only to find that she's lost all memory of herself and her past despite being otherwise mentally intact.

These cinematic depictions of amnesia are largely mirrored in the views of most Americans (O'Jile et al., 1997; Swift & Wilson, 2001). In one survey, 51% of Americans said that people with head injuries have more trouble remembering events that happened before than after the injury (Gouvier, Prestholdt, & Warner, 1988). In a more recent survey, 48% of Americans said that following a head injury, remembering things from one's past is harder than learning new things. Large percentages of Americans also believe that following head injuries, people routinely forget who they are and can't recognize anyone they know (Guilmette & Paglia, 2004).

Yet the popular psychology view of amnesia bears scant resemblance to its real-world counterpart. In fact, the primary problem among most people who experience a head injury or stroke isn't *retrograde amnesia* —loss of memory of the past—but rather *anterograde amnesia*—loss of memory for new information (Schachter, 1996). That is, people with amnesia typically have trouble forming new memories, although some have lost past memories too. The best known case of severe anterograde amnesia in the psychological literature is that of H.M., a lonely man (who died in 2008 at the age of 74) who underwent brain surgery in 1953 to halt his severe epilepsy, which hadn't responded to any other treatments. Following the surgery, which removed both of H.M.'s hippocampi (brain structures that are crucial to long-term memory), H.M. became virtually incapable of forming memories for new events, or what psychologists call "episodic memories" (Corkin, 2002). H.M. read the same magazines over and over again as though he'd never seen them before, routinely had no recollection of meeting people he'd been introduced to 5 minutes earlier, and experienced catastrophic grief each time his doctors informed him of his uncle's death (Milner, 1972; Shimamura, 1992). Although H.M. experienced some retrograde amnesia as well, anterograde amnesia was his primary problem, as it is for most amnesics.

In one of the rare exceptions in which American films got scientific psychology largely right, the brilliant 2000 thriller *Memento* showcases a character, Leonard (portrayed by Guy Pearce), who experiences severe anterograde amnesia following a head injury. Unable to create episodic memories, Leonard is exploited mercilessly by others, culminating in his murder of an innocent man. Cleverly, the scenes in the film unfold in reverse order, reflecting Leonard's sense of living almost completely in the present.

There's still another way in which the popular media usually gets amnesia wrong. Film portrayals to the contrary, so-called "generalized amnesia," in which people forget their identity and all details of their previous lives (American Psychiatric Association, 2000), is exceedingly rare. In the unusual cases in which generalized amnesia occurs, it's almost always believed to be associated with psychological causes, such as extreme stress, rather than head injury or other neurological causes (Baxendale, 2004). Nevertheless, some psychologists doubt that generalized amnesia due to psychological factors even exists (McNally, 2003). They may be right, because in these cases it's difficult to rule out the possibility that the apparent amnesia is due to malingering, that is, faking of symptoms to achieve an external goal, such as gaining financial compensation or avoiding military service (Cima, Merckelbach, Nijman, Knauer, & Hollnack, 2002).

We'd be remiss not to mention two further misconceptions regarding amnesia. First, perhaps inspired by scenes in many films (Baxendale, 2004), many people believe that, immediately after emerging from a prolonged coma, people can experience complete amnesia for their past yet otherwise be entirely normal. If we were to believe the typical Hollywood portrayal, such people can respond coherently to questions and talk in complete sentences, even if they believe the year is 1989—when they lost consciousness—rather than 2009. Indeed, in one survey a whopping 93% of respondents said that people with severe amnesia for virtually all of their pasts can be normal in every other way (Hux, Schram, & Goeken, 2006). Sadly, research demonstrates that this view amounts to little more than wishful thinking. People who emerge from comas with significant amnesia are almost always left with lasting and serious cognitive deficits, including problems in perception and learning (Hooper, 2006).

A second and more peculiar misconception is that following a head injury, one of the best ways to rid oneself of amnesia is to experience another head injury. This creative method of memory recovery is a plot device in many cartoons and films, including those featuring Tom the Cat and Tarzan (Baxendale, 2004). In the 1987 film *Overboard*, starring Kurt Russell and Goldie Hawn, Hawn's character loses her memory after bumping her head following a fall from a yacht, and regains her memory later in the film following a second bump on the head. This thinking may reflect a misapplication of the representativeness heuristic (see *Introduction*, p. 15): if a bump on the head can cause us to lose our memories, a second bump on the head can cause us to regain them. After all, if two heads are better than one, two head injuries might be too (Baxendale, 2004). Surveys indicate that anywhere from 38% to 46% of Americans and Canadians hold this misconception (Guilmette & Paglia, 2004). Like a number of other misconceptions in this book, this one isn't merely wrong, but backwards. By damaging brain circuitry, earlier head injuries typically leave patients more vulnerable to the adverse effects of later head injuries.

So the next time you see a film featuring a character who's lost all memories and all sense of who she is following a head injury, be sure not to "forget" a key point: The true amnesia is Hollywood's profound loss of memory for scientific evidence.

Chapter 3: Other Myths to Explore

Fiction	**Fact**
The memory of everything we've experienced is stored permanently in our brains, even if we can't access all of it.	There's no evidence for this claim; moreover, our brains aren't big enough to store memories of everything we've experienced.
Some people have true "photographic memories."	Even among people with "eidetic imagery," the closest approximation to photographic memory, there is evidence for memory errors and memory reconstruction.
With effort, we can remember events back to birth.	Because of the phenomenon of infantile amnesia, we can't recall anything prior to about age two or two and a half.
Memory is chemically transferable.	Attempts in the 1950s and 1960s to transfer learning in planaria worms by chopping them up and feeding them to other planaria were never replicated.

Fiction	Fact
The suggestibility of memory is only a problem for preschoolers.	The memory reports of all age groups can be affected by leading questions; in some cases, older children are even more vulnerable to suggestions than younger children.
People who can't recall what they had for lunch yesterday have a poor "short-term memory."	The duration of short-term memory is about 20 seconds or less; these people almost all have a poor long-term memory.
Rote memorization is the best way to retain information.	Information processed by its meaning is better retained than information that is merely repeated over and over again.
Almost all forgetting is due to decay of information in our brains.	Much of forgetting is due to interference as well as decay.
Gingko and other herbal remedies improve memory in normal individuals.	The effects of Gingko on normal memory are weak or nonexistent.

Sources and Suggested Readings

To explore these and other myths about memory, see Della Sala (1999, 2007); Gold, Cahill, and Wenk (2002); Loftus and Loftus (1980); McNally (2003); Schacter (2001); Solomon, Adams, Silver, Zimmer, and DeVeaux (2002); Turtle and Want (2008).

4 TEACHING OLD DOGS NEW TRICKS

Myths about Intelligence and Learning

Intelligence (IQ) Tests Are Biased against Certain Groups of People

Few icons of popular psychology are the subject of as many misconceptions as are tests of the intelligence quotient (IQ; Gottfredson, 1997). So before addressing what's perhaps the most widespread misconception, a tad bit of history is in order.

More than a century ago, Charles Spearman showed that scores on measures of many diverse cognitive abilities tend to be positively correlated. In a classic paper, he proposed a "general intelligence" factor to account for the commonality underlying these capacities (Spearman, 1904). Although Spearman recognized the existence of more specific abilities too, massive amounts of data show that mental abilities are underpinned by this factor (Carroll, 1993). Other terms for the general intelligence factor are general mental ability, IQ, and—in honor of its early proponent—Spearman's g. Most IQ tests, like the widely used Wechsler Adult Intelligence Scale (Wechsler, 1997), now in its fourth version, contain multiple subtests, like vocabulary and arithmetic. The positive associations among these subtests on these tests are consistent with Spearman's g, supporting the use of a single IQ score for many important purposes.

Far from being an arbitrary construct that depends entirely on how we choose to measure it, there's consensus among most experts that intelligence is:

a very general mental capability that, among other things, involves the ability to reason, plan, solve problems, think abstractly, comprehend complex ideas, learn quickly and learn from experience. It is not merely book learning, a narrow academic skill, or test-taking smarts. Rather, it reflects a broader and deeper capability for comprehending our surroundings—"catching on," "making sense" of things, or "figuring out" what to do. (Gottfredson, 1997, p. 13)

Some critics have charged that IQ tests predict performance only on other IQ tests. In a lively Internet discussion among faculty members regarding IQ tests, one participant commented that "IQ is a notoriously weak predictor of anything other than IQ" (http://chronicle.com/blogs/election/2456/can-iq-predict-how-well-a-president-will-perform; September 19, 2008). Yet the data show otherwise. Although far from perfect measures, IQ tests yield scores that are among the most valid and cost-effective predictors of academic achievement and job performance across just about every major occupation studied—factory worker, waiter, secretary, police officer, electrician, and on and on (Neisser et al., 1996; Sackett, Schmitt, Ellingson, & Kabin, 2001; Schmidt & Hunter, 1998). Dean Keith Simonton (2006) even showed that U.S. presidents' estimated IQs are good predictors of their success in office, as rated by historians. Because of their utility, decision-makers frequently use IQ tests in "high-stakes" (important in their real-world consequences) selection contexts, including admissions and hiring.

As the civil rights movement gathered steam in the 1960s, many researchers examined IQ score differences across racial and ethnic groups. It became popular to attribute differences among groups to test bias: Most researchers assumed that IQ tests favored white males (Anastasi & Urbina, 1997). The commonplace use of IQ tests and the weight assigned to applicants' IQ scores mean that if these tests are biased against women or minority group members, widespread and unfair discrimination could result. Potential test bias is far more than a question of hair-splitting or political correctness.

What's test bias, and how would we know it if we saw it? One widespread misunderstanding is that if any two groups score differently, the test is biased. We can find this misconception in a host of popular writings. It's a particularly frequent refrain among critics of IQ testing and other standardized tests. In the early 1980s, consumer advocate (and later multiple-time presidential candidate) Ralph Nader and his colleagues argued that the SAT (then called the Scholastic Aptitude Test) should be banned because poorer students and many students from minority groups tend to do worse on it than other students (Kaplan, 1982). Writing in *The Nation* magazine, Jay Rosner (2003) contended that consistent differences in SAT item performance between majority and minority students demonstrate that standardized tests are biased.

Many judges have similarly ruled that differences in the test scores of two groups, such as a majority versus a minority group, imply test bias. In the influential ruling of *Larry P. v. Riles* (1980), the 9th District court of Appeals in California ruled that an unbiased test by definition yields "the same pattern of scores when administered to different groups of people" (p. 955) and placed strict limits on the use of intelligence tests for classifying children as mildly mentally retarded for educational purposes (Bersoff, 1981). In another early court case, the Golden Rule Insurance Company sued the state licensing board and test publisher because a smaller proportion of black than white examinees responded correctly to some items on the licensing tests (*Golden Rule Insurance Company et al. v. Washburn et al.*, 1984). Many lawyers later filed court cases on the grounds that differences in test scores across groups prove that this test is biased.

But there's a serious problem with this popular view: The groups may actually differ in the trait being assessed (Anastasi & Urbina, 1997). Almost surely, a physician's records would show that the average weight of her adult male patients is greater than that of her adult female patients. This fact doesn't suggest that the scale used to measure patients' heights is biased, because men tend to be heavier than women. Differences between groups don't necessarily demonstrate bias, although they might suggest it in some cases. At least some of the reason for this misunderstanding may stem from a misapplication of the representativeness heuristic (see *Introduction*, p. 15). For much of American history, many outcomes that showed large group differences, like differences in school achievement across races or differences in job status between men and women, *were* due largely to societal bias. So today, when people see that a test yields group differences, they may automatically equate these differences with bias.

How can we know whether group differences in test scores are due to bias? The trick is to focus on the validity of a test's predictions. If we use an IQ test to predict performance in school or the workplace, we must collect data on the IQ scores of applicants and their performance. If group differences in IQ test scores are accompanied by roughly comparable differences in performance, the test is unbiased. An unbiased test neither underpredicts nor overpredicts performance for the members of any group. In contrast, if groups score differently on the IQ test but perform similarly, we can conclude that the test is biased. One consequence could be unfair discrimination in favor of the group whose performance is over-predicted and against the group whose performance is underpredicted.

Fortunately, many researchers have studied the possibility that IQ test scores are biased against women or minorities. Two panels assembled by the National Academy of Science (Hartigan & Wigdor, 1989; Wigdor & Garner, 1982) and a Task Force of the American Psychological Association (Neisser et al., 1996), each of which contained individuals representing a diverse range of expertise and opinions, reached the same conclusion: There's no evidence that IQ tests or other standardized tests, like the SAT, underpredict the performance of women or minorities. Today, most experts agree that the question of IQ test bias has been settled about as conclusively as any scientific controversy can be (Gottfredson, 1997, 2009; Jensen, 1980; Sackett et al., 2001; Sackett, Borneman, & Connelly, 2008).

It's crucial to understand, though, that the absence of test bias doesn't say anything about the *causes* of group differences in IQ; these differences could be due largely or entirely to environmental influences, like social disadvantages or prejudice. To the extent that we blame group differences in IQ on test bias, we may ignore the genuine causes of these differences, some of which we may be able to remedy with social and educational programs.

Despite the research evidence, some psychologists argue that the test bias claim contains a kernel of truth. Here's why. Researchers can evaluate potential bias not only at the level of a whole test, but at the level of the items making up a test. Just as a biased test would under-predict one group's ability relative to that of another, a biased test item would do the same. Psychologists refer to this phenomenon as *differential item functioning*, or DIF (Hunter & Schmidt, 2000). For any pair of groups (such as women versus men, or blacks versus whites), we can examine each item on an IQ test for DIF. If members of two groups perform about the same on the rest of the test but score differently on a particular item, this finding provides evidence of item bias. Researchers commonly find that a number of IQ test items meet criteria for DIF. Roy Freedle and Irene Kostin (1997) found DIF for a number of verbal analogy items on the SAT and GRE tests, including those with easy stems like "canoe: rapids" and hard stems like "sycophant: flattery." At first blush, finding DIF for many test items seems to call into question the verdict of no test bias. After all, how can the items themselves demonstrate DIF without scores on the whole test being biased?

It turns out that many or most instances of DIF are trivial in size (Sackett et al., 2001). Even among items that exhibit DIF, the direction of bias is inconsistent. Some items favor one group and other items favor the other group, so the effects tend to cancel out when the items are combined into the total score (Sackett et al., 2001). So DIF doesn't necessarily produce test bias (Freedle & Kostin, 1997).

As we've discovered throughout this book, the gulf between research and popular opinion is often wide, and this is especially the case in the domain of intelligence (Phelps, 2009). IQ tests validly predict performance in many important realms of everyday life, with no evidence of bias against women or minorities. The real bias occurs when we blame the "messengers"—that is, the IQ tests themselves—and neglect potential environmental explanations, such as cultural disadvantage, for differences in test scores across groups.

Myth # 16 If You're Unsure of Your Answer When Taking a Test, It's Best to Stick with Your Initial Hunch

Few phrases instill more fear into the hearts and minds of college students than those three dreaded words: "multiple choice test." Probably because many undergraduates would prefer sitting on a bed of nails to taking a multiple choice test, they're always on the lookout for tips to boost their performance on most professors' favorite weapon of intellectual torture. Fortunately, a handful of these test-taking pointers actually boast some scientific support. For example, on multiple-choice tests, longer answers are slightly more likely than other answers to be correct, as are more precise answers (for example, in response to the stem "The U.S. Constitution was adopted in ____", "1787" is more precise than "between 1770 and 1780") and "all of the above" answers (Geiger, 1997; Gibb, 1964).

Yet perhaps the most widely accepted piece of test-taking folklore is to stick with your original answer, especially if you're unsure whether it's right or wrong. Across various surveys, large proportions—between 68% and 100%—of college students say that changing their initial answers on a test won't improve their score. About three fourths say that changing their answers will actually lower their score (Ballance, 1977; Benjamin, Cavell, & Shallenberger, 1984). This myth—sometimes called the "first instinct fallacy"—isn't limited to undergraduates. In one study, among professors who gave their college students advice about changing answers on tests, 63% told them not to do so because it would tend to lower their scores. Among science and liberal arts professors, only 5–6% said that changing answers would tend to increase students' scores; the percentage among education professors was 30% (Benjamin et al., 1984).

What's more, scores of websites, including those designed to provide students with test-taking advice, inform readers that changing their initial answers is a bad strategy and encourage them to trust their first hunches. One website tells students, "Don't keep on changing your answer—usually your first choice is the right one, unless you misread the question" (TestTakingTips.com) and another advises them to "Trust your first hunch. When you answer a question, go with your first hunch —don't change your answer unless you're absolutely sure you're right" (Tomahawk Elementary School). Another goes further, even citing research support for this belief: "Be wary of changing your mind: There is evidence to suggest that students more frequently change right answers to wrong ones than wrong answers to right ones" (Fetzner Student-Athlete Academic Center).

What do the scientific findings actually say? With over 3 million high school students taking the SAT and ACT (interestingly, in the case of both tests the letters don't stand for anything) each year, this question is hardly trivial. In fact, the research evidence is surprisingly consistent, and it points to the *opposite* conclusion presented on these websites (Benjamin et al., 1984; Geiger, 1996; Skinner, 1983; Waddell & Blankenship, 1994). More than 60 studies lead to essentially the same verdict: When students change answers on multiple-choice tests (typically as judged by their erasures or cross-outs of earlier answers), they're more likely to change from a wrong to a right answer than from a right to a wrong answer. For each point that students lose when changing from a right to a wrong answer, they gain between two and three points on average in changing from a wrong to a right answer (Benjamin et al., 1984; Foote & Belinky, 1972; Geiger, 1996). In addition, students who change more answers tend to receive higher test scores than other students, although this finding is only correlational (see *Introduction*, p. 13) and may reflect the fact that frequent answer-changers are higher test performers to begin with (Geiger, 1997; Friedman & Cook, 1995). All of these conclusions hold not merely for multiple choice tests given in classes, but for standardized tests like the SAT and Graduate Record Exam (GRE).

Admittedly, there are two qualifications to the "when in doubt, change your answer" strategy. First, research suggests that students shouldn't change their answer if they're merely guessing this answer might be wrong; changing one's answer is beneficial only when students have a good reason to suspect their answer is wrong (Shatz & Best, 1987; Skinner,

1983). Second, there's some evidence that students who do poorly on multiple choice tests may benefit less from changing their answers than other students (Best, 1979). So these students may want to change their answers only when they're fairly certain these answers are wrong.

There's surprisingly little research addressing the question of why students believe that changing their initial answers is usually a bad idea. But three likely explanations come to mind. First, as we've seen, most professors who give their students advice about changing their answers advise them not to do so (Benjamin et al., 1984). So this mistaken belief is probably spread partly by word-of-mouth (Higham & Gerrard, 2005). Second, research suggests that students are more likely to remember items whose answers they changed from right to wrong than those they changed from wrong to right (Bath, 1967; Ferguson, Kreiter, Peterson, Rowat, & Elliott, 2002). Because the bitter taste of incorrect decisions lingers longer than the memory of correct decisions ("Why on earth did I change that answer? I had it right the first time"), our test-taking mistakes typically stick in our minds. As a consequence, a phenomenon called the *availability heuristic* may lead students to overestimate the risk of committing errors when changing answers. As we learned earlier (see *Introduction*, p. 15), a heuristic is a mental shortcut or rule of thumb. When we use the availability heuristic, we're estimating the likelihood of an event by how easily it comes to our minds. Indeed, research shows that students who change right answers to wrong answers recall these decisions much better than do students who change wrong answers to right answers, largely because the former changes create a more lasting emotional impact (Kruger, Wirtz, & Miller, 2005). Third, research indicates that most students overestimate how many answers they get right on multiple choice tests (Pressley & Ghatala, 1988), so they may assume that changing answers is likely to lower their score.

So to cut to the bottom line: When in doubt, we're usually best *not* trusting our instincts. After all, our first hunches are just that—hunches. If we have a good reason to believe we're wrong, we should go with our head, not our gut, and turn that pencil upside-down.

Myth #17 The Defining Feature of Dyslexia Is Reversing Letters

Humor often reveals our conceptions—and misconceptions—of the world. For example, few psychological conditions are the butt of as many jokes as dyslexia: "I'm an agnostic dyslexic with insomnia. I lay awake all night trying to work out if there really is a Dog." Or, "Dyslexics of the world, untie!"

Yet to people with dyslexia, these jokes aren't especially funny. Not only do they poke fun at people with a disability, but they reinforce inaccurate stereotypes of people with a genuine psychological condition. They also underscore just how distant the public's conception of dyslexia is from reality. Most people believe that the defining feature of dyslexia is "mirror writing" or "mirror reading" (Fiorello, 2001; Gorman, 2003). Indeed, many laypersons believe that dyslexics literally see letters backward. Two types of reversals are commonly associated in the public mind with dyslexia: (1) reversing letters themselves, like writing or seeing "b" instead of "d," and (2) reversing the order of letters within words, like writing "tar" instead of "rat." Even among educators, including university faculty, special education teachers, and speech therapists, 70% believe that the second problem is a defining feature of dyslexia (Wadlington & Wadlington, 2005). In another survey, about 75% of basic education teachers identified odd spellings, especially reversals of the order of letters within words, as a key sign of dyslexia (Kerr, 2001).

The belief that dyslexia is underpinned by letter reversals has early roots (Richardson, 1992). In the 1920s, American neurologist Samuel Orton (1925) coined the term *strephosymbolia* (meaning "twisted symbol") to refer to the tendency to reverse letters, and hypothesized that it was the underlying cause of dyslexia. He also claimed that some children with this condition could read more easily if they held writing up to a mirror. Orton's views helped to perpetuate the longstanding belief that letter reversals are central to dyslexia (Guardiola, 2001).

This view, or variants of it, is bolstered by media portrayals of—and jokes about—dyslexia. A 1984 ABC movie, *Backwards: The Riddle of Dyslexia*, stars a 13-year-old child, Brian Ellsworth (portrayed by the late River Phoenix), who reverses letters in words. The 1994 comedy film, *Naked Gun 33 1/3*, shows lead character Frank Drebin (portrayed by Leslie Nielsen) reading a newspaper featuring the headline "Dyslexia for Cure Found." In the 2001 film, *Pearl Harbor*, Captain Rafe McCauley (portrayed by Ben Affleck) informs the nurse administering an eye exam that he can't read letters because "I just get 'em backward sometimes." And on a *National Public Radio* show on dyslexia in 2007, the host stated that the "simplest explanation, I suppose, is that you see things backwards" (National Public Radio, 2007).

But what is dyslexia, anyway? Dyslexia (meaning "difficulty with words") is a learning disability marked by difficulties in processing written language (Shaywitz, 1996). Most often, dyslexics experience problems with reading and spelling despite adequate classroom instruction. Often, they find it challenging to "sound out" and identify printed words. About 5% of American children suffer from dyslexia. Despite what many people believe, dyslexia isn't an indicator of low mental ability, because dyslexia occurs in many highly intelligent people (Wadlington & Wadlington, 2005). Indeed, the formal psychiatric diagnosis of dyslexia (or more technically, "reading disorder") requires that children's overall intellectual ability be markedly superior to their reading ability (American Psychiatric Association, 2000).

The causes of dyslexia are controversial, although most researchers believe that dyslexics experience difficulty with processing *phonemes*, the smallest units of language that contain meaning (Stanovich, 1998; Vellutino, 1979). The English language, for example, contains 44 phonemes, such as the "c" in "cat" and the "o" in "four." Because dyslexics find it difficult to parse words into their constituent phonemes, they often make mistakes when identifying words (Shaywitz, 1996). Some researchers believe that a subset of dyslexics is marked by visual deficits in addition to deficits in phoneme processing (Badian, 2005; Everatt, Bradshaw, & Hibbard, 1999), but this view is not universally accepted (Wolff & Melngailis, 1996). In any case, there's no evidence that dyslexics literally "see" letters backward or in reverse order within words. Research on twins strongly suggests that dyslexia is partly influenced by genetic factors (Pennington, 1999).

More important, research conducted over the past few decades demonstrates that letter reversals are hardly distinctive to dyslexia. Both backward writing and letter reversals are commonplace in the early phases of spelling and writing of all children age 6 and younger (Liberman et al., 1971; Shaywitz, 1996), not merely dyslexic children. These errors decrease over time in both groups of children, although less so among dyslexic children. In addition, most research suggests that letter reversals are only slightly more frequent, and in some studies no more frequent, among dyslexic than non-dyslexic children (Cassar, Treiman, Moats, Pollo, & Kessler, 2005; Lachman & Geyer, 2003; Moats, 1983; Terepocki, Kruk, & Willows, 2002). Letter reversals also account for only a small minority of the errors that dyslexic children make, so they're hardly a defining feature of the condition (Guardiola, 2001; Terepocki et al., 2002). Finally, although dyslexic children are worse spellers than other children of their age, teachers who've worked extensively with dyslexic children can't distinguish their spellings from those of non-dyslexic, but younger, writers (Cassar et al., 2005). This finding supports the view that normal children make similar spelling errors to those of dyslexic children, but typically "outgrow" them.

So the next time someone asks you if you've heard the joke about the person with dyslexia who answers the phone by saying "O hell," you can politely reply that this view of dyslexia is now a few decades out of date.

Myth # 18 Students Learn Best When Teaching Styles Are Matched to Their Learning Styles

In the headline story "Parents of Nasal Learners Demand Odor-based Curriculum," writers at the satirical newspaper, *The Onion* (2000), poked good-natured fun at the idea that there is a teaching style to unlock every underperforming student's hidden potential (http://www.runet. edu/~thompson/obias.html). We've all observed students in the same classes learning in different ways. Many people believe that all students could achieve at the same level if only teachers would tailor their teaching styles to each student's learning style. As one parent in *The Onion* story put it, "My child is not stupid. There simply was no way for him to thrive in a school that only caters to traditional students who absorb educational concepts by hearing, reading, seeing, discussing, drawing, building, or acting out." An educational researcher noted that "Nasal learners often have difficulty concentrating and dislike doing homework . . . If your child fits this description, I would strongly urge you to get him or her tested for a possible nasal orientation." According to the story, we don't need to consider ability or motivation, because all students are equally capable. Any failure to learn means only that teachers haven't accommodated adequately to a student's learning style.

Of course, the nasal story was fiction, but it's not all that far from reality. Plug the words "learning styles" into an Internet search engine, and you'll find any number of websites claiming to diagnose your preferred learning style in a matter of minutes. One informs visitors that "Learning styles are a way to help improve your quality of learning. By understanding your own personal styles, you can adapt the learning process and techniques you use." It also directs them to a free "Learning Styles Inventory" that over 400,000 people have taken (http://www. learning-styles-online.com). There, you can find out whether you're primarily a visual learner, a social learner, an auditory (sound) learner, a physical learner, and so on. These sites are premised on a straightforward and widely accepted claim: Students learn best when teaching styles are matched to their learning styles.

It's understandable why this view is so popular: Rather than implying that some students are "better" or "worse" learners overall than others, it implies that all students can learn well, perhaps equally well, given just the right teaching style (Willingham, 2004). In addition, this view dovetails with the representative heuristic: like goes with like (see *Introduction*, p. 15). Advocates of this hypothesis claim that verbally oriented students learn best from teachers who emphasize words, visually oriented students learn best from teachers who emphasize images, and so on.

Ronald Hyman and Barbara Rosoff (1984) described the four steps of the learning styles (LS) approach: (1) Examine students' individual learning styles, (2) classify each style into one of a few categories, (3) match it to the teaching style (TS) of a teacher or request that teachers adjust their TS to match the student's LS, and (4) teach teachers to perform steps 1–3 in their training programs. These authors noted that each step imposes a requirement for the approach to work. These requirements include (a) a clear concept of LS, (b) a reliable and valid way to assess and classify students' LS, (c) knowledge of how LS and TS interact to influence learning, and (d) the ability to train teachers to adjust their TS to match students' LS. Writing in 1984, Hyman and Rosoff didn't believe that any of these requirements had been met. We'll soon see if their negative verdict has stood the test of time.

The notion that assessing students' LS is effective has become a virtual truism in educational theory and practice. It's been extolled in many popular books, such as *Teaching Students to Read through Their Individual Learning Styles* (Carbo, Dunn, & Dunn, 1986), and *Discover Your Child's Learning Style: Children Learn in Unique Ways* (Willis & Hodson, 1999). In an article entitled "Dispelling outmoded beliefs about student learning" in a popular educational journal, the authors debunked 15 myths about student learning, but began by proclaiming that the belief that "Students learn best when instruction and learning context match their learning style" was well supported (Dunn & Dunn, 1987, p. 55). In many school districts, questions about matching TS to LS are routine in interviews for aspiring teachers (Alferink, 2007). Many teachers share the field's enthusiasm: The results of one survey of 109 science teachers revealed that most displayed positive attitudes toward the idea of matching their TS to students' LS (Ballone & Czerniak, 2001). Not surprisingly, workshops on educating instructors about matching their styles to students' learning styles are popular, often attracting hundreds of teachers and principals (Stahl, 1999). In some schools, teachers have even asked children to wear shirts emblazoned with the letters V, A, K, which, as we'll soon learn, stand for three widely discussed learning styles—visual, auditory, and kinesthetic (Geake, 2008).

The prevalence of these beliefs is underscored by the sheer volume of articles published in the educational literature on LS, the vast number of LS models proposed, and the enormous commercial success of LS measures. An August, 2008 search of the ERIC database, which catalogues educational scholarship, revealed a whopping 1,984 journal articles, 919 conference presentations, and 701 books or book chapters on LS. In the most comprehensive review of the LS literature, Frank Coffield and his colleagues (Coffield, Moseley, Hall, & Ecclestone, 2004) counted no fewer than 71 LS models. For example, the "VAK" model targets visual, auditory, and kinesthetic learners, who allegedly learn best by seeing and reading, listening and speaking, or touching and doing, respectively. Peter Honey and Alan Mumford's (2000) model classifies students into four categories: "activists," who immerse themselves in new experiences, "reflectors," who sit back and observe, "theorists," who think through problems logically, and "pragmatists," who apply their ideas to the real world.

The LS movement has even embraced models and measures developed for very different purposes. Howard Gardner's (1983) influential theory of multiple intelligences is often considered an LS classification, and some teachers use the Myers–Briggs Type Indicator (Briggs & Myers, 1998), which was developed as a psychoanalytically oriented personality inventory (Hunsley, Lee, & Wood, 2003), to classify students' LS. Honey and Mumford's (2000) Learning Styles Questionnaire is popular, as are two different measures both called the Learning Styles Inventory (Dunn, Dunn, & Price, 1999; Kolb, 1999).

Among the 3,604 ERIC entries related to LS, less than one quarter are peer-reviewed articles. Likewise, Coffield et al. (2004) compiled a database of thousands of books, journal articles, theses, magazine articles, websites, conference papers, and unpublished literature. Few were published in peer-reviewed journals and fewer still were well-controlled studies. In other words, much of LS literature is flying "under the radar," bypassing anonymous critical feedback by expert scholars.

Fortunately, theory and research are available to address each of the four requirements spelled out by Hyman and Rosoff (1984). First, is there a clear concept of LS? The answer appears to be no. Among the most popular of the LS models Coffield et al. (2004) reviewed, the differences are much more striking than the similarities. For example, the VAK model is based on learners' preferred sensory modalities (visual, auditory, or kinesthetic), whereas the Honey–Mumford model, which divides students into activists, reflectors, theorists, and pragmatists, doesn't even address the issue of sensory modalities. There's no agreement on what LS is, despite decades of study.

Second, is there a reliable and valid way to assess students' LS? Again, the answer seems to be no (Snider, 1992; Stahl, 1999). Gregory Kratzig and Katherine Arbuthnott (2006) found no relationship between LS classifications and memory performance on visual, auditory, and kinesthetic versions of a task. Supposedly visual learners did no better at the visual version of the task than the auditory or kinesthetic versions, and the same was true for each preferred sensory modality. Perhaps one reason for the unsatisfactory reliability and validity of LS inventories is that these measures usually assess learning preferences devoid of context (Coffield et al., 2004; Hyman & Rosoff, 1984). In other words, models and measures of LS don't come to grips with the possibility that the best approaches to teaching and learning may depend on what students are trying to learn. Consider the first question on the Paragon Learning Style Inventory (http://www.oswego.edu/plsi/plsi48a.htm): "When you come to a new situation you usually (a) try it right away and learn from doing, or (b) like to watch first and try it later?" It's difficult to answer this question without knowing the type of new situation. Would you learn to read a new language, solve mathematical equations, and perform gymnastics routines using the same methods? If so, we'd certainly be concerned. Most LS models don't place learning into a meaningful context, so it's not surprising that measures based on these models aren't especially reliable or valid.

Third, is there evidence to support the effectiveness of matching instructors' TS to students' LS? From the 1970s onward, at least as many studies have failed to support this approach as have supported it (Kavale & Forness, 1987; Kratzig & Arbuthnott, 2006; Stahl, 1999; Zhang, 2006). That's mostly because certain TSs often yield better results than all others regardless of students' LS (Geake, 2008; Zhang, 2006). The 2007 film *Freedom Writers*, starring Hilary Swank as real-life teacher Erin Gruwell, illustrates this point. After a shaky beginning as a teacher with students torn by boundaries of race, Gruwell became engrossed in her students' lives and immersed them in the study of the Holocaust. By adopting a teaching style that went beyond ordinary classroom methods, she helped all of her students to appreciate and avoid the pitfalls of prejudice. Yet Gruwell didn't match her TS to students' LS. Instead, like many great teachers, she achieved outstanding results by developing an innovative TS to which the entire class responded enthusiastically.

Fourth, can educators train teachers to adapt their TS to match students' LS? Again, the commercial claims outstrip the scientific evidence. Coffield et al. (2004) noted minimal research support for this possibility, and positive results for using LS inventories to guide teaching training are at best weak. There are no clear implications for teaching practices because few well-conducted studies provide evidence, and those that do offer inconsistent advice.

So the popular belief that encouraging teachers to match their TS to students' LS enhances their learning turns out to be an urban legend of educational psychology. To the extent that this approach encourages teachers to teach to students' intellectual strengths rather than their weaknesses, it could actually backfire. Students need to correct and compensate for their shortcomings, not avoid them. Otherwise, their areas of intellectual weakness may grow still weaker. Because life outside the classroom doesn't always conform to our preferred styles of learning, good teaching must prepare us to confront real-world challenges. We agree with Frank Coffield, who said that "We do students a serious disservice by implying they have only one learning style, rather than a flexible repertoire from which to choose, depending on the context" (Henry, 2007).

Chapter 4: Other Myths to Explore

Fiction	Fact
Extremely intelligent people are more physically frail than other people.	With rare exceptions, extremely intelligent people tend to be in better physical health than other individuals.
IQ scores almost never change over time.	Although IQ scores tend to be quite stable in adulthood, they are unstable in childhood; moreover, even in adults, shifts of 5–10 points over a few months can occur.
IQ scores are unrelated to school performance.	IQ scores are moderately to highly predictive of grades in school, including high school and college.

Fiction	Fact
The SAT and other standardized tests are highly coachable.	Most studies show that total SAT scores increase an average of only about 20 points as a consequence of coaching.
There's a close link between genius and insanity.	There's no evidence that high IQ predisposes to psychotic disorders; to the contrary, the IQ scores of people with schizophrenia tend to be slightly lower than those of people in the general population.
Mental retardation is one condition.	There are over 500 genetic causes of mental retardation in addition to environmental causes, such as accidents during birth.
Most mentally retarded individuals are severely retarded.	About 85% of mentally retarded individuals are classified as mildly retarded.
There is no association between brain size and IQ.	Brain size and IQ are moderately correlated in humans.
Women are worse drivers than men.	Even after controlling for the fact that men drive more than women, men get into 70% more car accidents than women, perhaps because men take more risks as drivers.
Creative breakthroughs occur in sudden bursts of insight.	Brain imaging studies reveal that well before people suddenly report a creative answer to a problem, brain areas involved in problem-solving, such as the frontal lobes, have already been active.
Very high levels of motivation usually help when solving difficult problems.	Very high levels of motivation typically impair performance on difficult problems.
Negative reinforcement is a type of punishment.	Negative reinforcement and punishment are opposite in their effects; negative reinforcement increases the frequency of a behavior by withdrawing an aversive stimulus, whereas punishment decreases the frequency of a behavior.
Punishment is a highly effective means of changing long-term behavior.	Although punishment inhibits behavior in the short term, it tends to be less effective than reinforcement for shaping behavior in the long term.

Fiction	Fact
The best means of maintaining a behavior is to reward every response.	The best means of maintaining a behavior is to reward desired responses only intermittently.
B. F. Skinner raised his daughter in a "Skinner box," contributing to her psychosis later in life.	Skinner raised his daughter in a specially designed crib, not a Skinner box; moreover, she never developed a psychosis.
Small class sizes consistently promote better student achievement.	The association between class size and achievement is mixed and inconsistent, although small class size may exert small positive effects among poorly performing children.
Grouping students in classes by their ability levels promotes learning.	Most studies show that "ability grouping" produces few or no effects on student learning.
Holding immature or underperforming students back a grade can be helpful.	Most research suggests that grade retention is largely ineffective in enhancing achievement, and may result in poorer emotional adjustment.
Standardized test scores don't predict later grades.	Scores on the SAT and GRE are moderate to high predictors of later grades in samples with a broad range of SAT and GRE scores.
Direct and immediate feedback is the best means of ensuring long-term learning.	Irregularly provided feedback best promotes long-term learning.
"Discovery learning" (in which students must discover scientific principles on their own) is superior to direct instruction.	For tasks involving scientific reasoning, direct instruction is often superior to discovery learning.
The standardized test scores of U.S. students have been declining in recent decades.	Declines on the SAT and other standardized tests appear due largely or entirely to students with a broader range of abilities taking these tests in recent decades.
Students typically recall only 10% of what they read.	This is an urban legend with no scientific support.
Speed reading courses are effective.	Virtually all speed reading courses are ineffective, because they diminish comprehension.
Subvocalizing increases reading ability.	Subvocalizing slows down our reading speed, because we can read much more quickly than we can speak.

Fiction	Fact
Deaf people can understand most of what other people say by reading lips.	Even the best lip-readers can understand only about 30–35% of what speakers are saying.
Some people "speak in tongues."	There's no scientific evidence for genuine "glossolalia," that is, speaking in tongues.
Many identical twins have their own private language.	There's no evidence that twins have "cryptophasia" (secret language); reports to the contrary appear due to the fact that twins often share similar language impairments, which they accommodate in each other.
Albert Einstein had dyslexia.	There's no good evidence that Einstein was dyslexic.

Sources and Suggested Readings

To explore these and other myths about intelligence and learning, see Alferink (2007); DeBell and Harless (1992); Della Sala (2007); Druckman and Bjork (1991); Druckman and Swets (1988); Ehrenberg, Brewer, Gamoran, and Willms (2001); Furnham (1996); Greene (2005); Jimerson, Carlson, Rotert, Egeland, and Sroufe (1997); Lubinski, Benbow, Webb, and Bleske-Rechek (2006); Phelps (2009); Sternberg (1996); Willerman (1979).

5 ALTERED STATES

Myths about Consciousness

Myth #19
Hypnosis Is a Unique "Trance" State that Differs in Kind from Wakefulness

As you sink deeper and deeper into your chair, the hypnotist drones, "Your hand is getting lighter, lighter, it's rising, rising by itself, lifting off the resting surface." You notice that your hand lifts slowly, in herky-jerky movements, in sync with his suggestions. Two more hypnotic suggestions follow: one for numbness in your hand, after which you're insensitive to painful stimulation, and another to hallucinate a kitten on your lap. The cat seems so real you want to pet it. What's going on? What you've experienced seems so extraordinary that it's easy to conclude that you must have been in a trance. Were you?

The notion that a trance or special state of consciousness is central to the striking effects of hypnosis traces its origins to the earliest attempts to understand hypnotic phenomena. If you associate the term "mesmerized" with hypnosis, it's because Viennese physician Franz Anton Mesmer (1734–1815) provided early and compelling demonstrations of the power of suggestion to treat people who displayed physical symptoms, like paralyses, that actually stemmed from psychological factors. Mesmer believed an invisible magnetic fluid filled the universe and triggered psychological nervous illnesses when it became imbalanced. Mesmer may have been the model for the magician of The Sorcerer's Apprentice in the 1940 Walt Disney movie *Fantasia*. Dressed in a flowing cape, Mesmer merely had to touch his suggestible patients with a magnetic wand for them to experience wild laughter, crying, shrieking, and thrashing about followed by a stupor, a condition known as the "crisis." The crisis became the hallmark of mesmerism, and Mesmer's followers believed it was responsible for his dramatic cures.

Mesmer's theory was debunked in 1784 by a commission headed by the then American ambassador to France, Benjamin Franklin (by that time, Mesmer had decided to leave Vienna following a botched attempt to treat a blind musician and had moved to Paris). The investigators concluded that the effects of mesmerism were due to imagination and belief, or what today we would call the placebo effect—improvement resulting from the mere expectation of improvement (see *Introduction*, p. 14). Still, die-hard believers continued to claim that magnetism endowed people with supernatural powers, including the ability to see without their eyes and detect disease by seeing through their skin. Before doctors developed anesthetics in the 1840s, claims that doctors could use mesmerism to perform painless surgeries were fueled by James Esdaile's reports of successful surgical procedures in India performed using mesmerism alone (Chaves, 2000). By the mid 19th century, many far-fetched claims about hypnosis were greeted with widespread scientific skepticism. Even so, they contributed to the popular mystique of hypnosis.

The Marquis de Puysugaur discovered what later came to be regarded as a hypnotic trance. His patients didn't know they were supposed to respond to his inductions by going into a crisis, so they didn't. Instead, one of his patients, Victor Race, appeared to enter a sleep-like state when magnetized. His behavior in this state seemed remarkable, and as hypnotists became more interested in what they called "artificial somnambulism" ("somnambulism" means sleepwalking), the convulsive crisis gradually disappeared.

By the late 1800s, myths about hypnosis abounded, including the idea that hypnotized people enter a sleep-like state in which they forgo their willpower, are oblivious to their surroundings, and forget what happened afterwards (Laurence & Perry, 1988). The fact that the Greek prefix "hypno" means sleep probably helped to foster these misunderstandings. These misconceptions were widely popularized in George Du Maurier's novel *Trilby* (1894) in which Svengali, whose name today connotes a ruthless manipulator, uses hypnosis to dominate an unfortunate girl, Trilby. By placing Trilby in a hypnotic trance against her will, Svengali created an alternate personality (see also Myth #39) in which she performed as an operatic singer, allowing him to enjoy a life of luxury. Fast-forwarding to recent times, many of the same themes play to dramatic effect in popular movies and books that portray the hypnotic trance state as so powerful that otherwise normal subjects will (a) commit an assassination (*The Manchurian Candidate*); (b) commit suicide (*The Garden Murders*); (c) disfigure themselves with scalding water (*The Hypnotic Eye*); (d) assist in blackmail (*On Her Majesty's Secret Service*); (e) perceive only a person's internal beauty (*Shallow Hal*); (f) steal (*Curse of the Jade Scorpion*); and our favorite, (g) fall victim to brainwashing by alien preachers who use messages embedded in sermons (*Invasion of the Space Preachers*).

Recent survey data (Green, Page, Rasekhy, Johnson, & Bernhardt, 2006) show that public opinion resonates with media portrayals of hypnosis. Specifically, 77% of college students endorsed the statement that "hypnosis is an altered state of consciousness, quite different from normal waking consciousness," and 44% agreed that "A deeply hypnotized person is robot-like and goes along automatically with whatever the hypnotist suggests."

But research refutes these widely accepted beliefs. Hypnotized people are by no means mindless automatons. They can resist and even oppose hypnotic suggestions (see Lynn, Rhue, & Weekes, 1990), and they won't do things during or after hypnosis that are out of character, like harming people they dislike. So, Hollywood thrillers aside, hypnosis can't turn a mild-mannered person into a cold-blooded murderer. In addition, hypnosis bears no more than a superficial resemblance to sleep, because EEG (brain wave) studies reveal that hypnotized people are wide awake. What's more, individuals can be just as responsive to suggestions administered while they're alert and exercising on a stationary bicycle as they are following suggestions for sleep and relaxation (Banyai, 1991).

Stage hypnosis shows, in which zombie-like volunteers quack like ducks or play a wicked air guitar to the music of U-2, further contribute to popular stereotypes of hypnosis (Figure 5.1). But the wacky actions of people onstage aren't due to a trance. Before the show even gets under way, the hypnotist selects potential performers by noting how they respond to waking suggestions. Those whose outstretched hands fall down on command when asked to imagine holding a heavy dictionary are likely to be invited onstage, whereas the remaining audience members end up watching the show from their seats. Moreover, the hypnotized volunteers do outlandish things because they feel intense pressure to respond and entertain the audience. Many stage hypnotists also use the "stage whispers" technique of whispering suggestions ("OK, when I snap my fingers, bark like a dog") into the ears of subjects onstage (Meeker & Barber, 1971).

In the laboratory, we can easily produce all of the phenomena that people associate with hypnosis (such as hallucinations and insensitivity to pain) using suggestions alone, with no mention or even hint of hypnosis. The research literature is clear: No trance or discrete state unique

Figure 5.1 Stage hypnosis shows fuel the mistaken impression that hypnosis is a distinct "trance" state closely related to sleep.
Source: George Silk//Time Life Pictures/Getty Images.

to hypnosis is at work. Indeed, most people who undergo hypnosis later claim they weren't even in a trance. Kevin McConkey (1986) found that although 62% of participants endorsed the view that "hypnosis is an altered state of consciousness" before hypnosis, only 39% held this view afterwards.

If a trance isn't required for hypnosis, what determines hypnotic suggestibility? Hypnotic suggestibility depends on people's motivation, beliefs, imagination, and expectations, as well as their responsiveness to suggestions without hypnosis. The feeling of an altered state is merely one of the many subjective effects of suggestion, and it's not needed to experience any other suggested effects.

Evidence of a distinct trance or altered state of consciousness unique to hypnosis would require that researchers find distinctive physiological markers of subjects' responses to hypnotists' suggestions to enter a trance. Despite concerted efforts by investigators, no evidence of this sort has emerged (Dixon & Laurence, 1992; Hasegawa & Jamieson, 2000; Sarbin & Slagle, 1979; Wagstaff, 1998). So there's no reason to believe that hypnosis differs in kind rather than degree from normal wakefulness. Instead, hypnosis appears to be only one procedure among many for increasing people's responses to suggestions.

That said, hypnotic suggestions can certainly affect brain functioning. In fact, studies of the neurobiology of hypnosis (Hasegawa & Jamieson, 2000) point to the brain's anterior cingulate regions as playing a key role in alterations in consciousness during hypnosis. Although interesting, these findings "do not indicate a discrete state of hypnosis" (Hawegawa & Jamieson, 2000, p. 113). They tell us only that hypnosis changes the brain in some fashion. That's hardly surprising, because brain functioning also changes during relaxation, fatigue, heightened attention, and a host of other states that differ only in degree from normal awareness.

Still others have claimed that certain unusual behaviors are unique to the hypnotic state. But scientific evidence for this claim has been wanting. For example, American psychiatrist Milton Erickson (1980) claimed that hypnosis is marked by several unique features, including "literalism"—the tendency to take questions literally, such as responding "Yes" to the question "Can you tell me what time it is?" Yet research demonstrates that most highly hypnotizable subjects don't display literalism while hypnotized. Moreover, participants asked to simulate (role-play) hypnosis display higher rates of literalism than hypnotized subjects (Green et al., 1990).

So the next time you see a Hollywood movie in which the CIA transforms an average Joe into a sleepwalking zombie who prevents World War III by assassinating an evil dictator, be skeptical. Like most things that you see on the big screen, hypnosis isn't quite what it appears to be.

Myth #20 Researchers Have Demonstrated that Dreams Possess Symbolic Meaning

"When You Understand Your Own Dreams . . . You'll Be Stunned at How Quickly You Can Make LASTING, POSITIVE CHANGE In Your

Life! That's right! Your subconscious is trying very hard to TELL you something in your dreams. You just have to understand its SYMBOLIC LANGUAGE."

Lauri Quinn Loewenberg (2008) made this pitch on her website to promote her book on dream interpretation, which contains "7 secrets to understanding your dreams." Her site is one of many that tout the value of unraveling dreams' symbolic meaning. So-called dream dictionaries in books, on the Internet, and in "dream software" programs, which users can download to their computers, contain databases of thousands of dream symbols that promise to help readers decode their dreams' hidden meanings (Ackroyd, 1993). Movie and television plots also capitalize on popular beliefs about the symbolic meaning of dreams. In one episode of the HBO series, *The Sopranos*, Tony Soprano's friend appeared to Tony in a dream as a talking fish, leading Tony to suspect him as an FBI informant ("fish" is a slang term for informant) (Sepinwall, 2006).

Perhaps not surprisingly, the results of a recent *Newsweek* poll revealed that 43% of Americans believe that dreams reflect unconscious desires (Adler, 2006). Moreover, researchers who conducted surveys in India, South Korea, and the United States discovered that 56% to 74% of people across the three cultures believed that dreams can reveal hidden truths (Morewedge & Norton, 2009). In a second study, these investigators found that people were more likely to say they would avoid flying if they imagined they dreamt of a plane crashing on a flight they planned to take than if they had the conscious thought of a plane crashing, or received a governmental warning about a high risk of a terrorist attack on an airline. These findings demonstrate that many people believe that dreams contain precious nuggets of meaning that are even more valuable than waking thoughts.

Because many of us believe that dream symbols can foretell the future, as well as achieve personal insight, dream dictionaries liberally serve up heaping portions of predictions and advice. According to *Dream Central*'s dream dictionary, "If you abandon something bad in your dreams you could quite possibly receive some favorable financial news." In contrast, eating macaroni in a dream "could mean you are in for various small losses." The *Hyperdictionary of Dreams* warns that dreaming of an anteater "indicates that you might be exposed to new elements, people or events, that will threaten your business discipline and work ethic." Clearly, dreamers would do well to avoid anteaters eating macaroni, lest they risk financial trouble.

All kidding aside, many therapists trained in a Freudian tradition have long entertained the idea that the ever-changing and sometimes bizarre dream landscape is replete with symbols that, if properly interpreted, can surrender the psyche's innermost secrets. According to Freud, dreams are the *via regia*—the royal road to understanding the unconscious mind —and contain "the psychology of the neurosis in a nutshell" (Freud in a letter to Fleiss, 1897, in Jones, 1953, p. 355). Freud argued that the ego's defenses are relaxed during dreaming, leading repressed id impulses to knock at the gates of consciousness (for Freud, the "ego" was the part of the personality that interfaces with reality, the "id" the part of the personality that contains our sexual and aggressive drives). Nevertheless, these raging impulses rarely if ever reach the threshold of awareness. Instead, they're transformed by what Freud called the "dreamwork" into symbols that disguise forbidden hidden wishes and allow dreamers to sleep peacefully. If this censorship didn't occur, dreamers would be awakened by the unsettling eruption of repressed material—often of a sexual and aggressive nature.

Dream interpretation is one of the linchpins of the psychoanalytic method. Yet according to Freudians, dreams don't surrender their secrets without a struggle. The analyst's task is to go beyond the surface details of the dream, called the "manifest content," and interpret the "latent content," the deeper, cloaked, symbolic meaning of the dream. For example, the appearance of a scary monster in a dream (the manifest content) might symbolize the threat posed by a feared boss (the latent content). We draw dream symbols from our storehouse of life experiences, including the events we experience on the day prior to a dream, which Freud called the "day residue" (here, Freud was almost surely correct) as well as our childhood experiences.

According to Freud, dream interpretation should be guided by patients' free associations to various aspects of the dream, thereby leaving room for individually tailored interpretations of dream content. Although Freud warned readers that dream symbols don't bear a universal one-to-one relationship to psychologically meaningful objects, people, or events, he frequently came perilously close to violating this rule by interpreting the symbolic meaning of dreams with little or no input from his patients. For example, in his landmark book, *The Interpretation of Dreams* (1900), Freud reported that even though a woman generated no associations to the dream image of a straw hat with the middle piece bent upwards and the side piece hanging downwards, he suggested that the hat symbolized a man's genitals. Moreover, Freud noted that penetration into narrow spaces and opening locked doors frequently symbolize sexual activity, whereas hair cutting, the loss of teeth, and beheading frequently symbolize castration. So despite his cautions, Freud treated many dream symbols as essentially universal.

Freud's writings paved the way for a burgeoning cottage industry of dream interpretation products that shows no signs of loosening its chokehold on popular imagination. Still, most contemporary scientists reject the idea that specific dream images carry universal symbolic meaning. Indeed, close inspection of dream reports reveals that many dreams don't appear to be disguised by symbols. Indeed, in the early stages of sleep, before our eyes begin to dart back and forth in rapid eye movement (REM) sleep, most of our dreams mirror the everyday activities and concerns that occupy our minds, like studying for a test, shopping for groceries, or doing our taxes (Dorus, Dorus, & Rechtschaffen, 1971).

During REM sleep, our highly activated brains produce dreams that are sometimes illogical and charged with emotion (Foulkes, 1962; Hobson, Pace-Schott, & Stickgold, 2000). Does this occur because repressed material from the id somehow escapes censorship? Psychiatrist J. Allan Hobson doesn't think so. In fact, Hobson's theory of dreaming, which has garnered considerable scientific support, is so radically different from Freud's that some have called him "the anti-Freud" (Rock, 2004). Starting in the 1960s and 1970s, at Harvard's Laboratory of Neurophysiology, Hobson, along with Robert McCarley, developed the *activation-synthesis theory*, which ties dreams to brain activity rather than the symbolic expression of unconscious wishes (Hobson & McCarley, 1977).

According to this theory (Hobson et al., 2000), when we cycle through REM periods every 90 minutes or so during sleep, various neurotransmitters (chemical messengers) orchestrate a dramatic symphony of changes that generates dreams. More specifically, surges of acetylcholine hype the brain's emotional centers, while decreases in serotonin and norepinephrine tamp down brain areas that govern reason, memory, and attention. According to Hobson, REM dreams are our brain's best, if imperfect, efforts to cobble together a meaningful story based on a hodgepodge of random information transmitted by the pons, a structure at the base of the brain. Under these circumstances, images that bubble up lack symbolic meaning, so dream interpretation would be haphazard at best, much like attempting to derive pearls of wisdom from gibberish.

Still, to give Freud his due, he may have been right on at least two important counts: Our daily thoughts and feelings can influence our dreams, and emotion plays a powerful role in dreaming. Nevertheless, the fact that the emotional centers of the brain become supercharged during dreaming as the forebrain responsible for logical thinking shuts down (Solms, 1997, 2000) doesn't mean that dreams are attempts to fulfill the id's wishes. Nor does it mean that dreams use symbols to disguise their true meaning.

Rather than relying on a dream dictionary to foretell the future or help you make life decisions, it probably would be wisest to weigh the pros and cons of differing courses of action carefully, and consult trusted friends and advisers. Still, as far as your dreams go, it may be a good idea to avoid anteaters eating macaroni.

Myth # 21 People Can Learn Information, like New Languages, while Asleep

Imagine that you could learn all of the information in this book while getting just a few nights of sound sleep. You could pay someone to tape record the entire book, play the recording over the span of several weeknights, and voilà—you'd be all done. You could kiss goodbye to all of those late nights reading about psychological misconceptions.

As in many areas of psychology, hope springs eternal. Indeed, many proponents of *sleep-assisted learning*—learning new material while asleep (technically called "hypnopaedia")—have advanced many strong claims regarding this technique's potential. One website (http://www.sleeplearning.com/) informs visitors that:

> Sleep learning is a way to harness the power of your subconscious while you sleep, enabling you to learn foreign languages, pass exams, undertake professional studies and implement self-growth by using techniques based on research conducted all over the world with great success. . . . It's the most incredible learning aid for years.

The website offers a variety of CDs that can purportedly help us to learn languages, stop smoking, lose weight, reduce stress, or become a better lover, all while we're comfortably catching up on our *zzzzs*. The site even goes so far as to say that the CDs work better when people are asleep than awake. *Amazon.com* features a host of products designed to help us learn while sleeping, including CDs that claim to help us learn Spanish, Romanian, Hebrew, Japanese, and Mandarin Chinese while playing subliminal messages (see Myth #5) to us while we're sound asleep. Perhaps not surprisingly, the results of one survey revealed that 68% of undergraduates believed that people can learn new information while asleep (Brown, 1983).

Sleep-assisted learning is also a common fixture in many popular books, television programs, and films. In Anthony Burgess's (1962) brilliant but horrifying novel, *A Clockwork Orange*, later made into an award-winning film by director Stanley Kubrick, government officials attempt unsuccessfully to use sleep-assisted learning techniques to transform the main character, Alex, from a classic psychopath into a respectable member of society. In an episode of the popular television program, *Friends*, Chandler Bing (portrayed by Matthew Perry) attempts to quit smoking by playing a tape containing suggestions to stop smoking during sleep. Nevertheless, unbeknownst to him, the tape contained the suggestion, "You are a strong and confident woman," leading Chandler to behave in a feminine way in daily life.

But does the popular conception of sleep-assisted learning stack up to its advocates' impressive claims? One reason for initial optimism about sleep-assisted learning stems from findings that people sometimes incorporate external stimuli into their dreams. Classic research by William Dement and Edward Wolpert (1958) demonstrated that presenting dreaming subjects with stimuli, like squirts of water from a syringe, often leads them to weave these stimuli into their dreams. For example, in Dement and Wolpert's work, one participant sprayed with water reported a dream of a leaky roof after being awakened shortly thereafter. Later researchers showed that anywhere from 10–50% of participants appear to incorporate external stimuli, such as bells, red lights, and voices, into their dreams (Conduit & Coleman, 1998; Trotter, Dallas, & Verdone, 1988). Nevertheless, these studies don't really demonstrate sleep-assisted learning, because they don't show that people can integrate complex new information, like mathematical formulas or new words from foreign languages, into their dreams. Nor do they show that people can later recall these externally presented stimuli in everyday life if they're not awakened from their dreams.

To investigate claims regarding sleep-assisted learning, investigators must randomly assign some participants to hear audiotaped stimuli, like words from a foreign language, while sleeping and others to hear a "control" audiotape consisting of irrelevant stimuli, and later examine their knowledge of these stimuli on a standardized test. Interestingly, some early findings on sleep-assisted learning yielded encouraging results. One group of investigators exposed sailors to Morse code (a shorthand form of communication that radio operators sometimes use) while asleep. These sailors mastered Morse code three weeks faster than did other sailors

(Simon & Emmons, 1955). Other studies from the former Soviet Union also seemed to provide support for the claim that people could learn new material, such as words or sentences, while listening to tape recordings during sleep (Aarons, 1976).

Yet these early positive reports neglected to rule out a crucial alternative explanation: the tape recordings may have awakened the subjects! The problem is that almost all of the studies showing positive effects didn't monitor subjects' brain waves to ensure that they were actually asleep while listening to the tapes (Druckman & Bjork, 1994; Druckman & Swets, 1988). Better controlled studies that have monitored subjects' brain waves to make sure they're clearly asleep have offered little or no evidence for sleep-assisted learning (Logie & Della Sala, 1999). So to the extent that sleep-learning tapes "work," it's probably because subjects hear snatches of them while drifting in and out of sleep.

Listening to the tapes while fully awake is not only far more efficient but probably more effective. As for that quick fix for mastering new knowledge or reducing stress, we'd recommend saving your money about the tapes and just getting a good night's sleep.

Myth # 22   During "Out-of-Body" Experiences, People's Consciousness Leaves Their Bodies

Since biblical times, if not earlier, people have speculated that out-of-body experiences (OBEs) provide conclusive evidence that consciousness can leave the body. Consider the following example of an OBE reported by a woman who had an internal hemorrhage following an operation to remove her uterus:

> I was awake and aware of my surroundings. A nurse came in to take my blood pressure every half hour. On one occasion I remember her taking my blood pressure and then running out of the room, which I thought was unusual. I don't remember anything more after that consciously, but I was then aware of being above my body as if I was floating on the ceiling and looking down at myself in the hospital bed with a crowd of doctors and nurses around me. (Parnia, 2006, p. 54)

Or take this description from a woman on the operating table:

> . . . while I was being operated on I saw some very odd lights flashing and heard a loud keening noise. Then I was in the operating theatre above everyone else but just high enough to see over everyone's shoulders. I was

surprised to see everyone dressed in green . . . I looked down and wondered what they were all looking at and what was under the cover on the long table. I saw a square of flesh, and I thought, "I wonder who it is and what they are doing." I then realized it was me. (Blackmore, 1993, p. 1)

These reports are typical of OBEs, in which people claim to be floating above or otherwise disengaged from their bodies, observing themselves from a distance. Such fascinating alterations in consciousness prompted ancient Egyptians and Greeks, and others who experienced OBEs throughout history, to conclude that they reveal that consciousness can be independent of the physical body.

People in virtually all cultures report OBEs (Alcock & Otis, 1980). They're surprisingly common: About 25% of college students and 10% of members of the general population report having experienced one or more of them (Alvarado, 2000). Many people in the general public assume that OBEs occur most frequently when people are near death, such as when they're drowning or experiencing a heart attack. They're wrong. Although some OBEs occur during life-threatening circumstances (Alvarado, 2000), most occur when people are relaxed, asleep, dreaming, medicated, using psychedelic drugs, anesthetized, or experiencing seizures or migraine headaches (Blackmore, 1982, 1984; Green, 1968; Poynton, 1975). OBEs also occur in people who can spontaneously experience a wide variety of alterations in consciousness (Alvarado, 2000). People who often fantasize in their everyday lives to the extent that they lose an awareness of their bodies are prone to OBEs, as are those who report other strange experiences, like hallucinations, perceptual distortions, and unusual bodily sensations (Blackmore, 1984, 1986).

Some people report being able to create OBEs on command, and to mentally visit distant places or "spiritual realms" during their journeys out of body, a phenomenon called "astral projection" or "astral travel." One Internet site dubs the study of OBEs "projectiology," and claims, "Based on projectiological data, the projection of the consciousness is a real experience that takes place in a dimension other than the physical. Conscious projectors are able to temporarily leave the restriction of their physical body and access non-physical dimensions where they discover new aspects of the nature of consciousness" (Viera, 2002). Believers in "Eckankar," who claim to practice the "science of soul travel," contend that their senses are enhanced and that they experience ecstatic states of spiritual awareness during purposefully created OBEs. Instructions for producing OBEs to achieve spiritual enlightenment and to remotely view far-away places, including alien worlds, are widely available on the Internet, and in books and articles.

Tempting as it is to speculate that our consciousness can break free of the shackles of our physical bodies, research doesn't support this hypothesis. A straightforward way to test the notion that consciousness actually exits the body is to find out whether people can report accurately on what they "see" at a remote location during an OBE. Researchers typically test people who claim to be able to produce OBEs at will, and instruct them to "travel" to a pre-arranged location and describe what they observe when they return to their bodies. Scientists can determine the accuracy of the descriptions because they know what's physically at the site. Participants often report that they can "leave their bodies" when instructed, and that they can see what's happening at the target location, like a ledge in their apartment 10 feet above their bed. Yet investigators have found that their reports are almost always inaccurate, as gauged by judges' comparisons of these reports with the actual physical characteristics of the target locations. At best what they describe could just be a "good guess" in the rare cases that they've been accurate. Even when a few scattered researchers have reported seemingly positive results, others haven't replicated them (Alvarado, 2000).

If people don't actually leave their bodies during an OBE, what explains their dramatic alterations in consciousness? Our sense of "self" depends on a complex interplay of sensory information. One hypothesis is that OBEs reflect a disconnection between individuals' sense of their bodies and their sensations. Consistent with this possibility, research suggests that OBEs arise from the failure of different brain areas to integrate information from different senses (Blanke & Thut, 2007). When we reach for a knife and feel its sharp edges, we have a strong sense not only of its reality, but of ourselves as active agents.

Two studies suggest that when our senses of touch and vision are scrambled, our usual experience of our physical body becomes disrupted too. In Henrik Ehrsson's (2007) research, participants donned goggles that permitted them to view a video display of themselves relayed by a camera placed behind them. This setup created the weird illusion that their bodies, viewed from the rear, actually were standing in front of them. In other words, participants could literally "see" their bodies at a second location, separate from their physical selves. Ehrsson touched participants in the chest with a rod while he used cameras to make it appear that the visual image in the display was being touched at the same time. Participants reported the eerie sensation that their video double was also being touched, thus sensing they were at a location outside their physical bodies.

Bigna Lenggenhager and her colleagues (Lenggenhager, Tadi, Metzinger, & Blanke, 2007) concocted a similar virtual-reality setup. After participants viewed their virtual double, researchers touched them on their backs at the same time as they touched their projected alter egos. The researchers then blindfolded them, moved them from their original position, and asked them to return to the original spot. Interestingly, subjects repositioned themselves closer to the location where their double was projected than to the place where they stood initially. The fact that subjects were drawn to their alter egos suggests that they experienced their location outside their own bodies.

Numerous researchers have tried to pin down the brain location of OBEs. In the laboratory, several have successfully induced OBEs—reports of one's sense of self separated from one's body—by stimulating the temporal lobe, particularly the place where the brain's right temporal and parietal lobes join (Blanke, Ortigue, Landis, & Seeck, 2002; Persinger, 2001; Ridder, Van Laere, Dupont, Menovsky, & Van de Heyning, 2007).

One can certainly question the relevance of laboratory findings to OBEs that occur in everyday life, and it's possible that the latter stem from different causes than the former. Still, the fact that scientists can produce experiences that closely resemble spontaneously occurring OBEs suggests that our consciousness doesn't actually leave our bodies during an OBE, despite the striking subjective conviction that it does.

Chapter 5: Other Myths to Explore

Fiction	Fact
Relaxation is necessary for hypnosis to occur.	People can be hypnotized while exercising vigorously.
People are unaware of their surroundings during hypnosis.	Hypnotized people are aware of their surroundings and can recall the details of conversations overheard during hypnosis.
People have no memory for what took place while hypnotized.	"Posthypnotic amnesia" doesn't occur unless people expect it to occur.
Most modern hypnotists use a swinging watch to induce a hypnotic state.	Virtually no modern hypnotists use watches to induce hypnosis.
Some hypnotic inductions are more effective than others.	A wide range of hypnotic inductions are about equally effective.

Fiction	Fact
People who respond to many hypnotic suggestions are gullible.	People who respond to many hypnotic suggestions are no more gullible than people who respond to few suggestions.
Hypnosis can lead people to perform immoral acts they wouldn't otherwise perform.	There's little or no evidence that one can make hypnotized individuals engage in unethical acts against their will.
Hypnosis allows people to perform acts of great physical strength or skill.	These same acts can be performed by highly motivated subjects without hypnosis.
People can't lie under hypnosis.	Studies show that many subjects can lie while hypnotized.
The primary determinant of hypnosis is the skill of the hypnotist.	The main determinant of hypnosis is the subject's hypnotic suggestibility.
People can remain permanently "stuck" in hypnosis.	People can come out of a hypnotic state even if the hypnotist leaves.
Extremely high levels of motivation can allow people to firewalk over burning hot coals.	Firewalking can be accomplished by anyone who walks quickly enough, because coals are poor conductors of heat.
Dreams occur in only a few seconds, although they take much longer to recount later.	This belief, held by Sigmund Freud and others, is false; many dreams last a half hour or even more.
Our brains "rest" during sleep.	During rapid eye movement sleep, our brain is in a state of high activity.
Sleeping pills are a good long-term treatment for insomnia.	Prolonged use of sleeping pills often causes rebound insomnia.
"Counting sheep" helps people to fall asleep.	The results of one study show that asking insomniacs to count sheep in bed doesn't help them fall asleep.
Falling asleep the moment one's head hits the pillow is a sign of a healthy sleeper.	Falling asleep the moment one's head hits the pillow is a sign of sleep deprivation; most healthy sleepers take 10–15 minutes to fall asleep after going to bed.
Many people never dream.	Although many people claim that they never dream, virtually all people eventually report dreams when awakened from REM sleep.
Most dreams are about sex.	Only a small minority, perhaps 10% or less, of dreams contain overt sexual content.

Fiction	Fact
Most dreams are bizarre in content.	Studies show that most dreams are relatively realistic approximations of waking life.
People dream only in black and white.	Most people report color in their dreams.
Blind people don't dream.	Blind people do dream, although they only experience visual images in their dreams if they had sight prior to about age 7.
If we dream that we die, we'll actually die.	Many people have dreamt of their deaths and lived to tell about it.
Dreams occur only during REM sleep.	Dreams also occur in non-REM sleep, although they tend to be less vivid and more repetitive in content than REM dreams.
People can use lucid dreaming to improve their mental adjustment.	There's no research evidence that becoming aware of the fact that one is dreaming—and using this awareness to change one's dreams—can enhance one's psychological health.
Most sleepwalkers are acting out their dreams; most sleeptalkers are verbalizing them.	Sleepwalking and sleeptalking, which occur in non-REM sleep, aren't associated with vivid dreaming.
Sleepwalking is harmless.	Sleepwalkers often injure themselves by tripping or bumping into objects.
Sleepwalking is associated with deep-seated psychological problems.	There's no evidence that sleepwalking is associated with severe psychopathology.
Awakening a sleepwalker is dangerous.	Awakening a sleepwalker isn't dangerous, although sleepwalkers may be disoriented upon waking.
Transcendental meditation is a uniquely effective means of achieving relaxation.	Many studies suggest that meditation yields no greater physiological effects than rest or relaxation alone.

Sources and Suggested Readings

To explore these and other myths about consciousness, see Cardena, Lynn, and Krippner (2000); Harvey and Payne (2002); Hines (2003); Holmes (1984); Nash (1987); Nash (2001); Mahowald and Schenk (2005); Piper (1993); Squier and Domhoff (1998); Wagstaff (2008).

6 I'VE GOT A FEELING

Myths about Emotion and Motivation

Myth # 23 **The Polygraph ("Lie Detector") Test Is an Accurate Means of Detecting Dishonesty**

Have you ever told a lie?

If you answered "No," the odds are high you're lying. College students admit to lying in about one in every three social interactions—that's about twice a day on average—and people in the community about one in every five interactions—that's about once a day on average (DePaulo, Kashy, Kirkendol, Wyer, & Epstein, 1996).

Attempts to deceive others in everyday life are as difficult to detect as they are common (Ekman, 2001; Vrij & Mann, 2007). We might assume that as frequent as lying is, we'd be good at identifying it. If so, we'd be wrong. Contrary to what's depicted in the television show *Lie to Me*, starring Tim Roth as deception expert Dr. Cal Lightman, a large body of research reveals surprisingly few valid cues of deception (DePaulo et al., 2003). Moreover, most people, including those with special training in security professions, like judges and police officers, often do no better than chance at spotting lies (Ekman & O'Sullivan, 1991; Ekman, O'Sullivan, & Frank, 1999). Indeed, most of us are dead wrong about bodily cues that give away liars. For example, even though about 70% of people believe that shifty eyes are good indicators of lying, research shows otherwise (Vrij, 2008). To the contrary, there's evidence that psychopaths, who are pathological liars, are especially likely to stare others in the face when telling blatant fibs (Rime, Bouvy, Leborgne, & Rouillon, 1978).

If we can't determine who's lying or telling the truth by watching each other, what else can we do? History reveals a veritable parade of dubious methods to detect suspected liars, such as the "rice test" of the ancient Hindus (Lykken, 1998). Here's the idea: If deception leads to fear, and fear inhibits the secretion of saliva, then an accused individual shouldn't be able to spit out rice after chewing it because it will stick to the gums. In the 16th and 17th centuries, many accused witches were subjected to the "ordeal of water," also called the "dunking test." Accusers submerged the accused witch in a cold stream. If she floated to the surface, there was both good and bad news: She survived, but was deemed guilty—presumably because witches are supernaturally light or because water is so pure a substance as to repel a witch's evil nature—and therefore sentenced to death. In contrast, if she didn't float to the surface, there was again both good and bad news: She was deemed innocent but that was scant consolation to her because she'd already drowned.

Beginning in the 20th century, some enterprising researchers began to tinker with physiological measures to distinguish truth from lies. In the 1920s, psychologist William Moulton Marston invented a device —the first polygraph or so-called "lie detector" test—that measured systolic blood pressure (that's the number on the top of our blood pressure reading) to detect deception. Under the pen name Charles Moulton, he later created one of the first female cartoon superheroes, *Wonder Woman*, who could compel villains to tell the truth by ensnaring them in her magic lasso. For Marston, the polygraph was the equivalent of Wonder Woman's lasso: an infallible detector of the truth (Fienberg & Stern, 2005; Lykken, 1998). Beyond the pages of comic books, Marston's blood pressure device spurred the development of modern polygraph testing.

A polygraph machine provides a continuous record of physiological activity—such as skin conductance, blood pressure, and respiration— by plotting it on a chart. Contrary to the impression conveyed in such movies as *Meet the Parents* (2000) or such television shows as *The Moment of Truth*, the machine isn't a quick fix for telling us whether someone is lying, although the public's desire for such a fix almost surely contributes to the polygraph's enduring popularity (Figure 6.1). Instead, the examiner who asks questions typically interprets the polygraph chart and arrives at a judgment of whether the person is lying. Physiological activity may offer helpful clues to lying because it's associated with how anxious the examinee is during the test. For example, being nervous causes most of us to sweat, which increases how well our skin conducts electricity. Yet interpreting a polygraph chart is notoriously difficult for several reasons.

Figure 6.1 In the 2000 comedy, *Meet the Parents*, former CIA agent Jack Bynes (portrayed by Robert De Niro) administers a polygraph test to Greg Focker (portrayed by Ben Stiller) in an attempt to determine whether Focker would make a suitable son-in-law. Most portrayals of the lie detector in films and television programs erroneously portray the technique as essentially infallible.
Source: Photos 12/Alamy.

For starters, there are large differences among people in their levels of physiological activity (Ekman, 2001; Lykken, 1998). An honest examinee who tends to sweat a lot might mistakenly appear deceptive, whereas a deceptive examinee who tends to sweat very little might mistakenly appear truthful. This problem underscores the need for a baseline measure of physiological activity for each examinee. For investigating specific crimes, the most popular lie detector format is the Comparison Question Test (CQT; Raskin & Honts, 2002). This version of the polygraph test includes relevant questions concerning the alleged misdeed ("Did you steal $200 from your employer?") and comparison questions that try to force people to tell a lie that's irrelevant to the alleged misdeed ("Have you ever lied to get out of trouble?"). Almost all of us have fibbed to get out of trouble at least once, but because we wouldn't want to admit this awkward little fact during a polygraph test, we'd presumably need to lie about it. The rationale of the CQT is that the comparison questions provide a meaningful baseline for interpreting subjects' physiological activity to known lies.

But this rationale is dubious, because comparison questions don't control for a host of crucial factors. Moreover, as David Lykken (1998) noted, there's no evidence for a *Pinocchio response*: an emotional or physiological reaction uniquely indicative of deception (Cross & Saxe, 2001; Saxe, Dougherty, & Cross, 1985; Vrij, 2008). If a polygraph chart shows more physiological activity when the examinee responded to relevant than comparison questions, at most this difference tells us that the examinee was more nervous at those moments.

But here's the rub. This difference in anxiety could be due to actual guilt, indignation or shock at being unjustly accused, the realization that one's responses to relevant—but not comparison—questions may lead to one's being fired or imprisoned, or even the experience of unpleasant thoughts associated with the alleged misdeed (Ruscio, 2005). Not surprisingly, the CQT and related versions of the polygraph test suffer from a high rate of "false positives"—innocent people whom the test deems guilty (Iacono, 2008). As a consequence, the "lie detector" test is misnamed: It's an arousal detector, not a lie detector (Saxe et al., 1985; Vrij & Mann, 2007). This misleading name probably contributes to the public's belief in its accuracy. Conversely, some individuals who are guilty may not experience anxiety when telling lies, even to authorities. For example, psychopaths are notoriously immune to fear and may be able to "beat" the test in high pressure situations, although the research evidence for this possibility is mixed (Patrick & Iacono, 1989).

Further complicating matters is the fact that polygraph examiners are often prone to *confirmation bias* (Nickerson, 1998), the tendency to see what they expect to see. Examiners have access to outside information regarding the alleged misdeed and have often formed an opinion about examinees' guilt or innocence even before hooking them up. Gershon Ben-Shakhar (1991) noted that an examiner's hypothesis can influence the polygraph testing process at several stages: constructing the questions, asking these questions, scoring the chart, and interpreting the results. To illustrate the role of confirmation bias, he described an exposé aired by CBS News magazine *60 Minutes* in 1986. The *60 Minutes* producers hired three polygraph firms to determine who stole a camera from a photography magazine's office. Even though there was no actual theft, each polygraph examiner expressed supreme confidence that he'd identified a different employee who'd been subtly suggested as a suspect prior to testing.

Another reason why most polygraph examiners are convinced of the machine's accuracy probably stems from the undeniable fact that the polygraph is good for one thing: eliciting confessions, especially when people fail it (Lykken, 1998; Ruscio, 2005). As a consequence, polygraphers are selectively exposed to people who fail the polygraph and later admit they lied (although we'll learn in Myth #46 that some of these confessions may be false). What's more, these examiners often assume that people who flunk the test and don't admit they committed the crime must be lying. So the test seems virtually infallible: If the person fails and admits he lied, the test "worked," and if the person fails and doesn't admit he lied, the test also "worked." Of course, if the person passes, he'll essentially always agree that he was telling the truth, so the test again "worked." This "heads I win, tails you lose" reasoning renders the rationale underlying the polygraph test difficult or impossible to falsify. As philosopher of science Sir Karl Popper (1963) noted, unfalsifiable claims aren't scientific.

In a comprehensive review, the National Research Council (2003) criticized the CQT's rationale and the studies claiming to support its effectiveness. Most were laboratory investigations in which a relatively small number of college students performed simulated ("mock") crimes, like stealing a wallet, rather than field (real-world) studies with large numbers of actual criminal suspects. In the few field studies, examiners' judgments were usually contaminated by outside information (like newspaper reports about who committed the crime), rendering it impossible to distinguish the influence of case facts from polygraph test results. Moreover, participants usually weren't trained in the use of *counter-measures*, that is, strategies designed to "beat" the polygraph test. To use a countermeasure, one deliberately increases physiological arousal at just the right times during the test, such as by biting one's tongue or performing difficult mental arithmetic (like subtracting repeatedly from 1,000 by 17s) during the comparison questions. Information on countermeasures is widely available in popular sources, including the Internet, and would almost surely reduce the lie detector's real-world effectiveness.

Given these limitations, the National Research Council (2003) was reluctant to estimate the CQT's accuracy. David Lykken (1998) characterized an accuracy of 85% for guilty individuals and 60% for innocent individuals as charitable. That 40% of honest examinees appear deceptive provides exceedingly poor protection for innocent suspects, and this problem is compounded when polygraphers administer tests to many suspects. Let's suppose that intelligence information is leaked, evidence suggests

Mythbusting: A Closer Look

Is Truth Serum a Lie Detector?

We've seen that the polygraph test is far from a perfect tool for sorting truths from lies. But could truth serum be better? As early as 1923, an article in a medical journal referred to truth serum as a "lie detector" (Herzog, 1923). In a number of films, including *Jumping Jack Flash (1986), True Lies (1994), Meet the Parents* (2000), and *Johnny English* (2003), characters who've been hiding something suddenly begin uttering the truth, the whole truth, and nothing but the truth after taking a swig of truth serum. For decades, governmental intelligence agencies, such as the CIA and the former Soviet KGB, supposedly used truth serum to interrogate suspected spies. Even as recently as 2008, Indian police reportedly administered truth serum to Azam Kasir Kasab, the lone surviving terrorist in the devastating attacks in Mumbai, India (Blakely, 2008). Since the 1920s psychotherapists have occasionally used truth serum in an effort to excavate buried memories of trauma (Winter, 2005). For example, the 1994 sexual abuse charges against pop singer Michael Jackson emerged only after an anesthesiologist administered a truth serum to 13-year-old Jordan Chandler. Prior to receiving truth serum, Chandler denied that Jackson had sexually abused him (Taraborrelli, 2004).

Yet like the lie detector, "truth serum" is misnamed. Most truth serums are barbiturates, like sodium amytal or sodium penthothal. Because the physiological and psychological effects of barbiturates are largely similar to those of alcohol (Sudzak, Schwartz, Skolnick, & Paul, 1986), the effects of ingesting a truth serum aren't all that different from having a few stiff drinks. Like alcohol, truth serums make us sleepy and less concerned about outward appearances. And like alcohol, truth serums don't unveil the truth; they merely lower our inhibitions, rendering us more likely to report both accurate and inaccurate information (Dysken, Kooser, Haraszti, & Davis, 1979; Piper, 1993; Stocks, 1998). As a consequence, truth serums increase greatly the risk of erroneous memories and false confessions. Moreover, there's good evidence that people can lie under the influence of truth serum (Piper, 1993). So Hollywood aside, truth serums aren't any more likely than polygraphs to detect fibs.

it came from 1 of 100 employees who had access to this information, and all of them undergo polygraph testing. Using Lykken's estimates, there'd be an 85% chance of identifying the guilty individual, but about 40 other employees would be falsely accused! These numbers are worrisome given that the Pentagon has recently beefed up its efforts to screen all 5,700 of its current and future employees every year, partly in an attempt to minimize the risk of infiltration by terrorists (Associated Press, 2008).

Still, polygraph tests remain a popular icon in the public's imagination. In one survey, 67% of Americans in the general public rated the polygraph as either "reliable" or "useful" for detecting lies, although most didn't regard it as infallible (Myers, Latter, & Abdollahi-Arena, 2006). In Annette Taylor and Patricia Kowalski's (2003) survey of introductory psychology students, 45% believed that the polygraph "can accurately identify attempts to deceive" (p. 6). Moreover, polygraph testing has been featured prominently in more than 30 motion pictures and television shows, typically with no hint of its shortcomings. By the 1980s, an estimated 2 million polygraph tests were administered in the United States alone each year (Lykken, 1998).

Due to increasing recognition of their limited validity, polygraph tests are seldom admissible in courts. In addition, the federal Employee Polygraph Protection Act of 1988, passed by the federal government, prohibited most employers from administering lie detectors. Yet in a bizarre irony, the government exempted itself, allowing the polygraph test to be administered in law enforcement, military, and security agencies. So a polygraph test isn't deemed trustworthy enough to hire convenience store clerks, yet officials use it to screen employees at the FBI and CIA.

Were he still alive, William Moulton Marston might be disappointed to learn that researchers have yet to develop the psychological equivalent of Wonder Woman's magic lasso. For at least the foreseeable future, the promise of a perfect lie detector remains the stuff of science fiction and comic book fantasy.

Myth # 24 Happiness Is Determined Mostly by Our External Circumstances

As Jennifer Michael Hecht (2007) observed in her book, *The Happiness Myth*, virtually every generation has had its share of sure-fire prescriptions for how to attain ultimate happiness. From the vantage point of the early 21st century, some of these fads may strike us as positively bizarre. For example, throughout much of history, people have sought out a seemingly endless array of purported aphrodisiacs, such as the rhinoceros horn, Spanish fly, chili peppers, chocolate, oysters, or more recently, green M & M candies, to enhance their sex lives and drives (Eysenck, 1990). Yet research suggests that none of these supposed libido-lifters does much of anything beyond a placebo, that is, a sugar pill (Nordenberg, 1996). In late 19th century America, "Fletcherizing" was all the rage: according to champions of this dietary craze, chewing each piece of food precisely 32 times (that's one chew for each tooth) will bring us happiness and health (Hecht, 2007). Some of today's happiness fads may well strike early 22nd century Americans as equally odd. How will future generations perceive those of us who spend thousands of our hard-earned dollars on aromatherapy, *feng shui* (the Chinese practice of arranging objects in our rooms to achieve contentment), motivational speakers, or mood enhancing crystals? One has to wonder.

All of these fads reflect an underlying tenet central to much of popular psychology: Our happiness is determined mostly by our external circumstances. To achieve happiness, the story line goes, we must find the right "formula" for happiness, one that exists primarily outside of us. More often than not, this formula consists of lots of money, a gorgeous house, a great job, and plenty of pleasurable events in our lives. Indeed, as far back as the 18th century, British philosophers John Locke and Jeremy Bentham maintained that people's happiness is a direct function of the number of positive life events they experience (Eysenck, 1990). Today, one has to go only as far as *Amazon.com* to happen upon a treasure trove of advice books that instruct us how to achieve happiness through wealth, such as Laura Rowley's (2005) *Money and Happiness: A Guide to Living the Good Life*, Eric Tyson's (2006) *Mind over Money: Your Path to Wealth and Happiness*, and M. P. Dunleavy's (2007) *Money Can Buy Happiness: How to Spend to Get the Life You Want*. As American social critic Eric Hoffer commented wryly, "You can never get enough of what you don't need to make you happy."

Yet over 200 years ago, America's "First first lady," Martha Washington, offered a view sharply at odds with much of modern popular culture: "The greater part of our happiness or misery depends on our dispositions, not our circumstances." Indeed, in recent decades, psychologists have begun to question whether the "truism" that our happiness is mostly a function of what happens to us is really true. The late psychologist Albert Ellis (1977) insisted that one of the most prevalent—and pernicious—of all irrational ideas is the notion that our happiness and unhappiness derive mostly from our external circumstances rather than our interpretations of them. Ellis was fond of quoting Shakespeare's *Hamlet*, who said that "There is nothing either good or bad, but thinking makes it so." Psychologist Michael Eysenck (1990) even described the #1 myth about happiness as the notion that "Your level of happiness depends simply on the number and nature of the pleasurable events which happen to you" (p. 120).

Still, many of us are deeply resistant to the notion that our happiness is affected more by our personality traits and attitudes than our life experiences, and we're especially resistant to the notion that happiness is influenced substantially by our genetic make-up. In one survey, 233 high-school and college students gave a low rating (2.58 on a 7-point scale) to an item evaluating the perceived importance of genes to happiness (Furnham & Cheng, 2000).

So was Martha Washington right that our happiness "depends on our dispositions, not our circumstances"? Let's consider two provocative findings. First, Ed Diener and Martin Seligman screened over 200 undergraduates for their levels of happiness, and compared the upper 10% (the "extremely happy") with the middle and bottom 10%. Extremely happy students experienced no greater number of objectively positive life events, like doing well on exams or hot dates, than did the other two groups (Diener & Seligman, 2002). Second, Nobel Prize-winning psychologist Daniel Kahneman and his colleagues tracked the moods and activities of 909 employed women by asking them to record in detail their previous day's experiences (Kahneman, Krueger, Schkade, Schwarz, & Stone, 2004). They found that most major life circumstances, including women's household income and various features of their jobs (such as whether these jobs included excellent benefits), were correlated only minimally with their moment-by-moment happiness. In contrast, women's sleep quality and proneness toward depression were good predictors of their happiness.

Other research has offered support for what Philip Brickman and Donald Campbell (1971) called the *hedonic treadmill*. Just as we quickly adjust our walking or running speed to match a treadmill's speed (if we don't, we'll end up face first on the ground), our moods adjust quickly to most life circumstances. The hedonic treadmill hypothesis dovetails with research demonstrating that ratings of happiness are much more similar within pairs of identical twins, who are genetically identical, than within pairs of fraternal twins, who share only 50% of their genes on average (Lykken & Tellegen, 1996). This finding points to a substantial genetic contribution to happiness and raises the possibility that we're each born with a distinctive happiness "set point," a genetically influenced baseline level of happiness from which we bounce up and down in response to short-term life events, but to which we soon return once we've adapted to these events (Lykken, 2000).

More direct evidence for the hedonic treadmill comes from studies of people who've experienced either (1) extremely positive or (2) extremely negative, even tragic, life events. One might expect the first group of people to be much happier than the second. They are—but often for only a surprisingly brief period of time (Gilbert, 2006). For example, even though the happiness of big lottery winners reaches the stratosphere immediately after hitting the jackpot, their happiness pretty much falls back down to earth—and to the levels of most everybody else—about 2 months later (Brickman, Coates, & Janoff-Bulman, 1978). Most paraplegics—people paralyzed from the waist down—return largely (although not entirely) to their baseline levels of happiness within a few months of their accidents (Brickman et al., 1978; Silver, 1982). And although young professors who've been denied tenure (meaning they've lost their jobs) are understandably crushed after receiving the news, within a few years they're just about as happy as young professors who received tenure (Gilbert, Pinel, Wilson, Blumberg, & Wheatley, 1998). Most of us adapt fairly quickly to our life circumstances, both good and bad.

Research also calls into question the widespread belief that money buys us happiness (Kahneman, Krueger, Schkade, Schwarz, & Stone, 2006; Myers & Diener, 1996). As an illustration of the striking disconnect between money and happiness, the average life satisfaction of *Forbes* magazine's 400 richest Americans was 5.8 on a 7-point scale (Diener, Horowitz, & Emmons, 1985). Yet the average life satisfaction of the Pennsylvania Amish is also 5.8 (Diener & Seligman, 2004), despite the fact that their average annual salary is several *billion* dollars lower. It's true that to be happy we need to have *enough* money to be comfortable in life. Below about $50,000, household income is moderately related to happiness, probably because it's hard to be happy when we need to worry about putting food on the table or paying next month's rent. But above $50,000, the relation between money and happiness essentially vanishes (Helliwell & Putnam, 2004; Myers, 2000). Yet this fact didn't stop major league baseball players, whose average yearly salary was $1.2 million (not including commercial endorsements), from going on strike in 1994 for higher salaries.

Still, Martha Washington may not have been entirely right. Certain momentous life events can affect our long-term happiness for better or worse, although less powerfully than most of us believe. For example, getting divorced, widowed, or laid off from work seem to result in lasting and sometimes permanent decreases in happiness (Diener, Lucas, & Scollon, 2006). Yet even for divorce and death of a spouse, many people eventually adapt more or less completely over time (Clark, Diener, Georgellis, & Lucas, 2008).

So although our life circumstances certainly can affect our happiness in the short run, much of our happiness in the long run is surprisingly independent of what happens to us. More than we might wish to admit, happiness is at least as much a function of what we make of our lives as our lives themselves. As psychologist and happiness expert Ed Diener noted, "A person enjoys pleasures because he or she is happy, not vice-versa" (quoted in Eysenck, 1990, p. 120).

Myth # 25 Ulcers Are Caused Primarily or Entirely by Stress

Little more than two decades ago, it was virtually inconceivable that taking a pill would be the treatment of choice for *peptic ulcers*—sores in the lining of the stomach or small intestines. But breakthrough medical developments, a daring personal "experiment," and painstaking research transformed medical opinions about ulcers. Prior to the mid 1980s, most physicians and laypersons were convinced that ulcers were caused primarily by stress. They also believed that spicy foods, excess stomach acid, smoking, and alcohol consumption played important secondary roles in ulcer formation. Today, we know otherwise, thanks to the pioneering work of Barry Marshall and Robin Warren, who received the Nobel Prize for groundbreaking research that radically changed our thinking about ulcers and their treatment (Marshall & Warren, 1983).

Many psychologists influenced by the writings of Sigmund Freud once assumed that ulcers resulted from underlying psychological conflicts. Psychoanalyst Franz Alexander (1950) suggested that ulcers are linked to infantile cravings to be fed and feelings of dependency. In adulthood, these conflicts supposedly become rekindled and activate the gastrointestinal system (stomach and intestines), which is associated with feeding.

The idea that specific emotions and conflicts are associated with ulcers was discredited by research, only to be replaced by the popular belief that stress, along with eating habits and lifestyle choices, was the prime culprit. As Thomas Gilovich and Kenneth Savitsky (1996) noted, the belief that stress causes ulcers may stem from a misapplication of the representativeness heuristic (see *Introduction*, p. 15). Because stress often causes our stomachs to churn, it seems reasonable to suppose that stress can cause other stomach problems, including ulcers. Still, ulcers aren't limited to over-achieving executives of Fortune 500 companies. About 25 million Americans of all socioeconomic stripes will suffer the gnawing pain of ulcers during their lifetimes (Sonnenberg, 1994).

Despite the widespread public perception of an intimate link between stress and ulcers, a few scientists long suspected that an infectious agent might be responsible for at least some ulcers. Yet it wasn't until Marshall and Warren (1983) pinpointed a link between peptic ulcers and a curved bacterium—dubbed *Helicobacter (H.) pylori*—lurking in the lining of the stomach and intestines that scientists made real progress toward identifying a specific disease-causing agent.

Marshall and Warren first discovered that *H. pylori* infection was common in people with ulcers, but uncommon in people without ulcers. To demonstrate that the microscopic invader was the culprit in producing ulcers, Marshall bravely (some might say foolishly) swallowed a cocktail of the organisms and developed a stomach irritation known as gastritis for several weeks. Still, Marshall's daring stunt wasn't conclusive. He ended up with a wicked stomach ache, but no ulcer. So he was unable to show a direct tie between *H. pylori* and ulcer formation. This result actually isn't all that surprising given that although the bacterium is present in about half of all people, only about 10–15% of people who harbor the organism develop ulcers. Moreover, a single such demonstration, especially when conducted by the person who advances the hypothesis under study, can at best provide only suggestive evidence. The medical community, while intrigued and excited by these early findings, patiently awaited more convincing research.

The clincher came when independent researchers across the world cultured the bacterium, and demonstrated that treating the *H. pylori* infection with potent antibiotics reduced the recurrence of ulcers dramatically. This finding was important because drugs that merely neutralize or inhibit the production of stomach acid can effectively treat ulcers in the majority of cases, but 50–90% of ulcers recur after treatment stops (Gough et al., 1984). The fact that antibiotics decreased the recurrence of ulcers by 90–95% provided strong evidence that *H pylori* caused ulcers.

Nevertheless, as is so often the case, public opinion lagged behind medical discoveries. By 1997, 57% of Americans still believed that stress is the main cause of ulcers, and 17% believed that spicy foods cause ulcers (Centers for Disease Control and Prevention, 1997). Yet 3 years earlier, the U.S. National Institutes of Health had proclaimed the evidence that *H. pylori* caused ulcers convincing, and recommended antibiotics to treat people with ulcers and H. *pylori* infections (NIH Consensus Conference, 1994). Even today, the media promotes the singular role of negative emotions in generating ulcers. In the 2005 film, *The Upside of Anger*, Emily (played by Keri Russell) develops an ulcer after her father abandons the family and her mother frustrates her ambitions to become a dancer.

Because the great majority of people infected with *H. pylori* don't develop ulcers, scientists realized that other influences must play a role. Soon there was widespread recognition that excessive use of anti-inflammatory medications, like aspirin and ibuprofen, can trigger ulcers by irritating the stomach lining. Moreover, researchers didn't abandon their quest to identify the role of stress in ulcer formation. In fact, stress probably plays some role in ulcers, although studies show that the widespread belief that stress *by itself* causes ulcers is wrong. For example, psychological distress is associated with higher rates of ulcers in human and non-human animals (Levenstein, Kaplan, & Smith, 1997; Overmeier & Murison, 1997). Moreover, stress is linked to a poor response to ulcer treatment (Levenstein et al., 1996), and stressful events —including earthquakes and economic crises—are associated with increases in ulcers (Levenstein, Ackerman, Kiecolt-Glaser, & Dubois, 1999). Additionally, people with generalized anxiety disorder, a condition marked by worrying much of the time about many things, are at heightened risk for peptic ulcers (Goodwin & Stein, 2002). Nevertheless, it's possible that anxiety may not cause ulcers. Developing an ulcer and the pain associated with it may lead some people to worry constantly, or people may be predisposed to excessive anxiety and ulcers by genetic influences common to both conditions.

We can understand the fact that stress may contribute to the development of ulcers in terms of a *biopsychosocial perspective*, which proposes that most medical conditions depend on the complex interplay of genes, lifestyles, immunity, and everyday stressors (Markus & Kitayama, 1991; Turk, 1996). Stress may exert an indirect effect on ulcer formation by triggering such behaviors as alcohol use, and lack of sleep, which make ulcers more likely.

The verdict is still out regarding the precise role that stress plays in ulcer formation, although it's clear that stress isn't the only or even most important influence. In all likelihood, stress, emotions, and the damage wrought by disease-producing organisms combine to create conditions ripe for the growth of *H. pylori*. So if you're having stomach problems, don't be surprised if your doctor suggests that you learn to relax—as she pulls out a pen and pad to write you a prescription for powerful antibiotics.

Myth # 26 A Positive Attitude Can Stave off Cancer

Is cancer "all about attitude?" Perhaps negative thinking, pessimism, and stress create the conditions for the cells in our body to run amok and for cancers to develop. If so, then self-help books, personal affirmations, visualizing the body free of cancer, and self-help groups could galvanize the power of positive thinking and help the immune system to prevail over cancer.

Scores of popular accounts tout the role of positive attitudes and emotions in halting cancer's often ruthless progression. But this message has a subtle, more negative twist: If positive attitudes count for so much, then perhaps stressed-out people with a less than cheery view of themselves and the world are inflicting cancers on themselves (Beyerstein, 1999b; Gilovich, 1991; Rittenberg, 1995). The fact or fiction of the link between cancer and patients' attitudes and emotions, on the one hand, and cancer on the other, thus bears important consequences for the 12 million people worldwide diagnosed with cancer each year, and for those engaged in a protracted battle with the disease.

Before we examine the scientific evidence, let's survey some popular sources of information about whether psychological factors cause or cure cancer. Dr. Shivani Goodman (2004), author of the book, *9 Steps for Reversing or Preventing Cancer and Other Diseases,* wrote that one day she was able to "suddenly make sense" of her breast cancer. When she was a child, every morning she heard her father say the Jewish prayer: "Thank you, God, for not making me a woman" (p. 31). Her epiphany was that her breasts were her "symbol of femininity," and that unconsciously she was "rejecting being a woman, along with the notion that she deserved to live" (p. 32). Once she identified her toxic attitudes, she claimed "to change them into healing attitudes that created radiant health" (p. 32).

Similarly, in her book, *You Can Heal Your Life* (1984), Louise Hays boasted of curing her vaginal cancer with positive thinking. Hayes contended that cancer developed in her vagina because she experienced sexual abuse as a child. Her recommendation to chant self-affirmations like, "I deserve the best, I accept it now," to cure cancer stemmed from her belief that thoughts create reality. Rhonda Byrne (2006), author of the blockbuster bestseller, *The Secret* (which has sold over 7 million copies), gushed with a similar message. She related the tale of a woman who, after refusing medical treatment, cured her cancer by imagining herself cancer-free. According to Byrne, if we send out negative thoughts, we attract negative experiences into our lives. But by transmitting positive thoughts, we can rid ourselves of mental and physical ailments. After Oprah Winfrey plugged *The Secret* in 2007 on her popular television program, one viewer with breast cancer decided to stop her recommended medical treatments and use positive thoughts to treat her illness (on a later show, Oprah cautioned viewers against following in this viewer's footsteps). In *Quantum Healing*, self-help guru Deepak Chopra (1990) claimed that patients can achieve remission from cancer when their consciousness shifts to embrace the possibility they can be cured; with this shift, the cells in their bodies capitalize on their "intelligence" to defeat cancer.

The Internet overflows with suggestions for developing positive attitudes through healing visualizations, not to mention reports of seemingly miraculous cures of cancers of people who found meaning in their lives, quieted their turbulent emotions, or practiced visualization exercises to harness the power of positive thinking and reduce stress. For example, the website *Healing Cancer & Your Mind* suggests that patients imagine (a) armies of white blood cells attacking and overcoming cancer, (b) white blood cells as knights on white horses riding through the body destroying cancer calls, and (c) cancer as a dark color slowly turning paler until it's the same color as the surrounding tissue.

Self-described "healers" on the Internet offer manuals and advice on how to vanquish cancer. Brent Atwater, who claims to be a "Medical Intuitive and Distant Energy Healer," wrote a manual to "Help Survive Your Cancer Experience" containing the following advice:

(1) Separate YOUR identity from the Cancer's identity.
(2) You are a person, who is having a Cancer "experience." Recognize that an "experience" comes and goes!
(3) Your Cancer "experience" is your life's reset button! Learn from it.

Few would quibble with the idea that maintaining positive attitudes in the face of the most taxing life and death circumstances imaginable is a worthy goal. Yet many popular media sources imply that positive attitudes and stress reduction help to beat or slow down cancer. Does evidence support this claim? Many people who've had cancer certainly think so. In surveys of women who've survived breast cancer (Stewart et al., 2007), ovarian cancer (Stewart, Duff, Wong, Melancon, & Cheung, 2001), and endometrial and cervical cancer (Costanzo, Lutgendorf,

Bradley, Rose, & Anderson, 2005) for at least 2 years, between 42% and 63% reported they believed their cancers were caused by stress, and between 60% and 94% believed they were cancer-free because of their positive attitudes. In these studies, more women believed their cancers were caused by stress than by an array of influences, including genetic endowment and environmental factors, such as diet.

Yet meta-analyses of research studies (see p. 32) tell a different story. They contradict the popular belief in a link between stressful life events and cancer, with most studies revealing no connection between either stress or emotions and cancer (Butow et al., 2000; Duijts, Zeegers, & Borne, 2003; Petticrew, Fraser, & Regan, 1999). Interestingly, in a recent study of job stress (Schernhammer et al., 2004) among 37,562 U.S. female registered nurses who were followed for up to 8 years (1992–2000), researchers observed a 17% *lower* risk of breast cancer among women who experienced relatively *high* stress in their jobs compared with women who experienced relatively low job stress. Researchers who followed 6,689 women in Copenhagen for more than 16 years discovered that women who reported they were *highly* stressed were 40% *less* likely to develop breast cancer than those who reported lower stress levels (Nielsen et al., 2005). The once popular idea of a "cancer prone personality," a constellation of such personality traits as unassertiveness, shyness, and avoidance of conflict that supposedly predisposes to cancer, has similarly been discredited by controlled research (Beyerstein, Sampson, Stojanovic, & Handel, 2007).

Scientists have also failed to unearth any association between either positive attitudes or emotional states and cancer survival (Beyerstein et al., 2007). Over a 9-year period, James Coyne and his colleagues (Coyne et al., 2007b) tracked 1,093 patients with advanced head and neck cancer who suffered from non-spreading tumors. Patients who endorsed such statements as, "I am losing hope in my fight against my illness" were no less likely to live longer than patients who expressed positive attitudes. In fact, even the most optimistic patients lived no longer than the most fatalistic ones. Kelly-Anne Phillips and her associates (2008) followed 708 Australian women with newly diagnosed localized breast cancer for 8 years and discovered that people's negative emotions—depression, anxiety, and anger—and pessimistic attitudes bore absolutely no relation to life expectancy.

These and similar findings imply that psychotherapy and support groups geared to attitude and emotional adjustment aren't likely to stop cancer in its tracks or slow its progression. But psychiatrist David Spiegel and his colleagues' (Spiegel, Bloom, & Gottheil, 1989) widely publicized study of survival in breast cancer patients suggested otherwise. These researchers discovered that women with metastatic (spreading) breast cancer who participated in support groups lived almost twice as long as women who didn't attend support groups—36.6 months versus 18.9 months. Nevertheless, in the following two decades, researchers failed to replicate Spiegel's findings (Beyerstein et al., 2007). The accumulated data from psychotherapy and self-help groups show that psychological interventions, including support groups, can enhance cancer patients' quality of life, but can't extend their lives (Coyne, Stefanek, & Palmer, 2007a).

So why is the belief that positive attitudes can help to fight off cancer so popular? In part, it's almost surely because this belief appeals to people's sense of hope, especially among those who are seeking it desperately. In addition, cancer survivors who attribute their good outcomes to a positive attitude could be falling prey to post hoc, ergo propter hoc (after this, therefore because of this) reasoning (see *Introduction*, p. 14). The fact that someone maintained a positive attitude before their cancer remitted doesn't mean that this attitude caused the cause to remit; the link could be coincidental.

Finally, we may be more likely to hear about and remember cases of people who've fought off cancer with a positive outlook than cases of those who didn't survive cancer even with a positive outlook. The former cases make for better human interest stories, not to mention better subjects of television talk shows.

Although visualizations, affirmations, and unsubstantiated advice on the Internet probably won't cure or stave off cancer, that's not to say that a positive attitude can't help in *coping* with cancer. People with cancer can still do a great deal to relieve their physical and emotional burdens by seeking quality medical and psychological care, connecting with friends and family, and finding meaning and purpose in every moment of their lives. Contrary to widespread belief, people with cancer can take a measure of comfort in the now well-established finding that their attitudes aren't to blame for their illness.

Chapter 6: Other Myths to Explore

Fiction	Fact
Voice stress analyzers can help to detect lying.	Voice stress analyzers only detect vocal changes sometimes associated with arousal, not lying per se.

Fiction	Fact
"Positive thinking" is better than negative thinking for all people.	People with high levels of "defensive pessimism," for whom worrying is a coping strategy, tend to do worse on tasks when forced to think positively.
If we're upset about something, we should just try to put it out of our minds.	Research on "thought suppression" by Daniel Wegner and others suggests that trying to put something out of mind often increases its probability of reoccurrence.
Women have better social intuition than men.	Studies show that women are no better at accurately guessing the feelings of others than are men.
People are especially sad on Mondays.	Most research finds no evidence for this claim, which seems to be due to people's expectancies about feeling depressed on Mondays.
People who are prone to good moods tend to have fewer bad moods than other people.	The tendency toward positive moods (positive emotionality) is largely or entirely independent of the tendency toward negative moods (negative emotionality).
Most women's moods worsen during their premenstrual periods.	Studies in which women track their moods using daily diaries show that most don't experience mood worsening during premenstrual periods.
Living in modern Western society is much more stressful than living in undeveloped countries.	There's no systematic support for this belief.
Being placed in control of a stressful situation causes ulcers.	This claim, which derived largely from a flawed 1958 study on "executive monkeys" by Joseph Brady, is probably false; to the contrary, having control over a stressful situation is less anxiety-provoking than having no control.
Familiarity breeds contempt: we dislike things we've been exposed to more frequently.	Research on the "mere exposure effect" indicates that we typically prefer stimuli we've seen many times before to those we haven't.
Extreme fear can turn our hair white.	There's no scientific evidence for this belief, and no known mechanism that could allow it to occur.

Fiction	Fact
Sex makes advertisements more effective.	Sex makes people pay more attention to advertisements, but often results in less recall of the product's brand name.
Women have a "G-spot," a vaginal area that intensifies sexual arousal.	There's little or no scientific evidence for the G-spot.
Men think about sex an average of every 7 seconds.	This claim is an "urban legend" with no scientific support.
Beauty is entirely in the eye of the beholder.	There are large commonalities across cultures in their standards of physical attractiveness.
People are who most distinctive in certain physical features are typically viewed as most attractive by others.	People who are most statistically average in their physical features are typically viewed as most attractive by others.
Athletes shouldn't have sex prior to a big game.	Studies show that sex burns only about 50 calories on average and doesn't cause muscle weakness.
Exposure to pornography increases aggression.	Most studies show that pornography exposure does not increase risk for violence unless the pornography is accompanied by violence.
Most children who frequently "play doctor" or masturbate were sexually abused.	There's no scientific support for this belief.

Sources and Suggested Readings

To explore these and other myths about emotion and motivation, see Bornstein (1989); Croft and Walker (2001); Eysenck (1990); Gilbert (2006); Hines (2001); Ickes (2003); Lykken (1998); Nettle (2005); Norem (2001); O'Connor (2007); Radford (2007); Tavris (1992); Wegner (2002).

7 THE SOCIAL ANIMAL

Myths about Interpersonal Behavior

Myth #27 Opposites Attract: We Are Most Romantically Attracted to People Who Differ from Us

It's the Hollywood movie plot we've all come to know and love, and we can practically recite it by heart. Get out your popcorn, coke, and Raisinets, because the curtain is just about to rise.

Scene 1: The camera pans to a small, dingy, and messy bedroom. There, lying on the bed reading a biography of Ronald Reagan, we see a moderately overweight, balding, and rather unkempt man named Joe Cantgetadate. Joe is 37 years old, shy, nerdy, and completely lacking in self-confidence. Until recently he worked as a librarian but he's now out of a job. Joe hasn't dated anyone in over 3 years and he's feeling hopeless and lonely.

Scene 2: On his way out of his apartment an hour later, Joe bumps into (literally) a stunningly gorgeous 25-year-old woman named Candice Blondebombshell. In the process, Joe knocks all of the shopping bags out of Candice's hands, scattering them across the sidewalk, and he bends down to help her pick them up. Candice, it so happens, is not only beautiful, but outgoing, interpersonally skilled, and wildly popular. She works part-time as a waitress in an upscale restaurant and spends much of the rest of her time modeling for a top fashion agency. In contrast to Joe, who's a conservative Republican, Candice is a flaming liberal. Sheepishly, Joe asks Candice out for a date, but ends up making an embarrassing Freudian slip, asking her if she wants a "mate" rather than a "date." Candice laughs and tells Joe politely that she's romantically involved with a famous celebrity (Brad Crowe-Cruise) and can't see anyone else.

Scene 50: Forty-eight scenes, two and a half hours, and three buckets of popcorn later, Joe (who ended up bumping into Candice again 6 months later at the restaurant, this time knocking over all of the plates and drinks she was carrying) has somehow managed to win over Candice, who's just broken off her relationship with Brad Crowe-Cruise. Candice, initially put off by Joe's decided absence of stunning good lucks and awkward ways, now finds him adorable in a teddy-bear sort of way and utterly irresistible. Joe gets down on his knees, proposes to Candice, and she accepts. The credits scroll down the screen, the curtain closes, and you wipe the tears off your eyes with a Kleenex.

If this plot line seems awfully familiar, it's because the notion that "opposites attract" is a standard part of our contemporary cultural landscape. Films, novels, and TV sitcoms overflow with stories of diametrical opposites falling passionately in love. There's even an entire website devoted to "opposites attract" movies, such as *You've Got Mail* (1998), starring Tom Hanks and Meg Ryan, and *Maid in Manhattan* (2001), starring Jennifer Lopez and Ralph Fiennes (http://marriage.about.com/od/movies/a/oppositesmov.htm). The 2007 smash hit comedy, *Knocked Up*, starring Seth Rogen and Katherine Heigl, is perhaps Hollywood's latest installment in its seemingly never-ending parade of mismatched romantic pairings (for you diehard movie buffs out there, according to the site the top "opposites attract" movie of all time is the 1934 comedy flick *It Happened One Night*).

Many of us are convinced that people who are opposite from each other in their personalities, beliefs, and looks, like Joe and Candice, are especially likely to be attracted to each other (the technical term for the attraction of opposites is "complementarity"). Psychologist Lynn McCutcheon (1991) found that 77% of undergraduates agreed that opposites attract in relationships. In his popular book, *Opposites Attract*, writer Tim Lahaye informed readers that "Two people of the same temperament almost never get married. Why? Because like temperaments repel, they don't attract" (p. 43). This belief is also widespread in pockets of the ever-popular Internet dating community. On one Internet site called "Soulmatch," Harville Hendrix, Ph.D. states that "It's been my experience that *only* opposites attract because that's the nature of reality" (the italics are Hendrix's, not ours, by the way). "The great myth in our culture," he later says, "is that compatibility is the grounds for a relationship—actually, compatibility is grounds for boredom." Another Internet site, called "Dating Tipster," informs visitors that "The saying 'opposites attract' is definitely true in some instances. Perhaps it's the diversity of difference that creates the initial attraction . . . some people find the difference exciting."

Yet, for most proverbs, in folk psychology there's an equal and opposite proverb. So although you've almost certainly heard that "opposites attract," you've probably also heard that "birds of a feather flock together." Which saying is best supported by research evidence?

Unfortunately for Dr. Hendrix, research evidence suggests that he's gotten his myths backward. When it comes to interpersonal relationships, opposites *don't* attract. Instead, homophily (the fancy term for the tendency of similar people to attract each other) rather than complementarity is the rule. In this respect, Internet dating sites like *Match.com* and *eHarmony.com*, which try to match prospective partners on the basis of similarity in their personality traits and attitudes, are mostly on the right track (although there's not much research evidence on how successful these sites actually are in pairing people up).

Indeed, dozens of studies demonstrate that people with similar personality traits are more likely to be attracted to each other than people with dissimilar personality traits (Lewak, Wakefield, & Briggs, 1985). For example, people with a Type A personality style (that is, who are hard-driving, competitive, conscious of time, and hostile) prefer dating partners who also have a Type A personality, and the opposite goes for people with a Type B personality style (Morell, Twillman, & Sullaway, 1989). The same rule applies to friendships, by the way. We're considerably more likely to hang out with people with similar than dissimilar personality traits (Nangle, Erdley, Zeff, Stanchfield, & Gold, 2004).

Similarity in personality traits isn't merely a good predictor of initial attraction. It's also a good predictor of marital stability and happiness (Caspi & Herbener, 1990; Lazarus, 2001). Apparently, similarity on the personality trait of conscientiousness is especially important for marital satisfaction (Nemechek & Olson, 1999). So if you're a hopelessly messy and disorganized person, it's probably best to find someone who isn't a complete neat freak.

The "like attracts like" conclusion extends beyond personality to our attitudes and values. The classic work of Donn Byrne and his colleagues demonstrates that the more similar someone's attitudes (for example, political views) are to ours, the more we tend to like that person (Byrne, 1971; Byrne, London, & Reeves, 1968). Interestingly, this association approximates what psychologists call a "linear" (or straight line) function, in which proportionally more similarity in attitudes leads to proportionally more liking. So we're about twice as likely to be attracted to someone with whom we agree on 6 of 10 issues as someone with whom we agree on 3 of 10 issues. Nevertheless, at least some evidence suggests that *dissimilarity* in attitudes is even more important than similarity in predicting attraction (Rosenbaum, 1986). That is, although people with similar attitudes may be slightly more likely to be attracted to each other, people with dissimilar attitudes may be especially unlikely to be attracted to each other. In the case of attitudes, at least, it's not merely the case that opposites don't attract: They often repel.

Similarly, biologists Peter Buston and Stephen Emlen (2003) asked 978 participants to rank the importance of 10 characteristics they look for in a long-term mate, such as wealth, ambition, fidelity, parenting style, and physical attractiveness. They then asked these participants to rank themselves on the same 10 characteristics. The two sets of rankings were significantly associated, and were even more highly associated for women than for men, although the reason for this sex difference isn't clear. We shouldn't take the Buston and Emlen findings too far, as they're based entirely on self-report. What people say they want in a partner may not always correspond to what they actually want, and people are sometimes biased in how they describe themselves. Moreover, what people say they value in a potential partner may not always predict their initial attraction to others (after all, many of us have had the experience of falling for someone whom we knew was bad for us). Still, Buston and Emlen's results dovetail nicely with that of a great deal of other research demonstrating that when we seek out a soulmate, we seek out someone who matches our personalities and values.

How did the opposites attract myth originate? Nobody knows for sure, but we'll serve up three possibilities for your consideration. First, one has to admit that the myth makes for a darned good Hollywood story. Tales of Joe and Candice ending up together are almost always more intriguing than tales of two similar people ending up together. In most cases, these tales are also more heartwarming. Because we're more likely to encounter "opposites attract" than "similars attract" stories in films, books, and television programs, the former stories may strike us as commonplace. Second, we all yearn for someone who can make us "whole," who can compensate for our weaknesses. Bob Dylan wrote in one of his love songs (*The Wedding Song*, released in 1973) of the desire to find that "missing piece" that completes us, much like a missing piece in a jigsaw puzzle. Yet when push comes to shove, we may still be drawn to people who are most similar to us. Third and finally, it's possible that there's a tiny bit of truth to the "opposites attract" myth, because a few interesting differences between partners can spice up a relationship (Baron & Byrne, 1994). Being with someone who sees everything exactly the same way and agrees with us on every issue can be comforting, but boring. Still, no researchers have systematically tested this "similar people with a few differences here and there attract" hypothesis. Until they do, it's probably safest for the real-life version of Joe to find himself another overweight librarian.

Myth
28

There's Safety in Numbers: The More People Present at an Emergency, the Greater the Chance that Someone Will Intervene

Imagine the following two scenarios. *Scenario A*: Walking all alone late one night in a large city, you make a wrong turn into a long, dark alley. You turn the corner and see two men, one who is running toward you and the second, an unrelated passerby, who's about 15 feet behind the first man. Suddenly, the first man jumps on you, knocks you to the ground, and attempts to wrestle away your wallet. *Scenario B*: You find yourself all alone one sunny afternoon in the middle of a large city park. You see about 40 people in the midst of their daily activities; some are sitting on benches, others are taking a leisurely stroll, and still others are playing Frisbee. Suddenly, a man jumps on you, knocks you to the ground, and attempts to wrestle away your wallet.

Now close you eyes for a moment and ask yourself: In which scenario would you feel more frightened?

If you're like many laypersons and anywhere from one fifth to two fifths of psychology undergraduates (Furnham, 1992; Lenz, Ek, & Mills, 2009), you'd say Scenario A. After all, "there's safety in numbers," right? So in Scenario B, you could reasonably assume there's a much greater chance—probably 40 times greater—that you'd receive help. Yet as we've already discovered in this book, common sense is often a poor guide to psychological reality. In fact, most of the research evidence shows that you'd probably be safer in Scenario A; that is, there's actually danger rather than safety in numbers. How can this be?

To answer this question, let's first consider two horrifying incidents. On the morning of August 19, 1995, 33-year-old Deletha Word was driving across a bridge in Detroit, Michigan, when she accidentally hit the fender of a car driven by Martell Welsh. Welsh and the two boys with him jumped out of their car, stripped Deletha down to her underwear, and beat her repeatedly with a tire jack. At one point, Welsh even held Deletha up in the air and asked bystanders whether anyone wanted a piece of "the bitch." About 40 people drove by in their cars, but none intervened or called the police. In a desperate attempt to escape her attackers, Deletha jumped off the bridge into the river below, but drowned.

On May 30, 2008 in Hartford, Connecticut, a 78-year-old man on his way home from buying milk in a grocery store, Angel Arce Torres, was hit by a car in the middle of a busy street during rush hour. As Torres lay motionless, numerous bystanders merely watched and did nothing as nine cars swerved around him, not even bothering to stop. Oddly enough, one driver pulled over next to Torres but then continued on after doing nothing. Another man on a scooter circled around Torres briefly before departing. Not a single person paused to assist Torres before a police officer arrived on the scene. Today, Torres remains on a respirator, paralyzed from the waist down.

These two startling cases of bystander nonintervention seem difficult or impossible to explain. Following these deeply disturbing events, much of the news media routinely attempt to account for the nonresponsive behavior of bystanders by invoking the callousness or apathy of people in large cities. People in cities, they maintain, are so accustomed to seeing terrible things that they cease to notice or care when they witness crimes in progress.

Yet in the late 1960s, psychologists John Darley and Bibb Latane happened upon a very different explanation over a lunch meeting. They were discussing a similar widely publicized incident involving a young woman named Kitty Genovese, who was stabbed to death on March 13, 1964 in New York City, supposedly in full view of 38 eyewitnesses who did nothing (interestingly, later analyses of the police records from that day called into question several commonly accepted claims regarding the Genovese story, including the assertions that there were 38 eyewitnesses, that all eyewitnesses knew a murder was taking place, and that no eyewitnesses called the police; Manning, Levine, & Collins, 2007). Rather than blaming the causes of the Genovese murder and similar events on apathetic city-goers, Darley and Latane suspected that the causes of bystander nonintervention lay far more in commonplace psychological processes than in the interpersonal nature of the large urban environment. According to them, two key factors are at play in explaining bystander nonintervention.

First, Darley and Latane argued, a bystander needs to recognize that an emergency really *is* an emergency. Have you ever come across a person lying on the sidewalk and wondered whether that person needed help? Perhaps he or she was just drunk, or perhaps it was all part of a prank that you hadn't been let in on. If you looked around and noticed that no one else looked at all concerned, you probably assumed that the situation wasn't an emergency after all. Darley and Latane called this phenomenon *pluralistic ignorance*: the mistake of assuming that no one in the group shares your views ("No one is doing anything, so I guess I'm the only one who thinks this could be an emergency; well, I must be wrong"). One familiar example of pluralistic ignorance is the *silent classroom scenario*, which often occurs immediately after a lecture that's left all of the students bewildered. As soon as the lecture is over, the professor asks "Does anyone have any questions?" and not a single soul responds. Everyone in the classroom looks around nervously, sees all of the other students sitting quietly, and assumes mistakenly that everyone else except them understood the lecture.

According to Darley and Latane, there's a second process involved in bystander nonintervention. Even once it's crystal clear that the situation is an emergency, the presence of others still tends to inhibit helping. Why? Because the more people who are present at an emergency, the less each person feels individually responsible for the negative consequences of not helping. If you don't assist someone who's having a heart attack and that person later dies, you can always say to yourself, "Well, that's a terrible tragedy, but it wasn't really *my* fault. After all, there were lots of other people around who could have helped too." Darley and Latane called this phenomenon *diffusion of responsibility*, because the presence of other people makes each person feel less responsible for—and less guilty about—the outcome.

In an ingenious series of investigations, Darley, Latane, and their colleagues tested the notion that the presence of others inhibits helping in emergencies. In one study (Latane & Darley, 1968), participants entered a room to complete a series of questionnaires; in one condition, the participants were seated alone, in another, they were accompanied by two other participants. After a few minutes, smoke began pouring out of the vents into the room. When subjects were alone, they ran out of the room to report the smoke 75% of the time; when they were in groups, they did so only about half (38%) as often. When in groups, some subjects stayed in the smoke-filled room as long as 6 minutes—to the point at which they couldn't even see their questionnaires!

In another study (Latane & Rodin, 1969), a female experimenter greeted participants, escorted them to a room to complete some surveys, and went to work in a nearby office containing books and a ladder. In some cases participants were alone; in others they were accompanied by another participant. A few minutes later, participants heard the experimenter falling from a ladder, followed by the sound of her screaming voice: "Oh, my God, my foot . . . I . . . I . . . can't move it!" When participants were alone, they offered help 70% of the time; when they had a partner, one or both of them did so only 40% of the time. Researchers have replicated these kinds of findings many times using slightly different designs. In an analysis of almost 50 studies of bystander intervention involving almost 6,000 participants, Latane and Steve Nida (1981) found that participants were more likely help when alone than in groups about 90% of the time.

Yet even though there's usually danger rather than safety in numbers, many people do help even in the presence of others. In the Deletha Word tragedy, two men actually jumped into the water in an unsuccessful attempt to save Deletha from drowning. In the Angel Arce Torres tragedy, four good Samaritans did call the police. Although psychologists don't know for sure what makes some people more likely to help in emergencies than others, they've generally found that participants who are less concerned about social approval and less traditional are more likely to go against the grain and intervene in emergencies even when others are around (Latane & Darley, 1970).

There's another silver lining to this gray cloud: Research suggests that being exposed to research on bystander effects actually increases the chances of intervening in emergencies. This is an example of what Kenneth Gergen (1973) called an "enlightenment effect": Learning about psychological research can influence real-world behavior. One group of investigators (Beaman, Barnes, Klentz, & McQuirk, 1978) presented the research literature on bystander intervention effects to one psychology class (containing much of the same information you've just learned) but didn't present this literature to a very similar psychology class. Two weeks later, the students—accompanied by a confederate of the experimenters —came upon a person slumped over on a park bench (as you might guess, the experimenters had rigged this scenario). Compared with only 25% of students who hadn't received the lecture on bystander intervention, 43% of students who had received the lecture intervened to help the person. This study worked, probably because it imparted new knowledge and perhaps also because it made people more keenly aware of the importance of helping. So the few minutes you've spent reading this myth may have increased your chances of becoming a responsive bystander in emergencies. Although there may not be safety in numbers, there's often safety in knowledge.

**Men and Women Communicate in Completely
Different Ways**

Few topics have generated more spilt ink among poets, authors, and
song-writers than the age-old question of why men and women seem
not to understand each other. Even just confining ourselves to rock-and-
roll, the number of songs that describe male–female miscommunication
is probably too numerous to count. Take the lyrics of the *Genesis* song,
"Misunderstanding":

> There must be some misunderstanding
> There must be some kind of mistake
> I waited in the rain for hours
> You were late
> Now it's not like me to say the right thing
> But you could've called to let me know.

Of course, it's not just rock bands. Even famous personality theorists
have expressed exasperation at their failed efforts to comprehend the
opposite sex. No less an expert in human behavior than Sigmund Freud
told Marie Bonaparte (a psychoanalyst and the great grand-niece of
Napoleon Bonaparte) that:

> The great question that has never been answered, and which I have not
> yet been able to answer, despite my thirty years of research into the
> feminine soul, is "What does a woman want?" (Freud, quoted in Jones,
> 1955)

Of course, one harbors a sneaking suspicion that many women personality theorists hold similar views of men.

The belief that men and women communicate in completely different
ways, resulting in perennial misunderstandings, is deeply entrenched
in popular lore. Many television shows and cartoons, like *The Honey-
mooners*, *The Flintstones*, and more recently *The Simpsons* and *King of
the Hill*, capitalize heavily on the often unintentionally humorous communication differences between husbands and wives. The men in these
shows talk about sports, eating, hunting, and gambling, the women in
these shows about feelings, friendships, relationships, and home life.
Moreover, these shows typically depict men as less emotionally perceptive or, putting it a bit less charitably, "denser" than women.

Surveys suggest that college students similarly perceive men and women as differing in their communication styles. In particular, undergraduates see women as considerably more talkative than men and more skilled at picking up on subtle nonverbal cues during conversations (Swim, 1994).

Furthermore, if one were to read much of the current popular psychology literature, one might almost be tempted to conclude that men and women aren't merely different people, but different species. British linguist Deborah Tannen's book *You Just Don't Understand* (1991) reinforced this view by arguing—based largely on informal and anecdotal observations—that men's and women's styles of communication differ in kind rather than degree. In Tannen's words, "Women speak and hear a language of connection and intimacy, while men speak and hear a language of status and independence" (p. 42).

American pop psychologist John Gray took this view one step further, metaphorically likening men and women to creatures from different planets. In his enormously successful "Mars and Venus" series of self-help books, beginning with *Men are from Mars, Women are from Venus* (1992), extending to a host of related books, including *Mars and Venus in the Bedroom* (1996), *Mars and Venus on a Date* (1999), *Mars and Venus in the Workplace* (2001), and *Why Mars and Venus Collide* (2008), Gray has advanced the radical position that men and women have entirely different styles of communicating their needs, so different that they're continually misunderstanding each other. Wrote Gray (1992), "Not only do men and women communicate differently but they think, feel, perceive, react, respond, love, need, and appreciate differently. They almost seem to be from different planets, speaking different languages" (p. 5). Among other things, Gray claims that women's language focuses on intimacy and connectedness, men's on independence and competition (Barnett & Rivers, 2004; Dindia & Canary, 2006). In addition, says Gray, when they're upset, women express their feelings, whereas men withdraw into a "cave."

Gray's *Mars and Venus* books have sold over 40 million copies in 43 languages. *USA Today* named Gray's 1992 book one of the 25 most influential books of the 20th century, and according to one estimate, Gray's books were second only to the Bible during the 1990s in overall sales (http://www.ritaabrams.com/pages/MarsVenus.php). Gray has opened over 25 *Mars and Venus* Counseling Centers across the country, all with the goal of improving communication between the alien worlds of men and women. On Gray's website, one can find instructions for accessing a Mars and Venus dating service and phone helpline

(Cameron, 2007). And in 1997, Gray even transformed his *Mars and Venus* books into a musical comedy that opened on Broadway.

Although Gray and other pop psychologists haven't conducted any research to back up their claims, many other investigators have examined the evidence bearing on sex differences in communication. In particular, we can turn to the literature to address four major questions: (1) Do women talk more than men? (2) Do women disclose more about themselves than men? (3) Do men interrupt other people more than women? (4) Are women more perceptive of nonverbal cues than men (Barnett & Rivers, 2004; Cameron, 2007)?

In addition, we can pose a further question: To the extent that such differences exist, how large are they in size? To address this question, psychologists often rely on a metric called Cohen's *d*, named after statistician Jacob Cohen (1988), who popularized it. Without going into the gory statistical details, Cohen's *d* tells us how large the difference between groups is relative to the variability within these groups. As a rough benchmark, a Cohen's *d* of .2 is considered small, .5 medium, and .8 or bigger large. To provide a few yardsticks for comparison, the Cohen's *d* for the average difference between men and women in the personality trait of conscientiousness (with women being more conscientious) is about .18 (Feingold, 1994); for physical aggression (with men being more aggressive) it's about .60 (Hyde, 2005); and for height (with men being taller) it's about 1.7 (Lippa, 2005).

(1) *Do women talk much more than men?* Although the belief that women are more talkative than men has been popular for decades, psychiatrist Louann Brizendine lent it new credence in her bestselling book, *The Female Brain* (2006). There, Brizendine cited a claim that women speak an average of 20,000 words per day compared with only 7,000 for men, and scores of media outlets soon broadcast this difference as firmly established. Yet closer inspection of this report reveals that it's derived entirely from a self-help book and various second-hand sources, not from systematic research (Cameron, 2007; Liberman, 2006). Indeed, Brizendine dropped the claim from a later reprinting of her book. When psychologist Janet Hyde (2005) combined the results of 73 controlled studies into a meta-analysis (see p. 32), she found an overall Cohen's *d* of .11, reflecting greater talkativeness among women than men. Yet this difference is smaller than small, and barely noticeable in everyday life. Psychologist Matthias Mehl and his colleagues put another nail in the coffin of the talkativeness claim in a study tracking the

daily conversations of 400 college students who sported portable electronic recorders. They found that women and men both talked about 16,000 words per day (Mehl, Vazire, Ramirez-Esparza, Slatcher, & Pennebaker, 2007).

(2) *Do women disclose much more about themselves than men?* Contrary to the popular stereotype that women talk much more than men about matters of personal concern to them, Hyde (2005) found a Cohen's *d* of .18 across 205 studies. This finding is small in magnitude, and indicates that women are only slightly more self-disclosing than men.

(3) *Do men interrupt others much more often than women?* Yes, although across 53 studies of gender differences in conversations, Hyde (2005) again found the difference to be at most small in size, a Cohen's *d* of .15. Even this difference is hard to interpret, because research suggests that interruptions and turn-taking in conversation are partly a function of social status. In studies in which women are in charge, women tend to interrupt more often, take more turns, and talk longer than men (Aries, 1996; Barnett & Rivers, 2004).

(4) *Are women much more perceptive of nonverbal cues than men?* Here, the answer is somewhat clearer, and it's a qualified "yes." Meta-analyses (see p. 32) on adults by Judith Hall (1978, 1984) examining participants' ability to detect or differentiate emotions (like sadness, happiness, anger, and fear) in people's faces suggested a Cohen's *d* of about .40, although a meta-analysis on children and adolescents by Erin McClure (2000) suggested a smaller difference of only .13.

So, men and women indeed communicate in slightly different ways, and a few of these differences are sizeable enough to be meaningful. Yet for practical purposes, men and women are far more alike than different in their communication styles, and it's not clear how much the existing differences are due to intrinsic differences between the sexes as opposed to sex differences in power differentials (Barnett & Rivers, 2004; Cameron, 2007). Across studies, gender differences in communication seldom exceed the small range using Cohen's *d* (Aries, 1996). So John Gray's books, counseling centers, and Broadway musical notwithstanding, men aren't from Mars, nor are women from Venus. Instead, in the words of communication researcher Kathryn Dindia (2006), it's probably more accurate to say that "men are from North Dakota, women are from South Dakota" (p. 4).

Myth # 30
It's Better to Express Anger to Others than to Hold It in

Patrick Henry Sherrill has the dubious distinction of being the person who inspired the term "going postal" for committing one of the worst mass murders in American history. On August 20, 1986, Sherrill, enraged at the prospect that he'd be fired from his job as a postal worker, fired two guns that he hid in his mail pouch, killing 14 employees and wounding 6 others before taking his own life at the Edmond, Oklahoma Post Office. Many people now use the term "going postal" to describe a person's becoming uncontrollably angry and violent. "Road rage," a slang term referring to eruptions of anger on roadways, can likewise be deadly. On April 16, 2007, after flashing his headlights and tailgating Kevin Norman, Jason Reynolds cut in front of Norman and slammed on his brakes. When Norman swerved to avoid a collision, his vehicle rolled across the median, landed atop another vehicle, and killed Norman and the other driver (*The Washington Times*, 2007).

Could Sherrill and Reynolds have averted these lethal outbursts if they'd vented their pent-up emotions at home, say, by punching a pillow or using a plastic bat to swat away their anger? If you're like most people, you believe that releasing anger is healthier than keeping it bottled up. In one survey, 66% of undergraduates agreed that expressing pent-up anger is an effective means of reducing one's risk for aggression (Brown, 1983). This belief dates back to more than 2,000 years ago, when Greek philosopher Aristotle, in his classic *Poetics*, observed that viewing tragic plays provides the opportunity for *catharsis* (derived from the Greek word "katharsis")—a purging of anger and other negative emotions that provides a satisfying psychological cleansing experience.

Sigmund Freud (1930/1961), an influential proponent of catharsis, believed that repressed fury could build up and fester, much like steam in a pressure cooker, to the point that it caused psychological conditions like hysteria or trip-wired aggression. The key to therapy and rosy mental health, said Freud and his followers, is to dampen the pressure of negative feelings by talking about them and releasing them in a controlled manner in and out of treatment. The *Marvel* comic book and movie character, "The Hulk," is a metaphor for the consequences of the failure to control rage that always lurks at the fringes of consciousness. When mild-mannered Bruce Banner lets too much anger build up or is provoked, he morphs into his rampaging alter-ego, the Hulk.

Anger, popular psychology teaches us, is a monster we must tame. A host of films stoke the idea that we can do so by "letting off steam," "blowing our top," "getting things off our chest," and "getting it out of our system." In *Analyze This* (1999), a psychiatrist (played by Billy Crystal) advises a New York Gangster (played by Robert De Niro) to hit a pillow whenever he's angry. In *Network* (1976), an angry news anchor (played by Peter Finch) implores irate viewers, outraged by the high price of oil, the plummeting economy, and the country being on war footing, to release their frustrations by opening their windows and hollering, "I'm mad as hell and I'm not going to take it anymore." In response to his urgings, millions of Americans do just that. In *Anger Management* (2003), after the meek hero (played by Adam Sandler) is falsely accused of "air rage" on a flight, a judge orders him to attend an anger management group run by Dr. Buddy Rydell (played by Jack Nicholson). At Rydell's suggestion, Sandler's character fires dodgeball at schoolchildren and throws golf clubs to purge his anger.

Dr. Rydell's advice is similar to the counsel of authors of many self-help books on anger management. John Lee (1993) suggested that rather than "holding in poisonous anger," it's better to "Punch a pillow or a punching bag. And while you do it, yell and curse, and moan and holler. Punch with all the frenzy you can. If you are angry with a particular person, imagine his or her face on the pillow or punching bag, and vent your rage physically and verbally" (p. 96). Drs. George Bach and Herb Goldberg (1974) recommended an exercise dubbed "The Vesuvius" (named after the Italian volcano that caused the destruction of Pompeii in A.D. 79), in which ". . . individuals can vent their pent-up frustrations, resentments, hurts, hostilities, and rage in a full-throated, screaming outburst" (p. 180).

A variety of toys are available on the Internet to prevent anger melt-downs. One of our favorites is the "Choker Chicken." When you turn on the "Choker," you'll be treated to a lively rendition of the "Chicken Dance." When you choke the "Chicken," the reaction is immediate—his legs flail about as his eyes pop out and his cheeks redden. When you release his neck, you'll hear a speeded-up version of the "Chicken Dance," perhaps prompting you to engage in further "anger management." If you're not exactly enchanted by the prospect of choking a chicken (even a plastic one), perhaps consider the "Choking Strangler Boss" toy. When you press his left hand, the "Boss" taunts you with nasty criticisms, such as telling you that you need to work overtime even when you're feeling ill. But when you choke the "Boss," his eyes pop out, his arms and legs flail about, and he tells you that you deserve a raise or you can take some time off. Mission accomplished.

Techniques to deal with anger have even found a home in some psychotherapies. Some popular therapies encourage clients to scream, hit pillows, or throw balls against walls when they become angry (Lewis & Bucher, 1992). Proponents of "primal therapy," often informally called "primal scream therapy," believe that psychologically troubled adults must release the emotional pain produced by infant and childhood trauma by discharging this pain, often by screaming at the top of their lungs (Janov, 1970). Some cities, including Atlanta, Georgia, still have primal therapy centers. A website that advertises "The Center for Grieving Children" suggests using a "mad box" to help children deal with their emotions (http://www.cgcmaine.org/childrensactivities.html). The box is simple to construct, as follows: "(1). Fill the box with paper, you can cut pictures from a magazine or write down things that make you mad; (2). Tape the box shut; (3). Use a plastic bat, bataka, or jump on the box until it's in shreds; (4). Burn or recycle the remnants."

Some supposedly cathartic therapeutic approaches to cope with anger are arguably even more bizarre. People in the town of Castejon, Spain now practice "Destructotherapy" to relieve office stress: men and women destroy junked cars and household items with sledgehammers to the beat of a rock band playing in the background (Fox News, 2008; see Figure 7.1). This "therapy" may have been inspired by the film *Office Space* (1999), which includes a scene in which angry workers who hate their jobs and their boss take an office printer to a field and beat it mercilessly with a baseball bat.

These shenanigans aside, research suggests that the catharsis hypothesis is false. For more than 40 years, studies have revealed that encouraging the expression of anger directly toward another person or indirectly (such as toward an object) actually turns up the heat on aggression (Bushman, Baumeister, & Stack, 1999; Lewis & Bucher, 1992; Littrell, 1998; Tavris, 1988). In one of the earliest studies, people who pounded nails after someone insulted them were more, rather than less, critical of that person (Hornberger, 1959). Moreover, playing aggressive sports like football, which are presumed to promote catharsis, results in increases in aggression (Patterson, 1974), and playing violent videogames like *Manhunt*, in which bloody assassinations are rated on a 5-point scale, is associated with increased aggression in the laboratory and everyday life (Anderson & Bushman, 2002; Anderson, Gentile, & Buckley, 2007).

Figure 7.1 Participants in a 2005 "destructotherapy" session in Castejon, Spain, whack away at a car in a group effort to release their pent-up rage. But is destructotherapy an effective treatment for anger or a recipe for road rage?
Source: REUTERS/Vincent West.

So getting angry doesn't "let off steam": It merely fans the flames of our anger. Research suggests that expressing anger is helpful only when it's accompanied by constructive problem-solving designed to address the source of the anger (Littrell, 1998). So if we're upset at our partner for repeatedly showing up late for dates, yelling at him or her is unlikely to make us feel better, let alone improve the situation. But calmly and assertively expressing one's resentment ("I realize you probably aren't doing this on purpose, but when you show up late it hurts my feelings") can often go a long way toward resolving conflict.

The media may increase the likelihood that people will express anger: People may engage in aggressive acts because they believe they'll feel better afterward (Bushman, Baumeister, & Phillips, 2001). Brad Bushman and his colleagues (Bushman et al., 1999) provided participants with bogus newspaper stories claiming that acting aggressively is a good way to reduce anger, and then gave them critical comments on an essay they wrote on abortion ("This is one of the worst essays I have ever read!"). Contrary to the catharsis hypothesis, people who read the pro-catharsis story— which claimed that catharsis is a good way to relax and reduce anger —and then hit a punching bag became more aggressive toward the person who insulted them than did people who read an anti-catharsis newspaper story and hit a punching bag.

Why is the myth of catharsis still popular despite compelling evidence that anger feeds aggression? Because people sometimes feel better for a short time after they blow off steam, it may reinforce aggression and the belief that catharsis works (Bushman, 2002; Bushman et al., 1999). Also, people often mistakenly attribute the fact that they feel better after they express anger to catharsis, rather than to the fact that anger usually subsides on its own after a while. As Jeffrey Lohr and his colleagues (Lohr, Olatunji, Baumeister, & Bushman, 2007) observed, this is an example of the post hoc, ergo propter hoc (after this, therefore because of this) fallacy, the error of assuming that because one thing comes before another, it must cause it (see *Introduction*, p. 14). We agree with Carol Tavris (1988) that "It is time to put a bullet, once and for all, through the heart of the catharsis hypothesis" (p. 197). But after we pull the trigger, will we feel better—or worse—than before we fired the shot?

Chapter 7: Other Myths to Explore

Fiction	Fact
Large groups make less extreme decisions than individuals.	Research on the "risky shift" and, later, "group polarization" suggests that groups tend to make more extreme decisions than individuals.
Crowding consistently leads to more aggression.	Crowding sometimes reduces aggression, because people in crowded areas often try to limit their interactions with others.
People's attitudes are highly predictive of their behaviors.	In most cases, attitudes are only weak predictors of behaviors.
To reduce prejudice, we must first change people's attitudes.	Changing people's behaviors is often the best way to change their prejudiced attitudes.
"Brainstorming" new ideas in groups works better than asking people to generate ideas on their own.	Most studies show that the quality of ideas generated in brainstorming sessions is poorer than that of ideas generated by individuals.
High levels of anger in marriage are highly predictive of divorce.	Anger between partners tends not to be especially predictive of divorce, although levels of some other emotions, especially contempt, are.

Fiction	Fact
Poverty and poor education are major causes of terrorism, especially suicide bombings.	Many or most suicide bombers are well educated and financially comfortable.
Most members of cults are mentally disturbed.	Studies show that most cult members don't suffer from serious psychopathology.
The best way to change someone's attitude is to give him or her a large reward to do so.	Research on "cognitive dissonance" theory demonstrates the best way to change someone's attitude is to give him or her the smallest reward possible needed to do so.
Rewarding people for creative work always strengthens their motivation to produce more creative work.	In some cases, rewarding people for creative work may undermine their intrinsic motivation.
Basketball players shoot in "streaks."	Research suggests that the "hot hand" in basketball is an illusion, because making many shots in a row doesn't increase a player's chances of making his or her next shot.
Playing "hard to get" is a good way of getting someone interested in you romantically.	Research suggests that are men are less interested in women who are "standoffish" than women who are receptive to their advances.
When Kitty Genovese was murdered in New York City in 1964, no one came to her aid.	There's good evidence that some eyewitnesses called the police shortly after Genovese was attacked.

Sources and Suggested Readings

To explore these and other myths about interpersonal behavior, see de Waal, Aureli, and Judge (2000); Gilovich (1991); Gilovich, Vallone, and Tversky (1985); Kohn (1990); Manning, Levine, and Collins (2007); Myers (2008).

8 KNOW THYSELF

Myths about Personality

Raising Children Similarly Leads to
Similarities in Their Adult Personalities

How did you become who you are?

This is just about the most fundamental question we can ask about personality. Mull it over for a few minutes, and you're likely to generate a host of responses. If you're like most people, the odds are high that many of your answers pertain to how you were raised by your parents. "I'm a moral person because my parents taught me good values." "I'm a daredevil because my father wanted me to take risks in life."

Few beliefs about personality are as firmly held as what Judith Rich Harris (1988) termed "the nurture assumption," the idea that parenting practices make the personalities of children within a family more similar to each other—and to their parents (Pinker, 2002; Rowe, 1994). For example, in her 1996 book, *It Takes a Village*, former first-lady and now U.S. Secretary of State Hillary Clinton argued that parents who are honest with their children tend to produce children who are honest; parents who are unduly aggressive with their children tend to produce children who are aggressive; and so on (Clinton, 1996). Moreover, we can find this assumption in hundreds of scholarly articles and books. For example, in an early edition of his widely used personality textbook, Walter Mischel (1981) presented the outcome of a thought experiment:

> Imagine the enormous differences that would be found in the personalities of twins with identical genetic endowment if they were raised apart in two different families . . . Through social learning vast differences develop among people in their reactions to most stimuli they face in daily life. (Mischel, 1981, p. 311)

The nurture assumption also forms the bedrock of numerous theories that rely on parent-to-child socialization as a driving force of personality development (Loevinger, 1987). Sigmund Freud proposed that children learn their sense of morality (what he termed the "superego") by identifying with the same-sex parent and incorporating that parent's value system into their personalities. Albert Bandura's "social learning theory" holds that we acquire behaviors largely by emulating the actions of our parents and other authority figures. The fact that our personalities are molded largely by parental socialization is undeniable. Or is it?

It's true that children tend to resemble their parents to some extent on just about all personality traits. But this finding doesn't demonstrate that this resemblance is produced by environmental similarity, because biological parents and their children share not only environment but genes. To verify the nurture assumption, we must find systematic means of disentangling genes from environments.

One method of doing so capitalizes on a remarkable natural experiment. In about one of out every 250 births, the fertilized egg, or "zygote," splits into two copies called identical twins; for this reason, they're also called "monozygotic" twins. Identical twins therefore share 100% of their genes. By comparing the personalities of identical twins raised apart from birth with identical twins raised together, researchers can estimate the effect of *shared environment*: the combined environmental influences that increase the resemblance among family members.

The largest study of identical twins reared apart, conducted by University of Minnesota psychologist Thomas Bouchard and his colleagues, examined over 60 pairs of identical twins separated at birth and raised in different homes. Playfully termed the "Minnesota Twin" studies after the state's baseball team, this study reunited many adult twin pairs at the Minneapolis-St. Paul airport for the first time since their separation only a few days following birth.

Bouchard and his colleagues, including Auke Tellegen and David Lykken, found that these twins often exhibited eerie similarities in personality and habits. In one case of male twins raised in different countries, both flushed the toilet both before and after using it, read magazines from back to front, and got a kick out of startling others by sneezing loudly in elevators. Another pair consisted of two male twins who unknowingly lived only 50 miles apart in New Jersey. To their mutual astonishment, they discovered that they were both volunteer firefighters, big fans of John Wayne westerns and, although fond of beer, drinkers of only Budweiser. While attending college in different states, one installed fire detection devices, the other fire sprinkler devices. Amazing as these anecdotes are, they don't provide convincing evidence. Given enough pairings among unrelated individuals, one could probably detect a number of equally bizarre coincidences (Wyatt, Posey, Welker, & Seamonds, 1984).

More important was Bouchard and his colleagues' remarkable finding that on questionnaire measures of personality traits—like anxiety-proneness, risk-taking, achievement motivation, hostility, traditionalism, and impulsivity—identical twins raised apart were as similar as identical twins raised together (Tellegen et al., 1988). Being raised in entirely different families exerted little or no impact on personality similarity. Other studies of identical twins raised apart have yielded similar results (Loehlin, 1992). Walter Mischel was wrong. In fact, he deleted his thought experiment from later editions of his personality textbook.

Another method of investigating the nurture assumption takes advantage of what Nancy Segal (1999) called "virtual twins." Don't be fooled by this term, because they're not twins at all. Instead, virtual twins are unrelated individuals raised in the same adoptive family. Studies of virtual twins indicate that unrelated individuals raised in the same household are surprisingly different in personality. For example, one study of 40 children and adolescents revealed weak resemblance in personality traits, like anxiety-proneness, and most behavior problems within virtual twin pairs (Segal, 1999).

The results of identical and virtual twin studies suggest that the extent that you're similar to your parents in extraversion, anxiety, guilt-proneness, and other traits is due almost entirely to the genes you share with them. This research also suggests some counterintuitive advice to parents and would-be parents. If you're stress-prone and want your children to turn out to be stress-free as adults, don't stress out over it. It's unlikely that your parenting style will have as large a long-term impact on your children's anxiety levels as you think.

That's not to say that shared environment has no effect on us. For one thing, shared environment generally exerts at least some influence on *childhood* personality. But the effects of shared environment usually fade away once children leave the household and interact with teachers and peers (Harris, 1998). Interestingly, as Bouchard notes, this finding offers yet another example of how popular wisdom gets it backward. Most people believe that our environments exert increasing or even cumulative effects on us over time, whereas the opposite appears to be true, at least insofar as personality is concerned (Miele, 2008).

In addition, it's likely that extremely neglectful or incompetent parenting can produce adverse effects in later life. But within the broad range of what psychoanalyst Heinz Hartmann (1939) called the "average expectable environment," that is, an environment that affords children basic needs for nourishment, love, and intellectual stimulation, shared environmental influence on personality is nearly invisible. Finally, at least one important psychological characteristic seems to be influenced by shared environment: antisocial behavior (by the way, don't confuse "antisocial" behavior with "asocial" behavior, which means shyness or aloofness). Studies of children adopted into criminal homes often show that being raised by a criminal parent increases one's risk of criminality in adulthood (Lykken, 1995; Rhee & Waldman, 2002).

It's easy to see why most people, including parents, find the nurture assumption so plausible. We observe that parents and their children tend to be similar in personality, and we attribute this similarity to something we can see—parenting practices—rather than to something we can't—genes. In doing so, however, we're falling prey to post hoc, ergo propter reasoning, the mistake of assuming that because A comes before B, A causes B (see *Introduction*, p. 14). The fact that parenting practices precede the similarity between parents and children doesn't mean that they produce it.

Mythbusting: A Closer Look

Birth Order and Personality

The finding that shared environmental influences—those that make people within a family more similar—exert a minimal effect on adult personality doesn't imply that *nonshared influences*—those that make people within the same family different—aren't important. In fact, studies demonstrate that the correlations for all personality traits within identical twin pairs are considerably less than 1.0 (that is, considerably less than a perfect correlation), which strongly suggests that nonshared environmental influences are operating. Yet researchers have had a devil of a time pinpointing specific nonshared environmental influences on personality (Meehl, 1978; Turkheimer & Waldron, 2000).

One promising candidate for a nonshared influence on personality is birth order, a variable that's long been a darling of popular psychology. According to scores of self-help books, such as Kevin Leman's (1988) *The New Birth Order Book: Why You Are the Way You Are* and Cliff Isaacson

---

and Kris Radish's (2002) *The Birth Order Effect: How to Better Understand Yourself and Others*, birth order is a potent predictor of personality. First-borns, these books assure us, tend to be comformist and perfectionistic, middle-borns diplomatic and flexible, and later-borns nontraditional and prone to risk-taking.

Research paints a different picture. In most studies, the relations between birth order and personality has been inconsistent or nonexistent. In 1993, Swiss psychologists Cecile Ernst and Jules Angst surveyed over 1,000 studies of birth order and personality. Their conclusion, which surely produced angst (we couldn't resist the pun) among advocates of the birth order hypothesis, was that birth order is largely unrelated to personality (Ernst & Angst, 1993). More recently, Tyrone Jefferson and his colleagues examined the relations between birth order and the "Big Five" personality dimensions, which emerge from analyses of almost all broad measures of personality. These traits, which are conveniently recalled by the water-logged mnemonics CANOE or OCEAN, are conscientiousness, agreeableness, neuroticism (closely related to anxiety-proneness), openness to experience (closely related to intellectual curiosity), and extraversion. Jefferson and co-authors found no significant relations between birth order and self-reported measures of any of the Big Five traits. Using ratings from peers (such as friends and co-workers), they found modest associations between birth order and a few aspects of agreeableness, openness, and extraversion (with later-borns being more outgoing, inventive, and trusting than earlier-borns), but these findings didn't hold up using spouse ratings (Jefferson, Herbst, & McCrae, 1998).

On the basis of analyses of scientists' attitudes toward revolutionary theories, like Copernicus's theory of a sun-centered solar system and Darwin's theory of natural selection, historian Frank Sulloway (1996) argued that birth order is a predictor of rebelliousness, with later-borns being more likely to question conventional wisdom than earlier-borns. But others have found Sulloway's analyses unconvincing, in part because Sulloway wasn't "blind" to scientists' birth order when classifying their attitudes to scientific theories (Harris, 1998). Moreover, other investigators haven't been able to replicate Sulloway's claim that later-borns are more rebellious than earlier-borns (Freese, Powell, & Steelman, 1999).

So birth order may be weakly related to a few personality traits, although it's a far cry from the powerful predictor that folk psychology would have us believe.

Myth #32

The Fact that a Trait Is Heritable Means We Can't Change It

In the 1983 film *Trading Places*, two wealthy businessmen disagree about whether nature (genetic make-up) or nurture (environment) is responsible for success in life. To settle their dispute, they arrange for Louis Winthorpe III, an employee at their investment firm (played by Dan Aykroyd), to lose his job, home, money, and girlfriend. In his place, they hire Billy Ray Valentine, a con artist living on the street (played by Eddie Murphy), and give him the home and social status previously enjoyed by Winthorpe. If success depends on nature, Valentine should fail in his new position and end up back on the street, whereas Winthorpe should overcome temporary setbacks and rise again. The film reflects the perspective that was dominant at the time: Winthorpe became a victim of his new circumstances and Valentine thrived in his.

As recently as the early 1980s, the suggestion that genes could play a role in shaping human traits or behavior was exceedingly controversial. More than a century earlier, Charles Darwin (1859) had proposed his landmark theory of evolution by natural selection; two decades earlier, James Watson and Francis Crick (1953) had discovered the molecular structure of DNA (the genetic material). Yet many scholars dismissed these revolutionary discoveries as irrelevant to social and behavioral science. They simply assumed that our behavior was shaped only by our environments—cultural beliefs and practices, family members and other important people in our lives, physically or psychologically traumatic events, diseases, and the like. The question of how nature and nurture affect us wasn't up for debate. "Lower" animals might act on inherited instincts, but human behavior wasn't influenced by genes.

Of course, an awful lot has changed since then. Scientists have now firmly established the influence of genes on personality and many other aspects of human behavior. Even so, misconceptions about the heritability of psychological traits persist. Perhaps the most widespread myth is that heritable traits can't be changed, a message that might be discouraging if it were true. For example, in his well-regarded book *In the Name of Eugenics: Genetics and the Uses of Human Heredity*, Daniel Kevles (1985) wrote that the famous statistician Karl Pearson "outraged both physicians and temperance reformers . . . by his outspoken insistence that a tendency to contract tuberculosis was heritable—which made a mockery of public health measures to combat it" (p. 67). In their enormously controversial book, *The Bell Curve: Intelligence and Class*

Structure in American Life, Richard Herrnstein and Charles Murray (1994) also committed several errors when writing about heritability. In particular, they referred to "the limits that heritability puts on the ability to manipulate intelligence" and said that "even a heritability of [60%] leaves room for considerable change if the changes in environment are commensurably large" (p. 109). This statement suggests that a higher heritability wouldn't leave room for much change. These authors, like many others, implied mistakenly that highly heritable traits are difficult or impossible to change. As we'll soon discover, even a heritability of 100% doesn't imply unmodifiability. To see why, we need to understand what heritability means and how researchers study it.

Scientists define heritability as the percentage of individual differences (differences across people) in a trait that's due to genetic differences. Let's consider the trait of extraversion, or how outgoing and sociable someone is. If extraversion were 0% heritable, differences between shy and gregarious people would be due to environmental factors only, not genes. At the other extreme, if extraversion were 100% heritable, all differences on this trait would be produced genetically and unrelated to environmental factors. It turns out that extraversion, like most other personality traits, is about 50% heritable (Plomin & Rende, 1991). But what does it mean to say that something is partially heritable? Two aspects of the deceptively simple heritability concept are crucial to grasp.

First, despite what many people believe, heritability concerns differences *across* people, not within people. Even *The Bell Curve* co-author Charles Murray got this wrong in a 1995 interview on CNN: "When I—when we—say 60 percent heritability, it's not 60 percent of the variation. It is 60 percent of the IQ in any given person" (quoted in Block, 1995, p. 108). But heritability has no meaning within a "given person." Whatever your IQ, you can't say that you get 60% of this from your genes and the other 40% from your environment. Instead, this statistic means that across people in a population, 60% of their differences in IQ are due to differences in their genes and 40% to differences in their environments.

Second, heritability depends on the ranges of genetic and environmental differences in a sample. When studying the behavior of genetically identical organisms raised in different conditions, heritability would be 0%. Because there's no genetic variability across organisms, only environmental differences could exert any effect. Scientists sometimes attempt to minimize hereditary differences in behavior by working with specially bred strains of nearly genetically identical white mice. By eliminating just about all genetic variation, the effects of experimental manipulations are easier to detect. In contrast, when studying the behavior of genetically diverse organisms under exactly identical laboratory conditions, heritability would be 100%. Because there's no environmental variability, only genetic differences could exert any effect. Scientists comparing the yield of genetically different seed varieties can grow them in virtually identical soil, temperature, and lighting conditions to eliminate just about all environmental influences. To study the heritability of psychological traits, we should ideally include a broad range of genes and environments.

So how do scientists estimate heritability? It's not as simple as looking for similarities among members of intact families, because this approach confounds the influence of genes and environment. Children share not only their genes with their siblings, parents, and even other biological relatives, but also many aspects of their environment. The trick is to design a study in which genes and environments vary systematically and independently. For example, in most twin studies researchers test the similarities of siblings—who shared the same uterus and were born at virtually the same time—raised in the same homes. Specifically, they compare the similarity of identical twins, who share 100% of their genes, with that of fraternal twins, who share 50% of their genes on average (see Myth #31). Aspects of the environment relevant to the causes of personality traits are usually shared to a comparable extent by identical and fraternal twins. So we can treat environmental influences as about equal for each type of twin and test for differences due to shared genes. If identical twins are more similar to one another on a personality trait than are fraternal twins, this finding suggests that the trait is at least somewhat heritable; the larger the difference between identical and fraternal twins, the higher the heritability.

Using twin studies and other informative research designs, investigators have consistently found moderate heritability for personality traits like extraversion, conscientiousness, and impulsivity, as well as cognitive ability and vulnerability to psychopathology (Plomin & Rende, 1991). Even attitudes toward such political issues as abortion and such ideological positions as liberal or conservative are heritable, more so than affiliation with the Democratic or Republican political parties (Alford, Funk, & Hibbing, 2005). Judith Rich Harris (1995) reviewed evidence that the portion of individual differences in personality traits that's environmental has little to do with *shared* environmental factors, such as similar rearing by parents, and much more to do with *nonshared* environmental factors, such as differences in people's exposure to peers (see Myth #31).

The heritability of intelligence has been especially controversial. As early as the 1990s, there was strong agreement that IQ is heritable, but estimates of how much ranged from 40% to 80% (Gottfredson, 1997). Why is this range so large? Many factors can affect heritability estimates across studies, such as the socioeconomic status or age of participants. In a sample of 7-year-old children, Eric Turkheimer and his colleagues found that heritability was only 10% among the poorest families, but 72% among the richest families (Turkheimer, Haley, Waldron, D'Onofrio, & Gottesman, 2003). Other researchers have found that the heritability of IQ increases across the lifespan (Plomin & Spinath, 2004). As we develop into adults, our inherited traits and preferences exert an increasing influence on our environments. This phenomenon occurs both actively, as we select and create our own environments, and passively, as when people treat us differently. The net effect is that our inherited traits exert a greater impact on the development of our intelligence over time. Heritability estimates for IQ are low when our parents shape our environments, but they increase up to 80% by the time we're adults.

As our earlier examples illustrate, even knowledgeable authors have misunderstood what heritability means. Most critically, the heritability of a trait like IQ doesn't mean we can't modify it (Gottfredson, 1997). Instead, a high heritability means only that *current* environments exert a small effect on individual differences in a trait; it says nothing about the potential effects of *new* environments, nor does it imply that we can't successfully treat a disorder. For example, phenylketonuria (PKU) is a 100% heritable condition involving the inability to metabolize (break down) the amino acid phenylalanine. This condition can lead to irreversible problems in brain development, such as mental retardation. Products that contain phenylalanine, which includes anything made with the artificial sweetener aspartame (trade names Equal and Nutra-Sweet), include a warning on their labels for people with PKU; check the back of any Diet Coke can to see what we mean. By ridding their diets of phenylalanine, people with PKU can ward off harmful effects. So the fact that PKU is entirely heritable doesn't mean we can't modify it. We can.

In the same way, an enriched environment could stimulate the development of intellectual ability even if IQ is highly heritable. In fact, if research told us what constitutes an optimal learning environment and we provided this environment equally to all children in a study, the heritability of IQ would be 100% because only genetic variation would remain. So the good news is that we don't need to be troubled by high heritability. It doesn't mean we can't change a trait, and it may even indicate that we've made good progress in improving bad environments. Who knows—maybe in a few decades we'll use heritability estimates to measure the success of our programs!

Myth #33 Low Self-Esteem Is a Major Cause of Psychological Problems

On the morning of April 20, 1999—perhaps not coincidentally, Adolph Hitler's 110th birthday—two teenage students dressed in black trench coats strolled calmly into Columbine High School in Littleton, Colorado. Although essentially unknown prior to that morning, Eric Harris and Dylan Klebold were to become household names in America by the day's end. Armed with an assortment of guns and bombs, they gleefully chased down and slaughtered 12 students and a teacher before killing themselves.

No sooner did the Columbine tragedy occur than a parade of mental health experts and social commentators took to the airwaves to speculate on its causes. Although these pundits invoked a host of possible influences, one emerged as the clear front-runner: low self-esteem. The opinions expressed on one website were typical:

> The shootings at Columbine and other schools across the country continue the frightening pattern of kids shooting kids . . . While keeping guns out of the hands of our children is critical, teaching them to value themselves and others is even more important. (www.axelroadlearning.com/ teenvaluestudy.htm)

Others have explained the supposed recent epidemic of school shootings across America in terms of a marked decline in children's self-esteem (we say "supposed" because the claim that school shootings have been becoming more common is itself a myth; Cornell, 2006). The handful of mental health professionals who've questioned this prevailing wisdom publicly haven't always been well received. During a 1990s televised talk show, a psychologist patiently attempted to spell out the multiple causes underlying teen violence. One associate producer, believing the psychologist's arguments to be needlessly complicated, angrily waved a large card at her that read simply "SELF-ESTEEM!" (Colvin, 2000).

Indeed, many popular psychologists have long maintained that low self-esteem is a prime culprit in generating many unhealthy behaviors, including violence, depression, anxiety, and alcoholism. From Norman

Vincent Peale's (1952) classic *The Power of Positive Thinking* onward, self-help books proclaiming the virtues of self-esteem have become regular fixtures in bookstores. In a bestselling book, *The Six Pillars of Self-Esteem*, self-esteem guru Nathaniel Branden insisted that one:

> cannot think of a single psychological problem—from anxiety and depression, to fear of intimacy or of success, to spouse battery or child molestation —that is not traceable to the problem of low self-esteem. (Branden, 1994)

The National Association for Self-Esteem similarly claims that:

> A close relationship has been documented between low self-esteem and such problems as violence, alcoholism, drug abuse, eating disorders, school dropouts, teenage pregnancy, suicide, and low academic achievement. (Reasoner, 2000)

The perception that low self-esteem is detrimental to psychological health has exerted an impact on public policy. In 1986, California funded a Task Force on Self-Esteem and Personal and Social Responsibility to the tune of $245,000 per year. Its goal was to examine the negative consequences of low self-esteem and to find a means of remedying them. The prime mover behind this task force, California state assemblyman John Vasconcellos, argued that enhancing the self-esteem of California's citizens could help balance the state's budget (Dawes, 1994).

The self-esteem movement has also found its way into mainstream educational and occupational practices. Many American schoolteachers ask children to generate lists of what makes them good people in the hopes of enhancing their pupils' self-worth. Some athletic leagues award trophies to all schoolchildren to avoid making losing competitors feel inferior (Sommers & Satel, 2005). One elementary school in Santa Monica, California banned children from playing tag because the "children weren't feeling good about it" (Vogel, 2002), and still other schools refer to children who spell poorly as "individual spellers" to avoid hurting their feelings (Salerno, 2009). A number of U.S. companies have also leapt on the self-esteem bandwagon. The Scooter Store, Inc., in New Braunfels, Texas, hired a "celebrations assistant" who is assigned to toss 25 pounds of confetti each week to employees in an effort to boost their self-worth, and the Container Store has instituted "Celebration Voice Mailboxes" to provide continual praise to its workers (Zaslow, 2007).

Moreover, the Internet is chock full of educational books and products intended to boost children's self-esteem. One book, *Self-Esteem Games*

(Sher, 1998), contains 300 activities to help children feel good about themselves, such as repeating positive affirmations emphasizing their uniqueness, and another book, *501 Ways to Boost Your Children's Self-esteem* (Ramsey, 2002), encourages parents to give their children more say in family decisions, such as allowing them to choose how to be punished. One can order a "Self-Esteem Question Desk" of cards consisting of questions designed to remind oneself of one's accomplishments—like "What is a goal you have already achieved?" and "What honor have you received in the past that you are proud about?" Or one can even buy a self-esteem cereal bowl emblazoned with positive affirmations, like "I'm talented!" and "I'm good looking!"

But there's a fly in the ointment. Most research shows that low self esteem isn't strongly associated with poor mental health. In a painstaking—and probably painful!—review, Roy Baumeister, Jennifer Campbell, Joachim Krueger, and Kathleen Vohs (2003) canvassed all of the available evidence—over 15,000 studies worth—linking self-esteem to just about every conceivable psychological variable. Contrary to widespread claims, they found that self-esteem is minimally related to interpersonal success. Nor is self-esteem consistently related to smoking, alcohol abuse, or drug abuse. Moreover, they discovered that although self-esteem is positively associated with school performance, it doesn't seem to cause it (Mercer, 2010). Instead, better school performance appears to contribute to high self-esteem (Baumeister et al., 2003). It's likely that some earlier researchers had misinterpreted the correlation between self-esteem and school performance as reflecting a direct causal effect of self-esteem (see *Introduction*, p. 13). Furthermore, although self-esteem is associated with depression, this correlation is only moderate in size (Joiner, Alfano, & Metalsky, 1992). As a consequence, "low self-esteem is neither necessary nor sufficient for depression" (Baumeister et al., 2003, p. 6).

Still, readers with high self-esteem needn't despair. Self-esteem seems to afford two benefits (Baumeister et al., 2003). We say "seems" because the findings are merely correlational and may not be causal (see *Introduction*, p. 13). That said, self-esteem is associated with greater (1) initiative and persistence, that is, a willingness to attempt tasks and to keep at them when difficulties arise, and (2) happiness and emotional resilience.

Self-esteem is also related to a tendency to view oneself more positively than others do. High self-esteem individuals consistently regard themselves as smarter, more physically attractive, and more likeable than other individuals. Yet these perceptions are illusory, because people with high self-esteem score no higher than other people on objective measures of intelligence, attractiveness, and popularity (Baumeister et al., 2003).

When it comes to violence, the story becomes more complicated. There's some evidence that low self-esteem is associated with an elevated risk of physical aggression and delinquency (Donnellan, Trzesniewski, Robins, Moffitt, & Caspi, 2005). Yet high esteem doesn't protect people against violence. To the contrary, a subset of *high* self-esteem individuals—specifically, those whose self-esteem is unstable—is at highest risk for physical aggression (Baumeister, 2001). These individuals tend to be narcissistic and believe themselves deserving of special privileges, or so-called narcissistic "entitlements." When confronted with a challenge to their perceived worth, or what clinical psychologists term a "narcissistic injury," they're liable to lash out at others.

Interestingly, Harris and Klebold appeared to be anything but uncertain of themselves. Both were fascinated with Nazism and preoccupied with fantasies of world domination. Harris's diaries revealed that he saw himself as morally superior to others and felt contempt for almost all of his peers. Harris and Klebold had frequently been teased by classmates, and most commentators assumed that this mistreatment produced low self-esteem, bolstering Harris and Klebold's risk for violence. These commentators probably fell prey to post hoc, ergo propter hoc (after this, therefore because of this) reasoning (see *Introduction*, p. 14), which may be a key source of the low self-esteem myth. Tempting as it may be, we can't draw the inference that because teasing precedes violence, it necessarily produces it. Instead, Harris and Klebold's *high* self-esteem may have led them to perceive the taunts of their classmates as threats to their inflated sense of self-worth, motivating them to seek revenge.

In a series of clever experiments, Brad Bushman, in collaboration with Baumeister, asked participants to write essays expressing their attitudes toward abortion (see also Myth #30). A research assistant pretending to be another participant evaluated each essay. Unbeknownst to participants, this evaluation was a complete ruse. In fact, Bushman and Baumeister randomly assigned half of the participants to receive positive comments ("No suggestions, great essay!") comments, and half negative comments ("This is one of the worst essays I have read!"). Participants then took part in a simulated "competition" allowing them to retaliate against their essay evaluator with a loud and annoying blast of noise. Narcissistic participants responded to negative evaluations by bombarding their opponents with significantly louder noises than other participants. Positive essay evaluations produced no such effect (Bushman & Baumeister, 1998).

Consistent with these findings, bullies and some aggressive children tend to have overly positive perceptions of how others view them (Baumeister et al., 2003). Christopher Barry and his colleagues asked aggressive and nonaggressive children to estimate their popularity among their peers and compared their ratings with actual popularity ratings obtained from peers. Aggressive children were more likely than non-aggressive children to overestimate their popularity; this tendency was especially marked among narcissistic children (Barry, Frick, & Killian, 2003; Emler, 2001).

The implications of these findings are troubling, especially considering the popularity of self-esteem programs for at-risk teenagers. The National Association for Self-Esteem recommends 13 programs—many of which fly under the banner of "affective education programs"—designed to bolster the self-esteem of troubled youngsters (http://www.self-esteem-nase.org/edu.php). Moreover, many prisons have developed self-esteem programs to reduce repeat offending. The research we've described suggests that these programs could produce negative consequences, especially among participants at high risk for aggression. The one thing that Eric Harris and Dylan Klebold didn't need was higher self-esteem.

Myth # 34 Most People Who Were Sexually Abused in Childhood Develop Severe Personality Disturbances in Adulthood

"Scarred for life." Phrases like this appear in a seemingly endless parade of popular psychology books written for sexual abuse victims. The self-help literature is replete with claims that childhood sexual abuse produces lasting personality changes, including deep psychological wounds. Other popular psychology books, such as Jade Angelica's (1993) *A Moral Emergency*, refer to the "cycle of child sexual abuse." According to them, many or most sexually abused individuals become abusers themselves. Some self-help books go further, implying that sexual abuse leaves in its wake a distinctive "personality profile." Low self-confidence, intimacy problems, reluctance to commit to others in relationships, and fears of sex are among its tell-tale signs (Bradshaw, 1991; Frederickson, 1992).

The profound personality alterations induced by early sexual abuse are self-evident truths in many popular psychology circles. A popular article (Megan, 1997) maintained that "Like scar tissue, the effects of sexual abuse never go away, experts say, continuing to influence victims in various ways, such as by contributing to drug and alcohol abuse, low self-esteem, divorce and distrust." Or take *The Courage to Heal*, a 1988 self-help book by Ellen Bass and Laura Davis that's sold over a million copies. The authors informed readers that

> The long term effects of child sexual abuse can be so pervasive that it's sometimes hard to pinpoint exactly how the abuse affected you. It permeates everything: your sense of self, your intimate relationships, your sexuality, your parenting, your work life, even your sanity. Everywhere you look, you see its effects. (Bass & Davis, 1988, p. 37)

In addition, scores of Hollywood films, including *Midnight Cowboy* (1969), *The Color Purple* (1985), *Forrest Gump* (1994), *Antwone Fisher* (2002), and *Mystic River* (2003), powerfully depict adult characters who've experienced longstanding personality changes following sexual abuse in childhood.

Understandably, many laypersons believe that the close link between child sexual abuse and personality changes is well established. In one survey of 246 citizens of rural Oregon, 68% of males and 74% of females expressed the view that child sexual abuse "always" results in obvious behavioral changes (Calvert & Munsie-Benson, 1999).

There's little doubt that child sexual abuse, especially when extreme, can produce harmful effects (Nelson et al., 2002). Yet the most telling finding in the research literature on the apparent long-term consequences of child sexual abuse is the absence of findings. Numerous investigations demonstrate that the typical reaction to a history of child sexual abuse is not psychopathology, but resilience (also see "Mythbusting: A Closer Look").

In 1998, Bruce Rind and his colleagues conducted a meta-analysis (see p. 32) of the research literature on the correlates of child sexual abuse in college students. They had earlier conducted a similar review using community samples, which yielded almost identical results (Rind & Tromovitch, 1997). Their 1998 article appeared in the American Psychological Association's *Psychological Bulletin*, one of psychology's premier journals. Chock full of dense numerical tables and the technical details of statistical analyses, Rind and colleagues' article seemed an unlikely candidate for the centerpiece of a national political firestorm. Little did Rind and his colleagues know what was in store.

Rind and his co-authors reported that the association between a self-reported history of child sexual abuse and 18 forms of adult psychopathology—including depression, anxiety, and eating disorders—was weak in magnitude (Rind, Tromovitch, & Bauserman, 1998).

The average correlation between the two variables was a mere .09, an association that's close to zero. Moreover, a history of an adverse family environment, such as a highly conflict-ridden home, was a much stronger predictor of later psychopathology than was a history of sexual abuse. As Rind and his co-authors cautioned, the effects of early abuse are difficult to disentangle from those of a troubled family environment, particularly because each can contribute to the other. Surprisingly, they found that the relation between sexual abuse and later psychopathology was no stronger when the abuse was more severe or frequent.

The "Rind article," as it came to be known, provoked a furious media and political controversy. Radio talk-show personality Dr. Laura Schlessinger ("Dr. Laura") condemned the article as "junk science at its worst" and as a "not-so-veiled attempt to normalize pedophilia" (Lilienfeld, 2002). Several members of Congress, most notably Representatives Tom DeLay of Texas and Matt Salmon of Arizona, criticized the American Psychological Association for publishing an article that implied that sexual abuse isn't as harmful as commonly believed. On the floor of Congress, Salmon referred to the article as the "emancipation proclamation of pedophiles." Eventually, on July 12, 1999, the Rind article was denounced by the House of Representatives in a 355 to 0 vote, earning it the dubious distinction of becoming the first scientific article ever condemned by the U.S. Congress (Lilienfeld, 2002; McNally, 2003; Rind, Tromovitch, & Bauserman, 2000).

Several critics have raised thoughtful challenges to Rind and colleagues' findings, especially the extent to which they're generalizable to more severe samples. For example, college samples may not be ideal for studying the negative psychological effects of child sexual abuse, because people with severe personality disturbances may be less likely to attend college than other people (Dallam et al., 2001). Nevertheless, the central thrust of Rind and colleagues' conclusion, namely that many individuals escape from a history of early sexual abuse with few or no long-term psychopathological consequences, appears to hold up well (Rind, Bauserman, & Tromovitch, 2002; Ulrich, Randolph, & Acheson, 2006).

Nor is there evidence that survivors of child sexual abuse exhibit a unique profile of personality traits. In a 1993 review, Kathleen Kendall-Tackett and her co-authors found no evidence for the so-called "signature" of sexual abuse. Although some sexually abused individuals suffered from psychological problems in adulthood, no consistent pattern of specific symptoms emerged across abuse victims (Kendall-Tackett, Williams, & Finkelhor, 2003). Instead, different victims typically experienced very different symptoms.

Research calls into question other widely accepted claims regarding sexual abuse victims. For example, a 2003 article by David Skuse and his colleagues found only weak evidence for the oft-cited "cycle of child sexual abuse," the popular belief that the abused typically become abusers themselves. Slightly less than one eighth of their sample of 224 men who'd been sexually abused in childhood became sexual molesters as adults. Because the rate of sexual molesters among adults without a sexual abuse history was 1 in 20 in their sample, Skuse and co-authors' findings raise the possibility that early abuse increases one's risk of becoming an adult abuser. But their findings indicate that the cycle of abuse isn't close to being inevitable (Salter et al., 2003).

Perhaps not surprisingly, many therapists reacted to all of these findings, especially those of Rind and his colleagues, with disbelief. The claim that many child sexual abuse victims lead normal adult lives didn't jibe with their clinical experiences.

In attempting to explain this wide gulf between clinical perception and scientific reality, selection bias emerges as a major suspect. Because almost all individuals whom clinicians see in their everyday practices are distressed, including those who've been sexually abused, clinicians can be seduced into perceiving an illusory correlation (see *Introduction*, p. 12) between child sexual abuse and psychopathology (Chapman & Chapman, 1967; Cohen & Cohen, 1984). But this conclusion is almost certainly a consequence of the fact that most clinicians have minimal access to two crucial cells of "The Great Fourfold Table of Life," namely, those cells consisting of sexually abused and non-abused individuals

---

Mythbusting: A Closer Look

Underestimating Childhood Resilience

The research we've reviewed on child sexual abuse and later psycho-pathology imparts a valuable but often unappreciated lesson: Most children are resilient in the face of stressors (Bonanno, 2004; Garmezy, Masten, & Tellegen, 1984). Popular psychology has underestimated child-hood resilience, often portraying children as delicate creatures who are prone to "crack" when confronted with stressful events (Sommers & Satel, 2005). Yet this "myth of childhood fragility" (Paris, 2000) runs counter to scientific evidence.

For example, on July 15, 1976, 26 schoolchildren ranging in age from 5 to 14 were victims of a nightmarish kidnapping in Chowchilla, California. Along with their bus driver, they were taken hostage on a school bus for 11 hours and buried underground in a van for 16 hours. There, they managed to breathe through a few small air vents. Remarkably, the children and driver managed to escape, and all survived without injury. When found, most of the children were in shock, and some had soiled themselves. Two years later, although most were haunted by memories of the incident, virtually all were well adjusted (Terr, 1983).

To take a second example, much of the popular psychology literature informs us that divorce almost always exacts a serious long-run emotional toll on children. One website dealing with divorce says that "children really aren't 'resilient'" and that "divorce leaves children to struggle for a life-time with the residue of a decision their parents made" (Meyer, 2008). On September 25, 2000, *Time* magazine lent credibility to these claims with a cover story entitled "What Divorce Does to Kids," accompanied by the ominous warning that "New research says the long-term damage is worse than you thought." This story was sparked by a 25-year investigation by Judith Wallerstein (1989), who tracked a group of 60 divorced families in California. Wallerstein reported that although children in these families initially seemed to recover from their parents' divorces, the effects of divorce were subtle and enduring. Many years later, these children experienced difficulties with forming stable romantic relationships and establishing career goals. Yet Wallerstein's study didn't include a control group of families in which one or both parents had been separated from their children for reasons other than divorce, such as accidental death. As a result, her findings may reflect the effects of any kind of stressful disruption in the family rather than divorce itself.

In fact, most better-designed studies show that although children almost always find divorce stressful, the bulk of them survive divorces without much, if any, long-term psychological damage (Hetherington, Cox, & Cox, 1985). By and large, these investigations show that 75% to 85% of children are coping quite well in the wake of their parents' divorces (Hetherington & Kelly, 2002). Moreover, when parents experience severe conflict prior to the divorce, the apparent adverse effects of divorce appear to be minimal (Amato & Booth, 1997; Rutter, 1972). That's probably because children find the divorce to be a welcome escape from their parents' bitter arguing.

who do *not* experience psychological problems (again see *Introduction*, p. 12). If clinicians interacted in therapy with non-distressed individuals as much as they do with their distressed clients, they'd probably find that accounts of childhood sexual abuse would turn up just about as often.

Myth # 35 People's Responses to Inkblots Tell Us a Great Deal about Their Personalities

Is an inkblot always just an inkblot? Or can it be something far more, perhaps a secret passageway to hidden personality traits and psychological disorders?

The most familiar version of the inkblot test, developed by Swiss psychiatrist Hermann Rorschach, figures prominently in popular culture. Andy Warhol painted a series of mammoth inkblots inspired by the Rorschach Inkblot Test, and Mattel markets a game called "Thinkblot," which encourages players to generate creative responses to amoeboid black-and-white shapes. A successful rock band even calls itself "Rorschach Test." The 2009 film, *Watchmen*, stars a character named Rorschach, who sports a mask consisting of an inkblot.

We can trace the Rorschach Inkblot Test (often known simply as "The Rorschach") to Hermann Rorschach's dabblings with inkblots in childhood. Rorschach, a failed artist, apparently received the inspiration for the test that later bore his name from a popular European parlor game. First published in 1921, the Rorschach consists of 10 symmetrical inkblots, 5 in black and white, 5 containing color. Readers can view an inkblot similar to the Rorschach inkblots in Figure 8.1 (because of concerns about influencing test responses, the Rorschach's publisher cautions against reproducing the actual blots).

But the Rorschach is much more than an icon of popular culture. It's a cherished tool of clinicians, many of whom believe it can penetrate into the deepest and darkest recesses of the unconscious. In the 1940s and 1950s, psychologists Lawrence Frank and Bruno Klopfer referred to the Rorschach as a "psychological X-ray," and over half a century later many clinicians still regard it as an essential means of unearthing psychological conflicts (Wood, Nezworski, Lilienfeld, & Garb, 2003). One estimate places the number of Rorschach tests administered per year at 6 million worldwide (Sutherland, 1992). A 1995 survey of members of the American Psychological Association revealed that 82% of clinical psychologists use the Rorschach at least occasionally in their practice

Figure 8.1 A blot similar to the one of the 10 Rorschach inkblots (the test's publisher strongly discourages reproduction of the actual blots). According to Rorschach proponents, different kinds of responses are indicative of oppositionality, obsessiveness, and a host of other personality traits.
Source: Anastasi & Urbina (1997), p. 413.

and that 43% use it frequently or all of the time (Watkins, Campbell, Nieberding, & Hallmark, 1995). In 1998, the American Psychological Association's Board of Professional Affairs hailed the Rorschach as "perhaps the single most powerful psychometric instrument ever envisioned" (American Psychological Association Board of Professional Affairs, 1998, p. 392). Perhaps not surprisingly, 74% of undergraduates in one survey said that the Rorschach and closely related tests are helpful in psychiatric diagnosis (Lenz, Ek, & Mills, 2009).

The Rorschach is merely one of hundreds of *projective techniques*, most of which consist of ambiguous stimuli that clinicians ask respondents to interpret. Psychologists refer to these methods as "projective" because they assume that respondents project key aspects of their personalities onto ambiguous stimuli in the process of making sense of them. Using a kind of psychological reverse-engineering, test interpreters work backwards to try to infer respondents' personality traits. One of the first such techniques was the Cloud Picture Test developed around the turn of the century by German psychologist Wilhelm Stern, which asks respondents to report what they see in cloud-like images (Aiken, 1996; Lilienfeld, 1999). There's even a variant of the Rorschach test for blind individuals, the Cypress Knee Projective Technique, which asks respondents to place their hands around the knotty outgrowths of cypress tree roots and describe their mental imagery (Kerman, 1959).

Researchers subjected the Rorschach to a steady drumbeat of scientific criticism from the 1940s through the 1970s. They argued that the Rorschach was subjective in its scoring and interpretation and that almost none of its supposed personality correlates held up in careful research. One author, educational psychologist Arthur Jensen, commented in 1965 that "the rate of scientific progress in clinical psychology might well be measured by the speed and thoroughness with which it gets over the Rorschach" (Jensen, 1965, p. 509).

The modern version of the Rorschach, the "Comprehensive System" (CS) developed by psychologist John Exner in the 1974, was a heroic effort to rescue the Rorschach from a barrage of scientific attacks. The CS provides detailed rules for scoring and interpretation and yields over 100 indices that purportedly measure almost every imaginable feature of personality (Exner, 1974). For example, responses (see Figure 8.1 for this and the examples to follow) involving reflections ("I see a poodle looking at itself in the mirror") supposedly reflect narcissism. After all, the word narcissism derives from the Greek mythical character Narcissus, who fell in love with his reflection in the water. Responses involving unusual details ("That tiny speck of ink on the right part of the blot looks like a piece of dust") ostensibly indicate obsessiveness. And responses to the white space nestled within the blots rather than to the blots themselves ("That white area over there looks like a hand broom") ostensibly indicate rebelliousness toward authority.

Yet controlled research offers virtually no support for these assertions. James Wood and his colleagues found that the overwhelming majority of Rorschach scores are essentially unrelated to personality traits. The lone possible exception is dependency (Bornstein, 1996), which a few researchers have found to be associated with a higher than expected number of responses involving mouths and food (orthodox Freudians, who believe that excessive gratification during the oral stage of infancy produces dependency, would surely delight in this finding). Nor is the Rorschach especially useful for diagnostic purposes: Rorschach scores are negligibly related to clinical depression, anxiety disorders, or antisocial personality disorder, a condition marked by a history of criminal and irresponsible behaviors (Wood, Lilienfeld, Garb, & Nezworski, 2000).

Nevertheless, the Rorschach does a serviceable job of detecting conditions marked by thinking disturbances, such as schizophrenia and bipolar disorder (once known as manic depression) (Lilienfeld, Wood, & Garb, 2001). This fact isn't terribly surprising, because people who produce bizarre responses to inkblots (for example, "It looks like a giraffe's head exploding inside of a flying saucer" in response to the card in Figure 8.1) are more likely than other people to suffer from disordered thoughts. As psychologist Robyn Dawes (1994) noted, the use of the Rorschach for detecting thought disorder is actually *non-projective* in that it relies on the extent to which respondents *don't* perceive certain shapes in inkblots.

Moreover, the evidence that the Rorschach contributes to the detection of psychological characteristics above and beyond simpler methods —what psychologists call "incremental validity"—is weak. In fact, a few studies demonstrate that when clinicians who already have access to questionnaire or life history information examine Rorschach data, their predictive accuracy *decreases*. This is probably because they place excess weight on information derived from the Rorschach, which tends to be less valid than the data derived from the other sources (Garb, 1998; Lilienfeld et al., 2001, 2006).

Why is the Rorschach still enormously popular despite the meager evidence for its clinical utility? The phenomenon of illusory correlation (see *Introduction*, p. 12) probably contributes this test's mystique. When researchers have asked participants to peruse Rorschach protocols, these participants consistently perceive certain Rorschach indicators as linked to certain personality traits *even when the pairing of Rorschach indicators with personality traits in the protocols is entirely random* (Chapman & Chapman, 1969). In many cases, these participants are relying excessively on the representativeness heuristic (see *Introduction*, p. 15), erroneously leading them to conclude that certain Rorschach indicators are valid for detecting personality characteristics. For example, they may assume incorrectly that inkblot responses that contain morbid content, such as skeletons or dead bodies, are strongly associated with certain traits, such as depression, with which they share a superficial resemblance. Studies demonstrate that clinicians are vulnerable to the same mirages (Chapman & Chapman, 1969).

Second, studies show that the CS tends to make normal individuals appear disturbed. A 1999 study by Thomas Shaffer and his colleagues revealed that a sample of normal individuals comprising college students and blood bank volunteers obtained grossly pathological scores on the Rorschach. For example, 1 in 6 scored in the pathological range on the Rorschach Schizophrenia Index, purportedly a measure of schizophrenia (Shaffer, Erdberg, & Haroian, 1999). Paradoxically, the Rorschach's tendency to overpathologize individuals can mislead clinicians into concluding that it possesses remarkably sensitive diagnostic powers. Not infrequently, a clinician will find that a respondent produces normal results on questionnaires, but abnormal results on the Rorschach. The clinician may conclude from this discrepancy that the Rorschach is a "deep" test that uncovers hidden psychological disturbances that more "superficial" tests miss. More likely, the clinician is merely being fooled into perceiving psychopathology in its absence (Wood, Nezworski, Garb, & Lilienfeld, 2001).

So, returning to the question posed at the outset of this piece: To paraphrase Sigmund Freud, sometimes an inkblot *is* just an inkblot.

Myth # 36 Our Handwriting Reveals Our Personality Traits

"Cross your T's and dot your I's" is the universal refrain of teachers charged with the task of transforming their students' messy scribbles into legible penmanship. For many children, learning to write their name in cursive is a significant milestone. Yet pupils' handwriting somehow ends up being as distinctive as their fingerprints or earlobes. Therefore, it seems plausible that handwriting analysis—known as *graphology*—could help to reveal our psychological make-up.

Graphology is merely one branch of the group of pseudoscientific practices known as "character reading." At various times, character readers have assumed that they could acquire a window on our psychological make-up by interpreting the features of the face (physiognomy), creases on the hand (palmistry), bumps on the head (phrenology), features of the belly button (omphalomancy), patterns of forehead wrinkles (metoposcopy), patterns on tea leaves (tasseography), directions of light rays reflected from fingernails (onychomancy), or our favorite, the appearance of barley cakes (critomancy) (Carroll, 2003).

Graphologists have attracted legions of followers and persuaded much of the public that their craft is grounded in science. Until it went bankrupt recently, the Chicago-based International Graphoanalysis Society boasted a membership of about 10,000. Hundreds of graphologists have found gainful employment in Southern California, and graphology has even found a home in public schools. For example, in Vancouver, Canada, a graphologist claimed to have secretly identified actual and potential sexual molesters amidst the local teaching ranks. Many corporations, especially in Israel and some European countries, consult graphologists on personnel matters. Some financial institutions hire graphologists to determine whether applicants will prove to be trustworthy borrowers (Beyerstein & Beyerstein, 1992).

Graphology's modern history begins with the 17th century Italian physician, Camillo Baldi. Baldi inspired a group of Catholic clergy, among them the Abbé Jean-Hippolyte Michon, who coined the term "graphology" in 1875. Michon is the father of the "analytic" approach, which ascribes personality traits to writers based on specific writing "signs," such as the shapes or slants of letters. Michon's student, Crepieux-Jamin, broke with his mentor to found the "holistic" school. Rather than attending to individual elements of letters and lines, holists advocate an impressionistic approach in which the analyst intuits an overall "feel" for individuals' personalities on the basis of their writing. Although most modern graphologists embrace the analytic approach, many schools of graphology can't even agree on which signs are indicators of which traits. For instance, one well-known graphologist believes that a tendency to cross one's *t*s with whip-like lines indicates a sadistic personality, whereas another equally prominent analyst says that this style merely indicates a practical joker (there's no scientific evidence that either graphologist is right).

Proponents of the analytic approach claim to have identified hundreds of specific handwriting indicators of personality traits. Among them are little hooks on the letter *S*, which some graphologists claim reveal a willingness to snag others' belongings. Wide spacing between words supposedly denotes a tendency toward isolation. Writers whose sentences drift upward are optimists, whereas those whose lines sag downward are pessimists. Those who write with letters displaying different slants are unpredictable. Writers with large capital *I*s have big egos. A 2008 article in the *Los Angeles Times* claimed that then presidential candidate John McCain's tendency to sign his first name with letters slanted in opposing directions offered evidence of his "maverick" personality, whereas his opponent Barack Obama's tendency to shape his letters smoothly offered evidence of his flexibility (Iniquez, 2008). Perhaps our favorite is the claim that large, bulbous loops on *g*s, *y*s, and similar letters—ones that dangle below the lines—reveal a preoccupation with sex. Perhaps they do, although this preoccupation may lie more in the mind of the graphologist than of the writer (Beyerstein, 1992).

Some even embrace the bizarre claims of "graphotherapeutics," a New Age psychotherapy that claims to eliminate individuals' undesirable personality traits by removing problematic graphological signs from their writing. So, if you're a hopeless pessimist, you need do nothing more than start writing your sentences with an upward slant to change your attitude toward life.

Graphologists offer a variety of rationales for their practice; we'll examine the five most common of them here (Beyerstein & Beyerstein, 1992).

Writing is a form of expressive movement, so it should reflect our person-alities. Although research links a few global aspects of temperament to certain gestures, the kinds of characteristics loosely related to expressive body movements are far more general than the narrow traits graphologists claim to infer from writing. A general tendency to be irritable or domineering may be slightly correlated with body language, but the relationships are much too weak to allow us to draw conclusions about people's personalities.

Handwriting is brainwriting. True enough. Studies have shown that people's "footwriting" is similar to their handwriting (if you're skeptical, try signing your name on a piece of paper with a pencil stuck between the big toe and second toe of your preferred foot), suggesting that writing style is more a function of our brains than our limbs. Nevertheless, the fact that writing or, for that matter, sneezing and vomiting are controlled by the brain doesn't imply they're correlated with anything else the brain controls, such as personality traits.

Writing is individualized and personality is unique, so each must reflect the other. The fact that two attributes are idiosyncratic isn't grounds to conclude that they bear a specific relationship to one another. Faces are sufficiently different to serve as personal identification on a driver's license, but they say nothing about one's driving ability.

The police and courts use graphology, so it must be valid. This claim illustrates what logicians term the "bandwagon fallacy": If a belief is widespread, it must be correct. Of course, many convictions held by an overwhelming majority of people at some point in time, such as the belief that that the world is flat, have turned out to be just as flatly wrong. Moreover, much of graphology's undeserved positive reputation stems from the confusion of graphologists with questioned document examiners (QDEs). A QDE is a scientifically trained investigator who establishes for historians, collectors, or the courts the origins and authenticity of handwritten documents. QDEs pass judgment only on the probability that a given individual wrote the document in question, not on that individual's personality.

Personnel managers swear by graphologists' usefulness in selecting employees. Some do, but most don't. Furthermore, there are several reasons why managers may be falsely convinced of graphology's utility. First, graphologists often attend to many non-graphological clues that could point to the best candidate, even if they do so unintentionally. For instance, the contents of handwritten application letters are chock full of biographical information, some of which (like previous job history or a criminal record) can predict job performance. Second, for reasons of expense, employers rarely submit the scripts of all applicants to graphologists. Graphologists usually see the scripts of only short-listed applicants, those already selected using valid hiring criteria. Most people in this pool are already qualified for the job, and there's rarely an opportunity to determine whether the rejected applicants would have done as well or better.

Scientific tests of graphologists' ability to recognize job-relevant aptitudes are virtually unanimous. Well-controlled tests ask all participants to write the same sentences, and ask graphologists to offer personality judgments or behavioral predictions based on this writing. By asking all participants to transcribe the same sentences, researchers eliminate differences in content that could provide indirect cues to personality. In a thorough review, Richard Klimoski (1992) found that graphologists did no better than chance at predicting job performance. Geoffrey Dean (1992) conducted by far the most complete review of scientific tests of graphology. After performing a meta-analysis (see p. 32) over 200 studies, Dean found a clear failure on the part of graphologists to detect personality traits or forecast work performance.

Why are so many people convinced that graphology has merit? First, graphology appears compelling because it capitalizes on the representativeness heuristic (see *Introduction*, p. 15). We've already encountered claims that individuals whose sentences slant upward tend to be "uplifting" or optimistic. Another striking example is the assertion by some graphologists that people who cross their *t*s with the bar considerably above the stem are prone to daydreaming. Daydreamers, after all, seem to have their heads in the clouds.

Second, the assertions of graphologists can seem remarkably specific even when they're hopelessly vague. The mistaken sense that something profoundly personal has been revealed by a character reader stems from what Paul Meehl (1956) called the "The P. T. Barnum Effect," after the cynical circus entrepreneur who joked that he "liked to give a little something to everybody" in his acts. Researchers have discovered that most of us fall prey to this effect, which is the tendency of individuals to find statements that apply to just about everyone to be specific to them (Dickson & Kelly, 1985; Furnham & Schofield, 1987). The Barnum Effect works well because we're adept at finding meaning even in relatively meaningless information. In one study, participants rated descriptions about *someone else* generated by a certified graphologist as highly applicable to themselves, and just as applicable as Barnum statements crafted to be applicable to everyone.

Will future controlled research prove any kinder to graphology? Of course, it's always possible that some positive evidence will surface one day. But if the dismal scientific track record of graphology is any indication, we hope we can be forgiven for suggesting that the handwriting appears to be on the wall.

Chapter 8: Other Myths to Explore

Fiction	Fact
Astrology predicts people's personality traits at better than chance levels.	Astrology is useless for predicting people's personality traits.
People's drawings can tell us a great deal about their personalities.	Human figure drawing tests have low validity for detecting almost all normal and abnormal personality traits.
Positive self-affirmations ("I like myself") are a good way of boosting self-esteem.	Research suggests that positive affirmations are not especially helpful, particularly for people with low self-esteem.
Most people who were physically abused in childhood go to become abusers themselves (the "cycle of violence").	Most people who were physically abused as children don't become abusers as adults.

Fiction	Fact
There's strong evidence for the concept of "national character."	The evidence for "national character" stereotypes (such as the French are arrogant or the Germans rigid) is mixed and inconclusive.
Obese people are more cheerful ("jollier") than non-obese people.	There's little association between obesity and cheerfulness; in fact, most research suggests a slight positive association between obesity and depression.
Open-ended interviews are the best means of assessing personality.	Open-ended ("unstructured") interviews possess low or at best moderate validity for assessing personality, and tend to be less valid than structured interviews.
A clinician's number of years of experience using a personality test predicts his or her accuracy in clinical judgments from this test.	For most personality tests, number of years of experience in using the test is uncorrelated with accuracy.
More information is always preferable to less information when making diagnostic judgments.	In some cases, more assessment information leads to less accurate diagnostic judgments, because invalid assessment information can dilute the influence of valid information.
Anatomically correct dolls are a good way of determining whether a child was sexually abused.	Anatomically correct dolls misidentify large numbers of non-abused children as abused, because many non-abused children engage in sexualized doll play.

Sources and Suggested Readings

To explore these and other myths about personality, see Dean (1987); Furnham (1996); Garb (1998); Hines (2003); Jansen, Havermans, Nederkoorn, and Roofs (2008); Lilienfeld, Wood, and Garb (2000); McCrae and Terracciano (2006); Ruscio (2006).

9 SAD, MAD, AND BAD

Myths about Mental Illness

Psychiatric Labels Cause Harm by Stigmatizing People

How would you feel if your friends thought you had paranoid schizophrenia? David Rosenhan (1973b), a professor of psychology and law, posed this question as a means of suggesting that psychiatric diagnoses, or labels, are stigmatizing—meaning they cause us to view people who've received these labels negatively. He believed it self-evident that such labels as "paranoid schizophrenia" tainted patients with the stigma of mental illness, causing other people to treat them in prejudiced and even harmful ways. To reduce this stigma, Rosenhan argued that mental health professionals should avoid global diagnostic labels, such as "major depression," in favor of objective behavioral descriptions, like "looks sad," "cries a lot," and "walks and talks slowly."

In response, psychiatrist Robert Spitzer (1976) wondered whether this approach would really affect people's attitudes or behavior. He rephrased Rosenhan's question using behavioral terms rather than a diagnostic label: How would you feel if your colleagues thought that you had an unshakable but utterly false conviction that other people were out to harm you? Spitzer contended that the stigma of mental illness stems from people's reactions to aberrant thoughts and behaviors, such as paranoid delusions, not to the psychiatric diagnoses that professionals use to classify mental disorders. Who's right?

To many people, the answer to this question begins and ends with a famous paper by Rosenhan (1973a) entitled "On Being Sane in Insane Places." Eight mentally healthy individuals—including Rosenhan himself

—presented themselves to a total of 12 mental hospitals. According to plan, all pretended to exhibit mild anxiety and requested admission based on a supposed complaint of unusual auditory hallucinations, namely hearing voices that repeated the words "empty," "hollow," and "thud." Interestingly, all of these "pseudopatients" (fake patients) were admitted to the hospital: One was diagnosed with manic depression, the other 11 with schizophrenia. Once admitted, the pseudopatients stopped faking any symptoms of mental disorder. Aside from extensive note-taking for the purpose of data collection, the pseudopatients acted normally to see whether the hospital staff would discover their absence of illness and release them. Yet surprisingly, the pseudopatients were kept in the hospital for an average of 19 days, each with the same change in diagnosis. Their original condition was merely reclassified as "in remission," meaning "no longer displaying symptoms of illness." Rosenhan interpreted these findings to mean that mental health professionals can't distinguish normality from abnormality, because all patients retained their original diagnoses upon discharge.

The pseudopatients observed negligent and even abusive treatment of their fellow patients, much of which Rosenhan (1973a) attributed to the stigmatizing effects of labels. He claimed that "psychiatric diagnoses . . . carry with them personal, legal, and social stigmas" (p. 252) and cast patients in a hopeless light, as "the label sticks, a mask of inadequacy forever" (p. 257). Rosenhan concluded by conjecturing that "In a more benign environment, one that was less attached to global diagnosis, [the staff's] behaviors and judgments might have been even more benign and effective" (p. 257).

Rosenhan's study created a scientific and media sensation. In a flurry of comments on this article, scholars observed that Rosenhan (1973a) had used seriously flawed methodology, ignored relevant data, and reached unsound conclusions. In perhaps the most devastating critique, Spitzer (1976) contended that Rosenhan's own data ironically offered the best evidence against his claims. For example, recall that all 12 pseudopatients' discharge diagnoses were amended to "in remission." This change means that the abnormal behavior noted at intake was no longer present at discharge. Spitzer gathered data suggesting that "in remission" diagnoses were extremely rare, if not unheard of, in psychiatric hospitals. The fact that all 12 pseudopatients' diagnoses were changed in the same unusual way shows just how capably the staff recognized normal behavior when the pseudopatients stopped faking symptoms. As Spitzer noted, this fact counters Rosenhan's claim that mental health professionals can't distinguish normality from abnormality.

Even today, countless sources inform readers that psychiatric labels are stigmatizing and potentially harmful. A website sponsored by the U.S. Substance Abuse and Mental Health Services Administration (http://mentalhealth.samhsa.gov/publications/allpubs/SMA96-3118/default.asp) asserts that "labels lead to stigma" and that "words can be poison," listing "depressed, schizophrenic, manic, or hyperactive" as examples of hurtful labels. In a discussion of the dangers of diagnosis, sociologist Allan Horwitz and social worker Jerome Wakefield (2007) referred to the "vast evidence" that psychiatric diagnosis "leads to harmful stigma" (p. 23). Moreover, despite withering critiques, many scholarly texts still present Rosenhan's (1973a) study in an uncritical fashion. This study is among the most frequently cited studies in introductory psychology textbooks (Gorenflo & McConnell, 1991), has been reprinted in several edited books of classic readings in psychology (Heiner, 2008; Henslin, 2003; Kowalski & Leary, 2004), and has been cited in more than 1,100 journal articles (see also Ruscio, 2004). For example, in his widely used abnormal psychology text, Ronald Comer (2007) wrote that Rosenhan's study demonstrates "that the label 'schizophrenic' can itself have a negative effect not just on how people are viewed but on how they themselves feel and behave" (p. 432). In a lecture in the *Great Ideas of Psychology* audiotape series, psychologist Daniel Robinson (1997) told his listeners that "what Rosenhan's study made clear is that once one is diagnosed as being an X, one is going to be treated as an X . . . because the setting has established that you are an X, and you will be an X forever more."

Back in the 1970s, Spitzer had asked Rosenhan to provide access to his data to verify his conclusions. Granting access to data for an independent review by competent professionals is required by ethical standard 8.14 of the American Psychological Association (2002). Spitzer (1976) reported that Rosenhan agreed to provide the data once he completed a book about the study. But the book never materialized, and neither did Rosenhan's data. Thirty years later, writer Lauren Slater (2004) featured Rosenhan's work in a chapter of her book *Opening Skinner's Box: Great Psychological Experiments of the Twentieth Century.* She not only gave readers the impression that Rosenhan's conclusions were valid, but that she'd replicated them in a follow-up study in which she presented herself as a pseudopatient at various mental hospitals: "Let me tell you, I tried this experiment. I actually did it" (Slater, 2004, p. 89). Spitzer and several other prominent mental health researchers repeatedly asked Slater to provide copies of records from her hospital encounters, but she didn't comply. Only after Spitzer and his colleagues (Spitzer, Lilienfeld, & Miller, 2005) published a critique did Slater (2005) write that "I never did such a study; it simply does not exist" (p. 743). To this day, it's not clear whether Slater's claimed replication ever took place.

Even though Rosenhan and Slater never provided data for independent scientific review, many published studies have teased apart the influence of psychiatric diagnoses and aberrant behaviors on the stigma of mental illness. Some investigators have confounded these sources of evidence—John Ruscio (2004) discussed fatal flaws in the widely cited studies of Ellen Langer and Robert Abelson (1974) and Maurice Temerlin (1968)—but researchers have conducted a number of better-controlled experiments. For example, the written description of a target individual can include a psychiatric diagnosis (such as bipolar disorder), a behavioral description (such as alternating periods of clinically elevated and depressed moods), both, or neither. By varying labels and behaviors independently, investigators can determine how these two factors influence judgments about people with mental illnesses. One early review led its authors to conclude that "It seems likely that any rejection directed towards psychiatric patients comes from their aberrant behavior rather than from the label that has been applied to them" (Lehmann, Joy, Kreisman, & Simmens, 1976, p. 332). A number of later studies support this conclusion (Ruscio, 2004).

Even though a substantial body of evidence indicates that psychiatric labels themselves don't cause harm, the belief that diagnoses are responsible for the stigma associated with mental illness persists. Because the stigma itself is undeniably real, psychiatric diagnoses provide an easy target for the understandable frustrations experienced by those who suffer from mental illness and those who care for them. Yet the argument that diagnoses themselves, rather than the behaviors associated with them, produce this stigma was never plausible to begin with. First, let's consider the fact that the stigma of mental illness substantially predates all psychiatric classification systems. The *Diagnostic and Statistical Manual of Mental Disorders* (*DSM*), which is used by mental health practitioners around the world, was originally published in 1952, and the most recent edition was published in 2000 (American Psychiatric Association, 2000). Even though less formal classifications existed for a few decades prior to the first *DSM*, the stigma of mental illness has been present for centuries.

Further problems for the argument that diagnoses themselves cause stigma are that diagnoses are confidential and one needn't be diagnosed by a mental health professional to be stigmatized. Unless people care to share their formal diagnoses, others won't even know what these diagnoses are. For example, once released from mental hospitals, the pseudopatients in Rosenhan's (1973a) study would have had to tell people they'd been diagnosed with schizophrenia for anyone to know this information. Why would people concerned about being stigmatized tell others their diagnoses? In addition to or instead of the direct observation of aberrant behaviors, a plausible source of the stigma of mental illness is knowledge that someone has visited a mental health practitioner. It's not uncommon to assume that anyone who sees a therapist must suffer from a mental disorder, and laypersons informally label each other all the time using derogatory terms like "crazy," "loony," or "nuts." This process of "informal labeling," as some have called it, is often sufficient to give rise to the stigma associated with mental illness, whether or not one actually receives a psychiatric diagnosis or shares it with others (Gove, 1982).

Psychiatric diagnoses play important roles that would be difficult to fulfill if we abandoned them. Diagnoses are essential for many purposes, including communication among mental health professionals; the coordination of research activities around the world; the provision of mental health services; reimbursement from insurance companies; and connecting patients to the most effective treatments. Certainly, no one believes that the *DSM* is perfect. We should make every effort to improve the existing psychiatric classification system, but attacking it on the unsupported grounds that diagnoses are stigmatizing is counterproductive.

Suppose that people in your life observed that you had an unshakable but utterly false conviction that everybody was out to harm you. It's likely that any stigma associated with your mental illness would exist regardless of whether anybody knew you'd been diagnosed with paranoid schizophrenia. Rather than blaming stigma on psychiatric labels, Patrick Corrigan and David Penn (1999) discussed a number of more constructive ways to reduce stigma, including community-based educational and contact-oriented programs and compassionately conveying diagnoses in the context of humane and effective treatments.

Furthermore, several studies demonstrate that diagnostic labels can actually exert positive effects on stigma, probably because they provide observers with explanations for otherwise puzzling behaviors. In one study, peers rated essays written by children diagnosed with attention-deficit/hyperactivity disorders more positively than those written by non-diagnosed children (Cornez-Ruiz & Hendricks, 1993). In another study, adults rated mentally retarded children more favorably when they received a diagnostic label than when they didn't (Seitz & Geske, 1976). Similarly, Michelle Wood and Marta Valdez-Menchaca (1996) found positive effects of labeling children with expressive language disorder and suggested that a diagnostic label "may cause teachers to adopt a more supportive attitude toward the child . . . labeling can provide a more informative context in which to evaluate the relative strengths and weaknesses of a child with disabilities" (p. 587).

The history of clinical psychology and psychiatry reveals that as we come to better understand mental illnesses and as their treatment becomes more effective, stigma subsides. In the meantime, when individuals with mental illness experience stigma we should be careful not to place the blame where it doesn't belong—namely, on psychiatric diagnoses that can help to identify the source of their suffering.

Myth #38   Only Deeply Depressed People Commit Suicide

Before reading on, close your eyes and picture a suicidal person. What do you see?

Odds are you'll imagine a profoundly depressed individual, perhaps crying uncontrollably, contemplating whether life is worth living. There's certainly a large grain of truth to this description: Clinical depression —often called "major depression"—is a powerful predictor of suicide attempts and completions (Cheng, Chen, Chen, & Jenkins, 2000; Coppen, 1994; Harwitz & Ravizza, 2000; Moscicki, 1997). Indeed, the risk of suicide in the lifetime of a person with major depression is about 6% (Inskip, Harris, & Barracough, 1998). This percentage is considerably lower than the 15% figure that had long been previously accepted (Guze & Robins, 1970), but still far higher than the approximately 1% risk of suicide in the lifetime of a person drawn from the general population. Although friends, relatives, and loved ones sometimes think of depression as merely as a "passing phase," there's no doubt that it's often a life-threatening condition.

Yet many people who are aware of the link between depression and suicide assume that *only* depressed people take their own lives. For example, the director of a state suicide prevention foundation told a reporter "I didn't know he was depressed" after she learned of her husband's unexpected suicide (http://blog.cleveland.com/health/2008/03/boomers_suicide_trend_continue.html). In one study of 331 undergraduates enrolled in introductory psychology courses, 43% responded "True" to the item, "If assessed by a psychiatrist, everyone who commits suicide would be diagnosed as depressed" (Hubbard & McIntosh, 1992). A later study of undergraduate education majors revealed lower numbers, but still found that 25% endorsed this item (MacDonald, 2007).

Many people are therefore surprised to learn that people who aren't deeply depressed sometimes kill themselves. The belief that only clinically depressed people commit suicide is potentially dangerous, because friends, relatives, and significant others may assume erroneously that a person without serious depressive symptoms is "safe" and therefore doesn't require immediate psychological attention. Yet research shows that between 13% and 41% (depending on the investigation) of people who commit suicide don't meet diagnostic criteria for major depression. About 10% have diagnoses of either schizophrenia or substance use disorders, like alcoholism (Rihmer, 2007). In addition to depression, schizophrenia, and substance use disorders, other diagnoses significantly associated with suicide attempts, completions, or both are:

- *panic disorder* (Friedman, Jones, Chernen, & Barlow, 1992), a condition marked by sudden and unexpected surges of intense terror;
- *social phobia* (Schneier, Johnson, Hornig, Liebowitz, & Weissman, 1992), a condition marked by an extreme fear of situations that could be embarrassing or humiliating, like speaking or performing in public;
- *borderline personality disorder* (Soloff, Lynch, Kelly, Malone, & Mann, 2000), a condition marked by dramatic instability in mood, interpersonal relationships, impulse control, and identity;
- *antisocial personality disorder* (Douglas et al., in press), a condition marked by a longstanding history of irresponsible and often illegal behavior (see Myth #35);
- *gender identity disorder* (di Ceglie, 2000), a condition marked by extreme feelings of discomfort with one's gender, sometimes to the point of feeling "trapped" in the wrong body (American Psychiatric Association, 2000).

Still, there's some controversy regarding the relation of these conditions to suicide attempts and completions, because some of them are frequently "comorbid" with major depression, meaning they often co-occur with major depression within people. So at least some of the apparent association of these conditions with suicidal behavior may be due to their overlap with depression (Cox, Direnfeld, Swinson, & Norton, 1994; Hornig & McNally, 1995). Still, a number of researchers have found that even after accounting for depressive symptoms, at least some of these conditions still predict suicidal behavior. For example, patients with borderline personality disorder, either with or without depression, are about twice as likely to attempt suicide as patients with depression alone

(Kelly, Soloff, Lynch, Haas, & Mann, 2000). The evidence concerning whether panic disorder alone—that is, without comorbid depression—predicts suicide is more mixed (Vickers & McNally, 2004; Weissman et al., 1989).

For reasons that are mysterious, about 5–10% of people who commit suicide have no diagnosable mental disorder at all (Solomon, 2001). At least some of these individuals probably suffer from "subthreshold" symptoms of one or more mental disorders, meaning they barely fall short of meeting the formal diagnostic criteria for these conditions. But an undetermined number probably commit what some have termed "rational suicide," a carefully considered decision to end one's life in the face of terminal illness or severe and untreatable pain (Kleespies, Hughes, & Gallacher, 2000; Werth & Cobia, 1995).

There are other reasons to believe that depression isn't necessarily the only, or even most important, predictor of suicide. First, in some studies hopelessness has been a better predictor of suicide than depression itself (Beck, Brown, & Steer, 1989; Beck, Kovacs, & Weissman, 1975; Wetzel, 1976). That's probably because people are most likely to kill themselves when they see no means of escape from their psychological agony. Second, although depression actually tends to *decrease* in old age (see Myth #9), the rates of suicide *increase* sharply in old age, especially among men (Joiner, 2005). One likely reason for the striking discrepancy between the rates of depression and the rates of suicide with age is that the elderly are medically weakened and therefore less likely to survive suicide attempts, such as poisoning, than younger people. Nevertheless, another reason is that suicide attempts among the elderly tend to be more serious in intent (Draper, 1996). For example, compared with younger people, the elderly are more likely to use lethal means of attempting suicide, such as shooting themselves in the head (Frierson, 1991).

This discussion leads us to a closely related potential myth: Many people assume that the risk for suicide decreases as a severe depression lifts. In one survey of undergraduates, 53% responded "False" to the statement, "A time of high suicide risk in depression is when the person begins to improve" (Hubbard & McIntosh, 1992, p. 164). Yet there's actually evidence that suicide risk may sometimes *increase* as depression lifts (Isaacson & Rich, 1997; Keith-Spiegel & Spiegel, 1967; Meehl, 1973), perhaps because severely depressed people begin to experience a return of energy as they improve (Shea, 1998). During this time interval they may be in a hazardous "window" during which they're still depressed yet now possess sufficient energy to carry out a suicide attempt.

Nevertheless, the research support for this claim is mixed, because depressed patients who begin to experience improved mood but don't fully recover may be more suicidal to begin with than other depressed patients (Joiner, Pettit, & Rudd, 2004).

So improvement in mood may not *cause* increased suicide risk, although the issue isn't resolved. Still, it's safe to say that one should never assume that a deeply depressed person is "out of the woods" once his or her mood begins to brighten.

Myth #39 People with Schizophrenia Have Multiple Personalities

"Today, I'm feeling schizophrenic—of two minds, if you like."

"Most philosophers have a schizophrenic attitude toward the history of science."

"We face a dangerously schizophrenic approach to educating our young."

"There is, of course, an easy answer for this seeming moral schizophrenia: the distance between the principles and the policy . . . between the war on terror and the war in Iraq" (quotation from a journalist criticizing President George W. Bush's approach to the war in Iraq).

These quotations, pulled from various Internet sites, reflect a prevalent misconception, namely, that schizophrenia is the same thing as "split personality" or "multiple personality disorder." A popular bumper sticker and key chain even reads: "I was schizophrenic once, but we're better now"; another bumper sticker reads "I used to be a schizophrenic until they cured me—now I'm just lonely."

One prominent introductory psychology textbook goes so far as to say that "schizophrenia is probably the most misused psychological term in existence" (Carlson, 1990, p. 453). As this and other textbooks note, schizophrenia differs sharply from the diagnosis of *dissociative identity disorder* (DID), once known as multiple personality disorder (American Psychiatric Association, 2000). Unlike people with schizophrenia, people with DID supposedly harbor two or more distinct "alters"—personalities or personality states—within them at the same time, although this claim is scientifically controversial (Lilienfeld & Lynn, 2003). One familiar example of DID is the so-called "split personality," in which two alters, often opposite to each other in their personality traits, coexist. In the split personality, one alter might be shy and retiring, the other outgoing and flamboyant. Robert Louis Stevenson's classic 1886 novel, *The Strange Case of Dr. Jekyll and Mr. Hyde*, is probably the best-known illustration of the split personality in popular literature.

Nevertheless, many psychologists find the assertion that DID patients possess entirely distinct and fully formed personalities to be doubtful (Ross, 1990; Spiegel, 1993). It's far more likely that these patients are displaying different, but exaggerated, aspects of a single personality (Lilienfeld & Lynn, 2003).

Even some articles in scientific journals confuse schizophrenia with DID. One recent article published in a medical journal featured the subtitle *The dermatologist's schizophrenic attitude toward pigmented lesions* and went on to argue that although dermatologists have been on the forefront of educating the public about risk factors for skin cancer, many ignore patients' concerns about their skin blemishes (Dummer, 2003). An article entitled *Recent developments in the genetics of schizophrenia*, which appeared in a journal devoted to the genetics of brain disorders, stated that "Schizophrenia, which is also called 'split personality,' is a complex and multifactorial mental disorder with variable clinical manifestations" (Shastry, 1999, p. 149).

The schizophrenia–multiple personality misconception is surprisingly widespread. In one survey, 77% of students enrolled in introductory psychology courses endorsed the view that "a schizophrenic is someone with a split personality" (Vaughan, 1977, p. 139). Later studies found this number to be a bit lower—about 50% among college students, 40% among police officers, and nearly 50% among people in the community (Stuart & Arboleda-Florez, 2001; Wahl, 1987).

This misconception has also found its way into popular culture. The 2000 comedy film, *Me, Myself, and Irene*, starring Jim Carrey, features a man supposedly suffering from schizophrenia. Yet he actually suffers from a split personality, with one personality (Charlie) who's mellow and another (Hank) who's aggressive. In the film, Carrey's character switches unpredictably from "gentle" to "mental." After the NBC show, *My Own Worst Enemy*, starring Christian Slater as a spy with a split personality, debuted in October of 2008, numerous television critics erroneously referred to Slater's character as a schizophrenic (Perigard, 2008). The toy industry has contributed to the confusion too: one of G. I. Joe's action-figure enemies goes by the fear-inspiring name of Zartan, whom the toy makers describe as an "extreme paranoid schizophrenic" who "grows into various multiple personalities" (Wahl, 1997). Unfortunately, few articles on schizophrenia in popular magazines even discuss the confusion between schizophrenia and DID (Wahl, Borostovik, & Rieppi, 1995), making it difficult for the public to comprehend the difference.

The schizophrenia–DID myth almost surely stems in part from confusion in terminology. Swiss psychiatrist Eugen Bleuler coined the term "schizophrenia," meaning "split mind," in 1911. Many laypersons, and even some psychologists, soon misinterpreted Bleuler's definition. By schizophrenia, Bleuler (1911) meant that people afflicted with this serious condition suffer from a "splitting" both within and between their psychological functions, especially their emotion and thinking. For most of us, what we feel at one moment corresponds to what we feel at the next, and what we think at one moment corresponds to what we think at the next. If we feel sad at one moment, we often tend to feel sad a moment later; if we think sad thoughts at one moment, we often tend to think sad thoughts a moment later. In addition, what we feel at one moment usually corresponds to what we think at that moment; if we're feeling sad, we tend to think sad thoughts, and vice versa. Yet in schizophrenia, all of these linkages are frequently ruptured.

As Bleuler observed, people with schizophrenia don't harbor more than one coexisting personality; they possess a single personality that's been splintered or shattered (Arieti, 1968). In modern psychological and psychiatric lingo, schizophrenia is a severe psychotic disorder marked by a dramatic disruption in reality (American Psychiatric Association, 2000). People with this condition typically suffer from confused thinking and unpredictable moods, and often experience delusions (fixed false beliefs, like believing that one is being followed) and hallucinations (sensory experiences in the absence of any actual sensory stimulus, like hearing voices).

Ironically, the first misuse of schizophrenia as multiple personality in the popular press may have been by a prominent psychologist (McNally, 2007). In 1916, a *Washington Post* journalist described an interview with G. Stanley Hall, then a faculty member at the Johns Hopkins University and the first president of the American Psychological Association. "Schizophrenia," Dr. Hall told the reporter, "is a term much used by psychologists to describe a divided mind, of which the Jekyll–Hyde personality is one type" ("He calls it schizophrenia," p. A5). Only a few years later, the confusion between schizophrenia and multiple personality in popular culture proliferated, although the extent to which Hall's quotation fostered this confusion is unclear (Holzinger, Angermeyer, & Matschinger, 1998; McNally, 2007). By 1933, this confusion had even found its way into a dictionary article by well-known author T. S. Elliott, who wrote that "For a poet to be also a philosopher he would have to virtually be two men: I cannot think of any example of this thorough schizophrenia" (Turner, 1995, p. 350).

But should any of this matter? If people misuse the term schizophrenia, should we care? Regrettably, many people in the general public don't appreciate the fact that schizophrenia is often a profoundly disabling condition associated with a heightened risk for suicide, clinical depression, anxiety disorders, substance abuse, unemployment, homelessness, and other serious complications (American Psychiatric Association, 2000; Gottesman, 1991). Nor do many laypersons appreciate the often devastating effects of schizophrenia on family members, friends, and loved ones. Trivializing this condition, as do many Hollywood films, can lead us to underestimate its severity and minimize affected individuals' urgent need for effective treatment (Wahl, 1997). As psychologist Irving Gottesman (1991) noted, "everyday misuse of the terms schizophrenia or schizophrenic to refer to the foreign policy of the United States, the stock market, or any other disconfirmation of one's expectations does an injustice to the enormity of the public health problems and profound suffering associated with this most puzzling disorder of the human mind" (p. 8). Words matter.

Myth #40 Adult Children of Alcoholics Display a Distinctive Profile of Symptoms

Imagine that you've just seen a psychologist for an initial evaluation. You've been feeling out of sorts of late, and have been dissatisfied with your relationships, friendships, and job. "What's causing all of this?" you wonder. After keeping you waiting for a few anxious minutes in the waiting room, the psychologist calls you in to his office and asks you to sit down. He informs you that the results of his tests reveal that you're suffering from the following problems:

- Low self-esteem
- Shame and guilt
- Tendency to assume too much responsibility for others at certain times, and too little at other times
- Need for approval from others

- Difficulties with intimacy
- Excessive loyalty to others
- Feelings of powerlessness
- Problems with impulse control

What does this all mean, you ask sheepishly? The psychologist reassures you that these symptoms are entirely typical of someone with your family history. As the adult child of an alcoholic, he proclaims confidently, these problems are entirely to be expected. You breathe a sigh of relief, comforted by the realization that many of your previously inexplicable emotional difficulties stem from your father's alcoholism. Moreover, if you're totally honest with yourself, you're forced to admit that this personality profile fits you to a T.

Your psychologist's "diagnosis" is well in keeping with a great deal of popular literature. The symptoms listed above, along with a few others, comprise what's commonly believed to be a specific personality "profile" found among adult children of alcoholics (ACOAs) (Logue, Sher, & Frensch, 1992).

The ACOA symptom profile is one of the most firmly entrenched concepts in all of folk psychology. Over 220,000 websites contain the phrase "adult children of alcoholics," and hundreds of them advertise self-help groups and therapy programs intended to assist individuals with ACOA personality features. Such popular books as Wayne Kristberg's (1986) *The Adult Children of Alcoholics Syndrome*, Janet Woititz's (1983) *Adult Children of Alcoholics*, and Robert Ackerman's (2002) *Perfect Daughters* outline the hallmarks of the ACOA syndrome and describe techniques for alleviating or compensating for these problematic traits. Several widely publicized books have even attempted to account for the seemingly inexplicable behaviors of America's most famous ACOA, former U.S. President Bill Clinton, in terms of the ACOA profile (Fick, 1998). For example, David Maraniss's (1998) *The Clinton Enigma* attributed Clinton's notorious sexual escapades to the impulse control problems of ACOAs, and his intense political ambitions to the overpowering desire of ACOAs to solve others' problems.

When investigators have subjected the research literature on ACOAs to careful scrutiny, however, scientific support for this profile has evaporated. Kenneth Sher (1991) reviewed the major published studies on the personality characteristics of ACOAs and found surprisingly weak support for the ACOA syndrome. On average, children of alcoholics do exhibit some personality differences from children of nonalcoholics. For example, they tend to be somewhat more high-strung, outgoing, and prone to risk-taking than other individuals (Tarter, Alterman, & Edwards, 1985). Nevertheless, none of these differences map directly onto the standard ACOA profile, and most of the other features of the profile don't distinguish ACOAs from non-ACOAs.

In addition, there's little or no evidence that ACOAs display higher levels of "codependent" personality traits—that is, traits related to a tendency to help (or "enable") people who are dependent on alcohol or other substances—than do non-ACOAs, *The Oprah Winfrey Show* and many other popular TV programs notwithstanding. Nevertheless, ACOAs are significantly more likely than non-ACOA's to *label* themselves as codependent, perhaps because they've read or heard in popular psychology sources that ACOAs are often codependent (George, La Marr, Barrett, & McKinnon, 1999).

A 1992 study by Sher and two collaborators, Mary Beth Logue and Peter Frensch, sheds further light on the ACOA syndrome. They demonstrated that a self-report checklist consisting of supposed ACOA statements drawn from the popular psychology literature (for example, "In times of crisis you tend to take care of others," "You are sensitive to the difficulties of others") did no better than chance at distinguishing ACOAs from non-ACOAs (Logue et al., 1992). Interestingly, Sher and his co-authors found that ACOAs were just as likely to endorse a checklist of extremely vague and generalized statements (for example, "Variety and change may at times bother you," "You have too strong a need for others to admire you") as they were the checklist of ACOA statements. Moreover, about 70% of ACOAs and non-ACOAs reported that both checklists described them "very well" or better.

As we pointed out in Myth #36, psychologists refer to these kinds of exceedingly uninformative and ill-defined personality descriptors as "P. T. Barnum statements" and the tendency of people to find them accurate as the "Barnum Effect" (Meehl, 1956). People suffering from puzzling psychological problems may be especially vulnerable to this effect, because they're often searching for a neat and tidy explanation for their life difficulties. Psychologists term this phenomenon "effort after meaning." People want to figure out how they became who they are, and the Barnum Effect capitalizes on this understandable tendency.

Barnum statements come in several flavors. Some are "double-headed" because they apply to people who are either above or below average on a characteristic and by definition apply to essentially everyone (Hines, 2003). The third statement in the ACOA profile at the beginning of this piece, which describes taking both too much and too little responsibility for others, is a prime example. One website describes ACOAs as both afraid of getting close to people and overly dependent on people. Still other Barnum items refer to trivial weaknesses that are so prevalent in the general population as to be virtually meaningless for assessment purposes (for example, "I sometimes have difficulty making decisions") or to assertions that are impossible to disconfirm (for example, "I have a great deal of unrecognized potential"). The fourth statement in the ACOA profile, which refers to needs for approval, almost certainly fits the bill on both counts. Who doesn't sometimes desire approval, and how could we prove that someone who appears fiercely independent doesn't possess a deeply hidden need for approval?

The Barnum Effect probably accounts for much of the success of graphologists (see Myth #36), astrologers, crystal ball readers, palm readers, tarot card readers, and spirit mediums. All make extensive use of Barnum statements in their readings. You're also likely to observe the Barnum Effect at work during your next visit to a Chinese restaurant. To see what we mean, just crack open your fortune cookie and read the message.

The results of Sher and his colleagues probably help to explain why you found the ACOA profile at the beginning of this piece to fit you so well. Their findings confirm the popular belief that the personality features of this profile are true of ACOAs. There's only one little catch: They're true of just about everyone.

Myth #41   There's Recently Been a Massive Epidemic of Infantile Autism

Trying "googling" the phrase "autism epidemic," and you'll find about 85,000 hits referring to what many consider a self-evident truth: The past 15 years or so have witnessed an astonishing increase in the percentage of children with autism.

According to the most recent edition of the *Diagnostic and Statistical Manual of Mental Disorders* (DSM; American Psychiatric Association, 2000), autism is a severe disorder that first appears in infancy. About three fourths of individuals with autism are mentally retarded, and most are male. All suffer from marked language deficits, in severe cases resulting in complete muteness, and many don't establish close emotional bonds with others. Most engage in stereotyped and ritualized activities, such as hair twirling, hand fluttering, and head banging, and display pronounced negative reactions to even trivial changes in their environments.

Once assumed to be an exceedingly rare condition—prior to the 1990s, the best estimates put the prevalence of autism at about 1 in 2,500 (DeFrancesco, 2001)—autism is now believed to afflict about 1 in 150 people (Carey, 2007). Between 1993 and 2003, U.S. Department of Education statistics documented an astonishing 657% increase in the rates of autism nationwide (Lilienfeld & Arkowitz, 2007). Understandably, many people have attempted to pinpoint the sources of this baffling upsurge. Some of them, including consumer advocate Robert F. Kennedy Jr. (2005) and tens of thousands of parents of autistic children, have pointed the finger squarely at vaccines containing the preservative *thimerosal*, which are commonly administered shortly before many children develop autistic symptoms (Kirby, 2005). One of thimerosal's breakdown products is mercury, which can produce neurological damage at high doses (Figure 9.1). In one study, 48% of undergraduates agreed that "Autism is caused by immunization shots" (Lenz et al., 2009).

The claim that the rates of autism are skyrocketing has been popularized by a litany of high-profile media spokespersons. In 2005, NBC's *Meet the Press* devoted an entire show to the autism epidemic and to claims by bestselling author David Kirby that thimerosal-bearing vaccines

Figure 9.1 This T-shirt captures the sentiments of opponents of thimerosal-containing vaccines, whom most of whom believe that these vaccines explain the apparent recent epidemic of autism (*Hg* is the chemical symbol for mercury, which is a breakdown product of thimerosal).
Source: Photo courtesy of Zazzle.com.

are causing it. In 2008, actress and former Playboy Playmate Jenny McCarthy, who has an autistic son, called for the resignation of the head of the Centers for Disease Control and Prevention (CDC), Julie Gerberding, for her "incompetence during the autism epidemic" and called for a director "who recognizes that we are experiencing an epidemic of autism" (http://adventuresinautism.blogspot.com/2008/03/jenny-mccarthy-calls-for-julie.html). Former National Football League star quarterback Doug Flutie, who also has an autistic son, has similarly proclaimed publicly that the prevalence of autism is rising at an startling rate (http://www.dougflutiejrfoundation.org/About-Autism-What-is-Autism-.asp).

In addition, both major party candidates in the 2008 U.S. presidential election endorsed the view that autism is increasing dramatically in prevalence. In response to a question at a 2008 town hall meeting, John McCain replied that "It's indisputable that (autism) is on the rise amongst children, the question is what's causing it . . . there's strong evidence that indicates that it's got to do with a preservative in vaccines" (he reiterated the claim that autism is rising during the third presidential debate in October, 2008). Less than 2 months later, Barack Obama told supporters at a rally that "We've seen just a skyrocketing autism rate. Some people are suspicious that it's connected to the vaccines—this person included." Many Americans appear to share McCain's and Obama's views: according to one informal Internet poll in 2008 by CBS News' *60 Minutes*, 70% of respondents believe there's an epidemic of autism.

Yet there's serious reason to doubt that autism is becoming more common. A far more likely explanation for the findings is a pronounced loosening of diagnostic practices over time (Gernsbacher, Dawson, & Goldsmith, 2005; Grinker, 2007). The 1980 version of the *DSM* (*DSM-III*) required individuals to meet all 6 of 6 criteria to be diagnosed with autism. In contrast, the 1994 version (*DSM-IV*), which is still in use with minor modifications, requires individuals to meet any 8 of 16 criteria to be diagnosed with autism. In addition, whereas *DSM-III* contained only two diagnoses relevant to autism—autistic disorder and Asperger's syndrome, which is generally regarded as a mild form of autism—*DSM-IV* contains five such diagnoses, several of which describe relatively mild forms of autism. So the diagnostic criteria for autism have become considerably less stringent from 1980 to the present, resulting in more diagnoses of this condition (Gernsbacher et al., 2005).

Additional influences may be at play. Because of disabilities laws passed by the U.S. Congress in the early 1990s, schools are now required to provide precise counts of the number of children with disabilities, including autism. As a consequence, educational districts are now *reporting* far more cases of autism, although this increase doesn't necessary reflect any changes in autism's actual prevalence (Grinker, 2007; Mercer, 2010). Furthermore, the "Rain Man Effect," which refers to the public's heightened awareness of autism following the 1988 film of the same name (see "Mythbusting: A Closer Look"), may have made parents and teachers more likely to notice autistic symptoms in children (Lawton, 2005). The Rain Man Effect may produce what investigators term *detection bias*: heightened reporting of a condition resulting from a change in how readily observers detect it (Hill & Kleinbaum, 2005).

Indeed, several recent studies suggest that the autism epidemic may be an illusion. In one investigation, researchers tracked the prevalence of autism diagnoses between 1992 and 1998 in an area of England using *the same diagnostic criteria* at both time points (Chakrabarti & Fombonne, 2005). Contrary to what we'd expect if there were an autism epidemic, the authors found no increase whatsoever in the prevalence of autism over time. Another study found evidence for a phenomenon termed "diagnostic substitution": As rates of the autism diagnosis soared in the United States between 1994 and 2003, diagnoses of mental retardation and learning disabilities combined decreased at about an equal rate. This finding suggests that diagnoses of autism may be "swapping places" with other, less fashionable, diagnoses. The same trend may be unfolding in the case of diagnoses of language disorders, which have become less frequent as autism diagnoses have become more popular (Bishop, Whitehouse, Watt, & Line, 2008).

All of these studies offer no support for an autism epidemic: They suggest that diagnoses of autism are skyrocketing in the absence of any genuine increase in autism's prevalence. As a consequence, efforts to account for this epidemic by vaccines may be pointless. Putting that problem aside, there's no solid evidence for any link between autism and vaccinations—including either injections containing thimerosal or injections for MMR (measles, mumps, and rubella; Institute of Medicine, 2004; Offit, 2008). For example, several large American, European, and Japanese studies revealed that even as the rates of vaccinations stayed the same or went down, the rates of diagnosed autism increased (Herbert, Sharp, & Gaudiano, 2002; Honda, Shimizu, & Rutter, 2005). Even after the government removed thimerosal from vaccines in 2001, the rates of autism in California continued to climb rapidly until 2007 (Schechter & Grether, 2008), paralleling similar findings in Denmark (Madsen et al., 2002). Nor is there any evidence that vaccines containing stronger doses of thimerosal are associated with higher autism rates than vaccines containing weaker doses (Hviid, Stellfeld, Wohlfahrt, & Melbye, 2003).

None of these findings conclusively exclude the possibility that vaccines may increase the risk of autism in a tiny subset of children, as it's difficult to prove a negative in science. But they provide no evidence for a link between vaccines and autism (Offit, 2008). Moreover, they rule out the possibility that vaccines can explain the supposed autism epidemic, as any possible overall effect of vaccines is so miniscule that studies haven't been able to detect it.

Yet researchers haven't always found it easy to get the word out. One scientist who's published articles refuting the vaccine-autism link,

Mythbusting: A Closer Look

Do Most Autistic Individuals Possess Remarkable Intellectual Skills?

The purported epidemic of autism is merely one of a myriad of unsupported beliefs regarding this condition (Gernsbacher, 2007). One other rampant myth is that most people with autism are *savants* ("savant" means a wise person): individuals with one or more isolated pockets of remarkable intellectual ability, often called "splinter skills" (Miller, 1999; O'Connor & Hermelin, 1988). Among these skills are "calendar calculation," that is, the ability to name the day of the week given any past or future date (like March 8, 1602 or November 19, 2307), astonishing memory for specific facts (like knowing the exact batting averages for all major league baseball players over the past century), and exceptional musical talents (like being able to reproduce perfectly a complicated tune on a piano after hearing it only once). The belief that most people with autism possess remarkable abilities appears to be widespread, at least in the autism community. In one survey, parents (4.24 on a 6-point scale) and teachers (4.15 on a 6-point scale) of autistic children agreed mostly with the statement, "Most autistic children have special talents or abilities" (Stone & Rosenbaum, 1988, p. 410).

This belief almost surely stems in part from films, such the 1988 Academy Award-winning movie, *Rain Man*, starring Dustin Hoffman (see *Introduction*, pp. 17–18), that portray autistic individuals as savants. *Rain Man* was inspired by an actual savant named Kim Peek, who knows approximately 9,000 books by heart—he can read a page from a book in 8 to 10 seconds and recall details from it months later—and can operate as a human *Mapquest*, providing precise directions from any U.S. city to any other (Treffert & Christensen, 2005).

Yet studies show that among autistic individuals, savants are the exception rather than the rule. Although estimates vary, most studies show that no more than 10%, and perhaps less, of people with autism display savant abilities (Heaton & Wallace, 2004; Rimland, 1978). This figure compares with a rate of about 1% among individuals without autism. It's not known why only certain autistic individuals become savants, although research indicates that savants tend to have higher IQs than non-savants, suggesting that overall intellectual ability may play a role (Miller, 1999).

The misconception that most autistic individuals are savants may seem innocuous enough. But this belief may have contributed to a misguided treatment called *facilitated communication* (FC), which is premised on the unsubstantiated notion that autism is primarily a motor (movement) disorder, not a mental disorder. According to FC advocates, individuals with autism are essentially normal individuals trapped inside an abnormal body. Because of a motor impairment, they maintain, individuals with autism are unable to articulate words properly (Biklen, 1990). The existence of savants appears to provide a rationale for FC, because it implies that autistic individuals are often more intellectually capable than they superficially appear (Frontline, 1993).

Using FC, the argument goes, largely or entirely mute autistic individuals can type out words and sentences on a keyboard with the aid of a "facilitator," who guides their hands and thereby compensates for their presumed motor impairment. In the early 1990s, shortly after FC was introduced to the United States, scores of ecstatic facilitators reported astonishing success stories of previously uncommunicative autistic individuals typing out eloquent sentences, at times speaking of their sense of liberation upon at last being able to express their imprisoned feelings. Yet numerous controlled studies soon showed that FC was entirely a product of unintentional facilitator control over autistic children's hand movements. Without even realizing it, facilitators were leading children's fingers to the keys (Delmolino & Romancyzk, 1995; Jacobson, Mulick, & Schwartz, 1995). Regrettably, FC has raised false hopes among thousands of desperate parents of autistic individuals. In addition, it's led to dozens of uncorroborated accusations of sexual abuse against these parents—based entirely on typed communications that emerged with the aid of facilitators (Lilienfeld, 2005a; Margolin, 1994).

Paul Offit, has been called a "terrorist" by protesters and has received hundreds of hostile e-mails, including death threats. Other scientists have endured similar harassment (Hughes, 2007).

A great deal is at stake, as the public's misunderstanding of the autism–vaccine link may be dangerous. Following a widely publicized, but since discredited, 1998 British study proclaiming a link between MMR vaccines and autism, vaccination rates for MMR in England plummeted from 92% to 73%, resulting in sudden outbreaks of measles and at least one death (Smith, Ellenberg, Bell, & Rubin, 2008). Although this decline in vaccinations might have been coincidental, it's noteworthy that it immediately followed widespread media coverage of the autism–vaccine link. And the past several years have witnessed similar increases in measles in the United States, Italy, Switzerland, Austria, and Italy, all in areas in which many parents have refused to vaccinate their children (New York Times, 2008). Misconceptions matter.

Myth # 42 Psychiatric Hospital Admissions and Crimes Increase during Full Moons

We'll begin this myth with a riddle: Once every 29.53 days on average, an event of rather trivial astronomical significance occurs. But according to some writers, it's an event of enormous psychological significance. What is it?

The answer: A full moon. Over the years, authors have linked the full moon to a host of phenomena—strange behaviors, psychiatric hospital admissions, suicides, traffic accidents, crimes, heavy drinking, dog bites, births, crisis calls to emergency rooms and police stations, violence by hockey players . . . the list goes on and on (Carroll, 2003; Chudler, n.d.; Rotton & Kelly, 1985).

This belief is hardly new: the word "lunatic" (which in turn has given rise to the slang term "looney"), meaning a psychotic person, derives from the Latin term *luna*, or moon. Legends of werewolves and vampires, terrifying creatures that supposedly often emerged during full moons, date back at least to the ancient Greeks, including Hippocrates and Plutarch (Chudler, n.d.). These legends were also enormously popular in Europe during much of the Middle Ages and later eras. In his great play *Othello* (Act 5, Scene 2), Shakespeare wrote that "It is the very error of the moon. She comes more near the earth than she was wont. And makes men mad." In 19th century England, some lawyers even used a "not guilty by reason of the full moon" defense to acquit clients of crimes committed during full moons. Even today, Buddhism forbids participants from playing outdoor sports during full moons (Full Moon Rules out Play, 2001).

The notion that the full moon is tied to myriad strange occurrences—often called "The Lunar Effect or "Transylvania Effect"—is deeply embedded in modern culture as well. A 1995 study by investigators at the University of New Orleans revealed that up to 81% of mental health professionals believe in the lunar effect (Owens & McGowan, 2006), and a 2005 study of surgical nurses in Pittsburgh, Pennsylvania demonstrated that 69% believe that full moons are associated with increases in patient admissions (Francescani & Bacon, 2008). One study of Canadian college students revealed that 45% believe in the lunar effect (Russell & Dua, 1983). This belief has real-world implications; in 2007, the city of Brighton, England instituted a policy to place more police officers on the beat during full moon nights (Pugh, 2007).

The lunar effect is also a familiar fixture in scores of Hollywood films. For example, in the 1985 Martin Scorsese comedy, *After Hours*, one of the police officers mutters "There must be a full moon out there" after the main character behaves oddly late at night. In the 2009 film, *Underworld: Rise of the Lycans*, one of the human characters transforms himself repeatedly into a werewolf during full moons.

In recent decades, psychiatrist Arnold Lieber (1978, 1996) popularized the idea of a correlation between the full moon and behavior. For Lieber and his followers, much of the rationale for the lunar effect stems from the fact that the human body is four-fifths water. Because the moon affects the tides of the earth, so the argument goes, it's plausible that the moon would also affect the brain, which is, after all, part of the body. Yet on closer inspection, this argument doesn't "hold water," if you can forgive the pun. As astronomer George Abell (1979) noted, a mosquito sitting on your arm exerts a more powerful gravitational force on your body than does the moon. Similarly, the gravitational force of a mother holding her baby is about 12 million times greater than the gravitational force of the moon on that baby. Furthermore, the moon's tides are influenced not by its phase—that is, by how much of it is visible to us on earth—but by its distance from earth (Kelly, Laverty, & Saklofske, 1990). Indeed, during a "new moon," the phase at which the moon is invisible to us on earth, the moon exerts just as much gravitational influence as it does during a full moon.

These flawed explanations aside, we can still ask the question of whether the full moon exerts any meaningful effects on behavior. Because well over 100 published studies have examined this issue, scientists now have something close to a definitive answer. In 1985, psychologists James Rotton and Ivan Kelly reviewed all of the available research evidence on the lunar effect. Using meta-analytic techniques (see p. 32), they found no evidence that the full moon was related to much of anything—murders, other crimes, suicides, psychiatric problems, psychiatric hospital admissions, or calls to crisis centers (Rotton & Kelly, 1985). Rotton and Kelly did unearth a few scattered positive findings here and there, which isn't surprising given the dozens of studies they examined. Nevertheless, even these few positive findings were open to decidedly "non-lunar" explanations. For example, one team of investigators reported that traffic accidents were more common during full moon nights than other nights (Templer, Veleber, & Brooner, 1982). Yet as Rotton and Kelly pointed out, this finding was marred by a serious flaw. During the time period studied by the researchers, full moons fell more often on weekends—when there's more traffic—than on weekdays (Hines, 2003). When the researchers reanalyzed their data to take this confound into account, their positive findings vanished (Templer, Brooner, & Corgiat, 1983). Boldly flouting the conventional conclusion of psychology review articles that "more research is needed in this area," Rotton and Kelly ended their article by concluding that no further research on lunar effects was necessary (p. 302).

Later analyses of the lunar effect yielded equally negative results. Investigators have examined whether the full moon is linked to suicides (Gutiérrez-García & Tusell, 1997), psychiatric hospital admissions (Kung & Mrazek, 2005), dog bites (Chapman & Morrell, 2000), emergency room visits or runs by ambulances to emergencies (Thompson & Adams, 1996), births (Kelly & Martens, 1994), and heart attacks (Wake, Fukuda, Yoshiyama, Shimada, & Yoshikawa, 2007), and virtually all have come up empty-handed. There's also no evidence that emergency phone calls to operators or police departments go up during full moons (Chudler, n.d.). Because it's often difficult or impossible to prove a negative in science (see p. 199), determined proponents of the lunar effect can maintain that this effect will one day emerge with better data. Still, it's safe to say that if a lunar effect exists, it's so tiny in size as to be essentially meaningless (Campbell, 1982; Chudler, n.d.).

If so, why are so many intelligent people convinced of it? There are at least two potential reasons. First, psychologists have discovered that we're all prone to a phenomenon that Loren and Jean Chapman (1967, 1969) called illusory correlation, (see *Introduction*, p. 12). As you may recall, illusory correlation is the perception of an association between two events where none exists. It's a statistical mirage.

Although several factors probably give rise to illusory correlation (Lilienfeld, Wood, & Garb, 2006), one that deserves particular attention is the fallacy of positive instances. This fallacy refers to the fact that when an event confirms our hypotheses, we tend to take special note of it and recall it (Gilovich, 1991; see also p. 31). In contrast, when an event disconfirms our hypotheses, we tend to ignore it or reinterpret it in line with these hypotheses. So, when there's a full moon and something out of the ordinary happens, say, a sudden surge of admissions to our local psychiatric hospital, we're likely to remember it and tell others about it. In contrast, when there's a full moon and nothing out of the ordinary happens, we usually just ignore it (Chudler, n.d.). In still other cases, we might reinterpret the absence of any notable events during a full moon so that it's still consistent with the lunar hypothesis: "Well, there was a full moon and there weren't any psychiatric admissions tonight, but maybe that's because it's a holiday and most people are in a good mood."

The illusory correlation hypothesis dovetails with the findings of a study revealing that psychiatric hospital nurses who believed in the lunar effect wrote more notes about patients' strange behavior during a full moon than did nurses who didn't believe in the lunar effect (Angus, 1973). The nurses attended more to events that confirmed their hunches, which probably in turn bolstered these hunches.

A second explanation is more conjectural, but no less fascinating. Psychiatrist Charles Raison and his colleagues (Raison, Klein, & Steckler, 1999) speculated that modern society's belief in the lunar effect may stem from a correlation that once existed, and that some observers of the time misinterpreted as causation (see *Introduction*, p. 13 for a discussion of the confusion between correlation and causation). Prior to the advent of contemporary outdoor lighting, Raison and his collaborators suggested, the bright outdoor moon deprived people who were living outside, including homeless people with mental disorders, of sleep. Because sleep deprivation often triggers erratic behavior in patients with certain psychological conditions, especially bipolar disorder (once known as "manic depression"), and in patients with epilepsy, the full moon may once have been associated with a heightened rate of bizarre behaviors. Of course, it didn't directly *cause* these behaviors: It contributed to sleep deprivation, which in turn contributed to bizarre behaviors. Nowadays, according to Raison and his co-authors, we no longer find this correlation, at least in large cities, because outdoor lighting largely cancels out the effects of the full moon.

This clever explanation may turn out to be wrong. But it reminds us of a key principle: Even false beliefs may derive from what was once a kernel of truth (see *Introduction*, p. 17).

Chapter 9: Other Myths to Explore

Fiction	Fact
Psychiatric diagnoses are unreliable.	For most major mental disorders (such as schizophrenia and major depression), reliabilities are comparable with those of major medical disorders.
Most psychotic people in Western society would be viewed as "shamans" in non-Western cultures.	People in non-Western cultures clearly distinguish shamans from people with schizophrenia.
Hallucinations are almost always a sign of serious mental illness.	Ten percent or more or college students and community residents without psychotic disorders have experienced waking hallucinations while not on drugs.
Most people with agoraphobia can't leave their houses.	Only severe agoraphobia results in its sufferers becoming housebound.
Most people who experience severe trauma, like military combat, develop posttraumatic stress disorder (PTSD).	Even for the most severe traumas, only 25–35% of people typically develop PTSD.
The symptoms of PTSD were first observed following the Vietnam War.	Clear descriptions of PTSD date from at least the U.S. Civil War.
Most phobias are traceable directly to negative experiences with the object of the fear.	Most people with phobias report no direct traumatic experiences with the object of their fear.
People with fetishes are fascinated with certain objects.	People with fetishes obtain sexual arousal from certain objects, like shoes or stockings.
Psychosomatic disorders are entirely in "people's heads."	Psychosomatic disorders, now called psychophysiological disorders, are genuine physical conditions caused or exacerbated by stress and other psychological factors. They include asthma, irritable bowel syndrome, and some headaches.

Fiction	Fact
People with hypochondriasis are typically convinced they're suffering from many different illnesses.	People with hypochondriasis are typically convinced they're suffering from one serious undetected illness, like cancer or AIDS.
Most people with anorexia have lost their appetite.	Most patients with anorexia nervosa don't lose their appetites unless and until their illness becomes extremely severe.
All people with anorexia are female.	About 10% of people with anorexia are male.
Eating disorders, especially anorexia and bulimia, are associated with a history of child sexual abuse.	Controlled studies suggest that rates of child sexual abuse are probably no higher among eating disordered patients than patients with other psychiatric disorders.
Almost all people with Tourette's syndrome curse.	The proportion of Tourette's patients with coprolalia (uncontrollable cursing) ranges from 8% to 60% across studies.
The brains of children with attention-deficit/hyperactivity disorder (ADHD) are over-aroused.	Studies suggest that the brains of ADHD children are under-aroused.
Autistic individuals have a particular talent for generating prime numbers.	There's no good support for this claim, which derives from a few widely publicized examples.
All clinically depressed people suffer from extreme sadness.	Up to a third of clinically depressed people don't suffer from extreme sadness, but instead suffer from "anhedonia," an inability to experience pleasure.
Depressed people are less realistic than non-depressed people.	Mildly depressed people tend to be more accurate than non-depressed people on many laboratory tasks.
Depression has been demonstrated to be due to a "chemical imbalance" in the brain.	There's no scientific evidence for a genuine "imbalance" in any neurotransmitter in depression.
Children can't become seriously depressed.	There's strong evidence that clinical depression can occur in childhood.
The rates of depression in women increase dramatically during the postpartum period.	The rates of nonpsychotic depression are no higher immediately after giving birth than at other times, although the rates of psychotic depression are.
People with bipolar disorder, formerly called "manic depression," all experience both depressed and manic episodes.	Manic episodes alone are sufficient for the diagnosis of bipolar disorder.

Fiction	Fact
Suicide typically happens without warning.	Two thirds to three fourths of individuals who commit suicide had previously expressed their intentions to others.
Most people who commit suicide leave a suicide note.	Only a minority of people who commit suicide, about 15–25% in most studies, leave suicide notes.
People who talk a lot about suicide are extremely unlikely to commit it.	Talking repeatedly about suicide is one of the best predictors of killing oneself.
Asking people about suicide increases their risk for suicide.	Although no controlled experiment has examined this claim directly, there's no research support for it.
Suicides are especially likely during the Christmas holidays.	Suicide rates either remain the same or even decrease slightly during the Christmas holidays.
Suicide is especially common during the dark days of winter.	Across the world, suicide tends to be the most common during the warmest months.
The age group at highest risk for suicide is adolescents.	The age group at highest risk for suicide is the elderly, especially older men.
More women than men commit suicide.	More women than men attempt suicide, but more men than women succeed.
Families play a major role in causing or triggering schizophrenia.	Although familial criticism and hostility may trigger relapse in some cases of schizophrenia, there's no evidence that they play a causal role in the disorder's onset.
All people with catatonic schizophrenia are inactive, lying in a fetal position.	People with catatonic schizophrenia sometimes engage in frenzied and purposeless motor activity or perform odd gestures.
People with schizophrenia virtually never recover.	Follow-up studies suggest that one half to two thirds of people with schizophrenia improve markedly over time.
Virtually all people who use heroin become addicted to it.	Many regular heroin users never become addicted, and some previous addicts lose their addictions when they move to a new environment.
Most transvestites are homosexual.	True transvestites, who obtain sexual arousal from cross-dressing, are nearly all heterosexual males.

Sources and Suggested Readings

To explore these and other myths about mental illness, see American Psychiatric Association (2000); Finn & Kamphuis (1995); Furnham (1996); Harding and Zahniser (1994); Joiner (2005); Hubbard and McIntosh (1992); Matarazzo (1983); Murphy (1976); Raulin (2003); Rosen and Lilienfeld (2008).

10 DISORDER IN THE COURT

Myths about Psychology and the Law

Most Mentally Ill People Are Violent

Let's start off with a quick quiz for you movie buffs out there. What do the following Hollywood films have in common: *Psycho*, *Halloween*, *Friday the 13th*, *Misery*, *Summer of Sam*, *Texas Chain Saw Massacre*, *Nightmare on Elm Street*, *Primal Fear*, *Cape Fear*, and *Dark Knight*?

If you guessed that they all feature a mentally ill character who's violent, give yourself a point.

These films are the rule rather than the exception. About 75% of films depicting a character with a serious mental illness portray that character as physically aggressive, even homicidal (Levin, 2001; Signorielli, 1989; Wahl, 1997). Movies and television shows portraying "psychopathic killers" and "homicidal maniacs" have become a dime a dozen in Hollywood. Prime-time television programs depict characters with mental illness as engaging in violence about 10 times more often than other characters, and 10 to 20 times more often than the average person (Diefenbach, 1997; Stout, Villegas, & Jennings, 2004; Figure 10.1).

The coverage of mental illness in the news is scarcely different. In one study, 85% of news stories that covered ex-psychiatric patients focused on their violent crimes (Shain & Phillips, 1991). Of course, these findings won't come as any surprise to those familiar with the unspoken mottos of news organizations: "If it bleeds it leads; it if burns, it earns." The news media feeds on sensationalism, so stories of mentally ill people with histories of violence are virtually guaranteed to garner a hefty chunk of attention.

Figure 10.1 Many films fuel the public misperception of the mentally ill as frequently or even usually violent. Ironically, most psychopaths aren't even violent (see "Other Myths to Explore").
Source: Photofest.

Because of the *availability heuristic* (see p. 89), our tendency to judge the frequency of events with the ease with which they come to mind, this media coverage virtually guarantees that many people will think "violence" whenever they hear "mental illness" (Ruscio, 2000). This heuristic can contribute to illusory correlations (see *Introduction*, p. 12) between two phenomena, in this case violence and mental illness. Widespread media coverage of Andrea Yates' tragic drowning of her five children in 2001 and Seung-Hui Cho's horrific shootings of 32 students and faculty at Virginia Tech in 2007 have almost surely strengthened this connection in people's minds, as both Yates and Cho suffered from severe mental disorders (Yates was diagnosed with psychotic depression, and Cho apparently exhibited significant symptoms of schizophrenia). Indeed, in one study, reading a newspaper story about a murder of a 9-year-old by a mentally ill patient produced a significant increase in the perception that the mentally ill are dangerous compared with a control condition (Thornton & Wahl, 1996).

Not surprisingly, surveys reveal that the close link between mental illness and violence in the popular media is paralleled in the minds of the general public. One survey demonstrated that about 80% of Americans believe that mentally ill people are prone to violence (Ganguli, 2000). This perception of heightened risk holds across a broad range of disorders, including alcoholism, cocaine dependence, schizophrenia, and even depression (Angermeyer & Dietrich, 2006; Link, Phelan, Bresnahan, Stueve, & Pescosolido, 1999). In addition, between 1950 and 1996, the proportion of American adults who perceived the mentally ill as violent increased substantially (Phelan, Link, Stueve, & Pescosolido, 2000). This increase is ironic, because research suggests that the percentage of murders committed by the mentally ill has declined over the past four decades (Cutcliffe & Hannigan, 2001). Whatever the origins of this belief, it begins early in life. Studies show that many children as young as 11 to 13 years of age assume that most mentally ill people are dangerous (Watson et al., 2004).

Yet commonplace public beliefs about mental illness and violence don't square with the bulk of the research evidence (Applebaum, 2004; Teplin, 1985). Admittedly, most studies point to a modestly heightened risk of violence among people with severe mental illnesses, such as schizophrenia and bipolar disorder, once called manic depression (Monahan, 1992).

Yet even this elevated risk appears limited to only a relatively small subset of people with these illnesses. For example, in most studies, people with paranoid delusions (such as the false belief of being pursued by the Central Intelligence Agency) and substance abuse disorders (Harris & Lurigio, 2007; Steadman et al., 1998; Swanson et al., 1996), but not other mentally ill people, are at heightened risk for violence. Indeed, in some recent studies, severely mentally ill patients without substance abuse disorders showed no higher risk for violence than other individuals (Elbogen & Johnson, 2009). Nevertheless, psychiatric patients who take their medication regularly aren't at elevated risk for violence compared with members of the general population (Steadman et al., 1998). There's also some evidence that patients with "command hallucinations"—hearing voices instructing a person to commit an act like a murder—are at heightened risk for violence (Junginger & McGuire, 2001; McNiel, Eisner, & Binder, 2000).

Still, the best estimates suggest that 90% of more of people with serious mental illnesses, including schizophrenia, never commit violent acts (Hodgins et al., 1996). Moreover, severe mental illness probably accounts for only about 3–5% of all violent crimes (Monahan, 1996;

Walsh, Buchanan, & Fahy, 2001). In fact, people with schizophrenia and other severe mental disorders are far more likely to be victims than perpetrators of violence (Teplin, McClelland, Abram, & Weiner, 2005), probably because their weakened mental capacity renders them vulnerable to attacks by others. Furthermore, most major mental disorders, including major depression and anxiety disorders (such as phobias and obsessive-compulsive disorder), aren't associated with a heightened risk of physical aggression.

There is, though, a hint of a silver lining surrounding the huge gray cloud of public misunderstanding. Research suggests that the portrayal of mental illness in the news and entertainment media may gradually be changing. From 1989 to 1999, the percentage of news stories about the mentally ill that contained descriptions of violence decreased (Wahl, Wood, & Richards, 2002). In addition, recent films such as *A Beautiful Mind* (2001), which portray people with severe mental illnesses, such as schizophrenia, as nonviolent and as coping successfully with their psychiatric symptoms, may help to counter the public's erroneous perception of a powerful link between mental illness and violence. Interestingly, cross-cultural research suggests that the perception of a markedly heightened risk of violence among people with schizophrenia may be absent in some regions, including Siberia and Mongolia (Angermeyer, Buyantugs, & Kenzine, 2004), perhaps stemming from their limited access to media coverage. These findings give us further reason for hope that the perception of a greatly heightened risk for violence among the mentally ill isn't inevitable.

Myth #44 Criminal Profiling Is Helpful in Solving Cases

For most of October, 2002, the citizens of Virginia, Maryland, and Washington, D.C. were virtually held hostage in their homes. During 23 seemingly endless days, 10 innocent people were killed and 4 others wounded in a nightmarish series of shootings. One person was shot while mowing a lawn, another while reading a book on a city bench, another after leaving a store, another while standing in a restaurant parking lot, and several others while walking down the street or pumping gasoline. The shootings appeared entirely random: The victims included Whites and African Americans, children and adults, men and women. Terrified and bewildered, many residents of the Washington Beltway area avoided going out unless absolutely necessary, and dozens of schools ordered virtual lockdowns, cancelling all outdoor recesses and gym classes.

As the shooting spree continued with no clear end in sight, legions of criminal profilers took to the television airwaves to offer their conjectures about the sniper's identity. Criminal profilers are trained professionals who claim to be able to infer a criminal's personality, behavioral, and physical characteristics on the basis of specific details about one or more crimes (Davis & Follette, 2002; Hicks & Sales, 2006). In this way, they supposedly can help investigators identify the person responsible for the crime or crimes in question (Douglas, Ressler, Burgess, & Hartman, 1986). The U.S. Federal Bureau of Investigation (FBI) alone employs criminal profilers in about 1,000 cases every year (Snook, Gendreau, Bennell, & Taylor, 2008).

In the Beltway sniper case, most of the criminal profilers interviewed by the media agreed on one thing: The killer was probably a White male (Davis & Morello, 2002; Kleinfield & Goode, 2002). After all, these two characteristics matched the profile of most serial killers. Other profilers maintained that the killer didn't have children, and others that he wasn't a soldier, as a soldier would presumably have used highly accurate military bullets rather than the relatively crude bullets found at the shootings. Still other profilers speculated that the killer would be in his mid-20s, as the average age of sniper killers is 26 (Gettleman, 2002; Kleinfield & Goode, 2002).

Yet when "the sniper" was finally captured on October 24, most of the expert media profilers were in for a surprise. For one thing, "the sniper" wasn't one person: the murders had been committed by a team of two males, John Allen Muhammad and Lee Boyd Malvo. What's more, both men were African-American, not White. Contrary to what many profilers had predicted, Muhammad had four children and was a former soldier. And neither killer was in his mid-20s: Muhammad was 41, Malvo 17.

The infamous Beltway sniper case highlights two points. First, this case underscores the fact that criminal profiling has become an indelible part of the landscape of popular culture. The 1991 Academy Award-winning film, *The Silence of the Lambs*, starring Jodie Foster as a young intern in training as an FBI profiler, stoked many Americans' fascination with criminal profiling. At least nine other films, including *Copycat* (1995) and *Gothika* (2003), also feature criminal profilers in prominent roles. And several popular television series, most notably *Profiler*, *Millennium*, *Criminal Minds*, and *CSI: Crime Scene Investigation*, accord prominent billing to criminal profilers. Today, criminal profilers like Pat Brown and Clint van Zandt are featured routinely on television programs focused on crime investigations, such as Fox News' *On the Record* (hosted by

Greta van Susteren) and CNN's *Nancy Grace*. These films or programs seldom offer even a hint of skepticism regarding criminal profilers' predictive capacities (Muller, 2000).

The popularity of profiling in the media is mirrored by perceptions of its effectiveness among many mental health professionals and law enforcement officers. In a survey of 92 psychologists and psychiatrists with expertise in the law, 86% agreed that criminal profiling "is a useful tool for law enforcement," although only 27% believed it was scientifically established enough to be admitted into courts of law (Torres, Boccaccini, & Miller, 2006). In another survey of 68 U.S. police officers, 58% said that profiling was helpful in directing criminal investigations and 38% that it was helpful in fingering suspects (Trager & Brewster, 2001).

Second, the wildly inaccurate guesses of many profilers in the Beltway sniper case raise a crucial question: Does criminal profiling work? To answer this question, we need to address what we mean by "work." If we mean "Does criminal profiling predict perpetrators' characteristics better than chance?," the answer is probably yes. Studies show that professional profilers can often accurately guess some of the characteristics of criminals (such as whether they're male or female, young or old) when presented with detailed case file information regarding specific crimes, such as rapes and murders, and they perform better than we'd do by flipping a coin (Kocsis, 2006).

But these results aren't terribly impressive. That's because criminal profilers may be relying on "base rate information," that is, data on the characteristics of criminals who commit certain crimes that are readily available to anyone who bothers to look them up. For example, about 90% of serial killers are male and about 75% are White (Fox & Levin, 2001). So one needn't be a trained profiler to guess that a person responsible for a string of murders is probably a White male; one will be right more than two thirds of the time by relying on base rates alone. We can derive some base rate information even without consulting formal research. For example, it doesn't take a trained profiler to figure out that a man who brutally murdered his wife and three children by stabbing them repeatedly probably "had serious problems controlling his temper."

A better test of whether criminal profiling works is to pit professional profilers against untrained individuals. After all, profiling is supposedly a technique that requires specialized training. When one puts criminal profiling to this more stringent test, the results are decidedly unimpressive. In most studies, professional profilers barely do any better than untrained persons in inferring the personality traits of actual murderers from details about their crimes (Homant & Kennedy, 1998). In at least one study, homicide detectives with extensive experience in criminal investigation and police officers generated *less* accurate profiles of a murderer than did chemistry majors (Kocsis, Hayes, & Irwin, 2002).

A meta-analysis (see p. 32) of four well-controlled studies revealed that trained profilers did only slightly better than non-profilers (college students and psychologists) at estimating the overall characteristics of offenders from information about their crimes (Snook, Eastwood, Gendreau, Goggin, & Cullen, 2007). They fared no better or even slightly worse than non-profilers at gauging offenders' (a) physical characteristics, including gender, age, and race, (b) thinking processes, including motives and guilt regarding the crime, and (c) personal habits, including marital status and education. Even the finding that profilers did slightly better on overall offender characteristics than non-profilers is hard to interpret, as profilers may be more familiar than non-profilers with base rate information concerning criminals' characteristics (Snook et al., 2008). Non-profilers with just a bit of education regarding these base rates or motivation to look them up might do as well as profilers, although researchers haven't yet investigated this possibility.

Given that the scientific support for criminal profiling is so feeble, what accounts for its immense popularity? There are a host of potential reasons (Snook et al., 2008; in press), but we'll focus on three here. First, media reports on profilers' hits—that is, successful predictions—far outnumber their misses (Snook et al., 2007). This tendency is especially problematic because profilers, like police psychics, typically toss out scores of guesses about the criminal's characteristics in the hopes that at least a few of them will prove correct. As the old saying goes, "Throw enough mud at the wall and some of it will stick." For example, a few profilers guessed correctly that the Beltway sniper murders were conducted by two people (Gettleman, 2002). But it's not clear whether these guesses were anything more than chance hits.

Second, what psychologists have termed the "expertise heuristic" (Reimer, Mata, & Stoecklin, 2004; Snook et al., 2007) probably plays a role too. According to this heuristic (recall from the *Introduction*, p. 15, that a "heuristic" is a mental shortcut), we place particular trust in people who describe themselves as "experts." Because most profilers claim to possess specialized expertise, we may find their assertions especially persuasive. Studies show that police officers perceive profiles to be more accurate when they believe they're generated by professional profilers as opposed to non-experts (Kocsis & Hayes, 2004).

Third, the P. T. Barnum Effect—the tendency to find vague and general personality descriptions believable (Meehl, 1956; see Myths #36 and 40) is probably a key contributor to the popularity of criminal profiling (Gladwell, 2007). Most profilers sprinkle their predictions liberally with assertions that are so nebulous as to be virtually untestable ("The killer has unresolved self-esteem problems"), so general that they apply to just about everyone ("The killer has conflicts with his family"), or that rely on base rate information about most crimes ("The killer probably abandoned the body in or near a body of water"). Because many of their predictions are difficult to prove wrong or bound to be right regardless of who the criminal turns out to be, profilers may seem to be uncannily accurate (Alison, Smith, Eastman, & Rainbow, 2003; Snook et al., 2008). Consistent with this possibility, the results of one study revealed that police officers found a "Barnum" profile containing ambiguous statements (such as "the offender is an inappropriately immature man for his years" and "the offense . . . represented an escape from a humdrum, unsatisfying life") to fit an actual criminal just as well as a genuine profile constructed around factual details of the criminal's life (Alison, Smith, & Morgan, 2003).

Just as P. T. Barnum quipped that he liked to give "a little something to everybody" in his circus acts, many seemingly successful criminal profilers may put just enough in each of their profiles to keep law enforcement officials satisfied. But do profilers actually do better than the average person in solving crimes? At least at present, the verdict is "No, not beyond a reasonable doubt."

Myth # 45 A Large Proportion of Criminals Successfully Use the Insanity Defense

After giving a speech on the morning of March 30, 1981, U.S. President Ronald Reagan emerged from the Washington Hilton hotel in the nation's capital. Surrounded by security guards, a smiling Reagan walked toward his president limousine, waving to the friendly crowd gathered outside the hotel. Seconds later, six shots rang out. One of them hit a secret service agent, one hit a police officer, another hit the President's press secretary James Brady, and another hit the President himself. Lodged only a few inches from Reagan's heart, the bullet came perilously close to killing America's 40th President. Following surgery, the President recovered fully, but Brady suffered permanent brain damage.

The would-be assassin was a previously unknown 26-year-old man named John Hinckley. Hinckley, it turned out, had fallen in love from a distance with actress Jodie Foster, then a student at Yale University. Hinckley had recently seen the 1976 film *Taxi Driver*, which featured Foster as a child prostitute, and identified powerfully with the character of Travis Bickle (portrayed brilliantly by actor Robert De Niro), who harbored rescue fantasies toward Foster's character. Hinckley repeatedly left love notes for Foster and even reached her several times by phone in his dorm room at Yale, but his desperate efforts to woo her were to no avail. Hinckley's love for Foster remained unrequited. Hopelessly delusional, Hinckley believed that by killing the president he could make Foster come to appreciate the depth of his passion for her.

In 1982, following a combative trial featuring dueling psychiatric experts, the jury found Hinckley not guilty by reason of insanity. The jury's surprising decision generated an enormous public outcry; an ABC News poll revealed that 76% of Americans objected to the verdict. This negative reaction was understandable. Many Americans found the notion of acquitting a man who shot the president in broad daylight to be morally repugnant. Moreover, because the assassination attempt was captured on videotape, most Americans had witnessed the event with their own eyes. Many of them probably thought, "*Wait a minute; I saw him do it. How on earth could he be found not guilty?*" Yet the insanity defense doesn't deal with the question of whether the defendant actually committed the criminal act (what legal experts call *actus reas*, or guilty act) but rather with the question of whether the defendant was psychologically responsible for this act (what legal experts call *mens rea*, or guilty mind).

Since the Hinckley trial, Americans have witnessed numerous other high-profile cases featuring the insanity plea, including those of Jeffrey Dahmer (the Milwaukee man who killed and cannibalized a number of his victims) and Andrea Yates (the Texas woman who drowned five of her children). In all of these cases, juries struggled with the difficult question of whether an individual who committed murder was legally responsible for the act.

The first trick to understanding the insanity defense is to recognize that sanity and insanity are legal, not psychiatric, terms. Despite their informal use in everyday language ("That man on the street is talking to himself; he must be insane"), these terms don't refer to whether a person is psychotic—that is, out of touch with reality—but rather to whether that person was legally responsible at the time of the crime. Yet determining criminal responsibility is far from simple. There are several versions of the insanity verdict, each of which conceptualizes criminal responsibility a bit differently.

Most U.S. states use some variant of the *M'Naughten rule*, which requires that to be ruled insane, defendants must have either not known what they were doing at the time of the act or not known that what they were doing was wrong. This rule focuses narrowly on the question of *cognition* (thinking): Did the defendant understand the meaning of his or her criminal act? For example, did a man who murdered a gas station attendant understand that he was breaking the law? Did he believe that he was murdering an innocent person, or did he believe that he was murdering the devil dressed up as a gas station attendant?

For a time, several other states and most federal courts adopted the criteria outlined by the American Law Institute (ALI), which required that to be ruled insane, defendants must have either not understood what they were doing *or* been unable to control their impulses to conform to the law. The ALI guidelines broadened the M'Naughten rule to include both cognition and *volition*: the capacity to control one's impulses.

Because Hinckley was acquitted under the ALI guidelines, many states responded to this verdict by tightening these guidelines. Indeed, most states that use the insanity verdict have now returned to stricter M'Naughten-like standards. Moreover, following the Hinckley verdict, more than half of the states considered abolishing the insanity verdict entirely (Keilitz & Fulton, 1984) and four states—Montana, Idaho, Utah, and Kansas—have done so (Rosen, 1999). Still other states introduced a variant of the insanity verdict known as "guilty but mentally ill" (GBMI). Under GBMI, judges and juries can consider a criminal's mental illness during the sentencing phase, but not during the trial itself.

As the intense public reaction to the Hinckley verdict illustrates, many people hold strong opinions concerning the insanity defense. Surveys show that most Americans believe that criminals often use the insanity defense as a loophole to escape punishment. One study revealed that the average layperson believes that the insanity defense is used in 37% of felony cases, and that this defense is successful 44% of the time. This survey also demonstrated that the average layperson believes that 26% of insanity acquittees are set free, and that these acquittees spend only about 22 months in a mental hospital following their trials (Silver, Cirincione, & Steadman, 1994). Another survey indicated that 90% of members of the general public agreed that "the insanity plea is used too much. Too many people escape responsibilities for crimes by pleading insanity" (Pasewark & Seidenzahl, 1979).

Many politicians share these perceptions. For example, Richard Pasewark and Mark Pantle (1979) asked state legislators in Wyoming to estimate the frequency of use of the insanity defense in their state. These politicians estimated that 21% of accused felons had used this defense, and that they were successful 40% of the time. Moreover, many prominent politicians have lobbied strenuously against the insanity defense. In 1973, then U.S. President Richard Nixon made the abolition of the insanity defense the centerpiece of his nationwide effort to fight crime (because Nixon resigned over the Watergate scandal only a year later, this initiative never gathered much steam). Many other politicians have since called for an end to this verdict (Rosen, 1999).

Yet laypersons' and politicians' perceptions of the insanity defense are wildly inaccurate. Although most Americans believe that the use of the insanity defense is widespread, data indicate that this defense is raised in less than 1% of criminal trials and that it's successful only about 25% of the time (Phillips, Wolf, & Coons, 1988; Silver et al., 1994). For example, in the state of Wyoming between 1970 and 1972, a grand total of 1 (!) accused felon successfully pled insanity (Pasewark & Pantle, 1979). Overall, the public believes that this defense is used about 40 times more often than it actually is (Silver et al., 1994).

The misperceptions don't end there. Members of the general public also overestimate how many insanity acquittees are set free; the true proportion is closer to only 15%. For example, Hinckley has remained in St. Elizabeth's Hospital, a famous psychiatric facility in Washington, DC, since 1982. Moreover, the average insanity acquittee spends between 32 and 33 months in a psychiatric hospital, considerably longer than the public estimates (Silver et al., 1994). In fact, the results of several studies indicate that criminals acquitted on the basis of an insanity verdict typically spend at least as long, if not longer, in an institution (such as a psychiatric hospital) than criminals who are convicted (Rodriguez, 1983).

How did these misperceptions of the insanity defense arise? We Americans live increasingly in a "courtroom culture." Between *Court TV*, *CSI*, *Judge Judy*, *Law and Order*, *CNN's Nancy Grace*, and media coverage of the trials of celebrities (such as O. J. Simpson, Robert Blake, and Michael Jackson), we're inundated on an almost daily basis with information about the legal system and its innermost workings. Nevertheless, this information can be deceptive, because we hear far more about the sensational than the typical cases, which are, after all, typical. Indeed, the media devotes considerably more coverage to legal cases in which the insanity defense is successful, like Hinckley's, than to those in which it isn't (Wahl, 1997). Because of the *availability heuristic* (see

p. 89), we're more likely to hear about and remember successful uses of the insanity defense than unsuccessful uses.

As is so often the case, the best antidote to public misperception is accurate knowledge. Lynn and Lauren McCutcheon (1994) found that a brief fact-based report on the insanity defense, compared with a news program on crime featuring this defense, produced a significant decrease in undergraduates' misconceptions concerning the insanity defense (such as the notion that uses of the insanity defense are widespread in the criminal justice system and that most such uses are successful). These findings give us cause for hope, as they suggest that it may take only a small bit of information to overcome misinformation.

So the next time you hear friends or co-workers refer to someone who's acting strangely as "insane," you may want to pipe up and correct them politely. It could make more of a difference than you think.

Myth # 46 Virtually All People Who Confess to a Crime Are Guilty of It

We've all seen countless examples in the media of the "good-cop, bad-cop" game police play to extract confessions from criminal suspects. As the familiar routine goes, the "bad cop" confronts the suspect with overwhelming evidence of his guilt (it's usually a "he"), points out discrepancies in his testimony, questions his alibi, and intimidates him with the prospect of a long jail term if he doesn't confess. In contrast, the "good cop" offers sympathy and support, suggests possible justifications for the crime, and emphasizes the benefits of snitching on fellow criminals. As the scenario plays out, the suspect confesses to the crime, and there's no doubt about his guilt.

The belief that virtually all people who confess to a crime are guilty of it is comforting. Perhaps one reason why this idea is so appealing is that the bad guys get off the streets, and law and order prevail. Case closed.

Crime fighters claim to be accurate in ferreting out guilty parties. In one survey of American police investigators and Canadian customs officials, 77% of participants believed they were accurate at detecting whether a suspect was guilty (Kassin et al., 2007). Much of the news and entertainment media assume that criminal confessions are invariably accurate. Writing about the unsolved anthrax poisoning case that terrified much of America in late 2001, two *New York Times* reporters suggested that a confession on the part Dr. Bruce Ivins (a person pursued by the FBI who ending up committing suicide) would have provided "a definitive piece of evidence indisputably proving that Dr. Ivins mailed the letters" containing anthrax (Shane & Lichtblau, 2008, p. 24). The documentary film, *Confessions of Crime* (1991), regaled viewers with convicted killers' confessions to crimes on videotape, with the inscription "fact not fiction" emblazoned in bold letters on the video box. The violence portrayed may be disturbing, but we can sleep easier knowing that the evildoers wind up in prisons. In another documentary, *The Iceman—Confessions of a Mafia Hitman* (2002), Richard Kuklinski described in graphic detail the multiple murders he perpetrated while undercover as a businessman and family man. Yes, danger lurks out there, but we can be reassured that Kuklinski is now behind bars.

Television and movies hammer home the message that the people who confess to their nefarious deeds are almost always the real culprits. Yet the actual state of affairs is much more disturbing, and much less tidy: People sometimes confess to crimes they didn't commit. A case in point is John Mark Karr. In August 2006, Karr confessed to the 1996 murder of 6-year-old beauty queen JonBenet Ramsey. The Ramsey case captivated the media's attention for a decade, so hopes were raised that the murder would finally be solved. But following a frenzy of stories fingering Karr as the killer, the media soon reported that Karr couldn't have been the perpetrator because his DNA didn't match what investigators had found at the crime scene. Speculation was rampant about why Karr confessed. Was Karr, an alleged pedophile who was admittedly fascinated and perhaps obsessed with JonBenet, delusional or merely a publicity hound? More broadly, why do people confess to crimes they didn't commit?

We'll return to this question soon, but for now, we should point out that false confessions aren't uncommon in high-profile criminal cases. After world-famous aviator Charles Lindbergh's son was kidnapped in 1932, more than 200 people confessed to the crime (Macdonald & Michaud, 1987). Clearly, they couldn't all be guilty. In the late 1940s, the notorious "Black Dahlia" case—so named because Elizabeth Short, the aspiring actress who was murdered and mutilated, always dressed in black—inspired more than 30 people to confess to the crime. At least 29, and possibly all 30, of these confessions were false. To this day, Short's murder remains unsolved (Macdonald & Michaud, 1987).

Because so many people falsely confess to high-profile crimes, investigators keep the details of crime scenes from the media to weed out "false confessors." Truly guilty parties should be able to provide accurate information about the crime scene withheld by police and thereby prove their guilt. Henry Lee Lucas, who "confessed" to more than 600 serial murderers, was possibly the most prolific of all false confessors. He has the distinction of being the only person whose death sentence future U.S. president George W. Bush commuted of the 153 on which he passed judgment while Governor of Texas. Although Lucas may have murdered one or more people, most authorities are justifiably skeptical of his wild claims. Gisli Gudjonsson (1992) conducted a comprehensive evaluation of Lucas, and concluded that he said and did things for immediate gain and attention, eager to please and impress people. Clearly, these sorts of motivations may be at play in confessions regarding many well-publicized murders like the JonBenet Ramsey and Black Dahlia crimes.

People may confess voluntarily to crimes they didn't commit for a myriad of other reasons, including a need for self-punishment to "pay for" real or imagined past transgressions; a desire to protect the real perpetrator, such as a spouse or child; or because they find it difficult to distinguish fantasy from reality (Gudjonsson, 2003; Kassin & Gudjonsson, 2004). Unfortunately, when people come out of the woodwork to confess to crimes they didn't commit, or exaggerate their involvements in actual criminal investigations, it may hinder police attempts to identify the real perpetrator.

But an even more serious concern about false confessions is that judges and jurors are likely to view them as persuasive evidence of guilt (Conti, 1999; Kassin, 1998; Wrightsman, Nietzel, & Fortune, 1994). According to statistics compiled by the Innocence Project (2008), in more than 25% of cases in which DNA evidence later exonerated convicted individuals, they made false confessions or pled guilty to crimes they didn't commit. These findings are alarming enough, but the scope of the problem may be far greater because many false confessions are probably rejected as unfounded long before people get to trial because of suspected mental illness. Moreover, laboratory studies reveal that neither college students nor police officers are good at detecting when people falsely confess to prohibited or criminal activities (Kassin, Meissner, & Norwick, 2005; Lassiter, Clark, Daniels, & Soinski, 2004). In one study (Kassin et al., 2005), police were more confident in their ability to detect false confessions than were college students, although the police were no more accurate. In a condition in which participants listened to audiotaped confessions, police were more likely to believe that the false confessions were actually truthful. Thus, police may be biased to perceive people as guilty when they're innocent.

The following cases further underscore the difficulties with false confessions, and exemplify different types of false confessions. Beyond voluntary confessions, Saul Kassin and his colleagues (Kassin, 1998; Kassin & Wrightsman, 1985; Wrightsman & Kassin, 1993) categorized false confessions as either compliant or internalized. In the compliant type, people confess during interrogation to gain a promised or implied reward, escape an unpleasant situation, or avoid a threat (Kassin & Gudjonsson, 2004). The case of the "Central Park Five," in which five teenagers confessed to brutally beating and raping a jogger in New York City's Central Park in 1989, provides a good example of a compliant confession. The teenagers later recanted their confession, saying they believed they could go home if they admitted their guilt. After spending $5^{1}/_{2}$ to 13 years in prison, they were released after DNA evidence exonerated them. In 2002, 13 years after the crime was perpetrated, a serial rapist confessed to the crime.

Now consider the case of Eddie Joe Lloyd. Lloyd had a history of mental problems and made a practice of calling the police with suggestions about how to solve crimes. In 1984, a detective convinced him to confess to raping and murdering 16-year-old Michelle Jackson to trick the real rapist into revealing himself. Based on his confession, Lloyd was convicted and released 18 years later because his DNA didn't match that of the real rapist (Wilgoren, 2002).

In internalized confessions, vulnerable people come to believe they actually committed a crime because of pressures brought to bear on them during an interrogation. Police have tremendous latitude in interrogations and, at least in the U.S., can legally lie and distort information to extract a confession. For example, they can legally play the role of "bad cop" and confront suspects with false information about their alleged guilt, challenge their alibis, undermine suspects' confidence in their denials of criminal activity, and even falsely inform suspects that they'd failed a lie detector test (Leo, 1996).

Jorge Hernandez fell prey to such high-pressure techniques in the course of an investigation of the rape of a 94-year-old woman. Hernandez stated repeatedly that he couldn't remember what he was doing on the night of the crime several months earlier. Police claimed not only that they found his fingerprints at the crime scene, but that they had surveillance footage placing him at the scene of the crime. Confronted with this false evidence and told that the police would help him if he confessed, Hernandez began to doubt his own memory, and concluded that he must have been drunk and couldn't remember that he committed rape. Fortunately for Hernandez, after he spent 3 weeks in jail, he was released when authorities determined that his DNA didn't match samples taken from the crime scene.

Research indicates that many people are vulnerable to false confessions (Kassin & Kiechel, 1996). In an experiment supposedly concerning reaction time, investigators led subjects to believe they were responsible for a computer crash that occurred because they had pressed a key the research assistant had instructed them to avoid. Actually, the researchers had rigged the computer to crash; no subject touched the "forbidden" key. When a supposed witness was present and the pace was fast, all subjects signed a confession afterward admitting their "guilt." Moreover, 65% of these subjects internalized guilt, as indicated by their telling someone in a waiting room (actually a confederate) that they were responsible for the computer crash. When they returned to the lab to reconstruct what happened, 35% made up details consistent with their confession (such as "I hit the key with my right hand when you called out "A.").

Researchers have identified personal and situational characteristics that increase the likelihood of false confessions. People who admit to crimes they didn't commit are more likely to: (a) be relatively young (Medford, Gudjonnson, & Pearse, 2003), suggestible (Gudjonsson, 1992), and isolated from others (Kassin & Gudjonnson, 2004); (b) be confronted with strong evidence of their guilt (Moston, Stephenson, Williamson, 1992); (c) have a prior criminal history, use illicit drugs, and have no legal counsel (Pearse, Gudjonsson, Claire, & Rutter, 1998); and (d) be questioned by intimidating and manipulative interviewers (Gudjonsson, 2003).

Interestingly, the media may prove helpful in minimizing the risk of false confessions. Publicizing cases in which innocent people are wrongly imprisoned based on false confessions may spur efforts to create needed reforms in police interrogations, such as videotaping interviews from start to finish to evaluate the use and effects of coercive procedures. In fact, many police departments are already videotaping interrogations of suspects. We must "confess" we'd be pleased if this practice were implemented on a universal basis. And we stand by our confession.

Chapter 10: Other Myths to Explore

Fiction	**Fact**
Rehabilitation programs have no effect on the recidivism rates of criminals.	Reviews show that rehabilitation programs reduce the overall rate of criminal re-offending.

Fiction	Fact
Most pedophiles (child abusers) have extremely high rates of recidivism.	The majority of pedophiles don't re-offend within 15 years of their initial offense, or at least aren't caught doing so.
All pedophiles are untreatable.	Reviews of treatment studies show modest positive effects on re-offending among pedophiles.
The best approach to treating delinquents is "getting tough" with them.	Controlled studies show that boot camp and "Scared Straight" interventions are ineffective, and even potentially harmful, for delinquents.
The overwhelming majority of acts of domestic violence are committed by men.	Men and women physically abuse each other at about equal rates, although more women suffer injuries as a result.
The rates of domestic abuse against women increase markedly on Super Bowl Sunday.	There's no evidence for this widespread claim.
Being a postal worker is among the most dangerous of all occupations.	Being a postal worker is a safe occupation; the lifetime odds of being killed on the job are only 1 in 370,000 compared with 1 in 15,000 for farmers and 1 in 7,300 for construction workers.
Most psychopaths are violent.	Most psychopaths aren't physically violent.
Most psychopaths are out of touch with reality.	Most psychopaths are entirely rational and aware that their actions are wrong, but they don't care.
Psychopaths are untreatable.	Research provides little support for this claim; more recent evidence suggests that imprisoned psychopaths benefit from treatment as much as other psychiatric patients.
Serial killings are especially common among Whites.	The rates of serial killers are no higher among Whites than other racial groups.
Police officers have especially high rates of suicide.	Meta-analyses show that police officers aren't more prone to suicide than other people.
There is an "addictive personality."	No single personality "type" is at risk for addiction, although such traits as impulsivity and anxiety-proneness predict risk.

Fiction	Fact
Alcoholism is uniquely associated with "denial."	There's little evidence that people with alcoholism are more likely to deny their problems than people with most other psychological disorders.
Most rapes are committed by strangers.	Rapes by strangers comprise only about 4% of all rapes.
Police psychics have proven useful in solving crimes.	Police psychics do no better than anyone else in helping to solve crimes.
Homicide is more common than suicide.	Suicide is about one third more common than homicide.
"Insanity" is a formal psychological and psychiatric term.	Insanity and sanity are purely legal terms typically referring to the inability (or ability) to distinguish right from wrong or to know what one was doing at the time of the act.
The legal determination of insanity is based on the person's current mental state.	The legal determination of insanity is based on the person's mental state at the time of the crime.
Most people who plead insanity are faking mental illness.	Only a minority of individuals who plead insanity obtain clinically elevated scores on measures of malingering.
The insanity verdict is a "rich person's" defense.	Cases of extremely rich people who claim insanity with the support of high-priced attorneys are widely publicized but rare.

Sources and Suggested Readings

To explore these and other myths about psychology and the law, see Aamodt (2008); Arkowitz and Lilienfeld (2008); Borgida and Fiske (2008); Edens (2006); Nickell (1994); Phillips, Wolf, and Coons (1988); Silver, Circincione, and Steadman (1994); Ropeik and Gray (2002); Skeem, Douglas, and Lilienfeld (2009).

11 SKILLS AND PILLS

Myths about Psychological Treatment

Myth #47 Expert Judgment and Intuition Are the Best Means of Making Clinical Decisions

The title of an opinion piece in the satirical newspaper, *The Onion* (Kuhtz, 2004), read: "I want to fly a helicopter, not look at a bunch of crazy dials." The author described the challenges he confronted: "Things are spinning around and coming at you," such as "the telephone poles that keep popping up right in front of you." He longed to rely on his judgment and intuition rather than be forced to learn to use the mechanical aids he brushed off as "a bunch of dials, buttons, lights, and levers."

Flying a helicopter is hardly the only situation in which experts must process a complex array of confusing information. Psychotherapists and other mental professionals need to make equally difficult judgments and decisions virtually every day. Does this client suffer from a major depression? Should I treat this client myself or refer her to another therapist? Is this client suicidal? Would this client benefit from medication along with psychotherapy?

Whether it's diagnosing mental disorders or coming up with treatment plans, mental health professionals must consider an enormous amount of information. This information can include data gathered through interviews and questionnaires, some of it obtained from parents, spouses, teachers, employers, and a host of other sources. The task of putting all of this information together to reach a decision can be tricky. How trustworthy is each piece of information? How much weight should we give it? What should we do when the information isn't consistent?

In his blockbuster bestselling book *Blink: The Power of Thinking Without Thinking*, journalist Malcolm Gladwell (2005) argued that experts reach decisions by focusing on the most relevant information and making accurate snap judgments. They can recognize crucial details without being distracted by anything else, and combine this information using skilled intuition honed by years of training and experience. This model of expertise is what most people expect of mental health professionals. But is there a different way of making clinical decisions?

Over a half century ago, the brilliant clinical psychologist Paul Meehl (1954) provided an insightful analysis of clinical decision-making, outlining two approaches to this task. He referred to the traditional approach, which relies on judgment and intuition, as the *clinical method*. Meehl contrasted this approach with the *mechanical method*. When using the mechanical method, a formal algorithm (set of decision rules) such as a statistical equation or "actuarial table" is constructed to help make decisions in new cases. Insurance companies have used actuarial tables for decades to evaluate risk and set premiums. For example, they can use knowledge of someone's age, sex, health-related behaviors, medical history, and the like to predict how many more years he or she will live. Although actuarial predictions of mortality aren't perfectly accurate for everyone, they provide a decent basis for setting life insurance premiums. Meehl proposed that a mechanical approach would prove just as useful in clinical decision-making. Was he right?

Meehl (1954) reviewed the 20 studies available at the time to compare the accuracy of clinical and mechanical predictions when researchers supplied both the practitioner and the formula with the same information. To the shock of many readers, he found that mechanical predictions were at least as accurate as clinical predictions, sometimes more. Other reviewers have since updated this literature (Dawes, Faust, & Meehl, 1989; Grove et al., 2000), which now includes more than 130 studies that meet stringent criteria for a fair comparison between the two prediction methods. They've found that Meehl's central conclusion remains unchanged and unchallenged: Mechanical predictions are equally or more accurate than clinical predictions. This verdict holds true not only for mental health experts making psychiatric diagnoses, forecasting psychotherapy outcome, or predicting suicide attempts, but also for experts predicting performance in college, graduate school, military training, the workplace, or horse races; detecting lies; predicting criminal behavior; and making medical diagnoses or predicting the length of hospitalization or death. At present, there's no clear exception to the rule that mechanical methods allow experts to predict at least as accurately as the clinical method, usually more so.

How can this be? Let's consider the prior knowledge available for reaching decisions in new cases. For the clinical method, this knowledge consists of cases about which the expert has learned or worked with personally. For the mechanical method, this knowledge consists of cases drawn from the research literature, which is often a larger and more representative sample than is available to any clinician. In addition, even experts are subject to a host of biases when observing, interpreting, analyzing, storing, and retrieving events and information (Meehl, 1992). Mental health professionals, like the rest of us mere mortals, tend to give undue weight to their personal experience rather than the experience of other professionals or research findings (Ruscio, 2006). As a consequence, mechanical predictions usually assign more valid weights to new data than do clinical predictions. Meehl (1986) put it bluntly: "Surely we all know that the human brain is poor at weighting and computing. When you check out at a supermarket, you don't eyeball the heap of purchases and say to the clerk, 'Well it looks to me as if it's about $17.00 worth; what do you think?' The clerk adds it up" (p. 372).

Lewis Goldberg (1991) described several other advantages of mechanical prediction over clinical prediction. Whereas mechanical predictions are perfectly consistent—that is, reliable—clinical predictions aren't. For a variety of reasons, experts don't always agree with each other, or even with themselves when they review the same case the second time around. Even as clinicians acquire experience, the shortcomings of human judgment help to explain why the accuracy of their predictions doesn't improve much, if at all, beyond what they achieved during graduate school (Dawes, 1994; Garb, 1999).

Yet despite Meehl's verdict, many psychologists remain unconvinced. Still others aren't adequately informed. The results of a survey of members of the clinical psychology division (Division 12) of the American Psychological Association revealed that 22% believed that mechanical prediction methods were *inferior* to clinical prediction methods. Another 13% said they'd only heard of mechanical prediction methods but weren't well acquainted with them. Most remarkably, 3% had never heard of mechanical decision-making methods (Grove & Lloyd, in preparation)!

In addition to insufficient education, there are several reasons why many psychologists are reluctant to embrace mechanical decision-making methods in their clinical practice (Dawes et al., 1989). William Grove and Paul Meehl (1996) reviewed objections raised by opponents of these methods, some of which may help to explain the continued popularity of the myth of expert judgment. One concern is that a preference for mechanical prediction will lead to clinicians being replaced by computers. This fear is unfounded because mental health professionals do far more than process information to make decisions. They play essential roles in developing reliable and valid measures, knowing which data to collect, and providing services once they've reached a decision. Clinicians needn't worry about being put out to pasture, because no statistical equation or actuarial table can ever take their place in these essential tasks.

Some authors have argued that we shouldn't be comparing clinical and mechanical prediction methods, because practitioners should use both of them in conjunction. Although this argument may seem appealing at first, on closer inspection it just doesn't hold up. Consider a clinical psychologist who's provided years of intensive therapy for a violent sex offender and is asked by a parole board to recommend whether to grant or deny his request. If mechanical and clinical predictions agree, fine: It doesn't matter which method we use. But what if one method suggests that this prisoner poses no future risk, but the other method suggests that the prisoner poses a high future risk? Clearly, the psychologist can't recommend both granting and denying parole. The logical flaw in the "use both methods" objection is that these methods sometimes conflict. When they do, you can't use both.

Some object to mechanical prediction because "probability is irrelevant to the unique individual." In particular, they claim that knowing the outcomes for other people is of no use when making a decision for a new patient, because "every person is different." For example, research shows that the probability of successfully treating an individual's phobia is maximized through exposure-based treatment—treatment that exposes people systematically to their fears (Barlow, 2002). Yet some mental health experts engage in a "counterinductive generalization" (Dawes & Gambrill, 2003): They disregard this finding and recommend a different treatment on the grounds that group-level research doesn't apply to this unique person. There are two variations of this objection, but both are mistaken.

First, the clinician might think there's something so unusual about a given patient that he or she is an exception to the rule. No doubt this is sometimes true, but studies show that experts routinely identify too many counterexamples (Grove et al., 2000). They focus too heavily on unique aspects of each case and too little on what it shares with others. Their accuracy suffers as a result.

Second, the clinician might believe that any statement of probability is irrelevant to understanding or predicting an individual's behavior. A simple thought experiment, concocted by Meehl (1973), shows the fatal flaw—literally—in this reasoning. Suppose you're to play Russian roulette once, meaning you'll put a revolver to your head and pull the trigger. Would you prefer that there be one bullet and five empty chambers in the revolver, or five bullets and one empty chamber? We doubt seriously you'd respond, "Well, whether I die is only a matter of probabilities, so it doesn't matter." Instead, we'd be safe in assuming that, unless you're suicidal, you'd prefer the gun that will kill you 1 out of 6 times to the gun that will kill you 5 out of 6 times. Clearly, most of us recognize that probability matters when it comes to our own survival.

A final concern involves the allegedly "dehumanizing" nature of mechanical prediction methods, namely, that we shouldn't "treat people as mere numbers." This objection is both erroneous and irrelevant. For starters, there's no logical connection between how we interact with clients and how we combine information to reach clinical decisions. When we make decisions discreetly during or between sessions, a client typically won't even know what method we used. Even if clients feel we're treating them as numbers, feeling comfortable with a decision-making procedure is far less important than being diagnosed correctly and receiving the best treatment. As Meehl (1986) noted, "If I try to forecast something important about a college student, or a criminal, or a depressed patient by inefficient rather than efficient means, meanwhile charging this person or the taxpayer 10 times as much money as I would need to achieve greater predictive accuracy, that is not a sound ethical practice. That it feels better, warmer, and cuddlier to me as predictor is a shabby excuse indeed" (p. 374).

There's ample evidence to support the use of mechanical decision aids, yet mental health professionals rarely use them when they're readily available. That's a shame. Just as judgment and intuition alone aren't enough to hover, swoop, and steer clear of tall buildings when flying a helicopter, clinicians can make better decisions when they rely on more than just their judgment and intuition. And just as helicopter pilots must learn to use an airspeed indicator, an artificial horizon, and a bunch of "crazy dials," mental health professionals would serve their patients better if they developed and used statistical equations and actuarial tables to process information more effectively.

Abstinence Is the Only Realistic Treatment Goal for Alcoholics

If your aunt had a serious problem with drinking, would you be concerned if she had just one drink at a party? The idea that people who drink excessively need to abstain from alcohol completely is deeply etched into the popular imagination. The results of one survey revealed that only 29% of the general population believes that former alcoholics who've been treated successfully can later drink in moderation (Cunningham, Blomqvist, & Cordingley, 2007). The book *Alcoholics Anonymous* (1976) similarly presented a stark, yet still widely accepted, description of the possibility of an alcoholic ever drinking safely:

> ... here is a man who at 55 years found he was just where he left off at 30 (the man having taken his first drink in 25 years). We have seen the truth demonstrated again and again: "once an alcoholic, always an alcoholic." Commencing to drink after a period of sobriety, we are in short time as bad as ever. If we are planning to stop drinking, there must be no reservation of any kind, nor any lurking notion that someday we will be immune to alcohol. (p. 33)

The Alcoholics Anonymous (AA) view of "one drink, one drunk" is premised on the popular *disease model* of alcoholism. According to this model, alcoholism is a fatally progressive disease, caused by an "allergy" or other genetic vulnerability to lose control over drinking. From this perspective, even a single sip of liquor is often enough to trigger an uncontrollable binge (Fingarette, 1988). So, the argument continues, lifelong abstinence is the only acceptable treatment goal for alcoholics. This idea traces its roots to 19th century views of alcoholism, when the term was synonymous with "dipsomania," a disease-like condition of irresistible craving for alcohol (Miller, 1983).

By the early 20th century, the allure and destructive power of alcohol were front and center in the public eye. When movies were in their infancy, they were already capitalizing on the widespread view that alcohol can hijack people's willpower and shatter their lives. In 1909, D. W. Griffith directed two films, *What Drink Did* and *The Reformation of an Alcoholic*, that cautioned viewers about the evils of taking up a life of drinking. Charlie Chaplin's movie, *Charlie's Drunken Daze* (1915), was one of the first films to put a humorous spin on excessive drinking, but its comedic tension was fueled by the potential for tragedy. The decidedly grim movie, *The Lost Weekend* (1945), directed by Billy Wilder and based on the book with the same title (written by Charles Jackson), provided perhaps the most shocking depiction of the degradations of alcoholism, tracing the torturous path of a chronic alcoholic writer through a 5-day bourbon binge. More recent Academy Award-winning films, including *The Days of Wine and Roses* (1962) and *Leaving Las Vegas* (1995), have brought out the darker side of alcoholism by depicting alcohol's devastating effects on relationships and mental health, even the prospect of suicide.

Until quite recently, the idea that abstinence is the only treatment goal for alcoholics—people with a physical and psychological dependence on alcohol, and life problems stemming from drinking—was embraced not only by the general public, but by the alcohol treatment community, as exemplified by the popular AA program. Since stockbroker Bill Wilson and surgeon Bob Smith (better known as "Bill and Bob") founded AA in Akron, Ohio in 1935, it's become the largest organization for treating alcoholics, boasting nearly 2 million members worldwide (Humphreys, 2003). AA's famous 12-step program encourages members to admit they're powerless over alcohol. According to AA, to prevail over the all-consuming mental obsession to drink, members must commit to believing that a Higher Power greater than themselves (who's often, although not necessarily, God) can restore their "sanity" (Step 2), and turn their will and their lives over to the care of their Higher Power as they understand Him (Step 3).

Treatment programs in hospitals, clinics, and the community based on the 12 steps claim recovery rates as high as 85% (Madsen, 1989). Studies show that drinkers who join AA are more likely to get back on the wagon than those who receive no treatment (Kownacki & Shadish, 1999; Timko, Moos, Finney, & Lesar, 2000). Yet as many as two thirds of drinkers drop out within 3 months of joining AA (Emrick, 1987), and AA helps only about 20% of people abstain completely from alcohol (Levy, 2007). Not surprisingly, people who benefit most from AA are most active in the organization and most attracted to its spiritual emphasis. As helpful as AA may be for some people, AA and other programs based on the traditional disease model are far from successful in treating vast numbers of alcoholics.

Indeed, many researchers have challenged the idea that alcoholism is a progressive and incurable disease, along with the notion that abstinence is a necessary treatment goal for all alcoholics. A survey of 43,093 adults conducted by the National Institute of Alcohol Abuse and Alcoholism (NIAAA, 2001–2002) revealed that nearly 36% of respondents who were alcoholics at least a year before the survey were "fully recovered" when questioned. Interestingly, 17.7% of one-time alcoholics could drink in moderation without abusing alcohol, challenging the popular belief that "once an alcoholic, always an alcoholic."

Dramatic as these findings are, they weren't the first to suggest that a treatment goal of less than complete abstinence might be feasible. D. L. Davies' (1962) study showing that 7% of serious alcoholics could control their alcohol use for long as 11 years was one of the first to expose a sizable chink in the armor of the traditional view of alcoholism. Later, the Rand Report (Armor, Polich, & Stambul, 1976) of outcomes at 45 NIAAA treatment centers indicated that after a 4-year follow-up, 18% of patients were drinking moderately with no problems or dependence on alcohol.

Predictably, these studies created a hullabaloo among many researchers and mental health professionals, who suggested that not setting abstinence as a treatment goal was tantamount to medical blasphemy. But the controversy paled in comparison to the avalanche of criticism unleashed by Mark and Linda Sobell's (1973, 1976) reports of their successes in training hospitalized alcoholics to control their drinking. They found that at 3-year follow-up, patients trained to drink in moderation consumed less alcohol and had fewer adjustment problems than did those treated with the goal of abstinence. The Sobells' research was based on the behavioral viewpoint that excessive drinking is a learned habit maintained by a variety of social and physical reinforcers. Like other behaviors, alcohol use can be modified and, in some cases, brought under self-control short of total abstinence.

Some academics attacked the Sobells' findings on ethical, moral, and scientific grounds (Pendry, Maltzman, & West, 1982), with one researcher going so far as to accuse them of cooking up their findings (Maltzman, 1992). So passionate was the controversy that the media jumped into the thick of it. In 1983, an episode of the CBS news magazine *60 Minutes* started with reporter Harry Reasoner in a cemetery near the headstone of one of the Sobells' patients who was taught skills to control drinking, but who had died as result of alcoholism. Reasoner interviewed patients who'd relapsed in the controlled drinking condition, but didn't interview any patients in the abstinence condition. Nor did *60 Minutes* disclose that, over the same period, more patients assigned to the abstinence condition died than did those assigned to the controlled drinking condition (Sobell & Sobell, 1984). The program's presentation left viewers with the impression that controlled drinking could prove fatal. Along with the allegation of fraud, this program inspired a series of investigations into the Sobells' scientific conduct, which exonerated them.

Over the years, scientific controversy around controlled drinking ebbed, yet never disappeared. In the meantime, researchers amassed considerable evidence for the effectiveness of behavioral self-control training (BSCT) programs in studies that set moderate drinking as a treatment goal (Miller, Wilbourne, & Hettema, 2003). In BSCT programs (Miller & Hester, 1980), therapists train people who drink excessively to monitor their drinking, set appropriate limits for their alcohol consumption, control the rate of their drinking, and reinforce their progress. Some self-control programs emphasize teaching coping skills in situations in which drinkers had used alcohol as a coping mechanism (Monti, Abrams, Kadden, & Rohsenow, 1989) and preventing relapse by teaching drinkers to tolerate negative emotions (Marlatt & Gordon, 1985). These programs are at least as effective as 12-step programs (Project MATCH Research Group, 1998).

Relapse prevention (RP) programs run counter to the notion of "one drink, one drunk" by planning for the possibility that people may slip up and resume drinking (Larimer, Palmer, & Marlatt, 1999; Marlatt & Gordon, 1985). The credo of these programs is that a "lapse" needn't become a "relapse." To prevent relapse, the trick is for patients to avoid situations in which they might be tempted to drink. Moreover, they learn to understand that if they consume a single drink, it doesn't mean they're doomed to resume heavy drinking (Marlatt & Gordon, 1985; Polivy & Herman, 2002). RP programs teach people to think of a lapse as an opportunity to learn to cope with urges more effectively rather than thinking, "I've blown it so badly, I might as well keep drinking." A large body of research demonstrates that RP programs reduce the rates of alcohol relapse (Irvin, Bowers, Dunn, & Wang, 1999).

Like gloves and shoes, one size, or in this case one treatment, doesn't fit all. Fortunately, a wide range of treatment options is available to alcoholics, including medication, psychotherapy, and support groups. But the goal of abstinence versus controlled drinking may need to be tailored to individual patients. If your aunt at the party we described is severely dependent on alcohol, has a long history of alcohol abuse, or has physical and psychological problems from drinking, you have every reason to be concerned. Research suggests she'd probably be better served by a treatment program with the goal of abstinence (Rosenberg, 1993).

Yet even if controlled drinking isn't for all alcohol abusers, it probably works for some. The Institute of Medicine (1990) and the Ninth Special Report to Congress on Alcohol and Health (United States Department of Health and Human Services, 1977) endorsed moderation as a treatment goal for some people with drinking problems (MacKillop,

Lisman, Weinstein, & Rosenbaum, 2003). The availability of therapies with a controlled drinking goal may help problem drinkers seek help earlier than if abstinence were the only alternative. Controlled drinking is worth trying with patients who've failed repeatedly to achieve abstinence in programs that emphasize this goal. After all, people who try dieting, exercising, or other new ways of living often need to try several different approaches before they hit on one that works for them. Over the next decade, it's likely that researchers will develop more specific criteria to select heavy drinkers for diverse treatments with equally diverse treatment goals. In the meantime, one conclusion is clear: Abstinence isn't the only realistic treatment goal for all alcoholics.

Myth #49 All Effective Psychotherapies Force People to Confront the "Root" Causes of Their Problems in Childhood

When people think of psychotherapy, they usually conjure up a similar image: a client reclined comfortably on a couch, often recalling and processing painful memories of the distant past. Whether it's Billy Crystal in the film *Analyze This*, Robin Williams in the film *Good Will Hunting*, or Lorraine Bracco in the HBO series, *The Sopranos*, movie and television psychotherapists usually encourage their clients to look backwards, often decades backwards. Indeed, one of the most popular stereotypes of psychotherapy is that it forces patients to resurrect and confront childhood experiences that presumably are causing problems in adulthood. Moreover, numerous Hollywood films feature the tried-and-true formula of the "sudden cure," usually triggered by an emotionally charged recollection of a painful event from childhood, such as sexual or physical abuse (Wedding & Niemiec, 2003). That's not surprising, as the sudden cure makes for an emotionally gripping story line.

We can thank—or blame—Sigmund Freud and his followers for most, if not all, of these popular beliefs. One of Freud's (1915/1957) most enduring legacies is the idea that our ongoing difficulties are rooted in our childhood experiences, especially traumatic ones. According to this view, memories of early events are particularly revealing, and afford a window into current problems and a starting point for resolving them. Leon Saul, Thoburn Snyder, and Edith Sheppard (1956) similarly argued that early memories "reveal probably more clearly than any other single psychological datum, the central core of each person's psychodynamics, his chief motivations" (p. 229). Harry Olson (1979) affirmed a belief shared by many therapists and the general public: "early memories when correctly interpreted often reveal very quickly the basic core of one's personality . . ." (p. xvii). A related widely held idea is that insight into the childhood determinants of problems isn't merely helpful, but necessary, before enduring change can take place in psychotherapy.

Without question, understanding the history of a problem can sometimes help us appreciate the origins of our current maladaptive behaviors. Among other things, such understanding may help therapists to pinpoint problematic behavior patterns that planted their roots in childhood soil. Nevertheless, early memories sometimes yield a distorted picture of past events (Loftus, 1993). Moreover, there's no compelling evidence that all or even most adult psychological problems stem from childhood difficulties (Paris, 2000) and, as we'll soon learn, there's considerable evidence that insight isn't always needed to achieve enduring personal change.

For these and other reasons, increasing numbers of clinicians hailing from the more than 500 approaches to psychotherapy (Eisner, 2000) place little or no emphasis on rehashing the past or uncovering childhood memories. As psychologist John Norcross noted, "Average consumers who walk into psychotherapy expect to be discussing their childhood and blaming their parents for contemporary problems, but that's just not true any more" (Spiegel, 2006). Among the many contemporary schools of psychotherapy that focus primarily on present, but not past, issues are such self-help groups as Alcoholics Anonymous, group therapy, family therapy, and the major schools of therapy we'll consider next.

Psychodynamic therapists, known as "neo-Freudians," stood on Freud's intellectual shoulders, yet parted company with him in significant ways. In particular, many neo-Freudians placed less emphasis on unconscious functioning than their mentor did. Carl Jung (1933) and Alfred Adler (1922), both students of Freud, were among the first therapists to express concerns about conscious aspects of patients' functioning across the entire lifespan, and attempted to help patients understand how emotionally charged experiences, including those in recent life, contribute to current psychological conflicts.

Humanistic-existential therapists, including Carl Rogers (1942), Victor Frankl (1965), and Irvin Yalom (1980), stressed the importance of striving to reach our full potential in the present, rather than relentlessly scouring our memories for negative past experiences. For example, Frederick ("Fritz") Perls, the founder of Gestalt therapy, similarly insisted that the key to personal growth is encountering and accepting our feelings in the here-and-now (Perls, Hefferline, & Goodman, 1994/1951).

Gestalt therapy was the first of many experiential therapies that recognize the importance of current awareness, acceptance, and expression of feelings. For Perls, an excessive focus on the past can be unhealthy, because it often reflects a reluctance to confront our present difficulties head-on.

Behavior therapists focus on specific current behaviors that create patients' life problems and the variables that maintain these behaviors (Antony & Roemer, 2003). Behavior therapies are based on principles of classical and operant conditioning and observational learning, as well as rigorous research evidence regarding what works. Behavior therapists see the key to success in therapy as acquiring adaptive behaviors and strategies that clients can transfer to the real world. In most cases, they view achieving insight into the original causes of one's problems as largely unnecessary.

Cognitive-behavioral therapists, including Albert Ellis (Ellis, 1962) and Aaron Beck (Beck, Rush, Shaw, & Emery, 1979), place their money on identifying and changing irrational cognitions (beliefs), such as "I'm worthless." When people are freed from the tyranny of self-limiting beliefs, these therapists argue, they can more easily engage in new and healthier behaviors. For example, assigning a shy patient homework to strike up a conversation with 10 strangers over the course of a week can provide a powerful challenge to the irrational belief that "If someone rejects me, it will be catastrophic."

As we mentioned earlier, research demonstrates that achieving insight and delving into childhood experiences aren't needed to achieve gains in psychotherapy. In one study of psychoanalytic (Freudian) treatment (Bachrach, Galatzer-Levy, Skolnikoff, & Waldron, 1991), half of 42 patients improved but showed no increases in insight into their "core conflicts." Just as tellingly, the therapist's emotional support was more closely related to improvement than was insight.

Extensive research demonstrates that understanding our emotional history, however deep and gratifying it may be, isn't necessary or sufficient for relieving psychological distress (Bloom, 1994; Weisz, Donenberg, Han, & Weiss, 1995). In fact, treatments that place minimal emphasis on recovering or confronting unresolved feelings from childhood are typically equally effective as, or more effective than, past-oriented approaches. It's true that psychoanalytic and other insight-oriented approaches can help many people, and that relatively brief versions of psychodynamic treatments are more helpful than no treatment (Prochaska & Norcross, 2007). Nevertheless, reviews of controlled outcome studies show that behavioral and cognitive-behavioral treatments are: (a) effective for a wide array of psychological problems, (b) more effective than psychoanalytic and most other treatment approaches for anxiety disorders (Chambless & Ollendick, 2001; Hunsley & Di Giulio, 2002), and (c) more effective than other treatments for children and adolescents with behavior problems, such as lying, stealing, extreme defiance, and physical aggression (Garske & Anderson, 2003; Weisz, Weiss, Han, Granger, & Morton, 1995). Yet these treatments typically focus almost exclusively on the here-and-now.

A current trend in psychotherapy is for therapists to develop methods suited to the needs of clients based on an eclectic mix of techniques borrowed from diverse traditions, including insight-oriented, behavioral, and cognitive-behavioral approaches (Stricker & Gold, 2003). The good news is that a number of therapies, regardless of their focus on the past or present, can benefit many people, regardless of their socioeconomic status, gender, ethnicity, and age (Beutler, Machado, & Neufeldt, 1994; Petry, Tennen, & Affleck, 2000; Rabinowitz & Renert, 1997; Schmidt & Hancey, 1979). To improve, we don't need to look backward; looking forward will often do the trick.

Myth # 50 Electroconvulsive ("Shock") Therapy Is a Physically Dangerous and Brutal Treatment

If you've ever heard of electroconvulsive therapy (ECT), more popularly called "shock therapy," close your eyes for a moment and try to picture a typical treatment session. What do you see happening during the session? And what do you see right after it?

If you're like most Americans, you'll probably imagine an unwilling patient being dragged into a room, strapped to a narrow bed or gurney, receiving a powerful jolt of electric shock to his temples, and then convulsing violently while a team of doctors and nurses attempt to restrain him. When the patient finally "comes to," he acts dazed and confused, and he may have lost hefty chunks of his memory. As we'll soon discover, all of these stereotypes are erroneous, at least in the United States and other Western countries.

Indeed, few if any psychological treatments are the subject of as many misunderstandings as ECT (Kradecki & Tarkinow, 1992). To most people, ECT is a brutal, even barbaric, treatment. In many countries, including the United States, Australia, and European nations, substantial proportions of the general public regard ECT as physically dangerous and psychologically harmful (Dowman, Patel, & Rajput, 2005; Kerr,

McGrath, O'Kearney, & Price, 1982; Teh, Helmes, & Drake, 2007). In one study of 200 Americans, 59% stated that ECT is painful, 53% that it leads to nausea and vomiting, 42% that it's used regularly to punish misbehaving patients, and 42% that it destroys large numbers of brain cells. Sixteen percent believed ECT leaves patients in a permanent zombie-like state (Santa Maria, Baumeister, & Gouvier, 1998). Yet all of these beliefs are inaccurate. The results of another study revealed that 57% of 1,737 members of the Swiss population regarded ECT as harmful to patient's mental health; only 1% regarded it as helpful (Lauber, Nordt, Falcato, & Rössler, 2005). These negative views have had real-world consequences. In 1972, then U.S. Senator Thomas Eagleton withdrew under pressure as presidential candidate George McGovern's vice-presidential running mate after news surfaced that Eagleton had received ECT and other psychiatric treatments for severe depression. A decade later, the city of Berkeley, California voted to ban ECT and make its administration punishable by a fine, jail time, or both, although a court later overturned the ban.

People who know the least about ECT tend to view it most unfavorably (Janicak, Mask, Trimakas, & Gibbons, 1985), raising the possibility that education about ECT may reduce stereotypes about it. Yet even many people with medical training harbor negative views of ECT (Gazdag, Kocsis-Ficzere, & Tolna, 2005). A study of University of Arkansas second-year medical students revealed that 53% considered ECT painful, 32% unsafe and potentially fatal, and 20% "barbaric." Thirty-one percent believed that hospital staff often use ECT to punish aggressive or uncooperative patients (Clothier, Freeman, & Snow, 2001). It's therefore hardly surprising that ECT has long carried a negative stigma in the United States and other countries. With these widespread beliefs in mind, what are the truths about ECT?

It's indeed the case that early forms of ECT often produced violent convulsions, and occasionally resulted in broken bones, shattered teeth, and even death (Challiner & Griffiths, 2000). But that hasn't been true for the past five decades in the United States or most other Western countries, where the method of ECT administration has become far safer and more humane. Nor is it the case that physicians today use ECT to subdue difficult-to-manage patients.

Nowadays, patients who receive ECT—who usually suffer from severe depression or more rarely mania or schizophrenia—first receive a general anesthetic (such as methohexitol), a muscle relaxant (such as succinylcholine), and occasionally a substance (such as atropine) to block salivation (Sackeim, 1989). Then, a physician places electrodes on the patient's head, either on one side (unilateral ECT) or both sides (bilateral ECT), and delivers an electric shock. This shock induces a seizure lasting 45 to 60 seconds, although the anesthetic—which renders the patient unconscious—and muscle relaxant inhibit the patient's movements during the seizure.

Nevertheless, in some developing countries (Andrade, Shah, & Tharyan, 2003; Weiner, 1984), parts of Russia (Nelson, 2005), and modern-day Iraq (Goode, 2008), physicians sometimes administer ECT without anesthesia or muscle relaxants. In these countries, the poor reputation of ECT may be partly deserved, as ECT administered without these procedural advances is potentially dangerous.

Even today, there's no scientific consensus on how ECT works. Still, most controlled research suggests that ECT is helpful as a treatment for severe depression (Pagnin, de Queiroz, Pini, & Cassano, 2004), although it's typically recommended only as a last resort for this condition after other interventions, including psychotherapy and drug treatments, have failed repeatedly. This isn't to say, though, that ECT carries no risks. The death rate among patients who receive ECT is probably about 2 to 10 per 100,000 treatments, although this risk is no higher than the risk from anesthesia alone (Shiwach, Reid, & Carmody, 2001). Overall, the risk of dying from ECT is about 10 times lower than that of childbirth (Abrams, 1997). ECT is also associated with a heightened risk for unpleasant side effects, like headaches, muscle aches, nausea, and most notably, memory loss, mostly for events that take place immediately before each treatment (Sackeim, 1988). Nevertheless, there's also evidence that some memory loss persists for 6 months following treatment in at least some patients who receive ECT (Sackeim et al., 2007). ECT certainly isn't harmless, but it's far from the psychologically and physically dangerous treatment that many people assume.

Interestingly, one group of individuals seems to hold markedly less negative views of ECT than others: patients who've undergone ECT. In fact, most patients who've received ECT report that the treatment is less frightening than a trip to the dentist (Abrams, 1997; Pettinati, Tamburello, Ruetsch, & Kaplan, 1994). In one study, 98% of patients who received ECT said they'd undergo it again if their depression recurred (Pettinati et al., 1994); in another, 91% of patients who received ECT said that they viewed it positively (Goodman, Krahn, Smith, Rummans, & Pileggi, 1999). Kitty Dukakis, wife of former U.S. presidential candidate Michael Dukakis, is a case in point. In her co-authored book *Shock: The Healing Power of Electroconvulsive Therapy* (Dukakis & Tye, 2006), she eloquently recounts her experiences with ECT following severe depressive episodes that failed to respond to other treatments. According to Dukakis,

> It is not an exaggeration to say that electroconvulsive therapy has opened a new reality for me . . . Now I know there is something that will work and work quickly. It takes away the anticipation and the fear . . . It has given me a sense of control, of hope. (Dukakis & Tye, 2006, p. 120)

What, then, are the sources of the principal misconceptions regarding ECT? Certainly, some of these misconceptions are understandable given ECT's checkered past, and once relatively brutal method of administration. Moreover, some laypersons are probably troubled by the prospect of passing electricity through a person's brain, and assume this procedure must be hazardous (Kimball, 2007). In this case, they may be reasoning by representativeness (see *Introduction*, p. 15), and assuming that because electricity is often dangerous, anything containing electricity must damage the brain.

Nevertheless, much of ECT's sordid reputation surely stems from its inaccurate coverage in the entertainment media. From 1948 to 2001, at least 22 American films, including two that won Academy Awards as best picture—*One Flew over the Cuckoo's Nest* (1975) and *Ordinary People* (1980)—contained direct references to ECT, most of them strikingly negative (McDonald & Walter, 2001). In addition, the 2001 Academy Award-winning film, *A Beautiful Mind*, showed mathematician John Nash, portrayed by Russell Crowe, suffering violent convulsions following an ECT-like procedure (insulin coma therapy, an early and now outmoded form of convulsive therapy) that some movie reviewers (for example, Singleton, 2001; Stickland, 2002; http://plus.maths.org/issue19/reviews/book4/index.html) confused with ECT.

In many of the 22 films featuring ECT, hospital staff administered treatment not to deeply depressed patients, but to patients displaying severe antisocial or criminal behavior, especially those who were rebellious or disobedient. Some of the films depicted patients as fully conscious and even reacting in terror to the shock (Walter & McDonald, 2004). The most frequent ECT side effect portrayed in these films was acting like a zombie or losing one's memory or language. In six films, patients who received ECT became worse or even died. Probably no film transformed the American public's perception of ECT more than the 1977 movie, *One Flew Over the Cuckoo's Nest*. One unforgettable scene portrayed the main character, Randall McMurphy (played brilliantly by Jack Nicholson), receiving a brutal ECT treatment, complete with violent

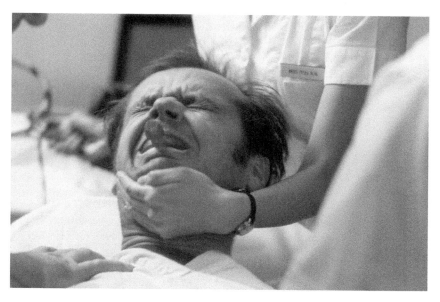

Figure 11.1 This powerful scene from the 1977 film, *One Flew over the Cuckoo's Nest*, featuring actor Jack Nicholson in an Academy Award-winning performance, almost certainly contributed to the public's negative perception of ECT.
Source: Photofest.

convulsions and grunting, after he led an unsuccessful patient revolt on the psychiatric unit (Figure 11.1).

Evidence suggests that viewing films about ECT may alter our perceptions of it. In one study, medical students who viewed clips from *One Flew over the Cuckoo's Nest*, *Ordinary People*, *Beverly Hillbillies*, and several other films featuring ECT or references to ECT ended up with less favorable attitudes toward this treatment (Walter, McDonald, Rey, & Rosen, 2002). Nevertheless, because the researchers didn't include a control group of medical students exposed to non-ECT films, the investigation doesn't allow us to draw definite causal conclusions. On the positive side, there's evidence that education concerning ECT can reduce myths about it. One team of researchers found that students who either viewed a video or read a pamphlet containing accurate information about ECT exhibited fewer misconceptions regarding ECT, such as beliefs that ECT is painful, causes long-term personality changes, and is used to control aggressive patients, than did a control group of students who received no corrective information (Andrews & Hasking, 2004).

The public's lingering misconceptions regarding ECT remind us of a central theme of this book: The popular psychology industry shapes the average person's stereotypes in powerful ways. At the same time, research on the effects of educational interventions on ECT gives us ample reason for hope, because it reminds us that the best means of combating psychological misinformation is providing people with accurate psychological information.

Chapter 11: Other Myths to Explore

Fiction	Fact
A psychologically caused disorder requires psychotherapy; a biologically caused disorder requires medication.	The cause of a disorder has no implications for its treatment, or vice versa; for example, headaches aren't caused by a deficiency of aspirin in the brain.
More experienced therapists tend to have much higher success rates than less experienced therapists.	Most research shows weak or even nonexistent associations between the number of years practicing as a therapist and therapeutic effectiveness.
Psychiatrists and psychologists are essentially identical.	Psychiatrists have M.D.s, whereas most psychologists have Ph.D.s or Psy.Ds; moreover, aside from two states (Louisiana and New Mexico), only psychiatrists can prescribe medications.
The "school of therapy" is the best predictor of treatment effectiveness.	For most disorders, the characteristics of therapists are better predictors of their effectiveness than their theoretical orientation.
All people who call themselves "psychotherapists" have advanced degrees in mental health.	In most U.S. states, the term "psychotherapist" isn't legally protected, so virtually anyone can open a clinical practice.
Most psychotherapy involves using a couch and exploring one's early past.	Most modern therapists no longer use a couch, and most don't focus excessively on childhood experiences.
Most modern therapies are based on the teachings of Sigmund Freud.	In recent surveys, only about 15% of psychologists and 35% of psychiatrists and social workers are predominantly psychoanalytic or psychodynamic in orientation.

Fiction	Fact
Psychotherapy did not exist prior to Freud.	Psychotherapies were present in the U.S. by the mid to late 1800s.
Psychotherapies can only help, not hurt.	At least some therapies, such as crisis debriefing for trauma-exposed individuals, sometimes produce negative effects.
Most psychotherapists use empirically supported therapies.	Surveys suggest that only a marked minority of therapists use empirically supported therapies for anxiety disorders, mood disorders, eating disorders, and other conditions.
Drug Resistance and Education (DARE) programs are effective.	Controlled studies demonstrate that DARE programs are ineffective in preventing drug use, and perhaps even slightly harmful.
People who've experienced a trauma must fully "process" the trauma to improve.	Many or most patients who've experienced a trauma get better on their own; moreover, some therapies that require such processing, like crisis debriefing, are ineffective or perhaps harmful.
Psychotherapies that don't address the "deeper causes" of problems result in symptom substitution.	There's no evidence that behavior therapies and other "symptom-focused" treatments result in symptoms being expressed in another disorder.
Few people can quit smoking on their own.	Studies of community samples show that many people quit smoking without formal psychological intervention.
Nicotine is far less addictive than other drugs.	Many researchers have rated nicotine as more addictive than heroin, cocaine, or alcohol.
Attention-deficit/hyperactivity disorder is caused by excess sugar in the diet.	There's no evidence that sugar exerts marked effects on children's hyperactivity or related behaviors.
Antidepressants greatly increase suicide risk.	Antidepressants may increase suicide risk slightly in some vulnerable individuals; nevertheless, they probably decrease suicide risk overall.
Antidepressants often turn people into "zombies."	Antidepressants don't make people extremely apathetic or unaware of their surroundings.

Fiction	Fact
Antidepressants are much more effective than psychotherapy for treating depression.	Both forms of treatment are about equally effective, and cognitive-behavioral therapy has often been found to be superior to medication for preventing relapse.
Most newer antidepressants, like Prozac and Zoloft, are more effective than older antidepressants.	Most newer antidepressants are no more effective than older antidepressants, although newer antidepressants generally produce fewer side effects and carry a lower risk of overdose.
Placebos influence only our imagination, not our brains.	Placebos exert genuine effects on brain functioning, including increases in the activity of dopamine and other neurotransmitters tied to reward.
Herbal remedies are superior to antidepressants for improving mood.	There's no evidence that any herbal remedies, such as St. John's Wort, are more effective than conventional antidepressants, although some herbal remedies may be helpful for mild depression.
The fact that a substance is "natural" means that it's safe.	Many substances found in nature, such as arsenic, mercury, and snake venom, are extremely dangerous.
Acupuncture works only if one inserts the needles in specific points in the body.	Researchers have generally found acupuncture to be equally effective when the needles are inserted in the "wrong" locations.
Electroconvulsive therapy is rarely administered today.	Over 50,000 Americans receive electroconvulsive therapy each year for severe depression that hasn't responded to other treatments.

Sources and Suggested Readings

To explore these and other myths about psychological treatment, see Bickman (1999); Cautin (in press); Dawes (1994); Dowman, Patel, and Rajput (2005); Gaudiano and Epstein-Lubow (2007); Lacasse and Leo (2005); Lilienfeld (2007); Lilienfeld, Lynn, and Lohr (2003); McNally, Bryant, and Ehlers (2003); Perry and Heidrich (1981); Tryon (2008).

POSTSCRIPT

Truth is Stranger than Fiction

In this book, we've surveyed the vast landscape of psychomythology and tried to persuade you to question your common sense when evaluating psychological claims. To accomplish this goal, we've focused on dispelling a wide array of mistaken beliefs about human behavior—beliefs that accord with our intuitions, but that are false. In the book's closing pages, we wish to accomplish this goal in a different, but complementary, way, namely, by highlighting a sampling of psychological findings that violate our intuitions, but that are true.

As Carl Sagan (1979) noted, one of the best antidotes to pseudoscience is genuine science. As Sagan reminded us, scientific fact is often far stranger—and more fascinating—than is scientific fiction. Indeed, we suspect that most people would be less susceptible to the seductive influence of psychological myths if they were sufficiently aware of genuine psychological knowledge. Such knowledge, as Sagan pointed out, fulfills our deep-seated needs for wonder, but has a decided advantage over mythology: It's true.

So here, in no particular order, is our own list of 10 difficult to believe, but true, psychological findings (for compilations of other remarkable or surprising psychological findings, see Furnham, 1996; Stine, 1990; Wiseman, 2007). Many of these findings may strike us as myths because they are counterintuitive, even bizarre. Yet they are much better supported by scientific research than the 50 beliefs we've examined over the preceding pages. They remind us to doubt our common sense.

Ten Psychological Findings that Are Difficult to Believe, but True

(1) Our brains contain about 3 million miles of neural connections, that is, connections among brain cells (Conlan, 1999). If lined up next to each other, these connections would stretch to the moon and back about 12 times.

(2) Patients who've experienced strokes in their brain's left frontal lobes, which result in severe language loss, are better at detecting lies than are people without brain damage (Etcoff, Ekman, Magee, & Frank, 2000). This may be because people who've lost language develop compensatory nonverbal skills that help them to spot deception in others.

(3) People with extreme forms of "anterograde amnesia," a memory disorder marked by an inability to consciously recall new information, may repeatedly (even over many years) express catastrophic shock when told of the death of the same family member, and re-read the same magazines dozens of times without remembering them (see p. 79). Yet they often exhibit "implicit" (unconscious) memory for certain events without being able to recall them consciously. For example, they may display a negative emotional reaction to a doctor who's been rude to them even though they have no recollection of having ever met him (Shimamura, 1992).

(4) People with a rare condition called "synesthesia" experience cross-modal sensations, that is, those that cut across more than one sensory modality. They may hear specific sounds when they see certain colors, or experience specific smells when they hear certain sounds. Still others may see certain words, like book, in certain colors, like blue (Cytowic, 1993). Brain imaging research demonstrates that synesthetes (people with synesthesia) display activity in multiple brain areas; for example, sound–color synesthetes display activity in both their auditory and visual regions when they hear sounds.

(5) Psychologists have taught pigeons to distinguish paintings by Monet from those of Picasso, and musical compositions by Bach from those of Stravinsky (Watanabe, Sakamoto, & Wakita, 1995), offering further evidence that the term "bird brained" may actually be a compliment rather than an insult. Over the course of many trials, the birds receive rewards for correct answers, and gradually learn to detect cues in the art and music that allow them to distinguish one creative genius' style from the other.

(6) People asked to hold a pencil with their teeth find cartoons funnier than do people asked to hold a pencil with their lips (Strack, Martin, & Stepper, 1988). If we think about it for a moment, we'll realize that people asked to hold a pencil with their teeth are forming a facial expression close to a smile, whereas people asked to hold a pencil with their lips are forming a facial expression close to a frown. One explanation for this peculiar finding is the "facial feedback hypothesis": the facial muscles feed back temperature information to our brains, which in turn influences our emotions (Zajonc, Murphy, & Inglehart, 1989). Interestingly, research shows that words that contain a "k" sound (which also make us smile when we say them)—like wacky, kooky, and quack —are especially likely to make us laugh (Wiseman, 2007).

(7) Research based on U.S. census reports suggests that an unusually large number of people live in places with names similar to their first names. For example, there are significantly more Georges living in Georgia than one would expect by chance, and the same holds for Louises living in Louisiana and Virginias living in Virginia (Pelham, Mirenberg, & Jones, 2002). This effect, which is small in magnitude, appears to result from people with certain names gravitating to places with similar names. This effect may reflect a form of "implicit egotism" in which people are drawn unconsciously to people, places, and things that resemble them.

(8) Compared with Dutch subjects asked to list the characteristics of trouble-making soccer fans, Dutch subjects asked to list the characteristics of professors later answered significantly more general knowledge questions derived from the game, *Trivial Pursuit* (Dijksterhuis & van Knippenberg, 1998). These findings suggest that even subtle mental representations can exert more of an impact on our behavior than psychologists have traditionally assumed.

(9) People's typical handshakes are revealing of their personality traits. For example, people with firm handshakes are more likely than other people to be extraverted and emotionally expressive, and less likely than other people to be shy and neurotic (Chaplin, Phillips, Brown, Clanton, & Stein, 2000). Among women, but not men, firm handshakes are predictive of the personality dimension of openness, which reflects intellectual curiosity and a willingness to seek out novel experiences.

(10) In isolated regions of some Asian countries, including Malaysia, China, and India, some people—usually males—are stricken

periodically with a bizarre psychological condition called "koro." Male victims of koro believe their penis and testicles are disappearing; female victims often believe their breasts are disappearing. Koro is typically spread by contagion; in one area of India in 1982, government officials took to the streets with loudspeakers to reassure hysterical citizens that their genitals weren't vanishing. These officials even measured male citizen's penises with rulers to prove their fears unfounded (Bartholomew, 1994).

As a special treat for those readers whose appetite for unusual psychological findings is still not whetted or who prefer their helpings as baker's dozens, we close with three "Honorable Mentions":

(11)   Although our memories can be quite fallible in some circumstances (see Myths #11–13), they can be astonishingly accurate in others. One research team showed undergraduate subjects 2,560 photographs of various scenes and objects for only a few seconds each. Three days later, they showed these subjects each of the original photographs they'd seen paired with a new one, and asked them to pick out the originals. They were right 93% of the time (Standing, Conezio, & Haber, 1970).

(12)   Some psychological research indicates that dogs resemble their owners. In one study, judges matched the faces of dog owners to their dogs at significantly better than chance levels, although this was true only of purebred, not mixed, breeds (Roy & Christenfeld, 2004).

(13)   Holding a warm object can make us feel "warmer" toward other people. In a recent investigation, two researchers asked subjects to hold either a cup of warm coffee or a cup of iced coffee for a few seconds as a favor for someone, and later asked them to rate a fictitious person on a series of attributes. Those asked to hold the warm cup of coffee were significantly more likely than other subjects to rate that person as higher on "warm" personality traits, such as "generosity" and "caring" (Williams & Bargh, 2008).

Closing Thoughts: Taking Mythbusting with You

As much as we intend our book to be a guide to evaluating psychomythology, we fervently hope it will serve as a lifelong guide to mythbusting in many other crucially important domains of your daily life, including medicine, the environment, politics, economics, and education. For example, the domain of medicine is rife with at least as many misconceptions as is psychology. Widespread beliefs that we need to drink at least eight glasses of water a day to stay healthy; reading in dim light can ruin our eyesight; hair and fingernails continue to grow after we die; shaving our hair makes it grow back faster; swimming less than 45 minutes after a meal can give us cramps; taking Vitamin C helps to prevent colds; we should feed a cold and starve a fever; cracking our knuckles causes arthritis; we lose most of our body heat through our heads; eating too many carrots makes our skin turn orange; and eating chocolate causes acne, have all been disconfirmed by medical research (O'Connor, 2007; Snyderman, 2008; Vreeman & Carroll, 2007, 2008; Wanjek, 2002). These popular but fallacious beliefs remind us that we need to take our mythbusting skills with us in evaluating all everyday life claims, not just those in psychology. Practicing and honing these skills can yield a useful payoff: better real-world decisions.

So as we bid you, the reader, adieu, we leave you with a few helpful summary pointers for taking mythbusting with you into everyday life:

- Although our first instincts and gut impressions may be helpful in "sizing up" people or in predicting our long-term emotional preferences, they're typically inadequate when it comes to evaluating scientific claims about the world.
- Many beliefs spread by "word-of-mouth" are nothing more than urban legends, so we shouldn't assume that widespread beliefs are accurate. We should be especially skeptical of any sentence that begins with "Everyone knows that . . ."
- Media coverage is often misleading, and can lead us to overestimate the frequency of sensational events and underestimate the frequency of less sensational events. Also, the media often tends to oversimplify complex phenomena with the aim of telling a good story. But good stories aren't always accurate stories.
- Biased samples can result in equally biased conclusions. If we're exposed primarily to one group of people (such as the mentally ill) in our line of work, our perceptions of the prevalence of certain traits in people at large will often be skewed.
- Certain biases, such as illusory correlation, confirmation bias, and the overuse of the representativeness and availability heuristics, can lead us to draw erroneous conclusions. Heuristics are helpful shortcuts and rules of thumb, but if we rely on them blindly and uncritically we'll often make mistakes.

- Correlation isn't causation, so a finding that two things are statistically associated doesn't tell us what's causing what. Also, merely because one thing comes before another doesn't mean it causes it.
- Carefully conducted scientific research, although rarely foolproof, is an invaluable gift that we should never take for granted, because it's our best safeguard against human error. As Albert Einstein reminded us, "all our science, measured against reality, is primitive and childlike—and yet it is the most precious thing we have" (quoted in Shermer, 2002, p. 43).

APPENDIX

Recommended Websites for Exploring Psychomythology

Reference List for Articles about Psychology Misconceptions:
http://cwx.prenhall.com/bookbind/pubbooks/morris2/chapter1/
medialib/demo/3.html

Student Misconceptions in the Psychology Classroom by Stephen Chew:
http://teachpsych.org/resources/e-books/eit2004/eit04-03.pdf

Myths about Famous Psychological Studies:
http://www.thepsychologist.org.uk/archive/archive_home.cfm?volumeID=
21&editionID=164&ArticleID=1394

Urban Legends Reference Page: http://www.snopes.com/

Student Misconceptions about the Psychology Major:
http://209.85.215.104/search?q=cache:kjTSkDR6-0oJ:psychclub.
monmouth.edu/assets/Career_Psychology%2520You%2520Think%
2520You%2520Know.doc+student+misconceptions+psychology+
major+monmouth&hl=en&ct=clnk&cd=1&gl=us

Common Statistical Myths (by Schulyer Huck):
http://www.psypress.com/statistical-misconceptions/

PsychBlog 10 Mind-Myths:
http://www.spring.org.uk/2008/04/10-mind-myths-do-any-of-these-
catch-you.php

Self-help Myths (by Annie Murphy Paul):
http://psychologytoday.com/articles/pto-20010301-000044.html

John Stossel's Top 10 Media Myths:
http://abcnews.go.com/2020/story?id=123606

Popular Medical Myths (Some Relevant to Psychology):
http://www.thepsychologist.org.uk/archive/archive_home.cfm?volumeID= 21&editionID=164&ArticleID=1394

Longview Community College "Critical Thinking across the Curriculum Project" featuring 12 widespread psychology misconceptions:
http://mcckc.edu/longview/ctac/psychology/commonsense3.htm

Time, etc., Ten Myths about the Brain:
http://www.time-etc.com/2007/06/ten-myths-about-brain.html

Memory and Learning: Myths and Facts:
http://www.supermemo.com/articles/myths.htm

Myths about Early Brain Development:
http://www.brainskills.co.uk/MythsFactsEarlyBrainDevelopment.html

Myths about False Memories:
http://www.bfms.org.uk/site_pages/myths_page.htm

Hypnosis Myths:
http://www.nhne.com/misc/hypnosis.html

Sleep Myths:
http://www.sleepfoundation.org/site/c.huIXKjM0IxF/b.2466811/k.4CDC/ Sleep_Myths__Fact_or_Fiction_Quiz.htm
http://longevity.about.com/od/lifelongenergy/tp/sleep_myths.htm

Myths about Sports Psychology:
http://www.mentalgamecoach.com/articles/SportsPsychologyMyths.html

John Grohol's Top Ten Myths of Mental Illness:
http://psychcentral.com/blog/archives/2008/06/13/10-myths-of-mental-illness/

Misconceptions about Eating Disorders:
http://www.healthyplace.com/eating-disorders/main/myths-and-misconceptions-about-eating-disorders/menu-id-58/

Alcohol and Alcoholism Myths:
http://www2.potsdam.edu/hansondj/AlcoholFactsandFiction.html
http://www.cnn.com/2007/EDUCATION/03/07/activity.alcohol.myths/ index.html

Common Misconceptions about Psychotherapy:
http://ezinearticles.com/?Common-Misconceptions-About-Psychotherapy&id=674132

REFERENCES

Aamodt, M. G. (2008). Reducing misconceptions and false beliefs in police and criminal psychology. *Criminal Justice and Behavior, 35*, 1231–1240.

Aamodt, S., & Wang, S. (2008). *Welcome to your brain: Why you lose your car keys but never forget how to drive and other puzzles of everyday life.* New York: Bloomsbury.

Aarons, L. (1976). Sleep-assisted instruction. *Psychological Bulletin, 83*, 1–40.

Abell, G. (1979, Spring). Review of the book, "The alleged lunar effect," by Arnold Lieber. *Skeptical Inquirer, 3*, 68–73.

Abrams, R. (1997). *Electroconvulsive therapy* (3rd ed.). New York: Oxford University Press.

Ackerman, R. J. (2002). *Perfect daughters.* Hollywood, FL: Health Communications.

Ackroyd, E. (1993). *A dictionary of dream symbols: With an introduction to dream psychology.* London: Blandford.

Adler, A. (1922). *Practice and theory of individual psychology.* London: Routledge & Kegan Paul.

Adler, J. (2006, March 27). Freud is not dead. *Newsweek, 147*, 42–46.

Aiken, L. R. (1996). *Personality assessment: Methods and practices.* Seattle: Hogrefe & Hube.

Alcock, J. E. (1990). *Science and supernature: A critical appraisal of parapsychology.* Amherst, NY: Prometheus.

Alcock, J., & Otis, L. P. (1980). Critical thinking and belief in the paranormal. *Psychological Reports, 46*, 479–482.

Alcoholics Anonymous. (1976). *Alcoholics Anonymous: The story of how many thousands of men and woman have recovered from alcoholism.* New York: Alcoholics World Services.

Alexander, F. (1950). *Psychosomatic medicine: Its principles and applications.* New York: W. W. Norton.

Alferink, L. (2007). Educational practices, superstitious behavior, and mythed opportunities. *Scientific Review of Mental Health Practice, 5*, 21–30.

Alford, J. R., Funk, C. L., & Hibbing, J. R. (2005). Are political orientations genetically transmitted? *American Political Science Review, 99,* 153–167.

Alison, L. J., Smith, M. D., Eastman, O., & Rainbow, L. (2003). Toulmin's philosophy of argument and its relevance to offender profiling. *Psychology, Crime, and Law, 9,* 173–183.

Alison, L. J., Smith, M. D., & Morgan, K. (2003). Interpreting the accuracy of offender profiles. *Psychology, Crime, and Law, 9,* 185–195.

Allen, W. (1976). *Without feathers.* New York: Ballantine Books.

Alvarado, C. S. (2000). Out-of-body experiences. In E. Cardena, S. J. Lynn, & S. Krippner (Eds.). *The varieties of anomalous experience* (pp. 183–218). Washington, DC: American Psychological Association.

Alvarez, C. X., & Brown, S. W. (2002). What people believe about memory despite the research evidence. *The General Psychologist, 37,* 1–6.

Amato, P. R., & Booth, A. (1997). *A generation at risk: Growing up in an era of family upheaval.* Cambridge, MA: Harvard University Press.

Ambady, N., & Rosenthal, R. (1992). Thin slices of expressive behavior as predictors of interpersonal consequences: A meta-analysis. *Psychological Bulletin, 111,* 256–274.

American Psychiatric Association. (2000). *Diagnostic and statistical manual of mental disorders* (4th ed., text rev). Washington, DC: Author.

American Psychological Association. (2002). Ethical principles of psychologists and code of conduct. Retrieved August 13, 2008 from http://www.apa.org/ethics/code2002.pdf

American Psychological Association Board of Professional Affairs. (1998). Awards for distinguished professional contributions: John Exner. *American Psychologist, 53,* 391–392.

Anastasi, A., & Urbina, S. (1997). *Psychological testing* (7th ed., p. 413). Upper Saddle River, NJ: Prentice Hall.

Anastasi, A., & Urbina, S. (1997). *Psychological testing.* Upper Saddle River, NJ: Prentice-Hall International.

Anderson, C. A., & Bushman, B. J. (2002). Media violence and the American Public revisited. *American Psychologist, 57,* 448–450.

Anderson, C. A., Gentile, D. A., & Buckley, K. E. (2007). *Violent video game effects on children and adolescents.* New York: Oxford University Press.

Anderson, D. R., & Pempek, T. A. (2005). Television and very young children. *American Behavioral Scientist, 48,* 505–522.

Andrade, C., Shah, N., & Tharyan, P. (2003). The dilemma of unmodified ECT. *Journal of Clinical Psychiatry, 64,* 1147–1152.

Andrews, M., & Hasking, P. A. (2004). The effect of two educational interventions on knowledge and attitudes towards electroconvulsive therapy. *Journal of ECT, 20,* 230–236.

Angelica, J. C. (1993). *A moral emergency: Breaking the cycle of child abuse.* Kansas City, MO: Sheed & Ward.

Angermeyer, M. C., & Dietrich, S. (2006). Public beliefs about and attitudes towards people with mental illness: A review of population studies. *Acta Psychiatric Scandinavica, 113*, 163–179.

Angermeyer, M. C., Buyantugs, L., & Kenzine, D. V. (2004). Effects of labeling on public attitudes toward people with schizophrenia: Are there cultural differences? *Acta Psychiatric Scandinavica, 109*, 420–425.

Angus, M. (1973). *The rejection of two explanations of belief of a lunar influence on behavior.* Unpublished Master's thesis, Simon Fraser University, Burnaby, British Columbia, Canada.

Antony, M. A., & Roemer, L. (2003). Behavior therapy. In A. S. Gurman & S. B. Messer. *Essential psychotherapies* (2nd ed., pp. 182–223). New York: Guilford Press.

Applebaum, P. S. (2004). One madman keeping loaded guns: Misconceptions of mental illness and their legal consequences. *Psychiatric Services, 55*, 1105–1106.

Arean, P. A., & Reynolds, C. F. (2005). The impact of psychosocial factors on late-life depression. *Biological Psychiatry, 58*, 277–282.

Aries, E. (1996). *Men and women in interaction.* New York: Oxford University Press.

Arieti, S. (1968). Schizophrenia. In *Encyclopedia Brittanica* (Vol. 19, p. 1162). London: William Benton.

Arkowitz, H., & Lilienfeld, S. O. (2008, April/May). Once a sex offender, always a sex offender? *Scientific American Mind, 18*(2), 78–79.

Armor, D. J., Polich, J. M., & Stambul, H. B. (1976). *Alcoholism and treatment.* Rand Corp: Santa Monica, CA.

Arnett, J. J. (1999). Adolescent storm and stress, reconsidered. *American Psychologist, 54*, 317–326.

Associated Press. (2008, August 24). Pentagon's intelligence arm stems up lie detecting efforts on employees. Retrieved August 24, 2008 from http://www.foxnews.com/story/0,2933,409502,00.html

Atwater, B. (n.d.). *Medical intuitive and distant energy healer.* Retrieved September 12, 2008 from http://www.brentenergywork.com/BOOKS.htm

Bach, G. R., & Goldberg, H. (1974). *Creative aggression.* New York: Doubleday.

Bachrach H., Galatzer-Levy, R., Skolnikoff, A., & Waldron, S. (1991). On the efficacy of psychoanalysis. *Journal of the American Psychoanalytic Association, 39*, 871–916.

Badian, N. (2005). Does a visual-orthographic deficit contribute to reading disability? *Annals of Dyslexia, 55*, 28–52.

Ballance, C. T. (1977). Students' expectations and their answer-changing behavior. *Psychological Reports, 41*, 163–166.

Ballone, L. M., & Czerniak, C. M. (2001). Teachers' beliefs about accommodating students' learning styles in science classes. *Electronic Journal of Science Education, 6*, 1–41.

Bandura, A. (1964). The stormy decade: Fact or fiction? *Psychology in the Schools, 1*, 224–231.

Bangerter, A., & Heath, C. (2004). The Mozart Effect: Tracking the evolution of a scientific legend. *British Journal of Social Psychology, 43*, 1–37.

Bányai, É. I. (1991). Toward a social-psychobiological model of hypnosis. In S. J. Lynn & J. W. Rhue (Eds.), *Theories of hypnosis: Current models and perspectives*. New York: Guilford Press.

Barlow, D. H. (2002). *Anxiety and its disorders: The nature and treatment of anxiety and panic* (2nd ed.). New York: Guilford Press.

Barnett, R., & Rivers, C. (2004). *Same difference: How gender myths are hurting our relationships, our children, and our jobs*. New York: Basic Books.

Baron, R. A., & Byrne, B. (1994). *Social psychology: Understanding human interaction* (7th ed.). Boston: Allyn & Bacon.

Barry, C. T., Frick, P. J., & Killian, A. L. (2003). The relation of narcissism and self-esteem to conduct problems in children: A preliminary investigation. *Journal of Clinical Child and Adolescent Psychology, 32*, 139–152.

Bartholomew, R. E. (1994). The social psychology of "epidemic" koro. *International Journal of Social Psychiatry, 40*, 46–60.

Basil, R. (Ed.). (1988). *Not necessarily the New Age: Critical essays*. Amherst, NY: Prometheus.

Bass, E., & Davis, L. (1988). *The courage to heal: A guide for women survivors of child sexual abuse*. New York: Harper & Row.

Bath, J. A. (1967). Answer-changing behavior on objective examinations. *Journal of Educational Research, 61*, 105–107.

Baumeister, R. F. (2001, April). Violent pride: Do people turn violent because of self hate, or self-love? *Scientific American, 284*(4), 96–101.

Baumeister, R. F., Campbell, J. D., Krueger, J. I., & Vohs, K. D. (2003). Does high self-esteem cause better performance interpersonal success, happiness, or healthier lifestyles? *Psychological Science in the Public Interest, 4*, 1–44.

Bausell, R. B. (2007). *Snake oil science: The truth about complementary and alternative medicine*. New York: Oxford University Press.

Baxendale, S. (2004). Memories aren't made of this: Amnesia at the movies. *British Medical Journal, 329*, 1480–1483.

Beaman, A., Barnes, P., Klentz, B., & McQuirk, B. (1978). Increasing helping rates through information dissemination: Teaching pays. *Personality and Social Psychology Bulletin, 4*, 406–411.

Beck, A. T., Brown, G., & Steer, R. A. (1989). Prediction of eventual suicide in psychiatric inpatients by clinical rating of hopelessness. *Journal of Consulting and Clinical Psychology, 57*, 309–310.

Beck, A. T., Kovacs, M., & Weissman, A. (1975). Hopelessness and suicidal behavior: An overview. *Journal of the American Medical Association, 234*, 1146–1149.

Beck, A. T., Rush, A. J., Shaw, B. F., & Emery, G. (1979). *Cognitive therapy of depression*. New York: Guilford Press.

Beins, B. (2008). Why we believe: Fostering critical thought and scientific literacy in research methods. In D. S. Dunn, J. S. Halonen, & R. A. Smith (Eds.), *Teaching critical thinking in psychology: A handbook of best practices* (pp. 199–210). Malden, MA: Wiley-Blackwell.

Bello-Hass, V. D., Bene, M. D., & Mitsumoto, H. (2002, December). End of life: Challenges and strategies for the rehabilitation professional. *Neurology Report*. Retrieved June 4, 2008 from http://findarticles.com/p/articles/mi_qa3959/is_200212/ai_n9159033

Bem, D. J., & Honorton, C. (1994). Does psi exist? Replicable evidence for an anomalous process of information transfer. *Psychological Bulletin, 115*, 4–18.

Benjamin, L. T., Jr., Cavell, T. A., & Shallenberger, W. R., III. (1984). Staying with initial answers on objective tests: Is it a myth? *Teaching of Psychology, 11*, 133–141.

Bennallack, O. (2006, April 24). Brain games aim to boost your IQ. BBC News. Retrieved August 8, 2008 from http://news.bbc.co.uk/2/hi/technology/4930996.stm

Ben-Shakhar, G. (1991). Clinical judgment and decision-making in CQT-polygraphy. *Integrative Physiological and Behavioral Science, 26*, 232–240.

Berke, R. L. (2000). Democrats see, and smell, "Rats" in G.O.P. ad. *The New York Times*, September 12, 2000.

Bersoff, D. N. (1981). Testing and the law. *American Psychologist, 36*, 1047–1056.

Best, J. B. (1979). Item difficulty and answer changing. *Teaching of Psychology, 8*, 228–230.

Beutler, L., Machado, P. P., & Neufeldt, S. A. (1994). Therapist variables. In A. E. Bergin & S. L. Garfield (Eds.), *Handbook of psychotherapy and behavior change* (4th ed.). New York: John Wiley & Sons.

Beyerstein, B. L. (1990). Brain scams: Neuromythologies of the New Age. *International Journal of Mental Health, 19*, 27–36.

Beyerstein, B. L., Sampson, W. I., Stojanovic, Z., & Handel, J. (2007). Can mind conquer cancer? In S. Della Sala (Ed.). *Tall tales about the mind and brain: Separating fact from fiction* (pp. 440–460). Oxford: Oxford University Press.

Beyerstein, B. L. (1985). The myth of alpha consciousness. *Skeptical Inquirer, 10*, 42–59.

Beyerstein, B. L. (1987). The brain and consciousness: Implications for psi phenomena. *The Skeptical Inquirer, 12*(2), 163–173.

Beyerstein, B. L. (1999a). Pseudoscience and the brain: Tuners and tonics for aspiring superhumans. In S. Della Sala (Ed.), *Mind myths: Exploring popular assumptions about the mind and brain* (pp. 59–82). Chichester: John Wiley & Sons.

Beyerstein, B. L. (1999b). Social and judgmental biases that make inert treatments seem to work. *The Scientific Review of Alternative Medicine, 3*(2), 16–29.

Beyerstein, B. L. (1999c). Whence cometh the myth that we only use ten percent of our brains? In S. Della Sala (Ed.), *Mind myths: Exploring popular assumptions about the mind and brain* (pp. 1–24). Chichester: John Wiley & Sons.

Beyerstein, B. L., & Beyerstein, D. F. (Eds.). (1992). *The write stuff: Evaluations of graphology—the study of handwriting analysis*. Amherst, NY: Prometheus.

Bickman, L. (1999). Practice makes perfect and other myths about mental health services. *American Psychologist, 54,* 965–999.

Biklen, D. (1990). Communication unbound: Autism and praxis. *Harvard Educational Review, 60,* 291–314.

Bishop, D. V., Whitehouse, A. J., Watt, H. J., & Line, E. A. (2008). Autism and diagnostic substitution: Evidence from a study of adults with a history of developmental language disorder. *Developmental Medicine and Child Neurology, 50,* 341–345.

Black, S. M., & Hill, C. E. (1984). The psychological well-being of women in their middle years. *Psychology of Women Quarterly, 8,* 282–292.

Blackmore, S. J. (1982). *Beyond the body: An investigation of out-of-the-body experience*. London: Heinemann.

Blackmore, S. J. (1984). A postal survey of OBEs and other experiences. *Journal of the Society for Psychical Research, 52,* 225–244.

Blackmore, S. J. (1986). Spontaneous and deliberate OBEs: A questionnaire survey. *Journal of the Society for Psychical Research, 53,* 218–224.

Blackmore, S. J. (1993). *Dying to live: Near-death experiences*. Amherst, NY: Prometheus.

Blakely, R. (2008, December 3). Mumbai police to use truth serum on "baby faced" terrorist Azam Amir Kasab. *Times Online*. Retrieved on January 24, 2009 from http://www.timesonline.co.uk/tol/news/world/asia/article5280084.ece

Blanke, O., Ortigue, S., Landis, T., & Seeck, M. (2002). Stimulating illusory own-body perceptions. *Nature, 419,* 269–270.

Blanke, O., & Thut, G. (2007). Inducing out-of-body experiences. In S. Della Sala (Ed.), *Tall tales about the mind and brain: Separating fact from fiction* (pp. 425–439). Oxford: Oxford University Press.

Bleuler, E. (1911). *Dementia praecox or the group of schizophrenias* (J. Zinkin, Trans.). New York: International Universities Press.

Block, N. (1995). How heritability misleads about race. *Cognition, 56,* 99–128.

Bloom, P. B. (1994). Is insight necessary for successful treatment? *American Journal of Clinical Hypnosis, 36,* 172–174.

Blume, S. E. (1990). *Secret survivors: Uncovering incest and its aftereffects in women*. Chichester: John Wiley & Sons.

Bohigian, G. M. (1998). The evil eye and its influence on medicine and social customs. *Skeptic, 6*(1), 43–47.

Bonanno, G. A. (2004). Loss, trauma, and human resilience: Have we underestimated the human capacity to thrive after extremely adverse events? *American Psychologist, 59,* 20–28.

Bonanno, G. A., Wortman, C. B., Lehman, D. R., Tweed, R. G., Haring, M., Sonnega, J., et al. (2002). Resilience to loss and chronic grief: A prospective study from preloss to 18 months postloss. *Journal of Personality and Social Psychology, 83,* 1150–1164.

Boorstin, D. J. (1983). *The discoverers: A history of man's search to know his world and himself.* London: Dent.

Borgida, E., & Fiske, S. T. (Eds.). (2008). *Beyond common sense: Psychological science in the courtroom.* Oxford: Wiley-Blackwell.

Bornstein, R. F. (1996). Construct validity of the Rorschach Oral Dependency Scale: 1967–1995. *Psychological Assessment, 8,* 200–205.

Bornstein, R. F. (1989). Exposure and affect: Overview and meta-analysis of research, 1968–1987. *Psychological Bulletin, 106,* 265–289.

Bowers, K. (1987). Revisioning the unconscious. *Canadian Psychology, 28*(2), 93–104.

Bradshaw, J. (1991). *Homecoming: Reclaiming and championing your inner child.* New York: Bantam.

Branden, N. (1994). *The six pillars of self-esteem.* New York: Bantam.

Brickman, P., & Campbell, D. T. (1971). Hedonic relativism and planning the good society. In M. H. Apley (Ed.), *Adaptation-level theory: A symposium* (pp. 287–302). New York: Academic Press.

Brickman, P., Coates, D., & Janoff-Bulman, R. (1978). Lottery winners and accident victims: Is happiness relative? *Journal of Personality and Social Psychology, 36,* 917–927.

Briggs, K. C., & Myers, I. B. (1998). *Myers–Briggs Type Indicator.* Palo Alto, CA: Consulting Psychologists Press.

Brim, O. G. (1992). *Ambition: How we manage success and failure throughout our lives.* New York: Basic Books.

Brim, O. G., Ryff, C. D., & Kessler, R. C. (2004). *How healthy are we? A national study of well-being at midlife.* The John D. and Catherine T. MacArthur Foundation Network on Mental Health and Development. Studies on Successful Midlife Development (R. C. Kessler, Ed.). Chicago: University of Chicago Press.

Brizendine, L. (2006). *The female brain.* New York: Broadway Books.

Bronowski, J. (1966). The logic of the mind. *American Scientist, 54,* 1–4.

Brown, D. F., Scheflin, A. W., & Hammond, C. (1998). *Memory, trauma treatment, and the law.* New York: W. W. Norton.

Brown, L. T. (1983). Some more misconceptions about psychology among introductory psychology students. *Teaching of Psychology, 10,* 207–210.

Brown, R., & Kulik, J. (1977). Flashbulb memories. *Cognition, 5,* 73–99.

Brownell, K., & Rodin, J. (1994). The dieting maelstrom: Is it possible and advisable to lose weight? *American Psychologist, 49,* 781–791.

Bruer, J. T. (1999). *The myth of the first three years*. New York: Free Press.

Brunvand, J. H. (1999). *Too good to be true: The colossal book of urban legends*. New York: W. W. Norton.

Buchanan, C. M., Eccles, J., & Becker, J. (1992). Are adolescents the victims of raging hormones? Evidence for activational effects of hormones on moods and behavior at adolescence. *Psychological Bulletin, 111*, 62–107.

Buckman, R. (1993). Communication in palliative care: A practical guide. In D. Doyle, G. W. C. Hanks, & N. McDonald (Eds.), *Oxford textbook of palliative care* (p. 51). Oxford: Oxford Medical Publications.

Burgess, A. (1962). *A clockwork orange*. New York: Penguin.

Bushman, B. J. (2002). Does venting anger feed or extinguish the flame? Catharsis, rumination, distraction, anger, and aggressive responding. *Personality and Social Psychology Bulletin, 28*, 724–731.

Bushman, B. J., & Baumeister, R. F. (1998). Threatened egotism, narcissism, self-esteem, and direct and displaced aggression: Does self-love or self-hate lead to violence? *Journal of Personality and Social Psychology, 75*, 219–229.

Bushman, B. J., Baumeister, R. F., & Phillips, C. M. (2001). Do people aggress to improve their mood? Catharsis, relief, affect regulation opportunity, and aggressive responding. *Journal of Personality and Social Psychology, 81*, 17–32.

Bushman, B. J., Baumeister, R. F., & Stack, A. D. (1999). Catharsis, aggression, and persuasive influence: Self-fulfilling or self-defeating prophecies. *Journal of Personality and Social Psychology, 76*, 367–376.

Buston, P. M., & Emlen, S. T. (2003). Cognitive processes underlying human mate choice: The relationship between self-perception and mate preference in Western society. *Proceedings of the National Academy of Sciences of the United States of America, 100*, 8805–8810.

Butow, P. N., Hiller, J. E., Price, M. A., Thackway, S. V., Kricker, A., & Tennant, C. C. (2000). Epidemiological evidence for a relationship between life events, coping style, and personality factors in the development of breast cancer. *Journal of Psychosomatic Research, 49*, 169–181.

Byrne, D. (1971). *The attraction paradigm*. New York: Academic Press.

Byrne, D., London, O., & Reeves, K. (1968). The effects of physical attractiveness, sex, and attitude similarity on interpersonal attraction. *Journal of Personality, 36*, 259–271.

Byrne, R. (2006). *The Secret*. New York: Atria Books.

Cacioppo, J. T. (2004). Common sense, intuition, and theory in personality and social psychology. *Personality and Social Psychology Review, 8*, 114–122.

Caldwell, B., & Woolley, S. (2008). Marriage and family therapists' endorsement of myths about marriage. *American Journal of Family Therapy, 36*, 367–387.

Calvert, J. F., & Munsie-Benson, M. (1999). Public opinion and knowledge about childhood sexual abuse in a rural community. *Child Abuse and Neglect, 23*, 671–682.

Cameron, D. (2007). *The myth of Mars and Venus*. New York: Oxford University Press.

Campbell, D. (1997). *The Mozart Effect*. New York: Avon Books.

Campbell, D. E. (1982). Lunar lunacy research: When enough is enough. *Environment and Behavior, 14,* 418–424.

Canfield, J., Hansen, M. V., McAdoo, C., & Evans, P. C. (2008). *Chicken soup for the soul. Empty nesters: 101 stories about surviving and thriving when the kids leave home.* New York: Simon & Schuster.

Carbo, M., Dunn, R., & Dunn, K. (1986). *Teaching students through their individual learning styles.* Englewood Cliffs, NJ: Prentice Hall.

Cardena, E., Lynn, S. J., & Krippner, S. (Eds.). (2000). *The varieties of anomalous experience.* Washington, DC: American Psychological Association.

Carey, B. (2007, February 9). Study puts rate of autism in 1 in 150 U.S. children. *New York Times.* Retrieved July 28, 2008 from http://www.nytimes.com/2007/02/09/health/09autism.html

Carlson, N. R. (1990). *Psychology* (5th ed.). Boston: Allyn & Bacon.

Carroll, J. B. (1993). *Human cognitive abilities: A survey of factor-analytic studies.* New York: Cambridge University Press.

Carroll, R. T. (2003). *The skeptic's dictionary: A collection of strange beliefs, amusing deceptions, and dangerous delusions.* New York: Wiley.

Carstensen, L. L., & Lockenhoff, C. E. (2003). Aging, emotion, and evolution: The bigger picture. *Annals of the New York Academy of Sciences, 1000,* 152–179.

Carver, R. P. (1987). Teaching rapid reading in the intermediate grades: Helpful or harmful? *Reading Research and Instruction, 26,* 65–76.

Caspi, A., & Herbener, E. S. (1990). Continuity and change: Assortative marriage and the consistency of personality in adulthood. *Journal of Personality and Social Psychology, 72,* 1440–1447.

Cassar, M., Treiman, R., Moats, L., Pollo, T. C., & Kessler, B. (2005). How do the spellings of children with dyslexia compare with those of nondyslexic children? *Reading and Writing, 18,* 27–49.

Cautin, R. L. (in press). The history of psychotherapy, 1860–1960. In J. C. Norcross, G. R. VandenBos, & D. K. Freedheim (Eds.). *History of psychotherapy* (2nd ed.). Washington, DC: American Psychological Association.

CBS 60 Minutes (Home Page). *A true confession? Interrogation techniques may lead to false confessions.* Retrieved September 12, 2008 from http://www.cbsnews.com/stories/2004/02/26/60minutes/main602401.shtml

Ceci, S. J., Crotteau-Huffman, M., Smith, E., & Loftus, E. F. (1994). Repeatedly thinking about non-events. *Consciousness and Cognition, 3,* 388–407.

Center for Grieving Children. Retrieved September 12, 2008 from http://www.cgcmaine.org/index.html

Centers for Disease Control and Prevention. (1997). Knowledge of peptic ulcer disease—United States, March–April 1997. *NNWR Weekly, 46,* 985–987.

Chabris, C. F. (1999). Prelude or requiem for the 'Mozart effect'? *Nature, 400,* 826–827.

Chakrabarti, S., & Fombonne, E. (2005). Pervasive developmental disorders in preschool children: Confirmation of high prevalence. *American Journal of Psychiatry, 162,* 1133–1141.

Challiner, V., & Griffiths, L. (2000). Electroconvulsive therapy: A review of the literature. *Journal of Psychiatric Mental Health Nursing, 7,* 191–198.

Chambless, D. L., & Ollendick, T. H. (2001). Empirically supported psychological interventions: Controversies and evidence. *Annual Review of Psychology, 52,* 685–716.

Chaplin, W. F., Phillips, J. B., Brown, J., Clanton, N. R., & Stein, J. L. (2000). Handshaking, gender, personality, and first impressions. *Journal of Personality and Social Psychology, 79,* 110–117.

Chapman, L. J., & Chapman, J. P. (1967). Genesis of popular but erroneous diagnostic observations. *Journal of Abnormal Psychology, 72,* 193–204.

Chapman, L. J., & Chapman, J. P. (1969). Illusory correlation as an obstacle to the use of valid psychodiagnostic signs. *Journal of Abnormal Psychology, 74,* 271–280.

Chapman, S., & Morrell, S. (2000). Barking mad? Another lunatic hypothesis bites the dust. *British Medical Journal, 321,* 1561–1563.

Chaves, J. F. (2000). Hypnosis. In A. E. Kazdin (Ed.), *Encyclopedia of psychology* (pp. 211–216). Washington, DC: American Psychological Association; New York: Oxford University Press.

Cheng, A. T. A., Chen, T. H. H., Chen, C-C., & Jenkins, R. (2000). Psychosocial and psychiatric risk factors for suicide. Case–control psychological autopsy study, *British Journal of Psychiatry, 177,* 360–365.

Chew, S. L. (2004, March). Student misconceptions in the psychology classroom. *E-xcellence in teaching.* PsychTeacher Electronic Discussion List.

Choker-Chicken-Animated-Dancing-Management. Retrieved September 12, 2008 from http://www.amazon.com

Choking Strangler Boss toy. Retrieved September 12, 2008 from http://www.kleargear.com/1085.html

Chopra, D. (1990). *Quantum healing: Exploring the frontiers of mind/body medicine.* New York: Bantam.

Chudler, E. (2006). Myths about the brain: 10 percent and counting. Everything Blog. Retrieved August 30, 2008 from http://everyravlik.blogspot.com/2006/10/myths-about-brain-10-percent-and.html

Chudler, E. (n.d.). Do we only use 10% of our brain? Retrieved September 12, 2008 from http://faculty.washington.edu/chudler/tenper.html

Cima, M., Merckelbach, H., Nijman, H., Knauer, E., & Hollnack, S. (2002). I can't remember your honour: Offenders who claim amnesia. *German Journal of Psychiatry, 5,* 24–34.

Clark, A., Diener, E., Georgellis, Y., & Lucas, R. (2008). Lags and leads in life satisfaction: A test of the baseline hypothesis. *Economic Journal, 118,* F222–F443.

Clarke, S. C. (1995). Advance report of final divorce statistics 1989 and 1990. *Monthly Vital Statistics Report, 43*(8, Suppl.). Hyattsville, MD: National Center for Health Statistics.

Clarke-Stewart, K. A. (1998). Historical shifts and underlying themes in ideas and rearing young children in the United States: Where have we been? Where are we going? *Early Development and Parenting, 7,* 101–117.

Clifasefi, S. L., Garry, M., & Loftus, E. F. (2007). Setting the record (or video camera) straight on memory: The video camera model of memory and other memory myths. In S. Della Sala (Ed.), *Tall tales about the mind and brain: Separating fact from fiction* (pp. 60–65). Oxford: Oxford University Press.

Clinton, H. (1996). *It takes a village: And other lessons children teach us.* New York: Simon & Schuster.

Clothier, J. L., Freeman, T., & Snow, L. (2001). Medical student attitudes and knowledge about ECT. *Journal of ECT, 17,* 99–101.

Coffield, F., Moseley, D., Hall, E., & Ecclestone, K. (2004). *Learning styles and pedagogy in post-16 learning: A systematic and critical review.* London: Learning and Skills Research Centre.

Cohen, J. (1988). *Statistical power analysis for the behavioral sciences* (2nd ed.). Hillsdale, NJ: Erlbaum.

Cohen, P., & Cohen, J. (1984). The clinician's illusion. *Archives of General Psychiatry, 41,* 1178–1182.

Colvin, R. (2000). Losing faith in self-esteem. *School Administrator, 57,* 28–33.

Comer, R. J. (2007). *Abnormal psychology* (6th ed.). New York: W. H. Freeman.

Conduit, R., & Coleman, G. (1998). Conditioned salivation and associated dreams from REM sleep. *Dreaming, 8,* 243–262.

Conlan, R. (1999). *States of mind: New discoveries about how our brains make us who we are.* New York: Dana Press.

Conti, R. (1999). The psychology of false confessions. *The Journal of Credibility Assessment and Witness Psychology, 2,* 14–36.

Copp, G. (1998). A review of current theories of death and dying. *Journal of Advanced Nursing, 28,* 382–390.

Coppen, A. (1994). Depression as a lethal disease: prevention strategies. *Journal of Clinical Psychiatry, 55*(Suppl.), 37–45.

Corballis, M. C. (1999). Are we in our right minds? In S. Della Sala (Ed.), *Mind myths: Exploring popular assumptions about the mind and brain* (pp. 25–42). Chichester: Wiley.

Corballis, M. C. (2007). The dual-brain myth. In S. Della Sala (Ed.), *Tall tales about the mind and brain: Separating fact from fiction* (pp. 291–314). Oxford: Oxford University Press.

Corkin, S. (2002). What's new with the amnesic patient H.M.? *Nature Reviews Neuroscience, 3,* 153–160.

Cornell, D. (2006). *School violence: Fears versus facts.* Mahwah, NJ: Erlbaum.

Cornez-Ruiz, S., & Hendricks, B. (1993). Effects of labeling and ADHD behaviors on peer and teacher judgments. *Journal of Educational Research, 86,* 349–355.

Corrigan, P. W., & Penn, D. L. (1999). Lessons from social psychology on discrediting psychiatric stigma. *American Psychologist, 54,* 765–776.

Costanzo, C., Lutgendorf, S. K., Bradley, S. L., Rose, S. L., & Anderson, B. (2005). Cancer attributions, distress, and health practices among gynecologic cancer survivors. *Psychosomatic Medicine, 67,* 972–980.

Cottrell, J. E., & Winer, G. A. (1994). Development in the understanding of perception: The decline of extramission beliefs. *Developmental Psychology, 30,* 218–228.

Cottrell, J. E., Winer, G. A., & Smith, M. C. (1996). Beliefs of children and adults about feeling stares of unseen others. *Developmental Psychology, 32,* 50–61.

Cox, B. J., Direnfeld, D. M., Swinson, R., & Norton, G. R. (1994). Suicidal ideation and suicide attempts in panic disorder and social phobia. *American Journal of Psychiatry, 151,* 882–887.

Coyne, J. C., Pajak, T. F., Harris, J., Konski, A., Movsas, B., Ang, K., et al. (2007b). Emotional well-being does not predict survival in head and neck cancer patients: A radiation therapy oncology group study. *Cancer, 110,* 2568–2575.

Coyne, J. C., Stefanek, M., & Palmer, S. C. (2007a). Psychotherapy and survival in cancer: The conflict between hope and evidence. *Psychological Bulletin, 133,* 367–394.

Crews, F. (1995). *The memory wars: Freud's legacy in dispute.* New York: New York Book Review.

Croft, G. P., & Walker, A. E. (2001). Are the Monday blues all in the mind? The role of expectancy in the subjective experience of mood. *Journal of Applied Social Psychology, 31,* 1133–1145.

Cromer, A. (1993). *Uncommon sense: The heretical nature of science.* New York: Oxford University Press.

Cross, T. P., & Saxe, L. (2001). Polygraph testing and sexual abuse: The lure of the magic lasso. *Child Maltreatment, 6,* 195–206.

Cuddy, A. J. C., & Fiske, S. T. (2002). Doddering but dear: Process, content, and function in stereotyping of older persons. In T. D. Nelson (Ed.), *Ageism: Stereotyping and prejudice against older persons* (pp. 3–26). Cambridge, MA: The MIT Press.

Cunningham, J. A., Blomqvist, J., & Cordingley, J. (2007). Beliefs about drinking problems: Results from a general population telephone survey. *Addictive Behaviors, 32,* 166–169.

Cutcliffe, J., & Hannigan, B. (2001). Mass media, monsters and mental health clients: The need for increased lobbying. *Journal of Psychiatric and Mental Health Nursing, 8,* 315–322.

Cytowic, R. E. (1993). *The man who tasted shapes.* New York: Putnam.

Dallam, S. J., Gleaves, D. H., Cepeda-Benito, A., Silberg, J. L., Kraemer, H. C., & Spiegel, D. (2001). The effects of child sexual abuse: Comment on Rind, Tromovitch, and Bauserman, 1998. *Psychological Bulletin, 127,* 715–733.

Darwin, C. (1859). *The origin of species.* London: John Murray.

Dasen, P. R. (2000). Rapid social change and the turmoil of adolescence: A cross-cultural perspective. *International Journal of Group Tensions, 29*(1/2), 17–49.

Davies, D. L. (1962). Normal drinking in recovered alcohol addicts. *Quarterly Journal of Studies on Alcohol, 23,* 94–104.

Davis, D., & Follette, W. C. (2002). Rethinking probative value of evidence: Base rates, intuitive profiling and the postdiction of behavior. *Law and Human Behavior, 26,* 133–158.

Davis, P., & Morello, C. (2002). Tarot card's message is a killer's cry for respect, experts say. *The Washington Post,* October 10, A22.

Dawes, R. M. (1994). *House of cards: Psychology and psychotherapy built on myth.* New York: Free Press.

Dawes, R. M., Faust, D., & Meehl, P. E. (1989). Clinical versus actuarial judgment. *Science, 243,* 1668–1674.

Dawes, R. M., & Gambrill, E. (2003). Ethics, science, and the helping professions: A conversation with Robyn Dawes. *Journal of Social Work Education, 39,* 27–42.

de Waal, F. B. M., Aureli, F., & Judge, P. G. (2000). Coping with crowding. *Scientific American, 282,* 76–81.

Dean, G. (1987). Does astrology need to be true? *Scientific Inquirer, 11*(3), 257–273.

Dean, G. (1992). Does astrology need to be true? In K. Frazier (Ed.), *The Hundredth Monkey and other paradigms of the paranormal* (pp. 279–319). Amherst, NY: Prometheus.

DeBell, C. S., & Harless, D. K. (1992). B. F. Skinner: Myth and misperception. *Teaching of Psychology, 19,* 68–73.

DeFrancesco, L. (2001). Scientists question rise in autism. *Nature Medicine, 7*(6), 1.

Della Sala, S. (Ed.). (2007). *Tall tales about the mind and brain.* Oxford: Oxford University Press.

Della Sala, S. (Ed.). (1999). *Mind myths: Exploring popular assumptions about the mind and brain.* Chichester: Wiley.

Delmolino, L. M., & Romancyzk, R. G. (1995). Facilitated communication: A critique. *Behavior Therapist, 18,* 27–30.

Dement, W., & Wolpert, E. A. (1958). The relation of eye movement, bodily motility, and external stimuli to dream content. *Journal of Experimental Psychology, 53,* 543–544.

DePaulo, B. M., Kashy, D. A., Kirkendol, S. E., Wyer, M. M., & Epstein, J. A. (1996). Lying in everyday life. *Journal of Personality and Social Psychology, 70,* 979–995.

DePaulo, B. M., Lindsay, J. J., Malone, B. E., Mulenbruck, L., Charlton, K., & Cooper, H. (2003). Cues to deception. *Psychological Bulletin, 129*, 74–118.

di Ceglie, D. (2000). Gender identity disorder in young people. *Advances in Psychiatric Treatment, 6*, 458–466.

Dickson, D. H., & Kelly, I. W. (1985). The 'Barnum Effect' in personality assessment: A review of the literature. *Psychological Reports, 57*, 367–382.

Diefenbach, D. L. (1997). The portrayal of mental illness on prime-time television. *Journal of Community Psychology, 25*, 289–302.

Diener, E., & Seligman, M. E. P. (2002). Very happy people. *Psychological Science, 13*, 81–84.

Diener, E., & Seligman, M. E. P. (2004). Beyond money: Toward an economy of well-being. *Psychological Science in the Public Interest, 5*, 1–31.

Diener, E., Horowitz, J., & Emmons, R. A. (1985). Happiness of the very wealthy. *Social Indicators, 16*, 263–274.

Diener, E., Lucas, R. E., & Scollon, C. N. (2006). Beyond the hedonic treadmill: Revisions to the adaptation theory of well-being. *American Psychologist, 61*, 305–314.

Dijksterhuis, A., & van Knippenberg, A. (1998). The relation between perception and behavior or how to win a game of Trivial Pursuit. *Journal of Personality and Social Psychology, 74*, 865–877.

DiLalla, L. F., & Gottesman, I. I. (1991). Biological and genetic contributors to violence—Widom's untold tale. *Psychological Bulletin, 109*, 125–129.

Dindia, K., & Canary, D. J. (Eds.). (2006). *Sex differences and similarities in communication* (2nd ed.). Mahwah, NJ: Erlbaum.

Dindia, K. (2006). Men are from North Dakota, Women are from South Dakota. In K. Dindia & D. J. Canary (Eds.), *Sex differences and similarities in communication* (2nd ed., pp. 3–20). Mahwah, NJ: Erlbaum.

Dixon, M., & Laurence, J-R. (1992). Two hundred years of hypnosis research: Questions resolved? Questions unanswered. In E. Fromm & M. R. Nash (Eds.), *Contemporary hypnosis research* (pp. 34–68). New York: Guilford Press.

Dobson, J. C. (2005). *Preparing for adolescence: How to survive the coming years of change.* Ventura, CA: Gospel Light Publications.

Doctors, S. R. (2000). Attachment-individuation: I. Clinical notes toward a reconsideration of adolescent turmoil. *Adolescent Psychiatry, 25*, 3–16.

Donnellan, M. B., Trzesniewski, K. H., Robins, R. W., Moffitt, T. E., & Caspi, A. (2005). Low self-esteem is related to aggression, antisocial behavior, and delinquency. *Psychological Science, 16*, 328–335.

Dorus, E., Dorus, W., & Rechtschaffen, A. (1971). The incidence of novelty in dreams. *Archives of General Psychiatry, 25*, 364–368.

Douglas, J. E., Ressler, R. K., Burgess, A. W., & Hartman, C. R. (1986). Criminal profiling from crime scene analysis. *Behavioral Sciences and the Law, 4*, 401–421.

Douglas, K. S., Lilienfeld, S. O., Skeem, J., Edens, J. E., Poythress, N. G., & Patrick, C. J. (in press). Relation of suicidal behavior to psychopathy and antisocial personality disorder. *Law and Human Behavior.*

Dowd, M. (2008, June 4). She's still here! *New York Times.* Available at http://www.nytimes.com/2008/06/04/opinion/04dowd.html?_r=2&hp&oref=slogin

Dowman, J., Patel, A., & Rajput, K. (2005). Electroconvulsive therapy: Attitudes and misconceptions. *Journal of ECT, 21,* 84–87.

Downe-Wamboldt, B., & Tamlyn, D. (1997). An international survey of death education trends in faculties of nursing and medicine. *Death Studies, 21,* 177–188.

Draper, B. (1996). Attempted suicide in old age. *International Journal of Geriatric Psychiatry, 11,* 577–588.

Dream central's dream dictionary. Retrieved March 14, 2008 from www.sleeps.com/dictionary/aaa.html.

Dream Symbols Software. Retrieved March 14, 2008 from Program URL.com www.programurl.com/software/dream-symbols.htm.

Druckman, D., & Bjork, R. J. (Eds.). (1991). *Learning, remembering, believing: Enhancing human performance.* Washington, DC: National Academy Press.

Druckman, D., & Swets, J. A. (Eds.). (1988). *Enhancing human performance: Issues, theories and techniques.* Washington, DC: National Academy Press.

Duijts, S. F. A., Zeegers, M. P. A., & Borne, B. V. (2003). The association between stressful life events and breast cancer risk: A meta-analysis. *International Journal of Cancer, 107,* 1023–1029.

Dukakis, K., & Tye, L. (2006). *Shock: The healing power of electroconvulsive therapy.* New York: Avery.

Dummer, R. (2003). About moles, melanomas, and lasers: The dermatologist's schizophrenic attitude toward pigmented lesions. *Archives of Dermatology, 139,* 1405.

Dunleavy, M. P. (2007). *Money can buy happiness: How to spend to get the life you want.* New York: Broadway.

Dunn, R., & Dunn, K. (1987). Dispelling outmoded beliefs about student learning. *Educational Leadership, 44,* 55–62.

Dunn, R., Dunn, K., & Price, G. (1999). *Learning style inventory grades 3–12.* Lawrence, KS: Price Systems.

Dysken, M. W., Kooser, J. A., Haraszti, J. S., & Davis, J. M. (1979). Clinical usefulness of sodium amobarbital interviewing. *Archives of General Psychiatry, 36,* 789–794.

Edens, J. F. (2006). Unresolved controversies concerning psychopathy: Implications for clinical and forensic decision-making. *Professional Psychology: Research and Practice, 37,* 59–65.

Editors of the American Heritage Dictionaries. (2000). *American Heritage Dictionary of the English Language* (4th ed.). Boston: Houghton-Mifflin.

Edwards, B. (1980). *Drawing on the right side of the brain.* Los Angeles: Jeremy P. Tarcher/Perigee.

Ehrenberg, R. G., Brewer, D. J., Gamoran, A., & Willms, J. D. (2001). Class size and student achievement. *Psychological Science in the Public Interest*, 2, 1–30.

Ehrsson, H. H. (2007). The experimental induction of out-of-body experiences. *Science*, 317, 1048.

Eich, E., & Hyman, R. (1991). Subliminal self-help. In D. Druckman & R. Bjork (Eds.), *In the mind's eye: Enhancing human performance* (pp. 107–119). Washington, DC: National Academy Press.

Eisner, D. A. (2000). *The death of psychotherapy: From Freud to alien abductions*. Westport, CT: Praeger.

Ekman, P. (2001). *Telling lies: Clues to deceit in the marketplace, politics, and marriage*. New York: W. W. Norton.

Ekman, P., & O'Sullivan, M. (1991). Who can catch a liar? *American Psychologist*, 46, 913–920.

Ekman, P., O'Sullivan, M., & Frank, M. G. (1999). A few can catch a liar. *Psychological Science*, 10, 263–266.

Elbogen, E. B., & Johnson, S. C. (2009). The intricate link between violence and mental disorder: Results from the National Epidemiological Survey on Alcohol and Related Conditions. *Archives of General Psychiatry*, 66, 152–161.

El-Hai, J. (2005). *The lobotomist: A maverick medical genius and his tragic quest to rid the world of mental illness*. New York: Wiley.

Elliott, J. (1965). Death and the mid-life crisis. *International Journal of Psychoanalysis*, 46, 502–514.

Ellis, A. (1962). *Reason and emotion in psychotherapy*. New York: Lyle Stuart.

Ellis, A. (1977). The basic clinical theory of rational-emotive therapy. In A. Ellis & R. Grieger (Eds.), *Handbook of rational-emotive therapy* (pp. 3–34). New York: Springer.

Emler, N. (2001). *Self-esteem: The costs and causes of low self-worth*. York, UK: Joseph Rowntree Foundation.

Emrick, C. D. (1987). Alcoholics Anonymous: Affiliation processes and effectiveness as treatment. *Alcoholism: Clinical and Experimental Research*, 11, 416–423.

Epley, N., Savitsky, K., & Kachelski, R. (1999). What every skeptic should know about subliminal persuasion. *The Skeptical Inquirer*, 23(5), 40–46.

Epstein, R. (2007). *The case against adolescence*. Sanger, CA: Quill Driver Books.

Erdelyi, M. (1994). Hypnotic hypermnesia: The empty set of hypermnesia. *International Journal of Clinical and Experimental Hypnosis*, 42, 379–390.

Erdelyi, M. (2006). The unified theory of repression. *Behavioral and Brain Sciences*, 29, 499–511.

Erdelyi, M. H. (1985). *Psychoanalysis: Freud's cognitive psychology*. New York: W. H. Freeman/Times Books/Henry Holt & Co.

Erickson, M. H. (1980). Literalness: An experimental study. In E. Rossi (Ed.), *The collected papers of Milton H. Erickson on hypnosis: Vol. 3. Hypnotic investigation of psychodynamic processes*. New York: Irvington.

Erikson, E. (1968). *Identity: Youth and crisis*. New York: W. W. Norton.

Ernst, C., & Angst, J. (1983). *Birth order: Its influence on personality*. Berlin: Springer.

ESP in the Silva Seminar. Retrieved June 23, 2005 from http://www.theunlimitedyou.com/lessons/7-esp.php

Etcoff, N. L., Ekman, P., Magee, J. J., & Frank, M. G. (2000). Lie detection and language comprehension. *Nature, 405*, 139.

Everatt, J., Bradshaw, M. F., & Hibbard, P. B. (1999). Visual processing and dyslexia. *Perception, 28*, 243–254.

Exner, J. E. (1974). *The Rorschach: A comprehensive system. Vol. 1*. New York: Wiley.

Eysenck, M. W. (1990). *Happiness: Fact and myths*. Hove, UK: Lawrence Erlbaum.

Falchikov, N. (1990). Youthful ideas about old age: An analysis of children's drawings. *International Journal of Aging and Human Development, 31*, 79–99.

False Memory Syndrome Foundation. (2008, Fall). Preliminary test of psychiatric Colin Ross's "eye beam energy" sends him back to the drawing board. *False Memory Syndrome Foundation Newsletter, 17*(4), 6.

Feingold, A. (1994). Gender differences in personality: A meta-analysis. *Psychological Bulletin, 116*, 429–456.

Ferguson, K. J., Kreiter, C. D., Peterson, M. W., Rowat, J. A., & Elliott, S. T. (2002). Is that your final answer? Relationship of changed answers to overall performance on a computer-based medical school course examination. *Teaching and Learning in Medicine, 14*, 20–23.

Fick, P. M. (1998). *The dysfunctional president: Understanding the compulsions of Bill Clinton*. Sacramento, CA: Citadel Press.

Fienberg, S. E., & Stern, P. C. (2005). In search of the magic lasso: The truth about the polygraph. *Statistical Science, 20*, 249–260.

Fingarette, H. (1988). *Heavy drinking: The myth of alcoholism as a disease*. Berkeley: University of California Press.

Finn, S. E., & Kamphuis, J. H. (1995). What a clinician needs to know about base rates. In J. Butcher (Ed.), *Clinical personality assessment: Practical approaches* (pp. 224–235). New York: Oxford University Press.

Fiorello, C. A. (2001, May/June). Common myths of children's behavior. *Skeptical Inquirer, 25*, 37–39, 44.

Fiske, S. T., Cuddy, A. J. C., Glick, P. S., & Xu, J. (2002). A model of (often mixed) stereotype content: Competence and warmth respectively follow from perceived status and competition. *Journal of Personality and Social Psychology, 82*, 878–902.

Flagel, D. C., & Gendreau, P. (2008). Sense, common sense, and nonsense. *Criminal Justice and Behavior, 35,* 1354–1361.

Flensmark, J. (2004). Is there an association between the use of heeled footwear and schizophrenia? *Medical Hypotheses, 63,* 740–747.

Foote, R., & Belinky, C. (1972). It pays to switch? Consequences of changing answers on multiple-choice examinations. *Psychological Reports, 31,* 667–673.

Foulkes, D. (1962). Dream reports from different stages of sleep. *Journal of Abnormal and Social Psychology, 65,* 14–25.

Fox News. (2008). Destruction therapy promises peace by sledgehammer. Retrieved June 21, 2008 from http://www.foxnews.com/story/0,2933,369885,00.html

Fox, J. A., & Levin, J. (2001). *The will to kill.* Boston: Allyn & Bacon.

Francescani, C., & Bacon, B. (2008, March 21). *Bad moon rising: The myth of the full moon.* ABC News. Retrieved March 22, 2008 from http://abcnews.go.com/TheLaw/story?id=3426758&page=1

Frankl, V. E. (1965). *The doctor and the soul: From psychotherapy to logotherapy.* New York: Alfred Knopf.

Frederickson, R. (1992). *Repressed memories.* New York: Fireside.

Freedle, R., & Kostin, I. (1997). Predicting Black and White differential item functioning in verbal analogy performance. *Intelligence, 24,* 417–444.

Freese, J., Powell, B., & Steelman, L. C. (1999). Rebel without a cause or effect: Birth order and social attitudes. *American Sociological Review, 64,* 207–231.

Freud, A. (1958). Adolescence. *Psychoanalytic Study of the Child, 13,* 255–278.

Freud, S. (1894). The psycho-neuroses of defense. *Standard Edition, 3,* 43–62.

Freud, S. (1900). *The interpretation of dreams.* New York: Macmillan.

Freud, S. (1915/1957). *The unconscious* (Standard ed., Vol. 14, pp. 159–215). London: Hogarth Press.

Freud, S. (1930/1961). *Civilization and its discontents* (Standard ed., p. 65). London: Norton.

Friedman, R., & James, J. W. (2008). The myth of the stages of dying, death, and grief. *Skeptic, 14*(2), 37–41.

Friedman, S., & Cook, G. (1995). Is an examinee's cognitive style related to the impact of answer-changing on multiple-choice tests? *Journal of Experimental Education, 63,* 199–213.

Friedman, S., Jones, J. C., Chernen, L., & Barlow, D. H. (1992). Suicidal ideation and suicide attempts among patients with panic disorder: A survey of two outpatient clinics. *American Journal of Psychiatry, 149,* 680–685.

Frierson, R. L. (1991). Suicide attempts by the old and the very old. *Archives of Internal Medicine, 151,* 141–144.

Frontline. (1993). *Prisoners of silence* (J. Palfreman, Producer). Public Broadcasting Service.

Frontline. (1995). *Divided memories.* Producer: Opra Bikel.

Fukuda, K., Ogilvie, R., Chilcott, L., Venditelli, A., & Takeuchi, T. (1998). High prevalence of sleep paralysis in Canadian and Japanese college students. *Dreaming, 8,* 59–66.

Full moon rules out play. (2001, December 28). BBC Sport. Retrieved March 21, 2008 from http://news.bbc.co.uk/sport1/hi/cricket/1729171.stm

Furnham, A. (1983). Social psychology as common sense. *Bulletin of the British Psychological Society, 36,* 105–109.

Furnham, A. (1992). Prospective psychology students' knowledge of psychology. *Psychological Reports, 70,* 375–382.

Furnham, A. (1996). *All in the mind: The essence of psychology.* New York: Taylor & Francis.

Furnham, A., Callahan, I., & Rawles, R. (2003). Adult's knowledge of general psychology. *European Psychologist, 8,* 101–116.

Furnham, A., & Cheng, H. (2000). Lay theories of happiness. *Journal of Happiness Studies, 1,* 227–246.

Furnham, A., & Schofield, S. (1987). Accepting personality test feedback: A review of the Barnum effect. *Current Psychological Research and Reviews, 6,* 162–178.

Galatzer-Levy, R. M. (1997). *Psychoanalysis, memory, and trauma.* London: Oxford University Press.

Ganguli, R. (2000, March 18). Mental illness and misconceptions. *Pittsburgh Post-Gazette.* Retrieved May 12, 2008 from http://www.post-gazette.com/forum/20000318gang1.asp

Garb, H. N. (1998). *Studying the clinician: Judgment research and psychological assessment.* Washington, DC: American Psychological Association.

Gardner, H. (1983). *Frames of mind: The theory of multiple intelligences.* New York: Basic Books.

Gardner, R. M., & Dalsing, S. (1986). Misconceptions about psychology among college students. *Teaching of Psychology, 13,* 32–34.

Gardner, R. M., & Hund, R. M. (1983). Misconceptions of psychology among academicians. *Teaching of Psychology, 10,* 20–22.

Garfield, B. (1994). CAA casts perfect spell in latest Coca-Cola ads. *Advertising Age,* February 14.

Garmezy, N., Masten, A. S., & Tellegen, A. (1984). The study of stress and competence in children: A building block for developmental psychopathology. *Child Development, 55,* 97–111.

Garske, J. P., & Anderson, T. (2003). Toward a science of psychotherapy research. In S. Lilienfeld, S. J. Lynn, & S. J. Lohr (Eds.), *Science and pseudoscience in clinical psychology* (pp. 145–175). New York: Guilford Press.

Gaudiano, B. A., & Epstein-Lubow, G. (2007). Controversies about antidepressants and the promotion of evidence-based treatment alternatives for depression. *Scientific Review of Mental Health Practice, 5,* 33–52.

Gazdag, G., Kocsis-Ficzere, N., & Tolna, J. (2005). Hungarian medical students' knowledge about and attitudes towards electroconvulsive therapy. *Journal of ECT, 21,* 96–99.

Gazzaniga, M. S. (1998, July). The Split brain revisited, *Scientific American, 279,* 50–55.

Geake, J. (2008). Neuromythologies in education. *Educational Research, 50,* 123–133.

Geiger, M. (1996). On the benefits of changing multiple-choice answers: Student perception and performance. *Education, 117,* 108–116.

Geiger, M. (1997). An examination of the relation between answer-changing, test-wiseness, and performance. *Journal of Experimental Education, 6,* 49–60.

Geller, U. (1996). *Uri Geller's mindpower kit.* New York: Penguin.

Gendreau, P., Goggin, C., Cullen, F. T., & Paparozzi, M. (2002). The common sense revolution and correctional policy. In J. McGuire (Ed.), *Offender rehabilitation and treatment: Effective programs and policies to reduce re-offending* (pp. 360–386). Chichester: Wiley.

George, W., La Marr, J., Barrett, K., & McKinnon, T. (1999). Alcoholic parent-age, self-labeling, and endorsement of ACOA-codependent traits. *Psychology of Addictive Behaviors, 12,* 39–48.

Gergen, K. J. (1973). Social psychology as history. *Journal of Personality and Social Psychology, 26,* 309–320.

Gernsbacher, M. A. (2007, January). *The science of autism: Beyond the myths and misconceptions.* Paper presented at the Annual Meeting of the National Institute of the Teaching of Psychology, St. Pete Beach, Florida.

Gernsbacher, M. A., Dawson, M., & Goldsmith, H. H. (2005). Three reasons not to believe in an autism epidemic. *Current Directions in Psychological Science, 14,* 55–58.

Gettleman, J. (2002, October 25). The hunt for a sniper: The profiling; A frenzy of speculation was wide of the mark. *New York Times.* Retrieved July 27, 2008 from http://query.nytimes.com/gst/fullpage.html?res=9C00E2D6103CF936A15753C1A9649C8B63

Gibb, B. G. (1964). *Test-wiseness as secondary cue response* (Doctoral Dissertation, Stanford University). Ann Arbor: University Microfilms, No. 64-7643.

Gigerenzer, G. (2007). *Gut feelings: The intelligence of the unconscious.* New York: Viking Press.

Gilbert, D. (2006). *Stumbling on happiness.* New York: Knopf.

Gilbert, D. T., Pinel, E. C., Wilson, T. D., Blumberg, S. J., & Wheatley, T. P. (1998). Immune neglect: A source of durability bias in affective forecasting. *Journal of Personality and Social Psychology, 75,* 617–638.

Gilovich, T. (1991). *How we know what isn't so: The fallibility of human reason in everyday life.* New York: Free Press.

Gilovich, T., & Savitsky, K. (1996, March/April). Like goes with like: The role of representativeness in paranormal belief. *Skeptical Inquirer, 20,* 34–40.

Gilovich, T., Vallone, R., & Tversky, A. (1985). The hot hand in basketball: On the misperception of random sequences. *Cognitive Psychology, 17,* 295–314.

Gladwell, M. (2005). *Blink: The power of thinking without thinking.* Boston: Little, Brown, & Company.

Gladwell, M. (2007, November 12). Dangerous minds: Criminal profiling made easy. *New Yorker,* 36–45.

Glass, R. M. (2001). Electroconvulsive therapy: Time to bring it out of the shadows. *Journal of the American Medical Association, 285,* 1346–1348.

Gold, P. E., Cahill, L., & Wenk, G. (2002). Ginkgo biloba: A cognitive enhancer? *Psychological Science in the Public Interest, 3,* 2–11.

Goldberg, L. R. (1991). Human mind versus regression equation: Five contrasts. In D. Cicchetti & W. M. Grove (Eds.), *Thinking clearly about psychology* (Vol. 1, pp. 173–184). Minneapolis: University of Minnesota Press.

Golden Rule Insurance Company et al. v. Washburn et al., 419–76 (stipulation for dismissal and order dismissing case, filed in the Circuit Court of the Seventh Judicial Circuit, Sangamon County, IL, 1984).

Golding, J. M., Sanchez, R. P., & Sego, S. A. (1996). Do you believe in repressed memories? *Professional Psychology: Research and Practice, 27,* 429–437.

Goode, E. (2008, May 20). War that traumatizes Iraqis takes toll on hospital that treats them. *New York Times,* A6, A14.

Goodman, G. S., Ghetti, S., Quas, J. A., Edelstein, R. S., Alexander, K. W., Redlich, A. D., et al. (2003). A prospective study of memory for child sexual abuse: New findings relevant to the repressed-memory controversy. *Psychological Science, 14,* 113–118.

Goodman, J. A., Krahn, L. E., Smith, G. E., Rummans, T. A., & Pileggi, T. S. (1999). Patient satisfaction with electroconvulsive therapy. *Mayo Clinics Proceedings, 74,* 967–971.

Goodman, S. (2004). *9 steps for reversing or preventing cancer and other diseases.* Franklin Lakes, NJ: Career Press.

Goodwin, R. D., & Stein, M. B. (2002). Generalized anxiety disorder and peptic ulcer disease among adults in the United States. *Psychosomatic Medicine, 64,* 862–866.

Gorchoff, S. M., John, O. P., & Helson, R. (2008). Conceptualizing change in marital satisfaction during middle age: An 18-year longitudinal study. *Psychological Science, 19,* 1194–1200.

Gorenflo, D. W., & McConnell, J. V. (1991). The most frequently cited journal articles and authors in introductory psychology textbooks. *Teaching of Psychology, 18,* 8–12.

Gorman, C. (2003, July 28). The new science of dyslexia. *Time, 162*(4), 52–59.

Gotlib, I., & Wheaton, B. (2006). *Stress and adversity over the life course: Trajectories and turning points.* Cambridge: Cambridge University Press.

Gottesman, I. I. (1991). *Schizophrenia genesis: The origins of madness*. New York: Freeman.

Gottfredson, L. S. (1997). Mainstream science on intelligence: An editorial with 52 signatories, history, and bibliography. *Intelligence, 24*, 13–23.

Gottfredson, L. S. (2009). Logical fallacies used to dismiss evidence on intelligence testing. In R. Phelps (Ed.). *Correcting fallacies about educational and psychological testing* (pp. 11–65). Washington, DC: American Psychological Association.

Gough, K. R., Korman, M. G., Bardhan, K. D., Lee, F. I., Crowe, J. P., Reed, P. I., et al. (1984). Ranitidine and cimetidine in prevention of duodenal ulcer relapse. A double-blind, randomized, multicentre, comparative trial. *Lancet, 2*(8404), 659–662.

Gould, S. J. (1996). *Full house: The spread of excellence from Plato to Darwin*. New York: Harmony Books.

Gouvier, W. D., Prestholdt, P. H., & Warner, M. S. (1988). A survey of common misconceptions about head injury and recovery. *Archives of Clinical Neuropsychology, 3*, 331–343.

Gove, W. R. (1982). The current status of the labeling theory of mental illness. In W. R. Gove (Ed.), *Deviance and mental illness* (pp. 273–300). Beverly Hills, CA: Sage.

Gray, C., & Della Sala, S. (2007). The Mozart effect: It's time to face the music! In S. Della Sala (Ed.), *Tall tales about the mind and brain* (pp. 148–157). Oxford: Oxford University Press.

Gray, J. (1992). *Men are from Mars, women are from Venus: A practical guide for improving communication and getting what you want in your relationships*. New York: HarperCollins.

Gray, J. (1996). *Mars and Venus in the bedroom: A guide to lasting romance and passion*. New York: HarperCollins.

Gray, J. (1996). *Mars and Venus on a date: A guide to navigating the 5 stages of dating to create a loving and lasting relationship*. New York: HarperCollins.

Gray, J. (2001). *Mars and Venus in the workplace: A practical guide to improving communication and getting results at work*. New York: HarperCollins.

Gray, J. (2008). *Why Mars and Venus collide: Improving relationships by understanding how men and women cope differently with stress*. New York: HarperCollins.

Greeley, A. M. (1987). Mysticism goes mainstream. *American Health, 6*, 47–49.

Green, C. E. (1968). *Out-of-the-body experiences*. London: Hamish Hamilton.

Green, J. P., Page, R. A., Rasekhy, R., Johnson, L. K., & Bernhardt, S. E. (2006). Cultural views and attitudes about hypnosis: A survey of college students across four countries. *International Journal of Clinical and Experimental Hypnosis, 54*, 263–280.

Green, J. P., & Lynn, S. J. (in press). Hypnosis vs. relaxation: Accuracy and confidence in dating international news events. *Applied Cognitive Psychology*.

Green, J. P., Lynn, S. J., Weekes, J. R., Carlson, B., Brentar, J., Latham, L., & Kurzhals, R. (1990). Literalism as a marker of hypnotic "trance": Disconfirming evidence. *Journal of Abnormal Psychology, 99,* 16–21.

Greenblatt, S. H. (1995). Phrenology in the science and culture of the 19th century. *Neurosurgery, 37,* 790–805.

Greene, J. (2005). *Education myths.* Lanham, MD: Rowman & Littlefield.

Greenwald, A. G., Spangenberg, E. R., Pratkanis, A. R., & Eskenazi, J. (1991). Double-blind tests of subliminal self-help audiotapes. *Psychological Science, 2,* 119–122.

Gregg, V. R., Winer, G. A., Cottrell, J. E., Hedman, K. E., & Fournier, J. S. (2001). The persistence of a misconception about vision after educational interventions. *Psychonomic Bulletin and Review, 8,* 622–626.

Grinker, R. R. (2007). *Unstrange minds: Remapping the world of autism.* New York: Basic Books.

Gross, C. G. (1999). The fire that comes from the eye. *The Neuroscientist, 5,* 58–64.

Grove, W. M., & Lloyd, M. (in preparation). *Survey on the use of mechanical prediction methods in clinical psychology.*

Grove, W. M., & Meehl, P. E. (1996). Comparative efficiency of informal (subjective, impressionistic) and formal (mechanical, algorithmic) prediction procedures: The clinical-statistical controversy. *Psychology, Public Policy, and Law, 2,* 293–323.

Grove, W. M., Zald, D. H., Lebow, B. S., Snitz, B. E., & Nelson, C. (2000). Clinical versus mechanical prediction: A meta-analysis. *Psychological Assessment, 12,* 19–30.

Guardiola, J. G. (2001). *The evolution of research on dyslexia.* Retrieved July 18, 2008 from http://ibgwww.colorado.edu/~gayan/ch1.pdf

Gudjonsson, G. H. (1992). *The psychology of interrogations, confessions, and testimony.* New York: Wiley.

Gudjonsson, G. H. (2003). *The psychology of interrogations and confessions: A handbook.* Chichester: John Wiley & Sons.

Guilmette, T. J., & Paglia, M. F. (2004). The public's misconceptions about traumatic brain injury: A follow up survey. *Archives of Clinical Neuropsychology, 19,* 183–189.

Gutiérrez-García, J. M., & Tusell, T. (1997). Suicides and the lunar cycle. *Psychological Reports, 80,* 243–250.

Guze, S. B., & Robins, E. (1970). Suicide and affective disorders. *British Journal of Psychiatry, 117,* 437–438.

Hall, G. S. (1904). *Adolescence: Its psychology and its relations to physiology, anthropology, sociology, sex, crime, religion, and education.* New York: Appleton.

Hall, J. A. (1978). Gender effects in decoding nonverbal cues. *Psychological Bulletin, 85,* 845–857.

Hall, J. A. (1984). *Nonverbal sex differences: Communication accuracy and expressive style.* Baltimore: Johns Hopkins University Press.

Hammer, D. (1996). More than misconceptions: Multiple perspectives on student knowledge and reasoning, and an appropriate role for education research. *American Journal of Physics, 64*, 1316–1325.

Harding, C. M., & Zahniser, J. H. (1994). Empirical correction of seven myths about schizophrenia with implications for treatment. *Acta Psychiatrica Scandinavica, 90*(Suppl. 384), 140–146.

Harkins, E. B. (1978). Effects of empty nest transition on self-report of psychological and physical well-being. *Journal of Marriage and the Family, 40*, 549–556.

Harris, A., & Lurigio, A. J. (2007). Mental illness and violence: A brief review of research and assessment strategies. *Aggression and Violent Behavior, 12*, 542–551.

Harris, J. R. (1995). Where is the child's environment? A group socialization theory of development. *Psychological Review, 102*, 458–489.

Harris, J. R. (1998). *The nurture assumption: Why children turn out the way they do*. New York: Free Press.

Hartigan, J. A., & Wigdor, A. K. (Eds.). (1989). *Fairness in employment testing: Validity generalization, minority issues, and the General Aptitude Test Battery*. Washington, DC: National Academy Press.

Hartmann, H. (1939). *Ego psychology and the problem of adaptation*. New York: International Universities Press.

Harvey, A. G., & Payne, S. (2002). The management of unwanted pre-sleep thoughts in insomnia: Distraction with imagery versus general distraction. *Behaviour Research and Therapy, 40*, 267–277.

Harwitz, D., & Ravizza, L. (2000). Suicide and depression. *Emergency Medical Clinics of North America, 18*, 263–271.

Hasegawa, H., & Jamieson, G. A. (2000). Conceptual issues in hypnosis research: Explanations, definitions, and the state/non-state debate. *Contemporary Hypnosis, 19*, 103–117.

Hays, L. (1984). *You can heal your life*. Carlsbad, CA: Hay House.

He calls it schizophrenia and places blame on war. (1916, July 16). *Washington Post*, p. A5.

Heaton, P., & Wallace, G. (2004). Annotation: The savant syndrome. *Journal of Child Psychology and Psychiatry, 45*, 899–911.

Hecht, J. M. (2007). *The happiness myth: Why what we think is right is wrong*. San Francisco: Harper.

Heiner, R. (2008). *Deviance across cultures*. New York: Oxford University Press.

Helliwell, J. F., & Putnam, R. D. (2004). The social context of well-being. *Philosophical Transactions of the Royal Society, 359*, 1435–1446.

Hendrix, H. (2005). *Do opposites attract?* Retrieved June 25, 2005 from http://www.beliefnet.com/story/149/story_14969_1.html

Henry, J. (2007, July 30). Professor pans "learning style" teaching method. [London] *Telegraph*. Retrieved on August 6, 2008 from http://www.telegraph.co.uk/news/uknews/1558822/Professor-pans-'learning-style'-teaching-method.html

Henslin, J. M. (2003). *Down to earth sociology: Introductory readings* (12th ed.). New York: Free Press.

Herbert, J. D., Sharp, I. A., & Gaudiano, B. A. (2002). Separating fact from fiction in the etiology and treatment of autism. *Scientific Review of Mental Health Practice, 1,* 23–43.

Herculano-Houzel, S. (2002). Do you know your brain? A survey on public neuroscience literacy at the closing of the decade of the brain. *Neuroscientist, 8*(2), 98–110.

Hermann, N. (1996). *The whole brain business book.* New York: McGraw Hill Professional.

Herrnstein, R. J., & Murray, C. (1994). *The bell curve: Intelligence and class structure in American life.* New York: Free Press.

Herzog, A. W. (1923). Scopolamine as a lie detector. *Medical-Legal Journal, 40,* 62–63.

Hess, J. L. (1991, July/August). Geezer-bashing: Media attacks on the elderly. *FAIR: Fairness and Accuracy in Reporting.* Available at http://www.fair. org/index.php?page=1511

Hetherington, E. M., & Kelly, J. (2002). *For better or for worse: Divorce reconsidered.* New York: W. W. Norton.

Hetherington, E. M., Cox, M., & Cox, R. (1985). Long-term effects of divorce and remarriage on the adjustment of children. *Journal of the American Academy of Child Psychiatry, 24,* 518–530.

Hewitt, W. (1996). *Psychic development for beginners.* St. Paul, MN: Llewellyn Worldwide Ltd.

Hicks, S. J., & Sales, B. D. (2006). *Criminal profiling: Developing an effective science and practice.* Washington, DC: American Psychological Association.

Higbee, K. L., & Clay, S. L. (1998). College students' beliefs in the ten-percent myth. *Journal of Psychology, 132,* 469–476.

Higham, P. A., & Gerrard, C. (2005). Not all errors are created equal: Metacognition and changing answers on multiple choice tests. *Canadian Journal of Experimental Psychology, 59,* 28–34.

Hill, H. A., & Kleinbaum, D. G. (2005). Detection bias. *Encyclopedia of biostatistics.* New York: John Wiley & Sons.

Hines, A. R., & Paulson, S. E. (2006). Parents' and teachers' perceptions of adolescent stress: Relations with parenting and teaching styles. *Adolescence, 41,* 597–614.

Hines, T. (2003). *Pseudoscience and the paranormal* (2nd ed.). Amherst, NY: Prometheus.

Hines, T. M. (2001). The G-spot: A modern gynecological myth. *American Journal of Obstetrics and Gynecology, 185,* 359–362.

Hobson, J. A., & McCarley, R. M. (1977). The brain as a dream state generator: An activation-synthesis hypothesis. *American Journal of Psychiatry, 134,* 1335–1348.

Hobson, J. A., Pace-Schott, E. F., & Stickgold, R. (2000). Dreaming and the brain: Toward a cognitive neuroscience of conscious states. *Behavior and Brain Sciences*, *23*, 793–842.

Hodgins, S., Mednick, S., Brennan, P. A., et al. (1996). Mental disorder and crime. Evidence from a Danish birth cohort. *Archives of General Psychiatry*, *53*, 489–496.

Holleman, W. L., Holleman, M. C., & Gershenhorn, S. (1994). Death education curricula in U.S. medical schools. *Teaching and Learning in Medicine*, *6*, 260–263.

Holmbeck, G., & Hill, J. (1988). Storm and stress beliefs about adolescence: Prevalence, self-reported antecedents, and effects of an undergraduate course. *Journal of Youth and Adolescence*, *17*, 285–306.

Holmes, D. S. (1984). Meditation and somatic arousal reduction: A review of the experimental evidence. *American Psychologist*, *39*, 1–10.

Holmes, D. S. (1990). The evidence for repression: An examination of sixty years of research. In J. L. Singer (Ed.), *Repression and dissociation: Implications for personality theory, psychopathology, and health* (pp. 85–102). Chicago: University of Chicago Press.

Holzinger, A., Angermeyer, M. C., & Matschinger, H. (1998). What do you associate with the word schizophrenia? A study of the social representation of schizophrenia. *Psychiatrische Praxis*, *25*, 9–13.

Homant, R. J., & Kennedy, D. B. (1998). Psychological aspects of crime scene profiling. *Criminal Justice and Behavior*, *25*, 319–343.

Honda, H., Shimizu, Y., & Rutter, M. (2005). No effect of MMR withdrawal on the incidence of autism: A total population study. *Journal of Child Psychology and Psychiatry*, *46*, 572–79.

Honey, P., & Mumford, A. (2000). *The Learning Styles Questionnaire: 80 item version*. Maidenhead, Berkshire, UK: Peter Honey Publications.

Hooper, S. R. (2006). Myths and misconceptions about traumatic brain injury: Endorsements by school psychologists. *Exceptionality*, *14*, 171–183.

Horgan, J. (2005, August 12). In defense of common sense. *New York Times*. Available at http://www.johnhorgan.org/in_defense_of_common_sense_46441.htm

Hornberger, R. H. (1959). The differential reduction of aggressive responses as a function of interpolated activities. *American Psychologist*, *14*, 354.

Hornig, C. D., & McNally, R. J. (1995). Panic disorder and suicide attempt. A reanalysis of data from the Epidemiologic Catchment Area Study. *British Journal of Psychiatry*, *167*, 76–79.

Horwitz, A. V., & Wakefield, J. C. (2007). *The loss of sadness: How psychiatry transformed normal sorrow into depressive disorder*. New York: Oxford University Press.

Houston, J. (1985). Untutored lay knowledge of the principles of psychology: Do we know anything they don't? *Psychological Reports*, *57*, 567–570.

Hubbard, R. W., & McIntosh, J. L. (1992). Integrating suicidology into abnormal psychology classes: The Revised Facts on Suicide Quiz. *Teaching of Psychology, 19*, 163–166.

Hughes, V. (2007). Mercury rising. *Nature Medicine, 13*, 896–897.

Humphreys, K. (2003). *Alcoholics Anonymous and 12-step alcoholism treatment programs*. New York: Kluwer Academic/Plenum Publishers.

Hunsley, J., & Di Giulio, G. (2002). Dodo bird, Phoenix, or urban legend? *Scientific Review of Mental Health Practice, 1*, 11–22.

Hunsley, J., Lee, C. M., & Wood, J. M. (2003). Controversial and questionable assessment techniques. In S. O. Lilienfeld, S. J. Lynn, & J. M. Lohr (Eds.), *Science and pseudoscience in clinical psychology* (pp. 39–76). New York: Guilford Press.

Hunter, J. E., & Schmidt, F. L. (2000). Racial and gender bias in ability and achievement tests: Resolving the apparent paradox. *Psychology, Public Policy, and Law, 6*, 151–158.

Hux, K., Schram, C. D., & Goeken, T. (2006). Misconceptions about brain injury: A survey replication study. *Brain Injury, 20*, 547–553.

Hviid, A., Stellfeld, M., Wohlfahrt, J., & Melbye M. (2003). Association between thimerosal-containing vaccines and autism. *Journal of the American Medical Association, 290*, 1763–1766.

Hyde, J. S. (2005). The gender similarities hypothesis. *American Psychologist, 60*, 581–592.

Hyman, I. E., Husband, T. H., & Billings, F. J. (1995). False memories of childhood experiences. *Applied Cognitive Psychology, 9*, 181–197.

Hyman, R. (1989). *The elusive quarry: A scientific appraisal of psychical research*. Amherst, NY: Prometheus.

Hyman, R., & Rosoff, B. (1984). Matching learning and teaching styles: The jug and what's in it. *Theory into Practice, 23*, 35–43.

Hyperdictionary. Dream dictionary. Retrieved March 14, 2008 from http://www. hyperdictionary.com/dream/aardvark. Paragraph 2.

HypnosisDownloads.com. Get rid of those midlife crisis feelings and grasp life by the horns again. Retrieved September 12, 2008 from http://www. hypnosisdownloads.com/downloads/hypnotherapy/midlife-crisis.html

Iacono, W. G. (2008). Effective policing: Understanding how polygraph tests work and are used. *Criminal Justice and Behavior, 35*, 1295–1308.

Ickes, W. (2003). *Everyday mind reading: Understanding what other people think and feel*. Amherst, NY: Prometheus.

Immunization Safety Review: Vaccines and Autism. (2004). *Immunization Safety Review Committee. Board of Health Promotion and Disease Prevention, Institute of Medicine*. New York: National Academy Press.

Ingram, R., Scott, W., & Siegle, G. (1999). Depression: Social and cognitive aspects. In T. Millon, P. H. Blaney, & R. D. Davis (Eds.), *Oxford textbook of psychopathology* (pp. 203–226). New York: Oxford University Press.

Iniquez, L. (2008, May 13). What's in a signature? *Los Angeles Times.* Retrieved January 22, 2009 from http://www.emergingimage.net/press/LATimes.pdf

Innocence Project. (2008). *Understand the causes: False confessions.* Retrieved January 22, 2009 from http://www.innocenceproject.org/understand/False-Confessions.php

Inskip, H. M., Harris, E. C., & Barracough, B. (1998). Lifetime risk of suicide for affective disorder, alcoholism, and schizophrenia. *British Journal of Psychiatry, 172,* 35–37.

Institute of Medicine. (1990). *Broadening the base of treatment for alcohol problems.* Washington, DC: National Academy Press.

Institute of Medicine. (2004). *Immunization safety review: Vaccines and autism.* Washington, DC: National Academies Review.

Irvin, J. E., Bowers, C. A., Dunn, M. E., & Wang, M. C. (1999). Efficacy of relapse prevention: A meta-analytic review. *Journal of Consulting and Clinical Psychology, 67,* 563–570.

Isaacson, C. E., & Radish, K. (2002). *The birth order effect: How to better understand yourself and others.* Avon, MA: Adams Media Corporation.

Isaacson, G., & Rich, C. (1997). Depression, antidepressants, and suicide: Pharmacoepidemiological evidence for suicide prevention. In R. Maris, M. Silverman, & S. Canetto (Eds.), *Review of suicidology* (pp. 168–201). New York: Guilford Press.

Jacobson, J. W., Mulick, J. A., & Schwarz, A. A. (1995). A history of facilitated communication: Science, pseudoscience, and antiscience. *American Psychologist, 50,* 750–765.

James, W. (1890). *The principles of psychology.* Cambridge, MA: Harvard University Press.

Janet, P. (1889/1973). *L'automatisme psychologique.* Paris: Alcan.

Janicak, P. G., Mask, J., Trimakas, K. A., & Gibbons, R. (1985). ECT: An assessment of health professionals' knowledge and attitudes. *Journal of Clinical Psychiatry, 46,* 262–266.

Janov, A. (1970). *The primal scream.* New York: Abacus.

Jansen, A., Havermans, R., Nederkoorn, C., & Roefs, A. (2008). Jolly fat or sad fat? Subtyping non-eating disordered overweight and obesity along an affect dimension. *Appetite, 51,* 635–640.

Jefferson, T., Herbst, J. H., & McCrae, R. R. (1998). Associations between birth order and personality traits: Evidence from self-reports and observer ratings. *Journal of Research in Personality, 32,* 498–509.

Jensen, A. R. (1980). *Bias in mental testing.* New York: Free Press.

Jensen, A. R. (1965). A review of the Rorschach. In O. K. Buros (Ed.), *Sixth mental measurements handbook* (pp. 501–509). Highland Park, NH: Gryphon.

Jimerson, S. R., Carlson, E., Rotert, M., Egeland, B., & Sroufe, L. A. (1997). A prospective, longitudinal study of the correlates and consequences of early grade retention. *Journal of School Psychology, 35,* 3–25.

Joiner, T. (2005). *Why people die by suicide*. Cambridge, MA: Harvard University Press.

Joiner, T., Pettit, J., & Rudd, M. D. (2004). Is there a window of heightened suicide risk if patients gain energy in context of continued depression? *Professional Psychology: Research and Practice, 35*, 84–89.

Joiner, T. E., Alfano, M. S., & Metalsky, G. I. (1992). When depression breeds contempt: Reassurance seeking, self-esteem, and rejection of depressed college students by their roommates. *Journal of Abnormal Psychology, 101*, 165–173.

Jones, E. (1953). *Sigmund Freud: Life and work. Vol. 1: The young Freud 1856–1900*. London: Hogarth Press.

Jones, E. (1955). *Sigmund Freud: Life and work. Vol. 2: The years of maturity 1901–1919*. London: Hogarth Press.

Jones, M. H., West, S. D., & Estell, D. B. (2006). The Mozart effect: Arousal, preference, and spatial performance. *Psychology and Aesthetics, 1*, 26–32.

Juan, S. (2006). *The odd brain: Mysteries of our weird and wonderful brains explained*. New York: HarperCollins.

Jung, C. G. (1933). *Modern man in search of a soul*. New York: Harcourt, Brace & World.

Junginger, J., & McGuire, L. (2001). The paradox of command hallucinations. *Psychiatric Services, 52*, 385.

Kagan, J. (1998). *Three seductive ideas*. Cambridge, MA: Harvard University Press.

Kahneman, D., Krueger, A., Schkade, D., Schwarz, N., & Stone, A. (2004). A survey method for characterizing daily life experience: The Day Reconstruction Method (DRM). *Science, 306*, 1776–1780.

Kahneman, D., Krueger, A., Schkade, D., Schwarz, N., & Stone, A. (2006). Would you be happier if you were richer? A focusing illusion. *Science, 312*, 1908–1910.

Kaplan, R. M. (1982). Nader's raid on the testing industry: Is it in the best interest of the consumer? *American Psychologist, 37*, 15–23.

Kassin, S. M. (1998). More on the psychology of false confessions. *American Psychologist, 53*, 320–321.

Kassin, S. M., Ellsworth, P. C., & Smith, V. L. (1989). The "general acceptance" of psychological research on eyewitness testimony. *American Psychologist, 8*, 1089–1098.

Kassin, S. M., & Gudjonsson, G. H. (2004). The psychology of confession evidence: A review of the literature and issues. *Psychological Science in the Public Interest, 5*, 33–67.

Kassin, S. M., & Kiechel, K. L. (1996). The social psychology of false confessions: Compliance, internalization, and confabulation. *Psychological Science, 7*, 125–128.

Kassin, S. M., Leo, R. A., Meissner, C. A., Richman, K. D., Colwell, L. H., Leach, et al. (2007). Police interviewing and interrogation: A self-report survey of police practices and beliefs. *Law and Human Behavior, 31*, 381–400.

Kassin, S. M., Meissner, C. A., & Norwick, (2005). "I'd know a false confession if I saw one": A comparative study of college students and police investigators. *Law and Human Behavior, 29,* 211–227.

Kassin, S. M., Tubb, A. V., Hosch, H. M., & Memon, A. (2001). On the "general acceptance" of eyewitness testimony research. *American Psychologist, 56,* 405–416.

Kassin, S. M., & Wrightsman, L. S. (1985). Confession evidence. In S. M. Kassin & L. S. Wrightsman (Eds.), *The psychology of evidence and trial procedure* (pp. 67–94). Beverly Hills, CA: Sage.

Kastenbaum, R. (1998). *Death, society, and human experience* (6th ed.). Boston: Allyn & Bacon.

Kastenbaum, R. (2004). *On our way: The final passage through life and death.* Berkeley: University of California Press.

Kavale, K. A., & Forness, S. R. (1987). Substance over style: A quantitative synthesis assessing the efficacy of modality testing and teaching. *Exceptional Children, 54,* 228–239.

Keilitz, I., & Fulton, J. P. (1984). *The insanity defense and its alternatives: A guide for policy-makers.* Williamsburg, VA: Institute on Mental Disability and the Law, National Center for State Courts.

Keith-Spiegel, P., & Spiegel, D. E. (1967). Affective states of patients immediately preceding suicide. *Journal of Psychiatric Research, 5,* 89–93.

Kelly, G. A. (1955). *The psychology of personal constructs, Vols. 1 and 2.* New York: W. W. Norton.

Kelly, I. W., Laverty, W. H., & Saklofske, D. H. (1990). Geophysical variables and behavior: LXIV. An empirical investigation of the relationship between worldwide automobile traffic disasters and lunar cycles: No relationship. *Psychological Reports, 67,* 987–994.

Kelly, I. W., & Martens, R. (1994). Lunar phase and birthrate: An update. *Psychological Reports, 75,* 507–511.

Kelly, T. M., Soloff, P. H., Lynch, K. G., Haas, G. L., & Mann, J. J. (2000). Recent life events, social adjustment, and suicide attempts in patients with major depression and borderline personality disorder. *Journal of Personality Disorders, 14,* 316–326.

Kendall-Tackett, K. A., Williams, L. M., & Finkelhor, D. (1993). Impact of sexual abuse on children: A review and synthesis of recent empirical studies. *Psychological Bulletin, 113,* 164–180.

Kennedy, R. F., Jr. (2005). Deadly immunity. *Rolling Stone,* June, 977–978.

Kerman, E. F. (1959). Cypress knees and the blind: Response of blind subjects to the Kerman cypress knee projective technic (KCK). *Journal of Projective Techniques, 23,* 49–56.

Kerr, H. (2001). Learned helplessness and dyslexia: A carts and horses issue? *Reading, Literacy, and Language, 35,* 82–85.

Kerr, R. A., McGrath, J. J., O'Kearney, T., & Price, J. (1982). ECT: Misconceptions and attitudes. *Australian and New Zealand Journal of Psychiatry, 16,* 43–49.

Kevles, D. J. (1985). *In the name of eugenics: Genetics and the uses of human heredity*. Berkeley: University of California Press.

Key, W. B. (1973). *Subliminal seduction*. New York: Signet.

Kihlstrom, J. F. (1987). The cognitive unconscious. *Science, 237*, 1445–1452.

Kimball, J. N. (2007). Electroconvulsive therapy: An outdated treatment, or one whose time has come? *Southern Medical Journal, 100*, 462–463.

Kirby, D. (2005). *Evidence of harm: Mercury in vaccines and the autism epidemic—A medical controversy*. New York: St. Martin's Press.

Kivela, S.-L., Pahkala, K., & Lappala, P. (1991). A one-year prognosis of dysthymic disorder and major depression in old age. *International Journal of Geriatric Psychiatry, 6*, 81–87.

Kleespies, P., Hughes, D., & Gallacher, F. (2000). Suicide in the medically and terminally ill: Psychological and ethical considerations. *Journal of Clinical Psychology, 56*, 1153–1171.

Kleinfield, N. R., & Goode, E. (2002, October 28). Retracing a trail: The sniper suspects. *New York Times*. Retrieved January 22, 2009 from http://query. nytimes.com/gst/fullpage.html?res=9503E1DD173FF93BA15753C1A9649C8B63

Klimoski, R. (1992). Graphology and personnel selection. In B. L. Beyerstein & D. F. Beyerstein (Eds.), *The write stuff: Evaluations of graphology—the study of handwriting analysis* (pp. 232–268). Amherst, NY: Prometheus.

Kluger, A. N., & Tikochinsky, J. (2001). The error of accepting the "theoretical" null hypothesis: The rise, fall and resurrection of common sense hypotheses in psychology. *Psychological Bulletin, 127*, 408–423.

Kocsis, R. N. (2006). *Criminal profiling: Principles and practice*. Totowa, NJ: Humana Press.

Kocsis, R. N., & Hayes, A. F. (2004). Believing is seeing? Investigating the perceived accuracy of criminal psychological profiles. *International Journal of Offender Therapy and Comparative Criminology, 48*, 149–160.

Kocsis, R. N., Hayes, A. F., & Irwin, H. J. (2002). Investigative experience and accuracy in psychological profiling of a violent crime. *Journal of Interpersonal Violence, 17*, 811–823.

Kohn, A. (1990). *You know what they say: The truth about popular beliefs*. New York: HarperCollins.

Kolb, B., & Whishaw, I. Q. (2003). *Fundamentals of human neuropsychology* (5th ed.). New York: Worth.

Kolb, D. A. (1999). *The Kolb Learning Style Inventory, Version 3*. Boston: Hay Resources Direct.

Kowalski, P., & Taylor, A. K. (in press). The effect of refuting misconceptions in the introductory psychology class. *Teaching of Psychology*.

Kowalski, R. M., & Leary, M. R. (2004). *The interface of social and clinical psychology: Key readings in social psychology*. New York: Psychology Press.

Kownacki, R. J., & Shadish, W. R. (1999). Does Alcoholics Anonymous work? The results from a meta-analysis of controlled experiments. *Substance Abuse and Misuse, 34*, 1897–1916.

Krackow, E., Lynn, S. J., & Payne, D. (2005–2006). The death of Princess Diana: The effects of memory enhancement procedures on flashbulb memories. *Imagination, Cognition, and Personality, 5/6*, 197–220.

Kradecki, D. M., & Tarkinow, M. L. (1992). Erasing the stigma of electroconvulsive therapy. *Journal of Anesthesia Nursing, 7*, 84–86.

Krakovsky, M. (2005, May). Dis-chord of the "Mozart effect". *Stanford Business Magazine*. Retrieved March 24, 2008 from http://www.gsb.stanford.edu/NEWS/bmag/sbsm0505/research_heath_psychology.shtml

Kratzig, G. P., & Arbuthnott, K. D. (2006). Perceptual learning style and learning proficiency: A test of the hypothesis. *Journal of Educational Psychology, 98*, 238–246.

Kristberg, W. (1986). *The adult children of alcoholics syndrome*. New York: Bantam.

Krueger, R. F., Hicks, B. M., & McGue, M. (2001). Altruism and antisocial behavior: Independent tendencies, unique personality correlates, distinct etiologies. *Psychological Science, 12*, 397–402.

Kruger, J., Wirtz, D., & Miller, D. (2005). Counterfactual thinking and the first instinct fallacy. *Journal of Personality and Social Psychology, 88*, 725–735.

Kübler-Ross, E. (1969). *On death and dying*. New York: Macmillan.

Kübler-Ross, E. (1974). *Questions and answers on death and dying*. New York: Macmillan.

Kübler-Ross, E., & Kessler, D. (2005). *On grief and grieving: Finding the meaning of grief through the five stages of loss*. New York: Scribner.

Kuhtz, R. (2004). I want to fly a helicopter, not look at a bunch of crazy dials. *The Onion*. Available at http://www.theonion.com/content/node/33928

Kung, S., & Mrazek, D. A. (2005). Psychiatric emergency department visits on full moon nights. *Psychiatric Services, 56*, 221–222.

Lacasse, J. R., & Leo, J. (2005). Serotonin and depression: A disconnect between the advertisements and the scientific literature. *PLoS Medicine, 2*(12), 101–106.

Lacey, H. P., Smith, D. M., & Ubel, P. A. (2006). Hope I die before I get old: Mispredicting happiness across the adult lifespan. *Journal of Happiness Studies, 7*, 167–182.

Lachman, M. E. (2003). Development in middle life. *Annual Review of Psychology, 55*, 305–331.

Lachman, M. E., Lewkowicz, C., Marcus, A., & Peng, Y. (1994). Images of midlife development among young, middle-aged, and older adults. *Journal of Adult Development, 1*, 201–211.

Lachmann, T., & Geyer, T. (2003). Letter reversals in dyslexia: Is the case really closed? A critical review and conclusions. *Psychology Science, 45*, 53–75.

Lahaye, T. (1998). *Opposites attract: Bringing out the best in your spouse's temperament*. Eugene, OR: Harvest House.

Lamal, P. A. (1979). College students' common beliefs about psychology. *Teaching of Psychology, 6*, 155–158.

Landau, J. D., & Bavaria, A. J. (2003). Does deliberate source monitoring reduce students' misconceptions about psychology? *Teaching of Psychology, 30,* 311–314.

Langer, E. J., & Abelson, R. P. (1974). A patient by any other name . . . : Clinician group difference in labeling bias. *Journal of Consulting and Clinical Psychology, 42,* 4–9.

Lanning, K. V., & Burgess, A. W. (1989). Child pornography and sex rings. In D. Zillmann & J. Bryant (Eds.), *Pornography: Research advances and policy considerations* (pp. 235–255). Hillsdale, NJ: Lawrence Erlbaum Associates.

Larimer, M. E., Palmer, R. S., & Marlatt, G. A. (1999). Relapse prevention: An overview of Marlatt's cognitive-behavioral model. *Alcohol Research and Health, 23,* 151–160.

Larry P. vs. Riles (1980, January 17). 495 F. Suppl. 926 (N.D. California 1979) appeal docketed, # 80–4027.

Larson, R., & Richards, M. H. (1994). *Divergent realities: The emotional lives of mothers, fathers, and adolescents.* New York: Basic Books.

Lassiter, G. D., Clark, J. K., Daniels, L. E., & Soinski, M. (2004, March). *Can we recognize false confessions and does the presentation format make a difference?* Paper presented at the meeting of the American Psychology-Law Society, Scottsdale, Arizona.

Latane, B., & Darley, J. M. (1968). Group inhibition of bystander intervention. *Journal of Personality and Social Psychology, 10,* 215–221.

Latane, B., & Darley, J. (1970). *The unresponsive bystander: Why doesn't he help?* New York: Appleton-Century-Crofts.

Latane, B., & Nida, S. (1981). Ten years of research on group size and helping. *Psychological Bulletin, 89,* 308–324.

Latane, B., & Rodin, J. (1969). A lady in distress: Inhibiting effects of friends and strangers on bystander intervention. *Journal of Experimental Social Psychology, 5,* 189–202.

Lauber, C., Nordt, C., Falcato, L., & Rössler, W. (2005). Can a seizure help? The public's attitude toward ECT. *Psychiatry Research, 134,* 205–209.

Laumann, E., Das, A., & Waite, L. (in press). Sexual dysfunction among older adults: Prevalence and risk factors from a nationally representative U.S. probability sample of men and women 57 to 85 years of age. *Journal of Sexual Medicine.*

Laurence, J. R., & Perry, C. W. (1988). *Hypnosis, will, and memory: A psycholegal debate.* New York: Guilford Press.

Laursen, B., Coy, K. C., & Collins, W. A. (1998). Reconsidering changes in parent–child conflict across adolescence: A meta-analysis. *Child Development, 69,* 817–832.

Lavigne, J. V. (1977). The pediatric hospital staff's knowledge of normal adolescent development. *Journal of Pediatric Psychology, 2,* 98–100.

Lawton, G. (2005, August 13). The autism epidemic that never was. *New Scientist, 2512,* 57–61.

Lazarus, A. A. (2001). *Marital myths revisited: A fresh look at two dozen mistaken beliefs about marriage.* Atascadero, CA: Impact Publishers.

Leahy, T. H., & Leahy, G. E. (1983). *Psychology's occult doubles: Psychology and the problem of pseudoscience.* New York: Nelson-Hall.

LeCrone, H. (2007, October 1). *The disease of adolescence. Pacifist War Games* retrieved July 22, 2008 from http://pacifistwargames.blogspot.com/2007/10/disease-of-adolescence.html

Lee, J. (1993). *Facing the fire: Experiencing and expressing anger appropriately.* New York: Bantam.

Lehman, D. R., Wortman, C. B., & Williams, A. F. (1987). Long-term effects of losing a spouse or child in a motor vehicle crash. *Journal of Personality and Social Psychology, 52,* 218–231.

Lehmann, S., Joy, V., Kreisman, D., & Simmens, S. (1976). Responses to viewing symptomatic behaviors and labeling of prior mental illness. *Journal of Community Psychology, 4,* 327–334.

Leman, K. (1988). *The birth order book: Why you are the way you are.* Old Tappan, NJ: Spire Books.

Lenggenhager, B., Tadi, T., Metzinger, T., & Blanke, O. (2007). Video ergo sum: Manipulating bodily self-consciousness. *Science, 317,* 1096–1099.

Lenz, M. A., Ek, K., & Mills, A. C. (2009, March 26). *Misconceptions in psychology.* Presentation at 4th Midwest Conference on Professional Psychology, Owatonna, Minnesota.

Leo, R. A. (1996). Inside the interrogation room. *The Journal of Criminal Law and Criminology, 86,* 621–692.

Levenson, R. (2005, April). Desperately seeking Phil. *APS Observer.* Retrieved March 20, 2008 from http://www.psychologicalscience.org/observer/getArticle.cfm?id=1749

Levenstein, S., Ackerman, S., Kiecolt-Glaser, J. K., & Dubois, A. (1999). Stress and peptic ulcer disease. *Journal of the American Medical Association, 281,* 10–11.

Levenstein, S., Kaplan, G. A., & Smith, M. (1997). Sociodemographic characteristics, life stressors, and peptic ulcer: A prospective study. *Journal of Clinical Gastroenterology, 21,* 185–92.

Levenstein, S., Prantera, C., Varvo, V., Scribano, M. L., Berto, E., Spinella, S., et al. (1996). Patterns of biologic and psychologic risk factors for duodenal ulcer. *Journal of Clinical Gastroenterology, 21,* 110–117.

Levin, A. (2001, May). Violence and mental illness: Media keep myths alive. *Psychiatric News, 36*(9), 10.

Levy, M. (2007). *Take control of your drinking . . . and you many not need to quit.* Baltimore, MD: Johns Hopkins University Press.

Lewak, R. W., Wakefield, J. A., Jr., & Briggs, P. F. (1985). Intelligence and personality in mate choice and marital satisfaction. *Personality and Individual Differences, 4,* 471–477.

Lewis, W. A., & Bucher, A. M. (1992). Anger, catharsis, the reformulated frustration–aggression hypothesis, and health consequences. *Psychotherapy, 29*, 385–392.

Liberman, I. Y., Shankweiler, D., & Orlando, C. (1971). Letter confusions and reversals of sequence in the beginning reader: Implications for Orton's theory of developmental dyslexia. *Cortex, 7*, 127–142.

Liberman, M. (2006, September 24). Sex on the brain. *Boston Globe*. Retrieved August 11, 2008 from http://www.boston.com/news/globe/ideas/articles/2006/09/24/sex_on_the_brain/

Lieber, A. L. (1978). *The lunar effect: Biological tides and human emotions*. Garden City, NJ: Anchor Press.

Lieber, A. L. (1996). *How the moon affects you*. Mamaroneck, NY: Hastings House.

Lilienfeld, S. O. (1999). New analyses raise doubts about replicability of ESP findings. *Skeptical Inquirer*, November/December.

Lilienfeld, S. O. (2002). When worlds collide: Social science, politics, and the Rind et al. (1998) child sexual abuse meta-analysis. *American Psychologist, 57*, 176–188.

Lilienfeld, S. O. (2005a). Scientifically supported and unsupported treatments for childhood psychopathology. *Pediatrics, 115*, 761–764.

Lilienfeld, S. O. (2005b, Fall). Challenging mind myths in introductory psychology courses. *Psychology Teacher Network, 15*(3), 1, 4, 6.

Lilienfeld, S. O. (2007). Psychological treatments that cause harm. *Perspectives on Psychological Science, 2*, 53–70.

Lilienfeld, S. O., & Arkowitz, H. (2007, April/May). Autism: An epidemic? *Scientific American Mind, 4*, 90–91.

Lilienfeld, S. O., & Arkowitz, H. (2008). Uncovering "brainscams." *Scientific American Mind, 19*(3), 80–81.

Lilienfeld, S. O., & Loftus, E. F. (1998). Repressed memories and World War II: Some cautionary notes. *Professional Psychology: Research and Practice, 29*, 471–475.

Lilienfeld, S. O., & Lynn, S. J. (2003). Dissociative identity disorder: Multiple personalities, multiple controversies. In S. O. Lilienfeld, S. J. Lynn, & J. M. Lohr (Eds.), *Science and pseudoscience in clinical psychology* (pp. 109–142). New York: Guilford Press.

Lilienfeld, S. O., Lynn, S. J., & Lohr, J. M. (Eds.). (2003). *Science and pseudoscience in clinical psychology*. New York: Guilford Press.

Lilienfeld, S. O., Wood, J. M., & Garb, H. N. (2000). The scientific status of projective techniques. *Psychological Science in the Public Interest, 1*, 27–66.

Lilienfeld, S. O., Wood, J. M., & Garb, H. N. (2006). Why questionable psychological tests remain popular. *Scientific Review of Alternative Medicine, 10*, 6–15.

Lindsay, D. S., & Read, J. D. (1994). Psychotherapy and memories of childhood sexual abuse: A cognitive perspective. *Applied Cognitive Psychology*, *8*, 281–338.

Link, B. G., Phelan, J. C., Bresnahan, M., Stueve, A., & Pescosolido, B. A. (1999). Public conceptions of mental illness: Labels, causes, dangerousness and social distance. *American Journal of Public Health*, *89*, 1328–1333.

Lippa, R. A. (2005). *Gender, nature, and nurture* (2nd ed.). Mahwah, NJ: Erlbaum.

Littrell, J. (1998). Is the re-experience of painful emotion therapeutic? *Clinical Psychology Review*, *18*, 71–102.

Loehlin, J. C. (1992). *Genes and environment in personality development.* Newbury Park, CA: Sage.

Loevinger, J. (1987). *Paradigms of personality.* New York: Freeman.

Loewenberg, L. Q. (2008). Ready to find out what your dreams really mean? The dream zone. Retrieved March 14, 2008 from http://www.thedreamzone.com

Loftus, E. F. (1993). The reality of repressed memories. *American Psychologist*, *48*, 518–537.

Loftus, E. F., & Ketcham, K. (1994). *The myth of repressed memory: False memories and accusations of sexual abuse.* New York: St. Martin's Press.

Loftus, E. F., & Loftus, G. R. (1980). On the permanence of stored information in the human brain. *American Psychologist*, *35*, 409–420.

Logie, R. H., & Della Sala, S. (1999). Repetita (non) luvant. In S. Della Sala (Ed.), *Mind myths: Exploring popular assumptions about the mind and brain* (pp. 125–137). Chichester: Wiley.

Logue, M. B., Sher, K. J., & Frensch, P. A. (1992). Purported characteristics of adult children of alcoholics: A possible "Barnum effect." *Professional Psychology: Research and Practice*, *23*, 226–232.

Lohr, J. M., Olatunji, B. O., Baumeister, R. F., & Bushman, B. J. (2007). The pseudopsychology of anger venting and empirically supported alternatives. *Scientific Review of Mental Health Practice*, *5*, 54–65.

Lubinski, D., Benbow, C. P., Webb, R. M., & Bleske-Rechek, A. (2006). Tracking exceptional human capital over two decades. *Psychological Science*, *17*, 194–199.

Lykken, D. T. (1995). The antisocial personalities. Hillsdale, NJ: Lawrence Erlbaum Associates.

Lykken, D. T. (1998). *A tremor in the blood: Uses and abuses of the lie detector* (2nd ed.). New York: Plenum.

Lykken, D. T. (2000). *Happiness: The nature and nurture of joy and contentment.* New York: St. Martin's Griffin.

Lykken, D. T., & Tellegen, A. (1996). Happiness is a stochastic phenomenon. *Psychological Science*, *7*, 186–189.

Lynn, R., Wilson, R. G., & Gault, A. (1989). Simple musical tests as measures of Spearman's *g. Personality and Individual Differences*, *10*, 25–28.

Lynn, S. J., Kirsch, I., Barabasz, A., Cardena, E., & Patterson, D. (2000). Hypnosis as an empirically supported adjunctive technique: The state of the evidence. *International Journal of Clinical and Experimental Hypnosis, 48*, 343–361.

Lynn, S. J., Neuschatz, J., Fite, R., & Rhue, J. R. (2001). Hypnosis and memory: Implications for the courtroom and psychotherapy. In M. Eisen & G. Goodman (Eds.), *Memory, suggestion, and the forensic interview*. New York: Guilford Press.

Lynn, S. J., & Rhue, J. W. (Eds.). (1994). *Dissociation: Clinical and theoretical perspectives*. New York: Gilford Press.

Lynn, S. J., Rhue, J., & Weekes, J. R. (1990). Hypnotic involuntariness: A social cognitive analysis. *Psychological Review, 97*, 169–184.

Macdonald, J. M., & Michaud, D. L. (1987). *The confession: Interrogation and criminal profiles for police officers*. Denver, CO: Apache.

MacDonald, M. G. (2007). Undergraduate education majors' knowledge about suicide. *Perceptual and Motor Skills, 105*, 373–378.

Machovec, F. J. (1976). The evil eye: Superstition or hypnotic phenomenon? *American Journal of Clinical Hypnosis, 19*, 74–79.

Maciejewksi, P. K., Zhang, B., Block, S. D., & Prigerson, H. G. (2007). An empirical examination of the stage theory of grief. *Journal of the American Medical Association, 297*, 716–723.

MacKillop, J., Lisman, S. A., Weinstein, A., & Rosenbaum, D. (2003). Controversial treatments for alcoholism. In S. O. Lilienfeld, S. J. Lynn, & J. W. Lohr (Eds.), *Science and pseudoscience in clinical psychology* (pp. 273–306). New York: Guilford Press.

Madsen, K. M., Hviid, A., Vestergaard, M., Schendel, D., Wohlfahrt, J., Thorsen, P., et al. (2002). A population-based study of measles, mumps, and rubella vaccination and autism. *New England Journal of Medicine, 347*, 1477–1482.

Madsen, W. (1989). Thin thinking about heavy drinking. *The Public Interest, Spring*, 112–118.

Magoffin, D. (2007). *Stereotyped seniors: The portrayal of older characters in teen movies from 1980–2006*. Doctoral Dissertation, Brigham Young University.

Mahoney, M. J., & DeMonbreun, B. G. (1977). Confirmatory bias in scientists and non-scientists. *Cognitive Therapy and Research, 1*, 176–180.

Mahowald, M. W., & Schenk, C. H. (2005). Insights from studying human sleep disorders. *Nature, 437*, 1279–1285.

Maltzman, I. (1992). The winter of scholarly science journals. *Professional Counselor, 7*, 38–39.

Manhart, K. (2005). Likely story. *Scientific American Mind, 16*(4), 58–63.

Manning, A. G. (1999). *Helping yourself with E.S.P.: Tap the power of extra sensory perception and make it work for you*. New York: Penguin.

Manning, R., Levine, M., & Collins, A. (2007). The Kitty Genovese murder and the social psychology of helping: The parable of the 38 witnesses. *American Psychologist, 62*, 555–562.

Maraniss, D. (1998). *The Clinton enigma*. New York: Simon & Schuster.

Margolin, K. N. (1994). How shall facilitated communication be judged? Facilitated communication and the legal system. In H. C. Shane (Ed.), *Facilitated communication: The clinical and social phenomenon* (pp. 227–258). San Diego, CA: Singular Press.

Marks, D., & Colwell, J. (2000, September/October). The psychic staring effect: An artifact of pseudo randomization. *Skeptical Inquirer, 24*, 41–49.

Marks, D., & Kammann, R. (1980). *The psychology of the psychic*. Amherst, NY: Prometheus.

Markus, H., & Kitayama, S. (1991). Culture and the self: Implication for cognition, emotion, and motivation. *Psychological Review, 98*, 224–253.

Marlatt, G. A., & Gordon, J. R. (Eds.). (1985). *Relapse prevention: Maintenance strategies in the treatment of addictive behaviors*. New York: Guilford Press.

Marshall, B., & Warren, J. R. (1983). Unidentified curved bacilli on gastric epithelium in active chronic gastritis. *Lancet, 1*, 1273–1275.

Martin, D. (2006, November 20). *The truth about happiness may surprise you*. Retrieved August 8, 2008 from http://www.cnn.com/2006/HEALTH/conditions/11/10/happiness.overview/index.html

Matarazzo, J. D. (1983). The reliability of psychiatric and psychological diagnosis. *Clinical Psychology Review, 3*, 103–145.

Mazzoni, G. A. L., Loftus, E. F., & Kirsch, I. (2001). Changing beliefs about implausible autobiographical events: A little plausibility goes a long way. *Journal of Experimental Psychology: Applied, 7*, 51–59.

Mazzoni, G. A. L., Loftus, E. F., Seitz, A., & Lynn, S. J. (1999). Changing beliefs and memories through dream interpretation. *Applied Cognitive Psychology, 13*, 125–144.

McCloskey, M. (1983). Naïve theories of motion. In D. Gentner & A. L. Stevens (Eds.), *Mental models* (pp. 299–324). Hillsdale, NJ: Erlbaum.

McClure, E. B. (2000). A meta-analytic review of sex differences in facial expression processing and their development in infants, children, and adolescents. *Psychological Bulletin, 126*, 424–453.

McConkey, K. M. (1986). Opinions about hypnosis and self-hypnosis before and after hypnotic testing. *International Journal of Clinical and Experimental Hypnosis, 34*, 311–319.

McConkey, K. M., & Jupp, J. J. (1986). A survey of opinions about hypnosis. *British Journal of Experimental and Clinical Hypnosis, 3*, 87–93.

McCrae, R. R., & Terracciano, A. (2006). National character and personality. *Current. Directions in Psychological Science, 15*, 156–161.

McCrone, J. (1999). "Right brain" or "left brain"—Myth or reality? *New Scientist, 2193*, 3 July.

McCutcheon, L. E. (1991). A new test of misconceptions about psychology. *Psychological Reports, 68*, 647–653.

McCutcheon, L. E., & McCutcheon, L. E. (1994). Not guilty by reason of insanity: Getting it right or perpetuating the myths? *Psychological Reports, 74*, 764–766.

McDonald, A., & Walter, G. (2001). The portrayal of ECT in American movies. *Journal of ECT, 17,* 264–274.

McKelvie, P., & Low, J. (2002). Listening to Mozart does not improve children's spatial ability: Final curtains for the Mozart effect. *British Journal of Developmental Psychology, 20,* 241–258.

McNally, K. (2007). Schizophrenia as split personality/Jekyll and Hyde: The origins of the informal usage in the English language. *Journal of the History of the Behavioral Sciences, 43,* 69–79.

McNally, R. J. (2003). *Remembering trauma.* Cambridge, MA: Harvard University Press.

McNally, R. J., Bryant, R. A., & Ehlers, A. (2003). Does early psychological intervention promote recovery from posttraumatic stress? *Psychological Science in the Public Interest, 4,* 45–79.

McNiel, D. E., Eisner, J. P., & Binder, R. L. (2000). The relationship between command hallucinations and violence. *Psychiatric Services, 51,* 1288–1292.

Medford, S., Gudjonsson, G. H., & Pearse, J. (2003). The efficacy of the appropriate adult safeguard during police interviewing. *Legal and Criminological Psychology, 8,* 253–266.

Meehl, P. E. (1954). *Clinical versus statistical prediction.* Minneapolis: University of Minnesota Press.

Meehl, P. E. (1956). Wanted: A good cookbook. *American Psychologist, 11,* 263–272.

Meehl, P. E. (1973). Why I do not attend case conferences. In P. E. Meehl (Ed.), *Psychodiagnosis: Selected papers* (pp. 225–302). Minneapolis: University of Minnesota Press.

Meehl, P. E. (1978). Theoretical risks and tabular asterisks: Sir Karl, Sir Ronald, and the slow progress of soft psychology. *Journal of Consulting and Clinical Psychology, 46,* 806–834.

Meehl, P. E. (1986). Causes and effects of my disturbing little book. *Journal of Personality Assessment, 50,* 370–375.

Meehl, P. E. (1992). Cliometric metatheory: The actual approach to empirical, history-based philosophy of science. *Psychological Reports, 71,* 339–467.

Meehl, P. E. (1993). Philosophy of science: Help or hindrance? *Psychological Reports, 72,* 707–733.

Meeker, W. B., & Barber, T. X. (1971). Toward an explanation of stage hypnosis, *Journal of Abnormal Psychology, 77,* 61–70.

Megan, K. (1997, February 23). The effects of sexual abuse. *Hartford Courant.* Available at http://www.smith-lawfirm.com/effects.htm

Mehl, M. R., Vazire, S., Ramirez-Esparza, N., Slatcher, R. B., & Pennebaker, J. W. (2007). Are women really more talkative than men? *Science, 317,* 82.

Memon, A., & Thomson, D. (2007). The myth of incredible eyewitness. In S. Della Salla (Ed.), *Tall tales about the mind and brain* (pp. 76–90). Oxford: Oxford University Press.

Mercer, J. (2010). *Child development: Myths and misunderstandings*. New York: Sage.

Merikle, P. M. (1992). Perception without awareness: Critical issues. *American Psychologist, 47*, 792–795.

Meyer, C. (2008). *Myths surrounding the effects of divorce on children*. Retrieved July 26, 2008 from http://divorcesupport.about.com/od/childrenanddivorce/p/childrenmyths.htm

Middlecamp, M., & Gross, D. (2002). Intergenerational daycare and pre-schoolers' attitudes about aging. *Educational Gerontology, 21*, 271–288.

Miele, F. (2008, Fall). En-twinned lives: Twins experts Thomas J. Bouchard, Jr. and Nancy L. Segal of the Minnesota Study of Twins Reared Apart re-unite to discuss behavior genetics and evolutionary psychology. *Skeptic*. Retrieved on January 24, 2009 from http://findarticles.com/p/articles/mi_kmske/is_3_14/ai_n31060470

Miller, L. K. (1999). The savant syndrome: Intellectual impairment and exceptional skill. *Psychological Bulletin, 125*, 31–46.

Miller, W. R. (1983). Controlled drinking: A history and a critical review. *Journal of Studies on Alcohol, 44*, 68–83.

Miller, W. R., & Hester, R. K. (1980). Treating the problem drinker: Modern approaches. In W. R. Miller (Ed.), *The addictive behaviors: Treatment of alcoholism, drug abuse, smoking and obesity* (pp. 111–141). New York: Plenum Press.

Miller, W. R., Wilbourne, P. L., & Hettema, J. E. (2003). What works? A summary of alcohol treatment outcome research. In R. K. Hester & W. R. Miller (Eds.), *Handbook of alcoholism treatment approaches: Effective alternatives* (3rd ed., pp. 13–63). Boston: Allyn & Bacon.

Milner, B. (1972). Disorders of learning and memory after temporal lobe lesions in man. *Clinical Neurosurgery, 19*, 421–446.

Milton, J., & Wiseman, R. (2001). Does psi exist? Reply to Storm and Ertel (2001). *Psychological Bulletin, 127*, 434–438.

Minow, N. (2005, December 14). Are "educational" baby videos a scam? Research lacking to support claims. *Chicago Tribune*. Available at http://nellminow.blogspot.com/2005/12/media-mom-column-on-baby-einstein.html

Mischel, W. (1981). *Introduction to personality*. New York: Holt, Rinehart, & Winston.

Moats, L. C. (1983). A comparison of the spelling errors of older dyslexics and second-grade normal children. *Annals of Dyslexia, 34*, 121–139.

Monahan, J. (1992). Mental disorder and violent behavior: Perceptions and evidence. *American Psychologist, 47*, 511–521.

Monahan, J. (1996). *Mental illness and violent crime*. Washington, DC: National Institute of Justice.

Monti, P. M., Abrams, D. B., Kadden, R. M., & Rohsenow, D. J. (1989). *Treating alcohol dependence: A coping skills training guide*. New York: Guilford Press.

Moore, D. (2005). *Three in four Americans believe in paranormal.* June 15, 2005, Gallup Organization.

Moore, T. E. (1992, Spring). Subliminal perception: Facts and fallacies. *Skeptical Inquirer, 16,* 273–281.

Morell, M. A., Twillman, R. K., & Sullaway, M. E. (1989). Would a Type A date another Type A? Influence of behavior type and personal attributes in the selection of dating partners. *Journal of Applied Social Psychology, 19,* 918–931.

Morewedge, C. K., & Norton, M. J. (2009). When dreaming is believing: The (motivated) interpretation of dreams. *Journal of Personality and Social Psychology, 96,* 249–264.

Moscicki, E. K. (1997). Identification of suicide risk factors using epidemiologic studies. *Psychiatric Clinics of North America, 20,* 499–517.

Moston, S., Stephenson, G. M., & Williamson, T. M. (1992). The effects of case characteristics on suspect behaviour during police questioning. *British Journal of Criminology, 32,* 23–40.

Motta, R. W., Little, S. G., & Tobin, M. I. (1993). The use and abuse of human figure drawings. *School Psychology Quarterly, 8,* 162–169.

Mroczek, D. K., & Kolarz, C. M. (1998). The effect of age on positive and negative affect: A developmental perspective on happiness. *Journal of Personality and Social Psychology, 75,* 1333–1349.

Mroczek, D. K., & Spiro, A. (2005). Change in lie satisfaction during adulthood: Findings from the Veteran Affairs normative aging study. *Journal of Personality and Social Psychology, 88,* 189–192.

Muller, D. A. (2000). Criminal profiling: Real science or just wishful thinking? *Homicide Studies, 4,* 234–264.

Murphy, C. (1990). New findings: Hold on to your hat. *The Atlantic, 265*(6), 22–23.

Murphy, J. M. (1976). Psychiatric labeling in cross-cultural perspective. *Science, 191,* 1019–1026.

Myers, B., Latter, R., & Abdollahi-Arena, M. K. (2006). The court of public opinion: Lay perceptions of polygraph testing. *Law and Human Behavior, 30,* 509–523.

Myers, D. (2008). *Psychology.* New York: Worth.

Myers, D. G. (2000). The funds, friends, and faith of happy people. *American Psychologist, 55,* 56–67.

Myers, D. G. (2002). *Intuition: Its powers and perils.* New Haven, CT: Yale University Press.

Myers, D. G., & Diener, E. (1996, May). The pursuit of happiness. *Scientific American, 274,* 54–56.

Nangle, D. W., Erdley, C. A., Zeff, K. R., Stanchfield, L. L., & Gold, J. A. (2004). Opposites do not attract: Social status and behavioral-style concordances among children and the peers who like or dislike them. *Journal of Abnormal Child Psychology, 32,* 425–434.

Nantais, K. M., & Schellenberg, E. G. (1999). The Mozart effect: An artifact of preference. *Psychological Science, 10*, 370–373.

Nash, M. R. (1987). What, if anything, is regressed about hypnotic age regression? A review of the empirical literature. *Psychological Bulletin, 102*, 42–52.

Nash, M. R. (2001, July). The truth and the hype of hypnosis. *Scientific American, 285*, 46–55.

Nass, C., Brave, S., & Takayama, L. (2006). Socializing consistency: From technical homogeneity to human epitome. In P. Zhang & D. Galletta (Eds.), *Human–computer interactions in management information systems: Foundations* (pp. 373–391). Armonk, NY: M. E. Sharpe.

National Institute on Alcohol Abuse and Alcoholism (NIAAA). (2001–2002). *National epidemiologic survey on alcohol and related conditions.* Retrieved June 2, 2008 from http://pubs.niaaa.nih.gov/publications/arh29-2/toc29-2.htm

National Public Radio. (2007, December 26). *Does dyslexia translate into business success?* Retrieved July 23, 2008 from http://www.npr.org/templates/story/story.php?storyId=17611066

National Research Council. (2003). *The polygraph and lie detection.* Washington, DC: National Academies Press.

Neath, I., & Surprenant, A. (2003). Memory development. In *Human memory* (2nd ed.). Pacific Grove, CA: Thomas-Wadsworth.

Neher, A. (1990). *The psychology of transcendence.* New York: Dover.

Neimeyer, R. (Ed.). (2001). *Meaning reconstruction and the experience of loss.* Washington, DC: American Psychological Association.

Neisser, U., Boodoo, G., Bouchard, T. J., Jr., Boykin, A. W., Brody, N., Ceci, S. J., et al. (1996). Intelligence: Knowns and unknowns. *American Psychologist, 51*, 77–101.

Neisser, U., & Harsch, N. (1992). Phantom flashbulbs: False recollections of hearing the news about Challenger. In E. Winograd & U. Neisser (Eds.), *Affect and accuracy in recall: Studies of "flashbulb" memories* (Vol. 4, pp. 9–31). New York: Cambridge University Press.

Neisser, U., & Hyman, I. (Eds.). (1999). *Memory observed: Remembering in natural contexts.* New York: Worth Publishers.

Nelson, A. (2005). A national survey of electroconvulsive therapy use in the Russian Federation. *Journal of ECT, 21*, 151–157.

Nelson, C. (2003, January 10). Mozart and the miracles. *The Guardian.* Retrieved September 12, 2008 from http://arts.guardian.co.uk/fridayreview/story/0,,871350,00.html

Nelson, E. C., Heath, A. C., Madden, P. A., Cooper, M. L., Dinwiddie, S. H., Bucholz, K. K., et al. (2002). Association between self-reported childhood sexual abuse and adverse psychosocial outcomes: Results from a twin study. *Archives of General Psychiatry, 59*, 139–145.

Nemechek, S., & Olson, K. R. (1999). Five-factor personality similarity and marital adjustment. *Social Behavior and Personality, 27*, 309–317.

Nettle, D. (2005). *Happiness: The science behind your smile.* Oxford: Oxford University Press.

New York Times. (2008, August 24). *Measles returns. New York Times.* Retrieved August 24, 2008 from http://www.nytimes.com/2008/08/24/opinion/24sun2.html

Nickerson, R. S. (1998). Confirmation bias: A ubiquitous phenomenon in many guises. *Review of General Psychology, 2,* 175–220.

Nielsen, N. R., Zhang, Z-F., Kristensen, T. S., Netterstrom, B., Schnor, P., & Gronbaek, M. (2005). Self-reported stress and risk of breast cancer: Prospective cohort study. *British Medical Journal, 331,* 548.

NIH Consensus Conference. (1994). Helicobacter pylori in peptic ulcer disease: NIH Consensus Development Panel on Helicobacter pylori in peptic ulcer disease. *Journal of the American Medical Association, 272,* 65–69.

Nisbett, R., & Wilson, T. (1977). Telling more than we can know: Verbal reports on mental processes. *Psychological Review, 84,* 231–259.

Nordenberg, T. (1996, January/February). The facts about aphrodisiacs. *FDA Consumer, 30,* 10–15.

Norem, J. K. (2001). *The positive power of negative thinking.* New York: Basic Books.

O'Connor, A. (2007). *Never shower in a thunderstorm: Surprising facts and misleading myths about our health and the world we live in.* New York: Henry Holt & Co.

O'Jile, J. R., Ryan, L. M., Parks-Levy, J., Gouvier, W. D., Betz, B., Haptonstahl, D. E., & Coon, R. C. (1997). Effects of head injury experience on head injury misconceptions. *International Journal of Rehabilitation and Health, 3,* 61–67.

O'Connor, N., & Hermelin, B. (1988). Low intelligence and special abilities. *Journal of Child Psychology and Psychiatry, 29,* 391–396.

Offer, D., Kaiz, M., Ostrov, E., & Albert, D. B. (2003). Continuity in family constellation. *Adolescent and Family Health, 3,* 3–8.

Offer, D., Ostrov, E., & Howard, K. I. (1981). The mental health profes- sional's concept of the normal adolescent. *Archives of General Psychiatry, 38,* 149–153.

Offer, D., & Schonert-Reichl, K. A. (1992). Debunking the myths of adoles- cence: Findings from recent research. *Journal of the American Academy of Child and Adolescent Psychiatry, 31,* 1003–1014.

Offit, P. (2008). *Autism's false prophets: Bad science, risky medicine, and the search for a cure.* New York: Columbia University Press.

Ollivier, F. J., et al. (2004). Comparative morphology of the tapetum lucidum (among elected species). *Veterinary Ophthalmology, 7,* 11–22.

Olson, H. A. (1979). The hypnotic retrieval of early recollections. In H. A. Olson (Ed.), *Early recollections: Their use in diagnosis and psychotherapy* (pp. 223– 229). Springfield, IL: Charles C. Thomas.

Orton, S. T. (1925). "Word-blindness" in school children. *Archives of Neuro- logy and Psychiatry, 14,* 581–615.

Osberg, T. M. (1991). Psychology is not just common sense: An introductory psychology demonstration. *Teaching of Psychology, 20,* 110–111.

Overmeier, J. B., & Murison, R. (1997). Animal models reveal the "psych" in the psychosomatics of peptic ulcer. *Current Directions in Psychological Science, 6,* 180–184.

Owens, M., & McGowan, I. W. (2006). Madness and the moon: The lunar cycle and psychopathology. *German Journal of Psychiatry.* Retrieved March 18, 2008 from http://www.gjpsy.uni-goettingen.de/gjp-article-owens.pdf

Packard, V. (1957). *The hidden persuaders.* New York: Pocket Books.

Pagnin, D., de Queiroz, V., Pini, S., & Cassano, G. B. (2004). Efficacy of ECT in depression: A meta-analytic review. *Journal of ECT, 20,* 13–20.

Panek, P. E. (1982). Do beginning psychology of aging students believe 10 common myths of aging? *Teaching of Psychology, 9,* 104–105.

Paris, J. (2000). *Myths of childhood.* New York: Brunner/Mazel.

Parnia, S. (2006). *What happens when we die? A groundbreaking study into the nature of life and death.* Carslbad, CA: Hay House, Inc.

Pasewark, R. A., & Seidenzahl, D. (1979). Opinions concerning the insanity plea and criminality among patients. *Bulletin of the American Academy of Psychiatry and Law, 7,* 199–202.

Pasewark, R. A., & Pantle, M. L. (1979). Insanity plea: Legislator's view. *American Journal of Psychiatry, 136,* 222–223.

Patrick, C. J., & Iacono, W. G. (1989). Psychopathy, threat, and polygraph test accuracy. *Journal of Applied Psychology, 74,* 347–355.

Patterson, A. H. (1974, September). *Hostility catharsis: A naturalistic experiment.* Paper presented at the annual convention of the American Psychological Association, New Orleans.

Peale, N. V. (1952). *The power of positive thinking.* New York: Simon & Schuster.

Pearse, J., Gudjonsson, G. H., Clare, I. C. H., & Rutter, S. (1998). Police interviewing and psychological vulnerabilities: Predicting the likelihood of a confession. *Journal of Community and Applied Social Psychology, 8,* 1–21.

Pelham, B. W., Mirenberg, M. C., & Jones, J. K. (2002). Why Susie sells seashells by the seashore: Implicit egotism and major life decisions. *Journal of Personality and Social Psychology, 82,* 469–487.

Pendry, M. L., Maltzman, I. M., & West, L. J. (1982). Controlled drinking by alcoholics? New findings and a reevaluation of a major affirmative study. *Science, 217,* 169–175.

Pennington, B. F. (1999). Toward an integrated understanding of dyslexia: Genetic, neurological, and cognitive mechanisms. *Development and Psychopathology, 11,* 629–654.

Perigard, M. A. (2008, October 13). Christian Slater is "Own Worst Enemy" playing dual roles as spy, dad. *Boston Herald.* Retrieved October 13, 2008 from http://www.bostonherald.com/entertainment/television/reviews/view.bg?articleid=1125156

Perls, F., Hefferline, R., & Goodman, P. (1994/1951). *Gestalt therapy: Excitement and growth in the human personality*. New York: Gestalt Journal Press.

Perry, S. W., & Heidrich, G. (1981). Placebo response: Myth and matter. *American Journal of Nursing, 81*, 720–725.

Persinger, M. M. (2001). The neuropsychiatry of paranormal experiences. *Neuropsychiatric Practice and Opinion, 13*, 521–522.

Petry, N. M., Tennen, H., & Affleck, G. (2000). Stalking the elusive client variable in psychotherapy research. In C. R. Snyder & R. Ingram (Eds.), *Handbook of psychological change* (pp. 88–109). New York: John Wiley & Sons.

Petticrew, M., Fraser, J. M., & Regan, M. F. (1999). Adverse life-events and risk of breast cancer: A meta-analysis. *British Journal of Health Psychology, 4*, 1–17.

Pettinati, H. M., Tamburello, B. A., Ruetsch, C. R., & Kaplan, F. N. (1994). Patient attitudes towards electroconvulsive therapy. *Psychopharmacology Bulletin, 30*, 471–475.

Phelan, J. C., Link, B. G., Stueve, A., & Pescosolido, B. A. (2000). Public conceptions of mental illness in 1950 and 1996: What is mental illness and is it to be feared? *Journal of Health and Social Behavior, 41*, 188–207.

Phelps, R. P. (2009). *Correcting fallacies about educational and psychological testing*. Washington, DC: American Psychological Association.

Phillips, K-A. (2008, Chicago). *Psychosocial factors and survival of young women with breast cancer*. Paper presented at the Annual Meeting of the American Society of Clinical Oncology, June.

Phillips, M., Wolf, A., & Coons, D. (1988). Psychiatry and the criminal justice system: Testing the myths. *American Journal of Psychiatry, 145*, 605–610.

Piaget, J. (1929). The child's conception of the world (J. Tomlinson & A. Tomlinson, Trans.). Totowa, NJ: Littlefield, Adams.

Pinker, S. (2002). *The blank slate: The modern denial of human nature*. New York: Penguin Putnam.

Piper, A. (1993). "Truth serum" and "recovered memories" of sexual abuse: A review of the evidence. *Journal of Psychiatry and Law, 21*, 447–471.

Piper, A. (1997). What science says—and doesn't say—about repressed memories: A critique of Scheflin and Brown. *Journal of Psychiatry and Law, 25*, 614–639.

Plomin, R., & Rende, R. (1991). Human behavioral genetics. *Annual Review of Psychology, 42*, 161–190.

Plomin, R., & Spinath, F. M. (2004). Intelligence: Genetics, genes, and genomics. *Journal of Personality and Social Psychology, 86*, 112–129.

Pohl, R. F. (2004). *Cognitive illusions: A handbook on fallacies and biases in thinking, judgment and memory*. New York: Psychology Press.

Polivy, J., & Herman, C. P. (2002). If you first don't succeed. False hopes of self-change. *American Psychologist, 57*, 677–689.

Polusny, M. A., & Follette, V. M. (1996). Remembering childhood sexual abuse: A national survey of psychologists' clinical practices, beliefs, and personal experiences. *Professional Psychology: Research and Practice, 27*, 41–52.

Poole, D. A., Lindsay, D. S., Memon, A., & Bull, R. (1995). Psychotherapists' opinions, practices, and experiences with recovery of memories of incestuous abuse. *Journal of Consulting and Clinical Psychology, 68*, 426–437.

Pope, H. G., Jr., Poliakoff, M. B., Parker, M. P., Boynes, M., & Hudson, J. L. (2006). Is dissociative amnesia a culture-bound syndrome? Findings from a survey of historical literature. *Psychological Medicine, 37*, 225–233.

Popper, K. R. (1963). Conjectures and refutations. London: Routledge & Kegan Paul.

Porter, S., Yuille, J. C., & Lehman, J. R. (1999). The nature of real, implanted, and fabricated childhood emotional events: Implications for the recovered memory debate. *Law and Human Behavior, 23*, 517–537.

Poynton, J. C. (1975). Results of an out-of-the-body survey. In J. C. Poynton (Ed.), *Parapsychology in South Africa* (pp. 109–123). Johannesburg: South African Society for Psychical Research.

Prager, D. (2002, June 19). The commencement address I would give. *Jewish World Review*. Retrieved on November 2, 2008 from http://www.jewishworldreview.com/0602/prager061902.asp

Pratkanis, A. R. (1992). The cargo-cult science of subliminal persuasion. *The Skeptical Inquirer*, Spring, 260–272.

Presley, S. (1997). Why people believe in ESP for the wrong reasons. *Independent Thinking Review, 2*(2).

Pressley, M., & Ghatala, E. S. (1988). Delusions about performance on multiple-choice comprehension test items. *Reading Research Quarterly, 23*, 454–464.

Prochaska, J. O., & Norcross, J. C. (2007). *Systems of psychotherapy: A transtheoretical approach* (6th ed.). Pacific Grove, CA: Brooks/Cole.

Project MATCH Research Group. (1998). Matching alcoholism treatments to client heterogeneity: Project MATCH three-year drinking outcomes. *Alcoholism: Clinical and Experimental Research, 22*, 1300–1311.

Proulx, C., & Helms, H. (2008). Mothers' and fathers' perceptions of change and continuity in their relationships with young adult sons and daughters. *Journal of Family Issues, 29*, 234–261.

Pugh, T. (2007, June 6). Police put more officers on the beat to tackle "full moon" violence. *The Independent* (London). Retrieved March 20, 2008 from http://findarticles.com/p/articles/mi_qn4158/is_6_27/ai_n19202774

Quart, A. (2006). Extreme parenting. *Atlantic Monthly*, July/August, 110–115.

Quick, D. C. (1999). Joint pain and weather. *Skeptical Inquirer, 23*, 49–54.

Quill, T. E. (2005). Terri Schiavo: A tragedy compounded. *New England Journal of Medicine, 352*(16), 1630–1633.

Rabbitt, P. (1999). When age is in, is the wit out? In S. Della Sala (Ed.), *Mind myths: Exploring popular assumptions about the mind and brain* (pp. 165–186). Chichester: Wiley.

Rabinowitz, J., & Renert, N. (1997). Clinicians' predictions of length of psychotherapy. *Psychiatric Services, 48,* 97–99.

Radford, B. (1999). The ten-percent myth. *The Skeptical Inquirer. 23 (2).* Retrieved September 12, 2008 from http://www.csicop.org/si/9903/ten-percent-myth.html

Radford, B. (2007, July). Might fright cause white? *Skeptical Inquirer, 31*(4), 26.

Raison, C. L., Klein, H. M., & Steckler, M. (1999). The moon and madness reconsidered. *Journal of Affective Disorders, 53,* 99–106.

Ramsey, R. D. (2002). *501 ways to boost your children's self-esteem.* New York: McGraw-Hill.

Raskin, D. C., & Honts, C. R. (2002). The Comparison Question Test. In M. Kleiner (Ed.), *Handbook of polygraph testing* (pp. 1–47). San Diego, CA: Academic Press.

Rassin, E., Merckelbach, H., & Spaan, V. (2001). When dreams become a royal road to confabulation: Realistic dreams, dissociation, and fantasy proneness. *Journal of Nervous and Mental Disease, 189,* 478–481.

Raulin, M. (2003). *Abnormal psychology.* Boston: Allyn & Bacon.

Rauscher, F. H., Shaw, G. L., & Ky, K. N. (1993). Music and spatial task performance. *Nature, 365,* 611.

Reasoner, R. (2000). The true meaning of self-esteem. Available at http://www.self-esteem-nase.org/whatisselfesteem.shtml

Reimer, T., Mata, R., & Stoecklin, M. (2004). The use of heuristics in persuasion: Deriving cues on source expertise from argument quality. *Current Research in Social Psychology, 10,* 69–83.

Reyna, V. F., & Farley, F. (2006). Risk and rationality in adolescent decision making: Implications for theory, practice, and public policy. *Psychological Science in the Public Interest, 7,* 1–44.

Rhee, S. H., & Waldman, I. D. (2002). Genetic and environmental influences on antisocial behavior: A meta-analysis of twin and adoption studies. *Psychological Bulletin, 128,* 490–529.

Rhine, J. B. (1933). *Extra-sensory perception.* Boston: Society for Psychical Research.

Richardson, S. (1992). Historical perspectives on dyslexia. *Journal of Learning Disabilities, 25,* 40–47.

Ridder, D. D., Van Laere, K. V., Dupont, P., Menovsky, T., & Van de Heyning, P. V. (2007). Visualizing out-of-body experience in the brain. *The New England Journal of Medicine, 357,* 1829–1833.

Riekse, R. J., & Holstege, H. (1996). *Growing older in America.* New York: McGraw-Hill.

Rihmer, Z. (2007). Suicide risk in mood disorders. *Current Opinion in Psychiatry, 20,* 17–22.

Rime, B., Bouvy, H., Leborgne, B., & Rouillon, F. (1978). Psychopathy and nonverbal behavior in an interpersonal setting. *Journal of Abnormal Psychology, 87,* 636–643.

Rimland, B. (1978). Savant capabilities of autistic children and their cognitive implications. In G. Serban (Ed.), *Cognitive defects in the development of mental illness* (pp. 44–63). New York: Brunner/Mazel.

Rind, B., Bauserman, R., & Tromovitch, P. (1998). A meta-analytic examination of assumed properties of child sexual abuse using college samples. *Psychological Bulletin, 124,* 22–53.

Rind, B., Bauserman, R., & Tromovitch, P. (2002). The validity and appropriateness of methods, analyses, and conclusions in Rind et al. (1998): A rebuttal of victimological critique from Ondersma et al. (2001) and Dallam et al. (2001). *Psychological Bulletin, 127,* 734–758.

Rind, B., & Tromovitch, P. (1997). A meta-analytic review of findings from national samples on psychological correlates of child sexual abuse. *Journal of Sex Research, 34,* 237–255.

Rind, B., Tromovitch, P., & Bauserman, R. (2000). Condemnation of a scientific article: A chronology and refutation of the attacks and a discussion of threats to the integrity of science. *Sexuality and Culture, 4,* 1–62.

Rittenberg, C. N. (1995). Positive thinking: An unfair burden for cancer patients? *Supportive Care in Cancer, 3*(1), 37–39.

Robinson, D. N. (1997). Being sane in insane places. In *The Great Ideas of Psychology* (audio series). Chantilly, VA: The Teaching Company.

Robinson, T., Callister, M., Magoffin, D., & Moore, J. (2007). The portrayal of older characters in Disney animated films. *Journal of Aging Studies, 21*(3), 203–213.

Rock, A. (2004). *The mind at night: The new science of how and why we dream.* New York: Basic Books.

Rodriguez, J. L. (1983). The insanity defense under siege: Legislative assaults and legal rejoinders. *Rutgers Law Journal, 14,* 397, 401.

Roediger, H. L., & McDermott, K. B. (1995). Creating false memories: Remembering words not presented in lists. *Journal of Experimental Psychology: Learning, Memory, and Cognition, 21,* 803–814.

Rogers, C. (1942). *Counseling and psychotherapy.* New York: Houghton Mifflin.

Ropeik, D., & Gray, G. (2002). *Risk: A practical guide for deciding what's really safe and what's really dangerous in the world around you.* Boston: Houghton Mifflin.

Rosen, G. M., & Lilienfeld, S. O. (2008). Posttraumatic stress disorder: An empirical analysis of core assumptions. *Clinical Psychology Review, 28,* 837–868.

Rosen, M. (1999). Insanity denied: Abolition of the insanity defense in Kansas. *The Kansas Journal of Law and Public Policy, 5,* 253–255.

Rosenbaum, M. E. (1986). The repulsion hypothesis: On the nondevelopment of relationships. *Journal of Personality and Social Psychology, 51,* 1156–1166.

Rosenberg, H. (1993). Prediction of controlled drinking by alcoholics and problem drinkers. *Psychological Bulletin, 113,* 129–139.

Rosenhan, D. L. (1973a). On being sane in insane places. *Science, 179*, 250–258.

Rosenhan, D. L. (1973b). Sane: Insane. *Journal of the American Medical Association, 224*, 1646–1647.

Rosenzweig, M. R., Breedlove, M. S., & Watson, N. V. (2005). *Biological psychology* (4th ed.). Sunderland, MA: Sinauer.

Rosner, J. (2003). On White preferences. *The Nation*, April 14, p. 24.

Ross, C. A. (1990). Twelve cognitive errors about multiple personality disorder. *American Journal of Psychotherapy, 44*, 348–356.

Ross, L., & Ward, A. (1996). Naive realism: Implications for social conflict and misunderstanding. In T. Brown, E. Reed, & E. Turiel (Eds.), *Values and knowledge* (pp. 103–135). Hillsdale, NJ: Erlbaum.

Rotton, J., & Kelly, I. W. (1985). Much ado about the full moon: A meta-analysis of lunar-lunacy research. *Psychological Bulletin, 97*, 286–306.

Rowe, D. C. (1994). *The limits of family influence: Genes, environment, and behavior*. New York: Guilford Press.

Rowley, L. (2005). *Money and happiness: A guide to living the good life*. New York: John Wiley & Sons.

Roy, M., & Christenfeld, N. (2004). Do dogs resemble their owners? *Psychological Science, 15*, 361–363.

Ruscio, J. (2000). Risky business: Vividness, availability, and the media paradox. *Skeptical Inquirer, 24*(2), 22–26.

Ruscio, J. (2004). Diagnoses and the behaviors they denote: A critical examination of the labeling theory of mental illness. *Scientific Review of Mental Health Practice, 3*, 5–22.

Ruscio, J. (2005). Exploring controversies in the art and science of polygraph testing. *Skeptical Inquirer, 29*, 34–39.

Ruscio, J. (2006). The clinician as subject: Practitioners are prone to the same judgment errors as everyone else. In S. O. Lilienfeld & W. O'Donohue (Eds.), *The great ideas of clinical science: 17 principles that every mental health researcher and practitioner should understand* (pp. 27–45). New York: Brunner-Taylor.

Russell, G. W., & Dua, M. (1983). Lunar influences on human aggression. *Social Behavior and Personality, 11*, 41–44.

Rutter, M. (1972). *Maternal dependence reassessed*. New York: Penguin.

Rutter, M., Graham, P., Chadwick, F., & Yule, W. (1976). Adolescent turmoil: Fact or fiction? *Journal of Child Psychiatry and Psychology, 17*, 35–56.

Sack, K. (1998, January 15). Georgia's governor seeks musical start for babies. *The New York Times*, A–12.

Sackeim, H. (1988). The efficacy of electroconvulsive therapy. *Annals of the New York Academy of Sciences, 462*, 70–75.

Sackeim, H. A. (1989). The efficacy of electroconvulsive therapy in the treatment of major depressive disorder. In S. Fisher & R. P. Greenberg

(Eds.), *The limits of biological treatments for psychological distress: Comparisons with therapy and placebo* (pp. 275–307). Hillsdale, N.J.: Lawrence Erlbaum.

Sackeim, H. A., Prudic, J., Fuller, R., Keilp, J., Lavori, P. W., & Olfson, M. (2007). The cognitive effects of electroconvulsive therapy in community settings. *Neuropsychopharmacology, 32,* 244–254.

Sackett, P. R., Borneman, M. J., & Connelly, B. J. (2008). High-stakes testing in higher education and employment: Appraising the evidence for validity and fairness. *American Psychologist, 63,* 215–227.

Sackett, P. R., Schmitt, N., Ellingson, J. E., & Kabin, M. B. (2001). High-stakes testing in employment, credentialing, and higher education: Prospects in a post-affirmative-action world. *American Psychologist, 56,* 302–318.

Sacks, O. (1985). *The man who mistook his wife for a hat and other clinical tales.* New York: Simon & Schuster/Summit.

Sagan, C. (1979). *Broca's brain: Reflections on the romance of science.* New York: Random House.

Sagan, C. (1995). *The demon-haunted world: Science as a candle in the dark.* New York: Random House.

Salerno, S. (2009). Positively misguided: The myths and mistakes of the positive thinking movement. *Skeptic, 14*(4), 30–37.

Salinger, J. D. (1951). *A catcher in the rye.* Boston: Little, Brown, and Company.

Salter, D., McMillan, D., Richards, M., Talbot, T., Hodges, J., Bentovim, A., et al. (2003). Development of sexually abusive behaviour in sexually victimized males: A longitudinal study. *Lancet, 361,* 471–476.

Santa Maria, M. P., Baumeister, A. A., & Gouvier, W. D. (1998). Public knowledge about electroconvulsive therapy: A demographically stratified investigation. *International Journal of Rehabilitation and Health, 4,* 111–116.

Sarbin, T. R., & Slagle, R. W. (1979). Hypnosis and psychophysiological outcomes. In E. Fromm & R. E. Shor (Eds.), *Hypnosis: Developments in research and new perspectives* (2nd ed., pp. 273–303). New York: Aldine.

Saul, L. J., Snyder, R. R., & Sheppard, E. (1956). On early memories. *Psychoanalytic Quarterly, 25,* 228–337.

Saxe, L., Dougherty, D., & Cross, T. (1985). The validity of polygraph testing: Scientific analysis and public controversy. *American Psychologist, 40,* 335–366.

Schachter, S. (1982). Recidivism and self-cure of smoking and obesity. *American Psychologist, 37,* 436–444.

Schacter, D. L. (1996). *Searching for memory: The brain, the mind, and the past.* New York: Basic Books.

Schacter, D. L. (2001). *The seven sins of memory.* Boston: Houghton-Mifflin.

Schechter, R., & Grether, J. K. (2008). Continuing increases in autism reported to California's developmental services system. *Archives of General Psychiatry, 65,* 19–24.

Scheflin, A. W., Brown, D., & Hammond, D. C. (1997). *Memory, therapy, and law.* Des Plaines, IL: American Society of Clinical Hypnosis.

Schernhammer, E. S., Hankinson, B., Rosner, B., Kroenke, C. H., Willett, W. C., Colditz, G. A., & Kawachi, I. (2004). Job stress and breast cancer risk: The Nurse's Health Study. *American Journal of Epidemiology, 160,* 1079–1086.

Schmidt, F. L., & Hunter, J. E. (1998). The validity and utility of selection methods in personnel psychology: Practical and theoretical implications of 85 years of research findings. *Psychological Bulletin, 124,* 262–274.

Schmidt, J. P., & Hancey, R. (1979). Social class and psychiatric treatment; Application of a decision-making model to use patterns in a cost-free clinic. *Journal of Consulting and Clinical Psychology, 47,* 771–772.

Schmolck, H., Buffalo, E. A., & Squire, L. R. (2000). Memory distortions develop over time. Recollections of the O. J. Simpson trial verdict after 15 and 32 months. *Psychological Science, 11,* 39–45.

Schneier, F. R., Johnson, J., Hornig, C. D., Liebowitz, M. R., & Weissman, M. M. (1992). Social phobia: Comorbidity in an epidemiological sample. *Archives of General Psychiatry, 49,* 282–288.

Schooler, J. W., Ambadar, Z., & Bendiksen, M. (1997). A cognitive corroborative case study approach for investigating discovered memories of sexual abuse. In J. D. Read & D. S. Lindsay (Eds.), *Recollections of trauma: Scientific evidence and clinical practice* (pp. 379–388). New York: Plenum.

Schwarz, N., Sanna, L., Skurnik, I., & Yoon, C. (2007). Metacognitive experiences and the intricacies of setting people straight: Implications for debiasing and public information campaigns. *Advances in Experimental Social Psychology, 39,* 127–161.

Segal, N. (1999). *Entwined lives: Twins and what they tell us about human behavior.* New York: Dutton.

Seitz, S., & Geske, D. (1976). Mothers' and graduate trainees' judgments of children: Some effects of labeling. *American Journal of Mental Deficiency, 81,* 362–370.

Sepinwall, A. The stuff that Tony's dreams are made of. *The Star Ledger.* March 6, 2006. Retrieved March 17, 2008 from http://www.nj.com/sopranos/ledger/index.ssf?/sopranos/stories/tonydreams_six.html

Shaffer, T. W., Erdberg, P., & Haroian, J. (1999). Current nonpatient data for the Rorschach, WAIS-R, and MMPI-2. *Journal of Personality Assessment, 73,* 305–316.

Shain, R., & Phillips, J. (1991). The stigma of mental illness: Labeling and stereotyping in the news. In L. Wilkins & P. Patterson (Eds.), *Risky business: Communicating issues of science, risk, and public policy* (pp. 61–74). New York: Greenwood Press.

Shane, S., & Lichtblau, E. (2008, September 7). Seeking details, lawmakers cite anthrax doubts. *New York Times,* 1, 24.

Shastry, B. S. (1999). Recent developments in. the genetics of schizophrenia. *Neurogenetics, 2*, 149–154.

Shatz, M. A., & Best, J. B. (1987). Students' reasons for changing answers on objective tests. *Teaching of Psychology, 14*, 241–242.

Shaywitz, S. E. (1996). Dyslexia. *Scientific American, 275*(5), 98–104.

Shea, S. C. (1998). *Psychiatric interviewing: The art of understanding* (2nd ed.). Philadelphia: W. B. Saunders Company.

Sheehy, G. (1976). *Passages: Predictable crises of adult life.* New York: Bantam.

Shek, D. T. L. (1996). Mid-life crisis in Chinese men and women. *Journal of Psychology, 130*, 109–119.

Sheldrake, R. (2003). *The sense of being stared at: And other aspects of the extended mind.* New York: Crown Publishers.

Shephard, R. N. (1990). *Mind sights.* New York: W. H. Freeman & Co.

Sher, B. (1998). *Self-esteem games: 300 fun activities that make children feel good about themselves.* San Francisco, CA: Jossey-Bass.

Sher, K. J. (1991). *Children of alcoholics: A critical appraisal of theory and research.* Chicago: The University of Chicago Press.

Shermer, M. (2002). *Why people believe weird things: Pseudoscience, superstition, andother confusions of our time.* New York: Henry Holt & Co.

Shermer, M. (October, 2005). Rupert's resonance: The theory of "morphic resonance" posits that people have a sense of when they are being stared at. What does the research show? *Scientific American.* Retrieved June 11, 2008 from http://www.sciam.com/article.cfm?id=ruperts-resonance&colID=13

Shimamura, A. P. (1992). Organic amnesia. In L. R. Squire (Ed.), *Encyclopedia of learning and memory* (pp. 30–35). New York: Macmillan.

Shiwach, R. S., Reid, W. H., & Carmody, T. J. (2001). An analysis of reported deaths following electroconvulsive therapy in Texas, 1993–1998. *Psychiatric Services, 52*, 1095–1097.

Shobe, K. K., & Kihlstrom, J. F. (1997). Is traumatic memory special? *Current Directions in Psychological Science, 6*, 70–74.

Signorielli, N. (1989). Television and conceptions about sex roles: Maintaining conventionality and the status quo. *Sex Roles, 21*, 341–360.

Silver, E., Cirincione, C., & Steadman, H. J. (1994). Demythologizing inaccurate perceptions of the insanity defense. *Law and Human Behavior, 18*, 63–70.

Silver, R. L. (1982). *Coping with an undesirable life event: A study of early reactions to physical disability.* Unpublished doctoral dissertation, Northwestern University, Evanston, IL.

Simon, C. W., & Emmons, W. H. (1955). Learning during sleep. *Psychological Bulletin, 52*, 328–342.

Simonton, D. K. (2006). Presidential IQ, openness, intellectual brilliance, and leadership: Estimates and correlations for 42 U.S. chief executives. *Political Psychology, 27*, 511–526.

Singleton, G. O. (2001). *An alternate reality*. Reel Movie Critic.com. Retrieved May 13, 2008 from http://www.reelmoviecritic.com/2001/id1846.htm

Skeem, J. L., Douglas, K. S., & Lilienfeld, S. O. (2009). *Psychological science in the courtroom: Consensus and controversies*. New York: Guilford Press.

Skinner, N. F. (1983). Switching answers on multiple-choice questions: Shrewdness or shibboleth? *Teaching of Psychology, 10*, 220–222.

Skurnik, I., Yoon, C., Park, D. C., & Schwarz, N. (2005). How warnings about false claims become recommendations. *Journal of Consumer Research, 31*, 713–724.

Slater, L. (2004). *Opening Skinner's box: Great psychological experiments of the twentieth century*. New York: W. W. Norton.

Slater, L. (2005). Reply to Spitzer and colleagues. *Journal of Nervous and Mental Disease, 193*, 743–744.

Smith, M. J., Ellenberg, S. S., Bell, L. M., & Rubin, D. M. (2008). Media coverage of the Measles-Mumps-Rubella vaccine and autism controversy and its relationship to MMR immunization rates in the United States. *Pediatrics, 121*, 836–843.

Smith, S. M., Lindsay, R. C. L., Pryke, S., & Dysart, J. E. (2001). Postdictors of eyewitness errors: Can false identifications be diagnosed in the cross race situation? *Psychology, Public Policy, and Law, 7*, 153–169.

Snider, V. E. (1992). Learning styles and learning to read: A critique. *Remedial and Special Education, 13*, 6–18.

Snook, B., Cullen, R. M., Bennell C., Taylor, P. J., & Gendreau, P. (in press). The criminal profiling illusion: What's behind the smoke and mirrors? *Criminal Justice and Behavior*.

Snook, B., Eastwood, J., Gendreau, P., Goggin, C., & Cullen, R. M. (2007). Taking stock of criminal profiling: A narrative review and meta-analysis. *Criminal Justice and Behavior, 34*, 437–453.

Snook, B., Gendreau, P., Bennell, C., & Taylor, P. J. (2008). Criminal profiling: Granfalloons and gobbledygook. *Skeptic, 14*, 36–41.

Snyder, M., & Uranowitz, S. W. (1978). Reconstructing the past: Some cognitive consequences of person perception. *Journal of Personality and Social Psychology, 36*, 941–950.

Snyderman, N. (2008). *Medical myths that can kill you: And the 101 truths that will save, extend, and improve your life*. New York: Random House.

Sobell, M. B., & Sobell, L. C. (1973). Alcoholics treated by individualized behavior therapy: One year treatment outcome. *Behaviour Research and Therapy, 11*, 599–618.

Sobell, M. B., & Sobell, L. C. (1976). Second year treatment outcome of alcoholics treated by individualized behavior therapy: Results. *Behaviour Research and Therapy, 14*, 195–215.

Sobell, M. B., & Sobell, L. C. (1984). The aftermath of heresy; A response to Pendry et al.'s 1982 critique of "Individualized behavior therapy for alcoholics." *Behavior Therapy and Research, 22*, 413–440.

Solms, M. (1997). *The neuropsychology of dreams: A clinico-anatomical study.* Mahwah, NJ: Lawrence Erlbaum Associates.

Solms, M. (2000). Dreaming and REM sleep are controlled by different brain mechanisms. *Behavioral and Brain Sciences, 23,* 843–850.

Soloff, P. H., Lynch, K. G., Kelly, T. M., Malone, K. M., & Mann, J. J. (2000). Characteristics of suicide attempts of patients with major depressive episode and borderline personality disorder: A comparative study. *American Journal of Psychiatry, 157,* 601–608.

Solomon, A. (2001). The noonday demon: An atlas of depression. New York: Simon & Schuster.

Solomon, P. R., Adams, F., Silver, A., Zimmer, J., & DeVeaux, R. (2002). Ginkgo for memory enhancement: A randomized controlled trial. *Journal of the American Medical Association, 288,* 835–840.

Sommers, C. H., & Satel, S. (2005). *One nation under therapy: How the helping culture is eroding self-reliance.* New York: St. Martin's Press.

Sonnenberg, A. (1994). Peptic ulcer. In J. E. Everhart (Ed.), *Digestive diseases in the United States: Epidemiology and impact* (pp. 359–408). NIH publication no. 94-1447. Washington, DC: U.S. Department of Health and Human Services, Public Health Service, National Institutes of Health.

Spanos, N. P. (1996). *Multiple identities and false memories: A sociocognitive perspective.* Washington, DC: American Psychological Association.

Spanos, N. P., Menary, E., Gabora, M. J., DuBreuil, S. C., & Dewhirst, B. (1991). Secondary identity enactments during hypnotic past-life regression: A sociocognitive perspective. *Journal of Personality and Social Psychology, 61,* 308–320.

Spearman, C. (1904). "General intelligence," objectively determined and measured. *American Journal of Psychology, 15,* 201–292.

Spiegel, A. (2006, February 14). More and more, favored psychotherapies let bygones be bygones. *New York Times.* Retrieved March 29, 2008 from http://www.biopsychiatry.com/misc/psychotherapy.html

Spiegel, D. (1993, May 20). Letter to the Executive Council, International Study for the Study of Multiple Personality and Dissociation. *News, International Society of the Study of Multiple Personality and Dissociation, 11,* 15.

Spiegel, D., Bloom, J. R., & Gottheil, E. (1989). Effects of psychosocial treatment on survival of patients with metastatic breast cancer. *Lancet, 2,* 888–891.

Spitzer, R. L. (1976). More on pseudoscience in science and the case for psychiatric diagnosis. *Archives of General Psychiatry, 33,* 459–470.

Spitzer, R. L., Lilienfeld, S. O., & Miller, M. B. (2005). Rosenhan revisited: The scientific credibility of Lauren Slater's pseudopatient diagnosis study. *Journal of Nervous and Mental Disease, 193,* 734–739.

Springer, S. P., & Deutsch, G. (1997). *Left brain, right brain* (5th ed.). New York: W. H. Freeman & Co.

Squier, L. H., & Domhoff, G. W. (1998). The presentation of dreaming and dreams in introductory psychology textbooks: A critical examination with suggestions for textbook authors and course instructors. *Dreaming, 8,* 149–168.

Stahl, S. (1999). Different strokes for different folks? A critique of learning styles. *American Educator, Fall,* 27–31.

Standing, L., Conezio, J., & Haber, R. N. (1970). Perception and memory for pictures: Single-trial learning of 2500 visual stimuli. *Psychonomic Science, 19,* 73–74.

Standing, L. G., & Huber, H. (2003). Do psychology courses reduce belief in psychology myths? *Social Behavior and Personality, 31,* 585–592.

Stanovich, K. (1998). Twenty-five years of research on the reading process: The grand synthesis and what it means for our field. In T. Shanahan & F. Rodriguez-Brown (Eds.), *Forty-seventh yearbook of the National Reading Conference* (pp. 44–58). Chicago: National Reading Conference.

Stanovich, K. (2007). *How to think straight about psychology.* Boston: Allyn & Bacon.

Steadman, H. J., Mulvey, E. P., Monahan, J., et al. (1998). Violence by people discharged from acute psychiatric impatient facilities and by others in the same neighborhoods. *Archives of General Psychiatry, 55,* 393–401.

Steblay, N. M., & Bothwell, R. K. (1994). Evidence for hypnotically refreshed testimony: The view from the laboratory. *Law and Human Behavior, 18,* 635–651.

Steele, K. M. (2000). Arousal and mood factors in the "Mozart effect". *Perceptual and Motor Skills, 91,* 188–190.

Steele, K. M., Bass, K. E., & Crook, M. D. (1999). The mystery of the Mozart effect: Failure to replicate. *Psychological Science, 10,* 366–369.

Steinberg, L. (2007). Risk-taking in adolescence: New perspectives from brain and behavioral science. *Current Directions in Psychological Science, 16,* 55–59.

Sternberg, R. J. (1996). Myths, countermyths, and truths about human intelligence. *Education Researcher, 25*(2), 11–16.

Stewart, D. E., Cheung, A. M., Duff, S., Wong, F., McQuestion, M., Cheng, T., et al. (2007). Attributions of cause and recurrence in long-term breast cancer survivors. *Psychooncology, 10,* 179–183.

Stewart, D. E., Duff, S., Wong, F., Melancon, C., & Cheung, A. M. (2001). The views of ovarian cancer survivors on its cause, prevention, and recurrence. *MedGenMed, 3*(4) [formerly published in Medscape Women's Health Journal, 6(5), 2001]. Retrieved September 12, 2008 from http://www.medscape.com/viewarticle/408950

Stickland, A. (2002). A beautiful mind. *Plus Magazine.* Retrieved May 13, 2008 from http://plus.maths.org/issue19/reviews/book4/index.html

Stine, J. M. (1990). *The holes in your head: And other humorous and astounding facts about our human mind and psychology.* Renaissance ebooks: Pageturner Publications.

Stocks, J. T. (1998). Recovered memory therapy: A dubious practice technique. *Social Work, 43,* 423–436.

Stone, W., & Rosenbaum, J. (1988). A comparison of teacher and parent views of autism. *Journal of Autism and Developmental Disorders, 18,* 403–414.

Storm, L., & Ertel, S. (2001). Does psi exist? Comments on Milton and Wiseman's (1999) meta-analysis of ganzfeld research. *Psychological Bulletin, 127,* 424–433.

Stout, P. A., Villegas, J., & Jennings, N. A. (2004). Images of mental illness in the media: Identifying gaps in the research. *Schizophrenia Bulletin, 30,* 543–561.

Stover, S., & Saunders, G. (2000). Astronomical misconceptions and ethe effectiveness of science museums in promoting conceptual change. *Journal of Elementary Science Education, 12,* 41–52.

Strack, F., Martin, L., & Stepper, S. (1988). Inhibiting and facilitating conditions of the human smile: A nonobtrusive test of the facial feedback hypothesis. *Journal of Personality and Social Psychology, 54,* 768–777.

Stricker, G., & Gold, J. (2003). Integrative approaches to psychotherapy. In A. S. Gurman & S. Messer (Eds.), *Essential psychotherapies* (pp. 317–349). New York: Guilford Press.

Stuart, H., & Arboleda-Florez, J. (2001). Community attitudes toward people with schizophrenia. *Canadian Journal of Psychiatry, 46,* 245–252.

Sudzak, P. D., Schwartz, R. D., Skolnick, O., & Paul, S. M. (1986). Ethanol stimulates gamma-aminobutyric acid receptor mediated chloride transport in rat brain synaptoneurosomes. *Proceedings of the National Academy of Sciences, 83,* 4071–4075.

Sulloway, F. J. (1996). *Born to rebel: Birth order, family dynamics, and creative lives.* New York: Pantheon.

Sutherland, S. (1992). *Irrationality: Why we don't think straight!* New Brunswick, NJ: Rutgers University Press.

Swanson, J. W., Estroff, S., Swartz, M., et al. (1996). Violence and severe mental disorder in clinical and community populations: The effects of psychotic symptoms, comorbidity, and lack of treatment. *Psychiatry, 60,* 1–22.

Swift, T. L., & Wilson, S. L. (2001). Misconceptions about brain injury among the general public and non-expert health professionals: An exploratory study. *Brain Injury, 15,* 149–165.

Swim, J. K. (1994). Perceived versus meta-analytic effect sizes: An assessment of the accuracy of gender stereotypes. *Journal of Personality and Social Psychology, 66,* 21–36.

Tan, Z. S. (2008). *Age-proof your mind: Detect, delay and prevent memory loss before it's too late.* New York: Warner Wellness.

Tannen, D. (1991). *You just don't understand: Women and men in conversation.* New York: Ballantine Books.

Taraborrelli, J. R. (2004). *The magic and the madness.* London: Pan MacMillan.

Tarter, R. E., Alterman, A. I., & Edwards, K. L. (1985). Vulnerability to alcoholism in men: A behavior-genetic perspective. *Journal of Studies on Alcohol, 46*, 329–356.

Tavris, C. (1988). Beyond cartoon killings: Comments on two overlooked effects of television. In S. Oskamp (Ed.), *Television as a social issue* (pp. 189–197). Newbury Park, CA: Sage.

Tavris, C. (1992). *The mismeasure of woman: Why women are not the better sex, the inferior sex, or the opposite sex.* New York: Touchstone.

Taylor, A. K., & Kowalski, P. (2003, August). *Media influences on the formation of misconceptions about psychology.* Poster presented at the Annual Conference of the American Psychological Association. Toronto, Canada.

Taylor, A. K., & Kowalski, P. (2004). Naïve psychological science: The prevalence, strength, and sources of misconceptions. *Psychological Record, 54,* 15–25.

Teh, S. P. C., Helmes, E., & Drake, D. G. (2007). A Western Australian survey on public attitudes toward and knowledge of electroconvulsive therapy. *International Journal of Social Psychiatry, 53,* 247–273.

Tellegen, A., Lykken, D. T., Bouchard, T. J., Wilcox, K. J., Segal, N. L., & Rich, S. (1988). Personality similarity in twins reared apart and together. *Journal of Personality and Social Psychology, 54,* 1031–1039.

Temerlin, M. K. (1968). Suggestion effects in psychiatric diagnosis. *Journal of Nervous and Mental Disease, 147,* 349–353.

Templer, D. I., Brooner, R. K., & Corgiat, M. D. (1983). Geophysical variables and behavior XIV. Lunar phase and crime: Fact or artifact. *Perceptual and Motor Skills, 57,* 993–994.

Templer, D. I., Veleber, D. M., & Brooner, R. K. (1982). Geophysical variables and behavior VI. Lunar phase and accident injuries: A difference between night and day. *Perceptual and Motor Skills, 55,* 280–282.

Teplin, L. A. (1985). The criminality of the mentally ill: A deadly misconception. *American Journal of Psychiatry, 142,* 593–598.

Teplin, L. A., McClelland, G. M., Abram, K. M., & Weiner, D. A. (2005). Crime victimization in adults with severe mental illness: Comparison with the National Crime Victimization Survey. *Archives of General Psychiatry, 62,* 911–921.

Terepocki, M., Kruk, R. S., & Willows, D. M. (2002). The incidence and nature of letter orientation errors in reading disability. *Journal of Learning Disabilities, 35,* 214–233.

Terr, L. C. (1983). Chowchilla revisited: The effects of psychic trauma four years after a school-bus kidnapping. *American Journal of Psychiatry, 140,* 1543–1550.

The Washington Times. (2007). *Road-rage deaths draw 2 life terms.* April 16, 2007. Retrieved September 12, 2008 from http://washingtontimes.com/news/2007/apr/16/20070416-111446-1166r/

Thompson, D. A., & Adams, S. L. (1996). The full moon and ED patient volumes: Unearthing a myth. *American Journal of Emergency Medicine, 14,* 161–164.

Thompson, W. F., Schellenberg, E. G., & Husain, G. (2001). Arousal, mood, and the Mozart effect. *Psychological Science, 12,* 248–251.

Thornton, J. A., & Wahl, O. F. (1996). Impact of a newspaper article on attitudes toward mental illness. *Journal of Community Psychology, 24,* 17–25.

Timko, C., Moos, R. H., Finney, J. W., & Lesar, M. D. (2000). Long-term outcomes of alcohol use disorders: Comparing untreated individuals with those in Alcoholics Anonymous, and formal treatment. *Journal of Studies on Alcohol, 61,* 529–540.

Tomatis, A. A. (1991). *The conscious ear.* Barrytown, NY: Station Hill Press.

Torres, A. N., Boccaccini, M. T., & Miller, H. A. (2006). Perceptions of the validity and utility of criminal profiling among forensic psychologists and psychiatrists. *Professional Psychology: Research and Practice, 37,* 51–58.

Towbin, M. A., Haddock, S. A., Zimmerman, T. S., Lund, L. K., & Tanner, L. R. (2003). Images of gender, race, age, and sexual orientation in Disney feature-length animated films. *Journal of Feminist Family Therapy 15,* 19–44.

Trager, J., & Brewster, J. (2001). The effectiveness of psychological profiles. *Journal of Police and Criminal Psychology, 16,* 20–25.

Treffert, D. A., & Christensen, D. D. (2005). Inside the mind of a savant. *Scientific American, 293*(6), 108–113.

Trotter, K., Dallas, K., & Verdone, P. (1988). Olfactory stimuli and their effect on REM dreams. *Psychiatric Journal of the University of Ottawa, 13,* 94–96.

Tryon, W. W. (2008). Whatever happened to symptom substitution? *Clinical Psychology Review, 28,* 963–968.

Turk, D. (1996). Psychological aspects of pain and disability. *Journal of Musculoskeletal Pain, 4,* 145–154.

Turkheimer, E., & Waldron, M. C. (2000). Nonshared environment: A theoretical, methodological, and quantitative review. *Psychological Bulletin, 126,* 78–108.

Turkheimer, E., Haley, A., Waldron, M., D'Onofrio, B., & Gottesman, I. I. (2003). Socioeconomic status modifies heritability of IQ in young children. *Psychological Science, 14,* 623–628.

Turner, T. (1995). Schizophrenia (social section). In G. E. Berrios & R. Porter (Eds.), *A history of clinical psychiatry: The origin and history of psychiatric disorders* (pp. 349–359). London: The Athlone Press.

Turtle, J., & Want, S. C. (2008). Logic and research versus intuition and past practice as guides to gathering and evaluating eyewitness evidence. *Criminal Justice and Behavior, 35,* 1241–1256.

Tversky, A., & Kahneman, D. (1974). Judgments under uncertainty: Heuristics and biases. *Science, 185,* 1124–1131.

Tyson, E. (2006). *Mind over money: Your path to wealth and happiness*. New York: CDS Books.

Ullman, M., Krippner, S., & Vaughan, A. (1973). *Dream telepathy*. New York: Macmillan.

Ulrich, H., Randolph, M., & Acheson, S. (2006). Child sexual abuse: Replication of the meta-analytic examination of child sexual abuse by Rind, Tromovitch, and Bauserman (1998). *Scientific Review of Mental Health Practice*, 4(2), 37–51.

United States Department of Health and Human Services. (1997). *Ninth special report to the U.S. Congress on alcohol and health*. (NIH Publication No. 97–4017). Washington, DC: Author.

United States Department of Health and Human Services. (2007). *Alzheimer's disease*. Retrieved July 29, 2008 from http://www.healthfinder.gov/scripts/SearchContext.asp?topic=36

Uttal, W. R. (2003). *Psychomythics: Sources of artifacts and misconceptions in psychology*. Hillsdale, NJ: Erlbaum.

van Zuilen, M. H., Rubert, M. P., Silverman, M., & Lewis, J. (2001). Medical students' positive and negative misconceptions about the elderly: The impact of training in geriatrics. *Gerontology and Geriatrics Education, 21*, 31–40.

Vaughan, E. D. (1977). Misconceptions about psychology among. introductory psychology students. *Teaching of Psychology, 4*, 138–141.

Vellutino, F. R. (1979). *Dyslexia: Theory and research*. Cambridge, MA: MIT Press.

Vickers, K., & McNally, R. J. (2004). Panic disorder and suicide attempt in the National Comorbidity Survey. *Journal of Abnormal Psychology, 113*, 582–591.

Viera, W. (2002). Projectiology: A panorama of experiences of consciousness outside of the body. Retrieved December 16, 2007 from http://www.iacworld.org/English/Sciences/Projectiology.asp

Vogel, A. (2002, June 20). *School says game of tag is out*. FoxNews.com. Retrieved July 26, 2008 from http://www.foxnews.com/story/0,2933,55836,00.html

Vokey, J. R., & Read, J. D. (1985). Subliminal messages: Between the devil and the media. *American Psychologist, 40*, 1231–1239.

Voltaire. (1764). *Philosophical dictionary*. Paris: Editions Garnier.

Vreeman, R. C., & Carroll, A. E. (2007). Medical myths. *British Medical Journal, 335*, 1288–1289.

Vreeman, R. C., & Carroll, A. E. (2008). Festive medical myths. *British Medical Journal, 337*, a2769.

Vrij, A. (2008). *Detecting lies and deceit: Pitfalls and opportunities*. New York: Wiley.

Vrij, A., & Mann, S. (2007). The truth about deception. In S. Della Sala (Ed.), *Tall tales about the mind and brain: Separating fact from fiction* (pp. 271–288). Oxford. Oxford University Press.

Vygotsky, L. (1978). Interaction between learning and development (pp. 79–91). In *Mind in society* (M. Cole, Trans.). Cambridge, MA: Harvard University.

Wachtel, P. (1977). *Psychoanalysis, behavior change, and the relational world.* Washington, DC: American Psychological Association.

Waddell, D. L., & Blankenship, J. C. (1994). Answer changing: A meta-analysis of the prevalence and patterns. *Journal of Continuing Education in Nursing, 25,* 155–158.

Wade, C. (2008). Critical thinking: Needed now more than ever. In D. S. Dunn, J. S. Halonen, & R. A. Smith (Eds.), *Teaching critical thinking in psychology: A handbook of best practices* (pp. 11–21). Malden, MA: Wiley-Blackwell.

Wade, K. A., Garry, M., Read, J. D., & Lindsay, D. S. (2002). A picture is worth a thousand lies: Using false photographs to create false childhood memories. *Psychonomic Bulletin and Review, 9,* 597–603.

Wadlington, E. M., & Wadlington, P. L. (2005). What educators really believe about dyslexia. *Reading Improvement, 42,* 16–33.

Wagner, M. W., & Monnet, M. (1979). Attitudes of college professors toward extra-sensory perception. *Zetetic Scholar, 5,* 7–16.

Wagstaff, G. F. (1998). Hypnosis and forensic psychology. In I. Kirsch, A. Capafons, E. Cardena-Buelna, & S. Amigo (Eds.), *Clinical hypnosis and self regulation.* Washington, DC: American Psychological Association.

Wagstaff, G. F. (2008). Hypnosis and the law: Examining the stereotypes. *Criminal Justice and Behavior, 35,* 1277–1294.

Wahl, O. F. (1987). Public vs. professional conceptions of schizophrenia. *Journal of Community Psychology, 15,* 285–291.

Wahl, O. F. (1997). *Media madness: Public images of mental illness.* New Brunswick, NJ: Rutgers University Press.

Wahl, O. F., Borostovik, L., & Rieppi, R. (1995). Schizophrenia in popular periodicals. *Community Mental Health Journal, 31,* 239–248.

Wahl, O. F., Wood, A., & Richards, R. (2002). Newspaper coverage of mental illness: Is it changing? *Psychiatric Rehabilitation Skills, 6,* 9–31.

Wake, R., Fukuda, D., Yoshiyama, M., Shimada, K., & Yoshikawa, J. (2007). The effect of the gravitation of the moon on acute myocardial infarction. *American Journal of Emergency Medicine, 25,* 256–258.

Wallerstein, J. (1989). Children after divorce: Wounds that don't heal. *Perspectives in Psychiatric Care, 25,* 107–113.

Walsh, E., Buchanan, A., & Fahy, T. (2001). Violence and schizophrenia: Examining the evidence. *British Journal of Psychiatry, 180,* 490–495.

Walsh, F. (1999). Families in later life: Challenges and opportunities. In B. Carter & M. McGoldrick (Eds.), *The expanded family cycle: Individual, family and social perspectives* (3rd ed., pp. 307–326). Boston: Allyn & Bacon.

Walter, G., & McDonald, A. (2004). About to have ECT? Fine, but don't watch it in the movies: The sorry portrayal of ECT in film. *Psychiatric Times, 21,* 1–3.

Walter, G., McDonald, A., Rey, J. M., & Rosen, A. (2002). Medical student knowledge and attitudes regarding ECT prior to and after viewing ECT scenes from movies. *Journal of ECT, 18*, 43–46.

Wanjek, C. (2002). *Bad medicine: Misconceptions and misuses revealed, from distance healing to Vitamin O.* New York: John Wiley & Sons.

Watanabe, S., Sakamoto, J., & Wakita, M. (1995). Pigeons' discrimination of paintings by Monet and Picasso. *Journal of the Experimental Analysis of Behavior, 63*, 165–174.

Watkins, C. E., Campbell, V. L., Nieberding, R., & Hallmark, R. (1995). Contemporary practice of psychological assessment by clinical psychologists. *Professional Psychology: Research and Practice, 26*, 54–60.

Watson, A. C., Otey, E., Westbrook, A. L., et al. (2004). Changing middle schoolers' attitudes about mental illness through education. *Schizophrenia Bulletin, 30*, 563–572.

Watson, J. D., & Crick, F. H. C. (1953). Molecular structure of nucleic acids. *Nature, 171*, 737–738.

Weaver, K., Garcia, S. M., Schwarz, N., & Miller, D. T. (2007). Inferring the popularity of an opinion from its familiarity: A repetitive voice can sound like a chorus. *Journal of Personality and Social Psychology, 92*, 821–833.

Wechsler, D. (1997). *WAIS–III: Wechsler Adult Intelligence Scale—third edition administration and scoring manual.* San Antonio, TX: Psychological Corporation.

Wedding, D., & Niemiec, R. M. (2003). The clinical use of films in psychotherapy. *Journal of Clinical Psychology/In Session, 59*, 207–215.

Wegner, D. M. (2002). *The illusion of conscious will.* Cambridge, MA: MIT Press.

Weiner, R. D. (1984). Does electroconvulsive therapy cause brain damage? *Behavioral and Brain Sciences, 7*, 1–22.

Weiss, B. L. (1988). *Many lives, many masters.* New York: Simon & Schuster.

Weissman, M. M., Klerman, G. L., Markowitz, J. S., et al. (1989). Suicidal ideation and suicide attempts in panic disorder and attacks. *New England Journal of Medicine, 321*, 1209–1214.

Weisz, J. R., Donenberg, G. R., Han, S. S., & Weiss, B. (1995). Bridging the gap between laboratory and clinic in child and adolescent psychotherapy. *Journal of Consulting and Clinical Psychology, 63*, 542–549.

Weisz, J. R., Weiss, B., Han, S. S., Granger, D. A., & Morton, T. (1995). Effects of psychotherapy with children and adolescents revisited: A meta-analysis of treatment outcome studies. *Psychological Bulletin, 117*, 450–468.

Wells, G. L., & Bradford, A. L. (1998). "Good you identified the subject": Feedback to eyewitnesses distorts their reports of the witnessing experience. *Journal of Applied Psychology, 83*, 360–376.

Werth, J. L., Jr., & Cobia, D. C. (1995). Empirically based criteria for rational suicide: A survey of psychotherapists. *Suicide and Life-Threatening Behavior, 25*, 231–240.

Wethington, E. (2000). Expecting stress: Americans and the "midlife crisis." *Motivation and Emotion, 24*, 85–103.

Wetzel, R. D. (1976). Hopelessness, depression, and suicide intent. *Archives of General Psychiatry, 33*, 1069.

Whitbourne, S. K. (1996). Multiple stereotypes of elderly and young adults: A comparison of structure and evaluations. In J. Cavanaugh & S. K. Whitbourne (Eds.), *Gerontology: An interdisciplinary perspective* (pp. 65–90). New York: Oxford Press.

Whitehouse, W. G., Orne, E. C., Orne, M. T., & Dinges, D. F. (1991). Distinguishing the source of memories reported during prior wakening and hypnotic recall attempts. *Applied Cognitive Psychology, 5*, 51–59.

Widom, C. S. (1989). The cycle of violence. *Science, 244*, 160–166.

Wigdor, A. K., & Garner, W. R. (Eds.). (1982). *Ability testing: Uses, consequences, and controversies.* Washington, DC: National Academy Press.

Wilgoren, J. (2002, August 26). Confession had his signature; DND did not. *The New York Times on the Web.* Retrieved August 3, 2008 from http://www.truthinjustice.org/eddie-lloyd.htm

Willerman, L. (1979). *The psychology of individual and group differences.* San Francisco: W. H. Freeman.

Williams, L. E., & Bargh, J. A. (2008). Experiencing physical warmth promotes interpersonal warmth. *Science, 322*, 606–607.

Williams, W. M., & Ceci, S. (1998). *Escaping the advice trap: 59 tough relationship problems solved by the experts.* Kansas City, MO: Andrews McMeel Publishing.

Willingham, D. (2004). Reframing the mind: Howard Gardner became a hero among educators simply by redefining talents as "intelligences." *Education Next, 4*, 18–24.

Willis, M., & Hodson, V. K. (1999). *Discover your child's learning style: Children learn in unique ways.* New York: Crown Publishing.

Wilson, L., Greene, E., & Loftus, E. F. (1986). Beliefs about forensic hypnosis. *International Journal of Clinical and Experimental Hypnosis, 34*, 110–121.

Wilson, N. (2003). Commercializing mental health issues: Entertainment, advertising, and psychological advice. In S. O. Lilienfeld, S. J. Lynn, & J. M. Lohr (Eds.), *Science and pseudoscience in clinical psychology* (pp. 425–459). New York: Guilford Press.

Wilson, T. (2004). *Strangers to ourselves: Discovering the adaptive unconscious.* Cambridge, MA: Harvard University Press.

Winer, G. A., & Cottrell, J. E. (1996a). Does anything leave the eye when we see? Extramission beliefs of children and adults. *Current Directions in Psychological Science, 5*, 137–142.

Winer, G. A., & Cottrell, J. E. (1996b). Effects of drawing on directional representations of the process of vision. *Journal of Educational Psychology, 88*, 704–714.

Winer, G. A., Cottrell, J. E., Gregg, V. R., Foumier, J. S., & Bica, L. A. (2002). Fundamentally misunderstanding visual perception: Adults' belief in visual emissions. *American Psychologist, 57,* 417–424.

Winer, G. A., Cottrell, J. E., Karefilaki, K., & Chronister, M. (1996). Conditions affecting beliefs about visual perception among children and adults. *Journal of Experimental Child Psychology, 61,* 93–115.

Winer, G. A., Cottrell, J. E., Karefilaki, K., & Gregg, V. R. (1996). Images, words and questions: Variables that influence beliefs about vision in children and adults. *Journal of Experimental Child Psychology, 63,* 499–525.

Winer, G. A., Rader, A. W., Cottrell, J. E. (2003). Testing different interpretations for the mistaken belief that rays exit the eyes during vision. *The Journal of Psychology, 137,* 243–261.

Winter, A. (2005). The making of "truth serum." *Bulletin of the History of Medicine, 79,* 500–533.

Wise, R. A., & Safer, M. A. (2004). What U.S. judges know and believe about eyewitness testimony. *Applied Cognitive Psychology, 18,* 427–443.

Wiseman, R. (2007). *Quirkology: How we discover the big truths in small things.* New York: Basic Books.

Witt, S. (1983). *How to be twice as smart: Boosting your brainpower and unleashing the miracles of your mind.* Englewood Cliffs, NJ: Prentice Hall.

Woititz, J. G. (1983). *Adult children of alcoholics.* Hollywood, FL: Health Communications.

Wolff, P. H., & Melngailis, J. (1996). Reversing letters and reading transformed text in dyslexia: A reassignment. *Reading and Writing: An Interdisciplinary Journal, 8,* 341–355.

Wolpert, L. (1992). *The unnatural nature of science.* London: Faber and Faber.

Wood, J. M., Lilienfeld, S. O., Garb, H. N., & Nezworski, M. T. (2000). The Rorschach Test in clinical diagnosis: A critical review, with a backward look at Garfield (1947). *Journal of Clinical Psychology, 56,* 395–430.

Wood, J. M., Nezworski, M. T., Garb, H. N., & Lilienfeld, S. O. (2001). Problems with the norms of the Comprehensive System for the Rorschach: Methodological and conceptual considerations. *Clinical Psychology: Science and Practice, 8,* 397–402.

Wood, J. M., Nezworski, M. T., Lilienfeld, S. O., & Garb, H. N. (2003). *What's wrong with the Rorschach? Science confronts the controversial inkblot test.* New York: Jossey-Bass.

Wood, M., & Valdez-Menchaca, M. C. (1996). The effect of a diagnostic label of language delay on adults' perceptions of preschool children. *Journal of Learning Disabilities, 29,* 582–588.

Wortman, C. B., & Boerner, K. (2006). Reactions to the death of a loved one: Myths of coping versus scientific evidence. In H. S. Friedman, & R. C. Silver (Eds.), *Foundations of health psychology* (pp. 285–324). Oxford: Oxford University Press.

Wortman, C. B., & Silver, R. C. (1989). The myths of coping with loss. *Journal of Consulting and Clinical Psychology, 57,* 349–357.

Wrightsman, L. S., & Kassin, S. M. (1993). *Confessions in the courtroom.* Newbury Park, CA: Sage.

Wrightsman, L. S., Nietzel, M. T., & Fortune, W. H. (1994). *Psychology and the legal system* (3rd ed.). Pacific Grove, CA: Brooks/Cole.

Wyatt, W., Posey, A., Welker, W., & Seamonds, C. (1984). Natural levels of similarities between identical twins and between unrelated people. *Skeptical Inquirer, 9,* 62–66.

Yalom, I. (1980). *Existential psychotherapy.* New York: Basic Books.

Yang, Y. (2008). Social inequalities in happiness in the United States, 1972 to 2004: An age-period cohort analysis. *American Sociological Review, 73,* 204–226.

Yang, Z. (2007, March). *Learning experiences and misconceptions of vision.* Senior honors thesis, Department of Psychology, Ohio State University.

Yapko, M. (1994). *Suggestions of abuse: True and false memories of childhood sexual trauma.* New York: Simon & Schuster.

Yapko, M. D. (1994). Suggestibility and repressed memories of abuse: A survey of psychotherapists' beliefs. *American Journal of Clinical Hypnosis, 36,* 163–171.

Zajonc, R. B., Murphy, S. T., & Inglehart, M. (1989). Feeling and facial efference: Implications of the vascular theory of emotions. *Psychological Review, 96,* 395–416.

Zaslow, J. (2007, April 20). The most-praised generation goes to work. *Wall Street Journal.* Retrieved October 17, 2008 from http://rricketts.ba.ttu.edu/The%20Most%20Praised%20Generation%20Goes%20to%20Work.doc

Zhang, L. (2006). Does student–teacher thinking style match/mismatch matter in students' achievement? *Educational Psychology, 26,* 395–409.

INDEX